Mountain Biking Europe

Rowan Sorrell, Chris Moran and Ben Mondy

N

200 km
200 miles

FINLAND

Helsinki

Bergen

Oslo
NORWAY

Stockholm

SWEDEN

Gothenburg

SCOTLAND

Glasgow
Edinburgh

Newcastle
upon Tyne

Manchester

Berlin

GERMANY

WALES

Birmingham

ENGLAND

Prague

CZECH REPUBLIC

Cardiff
London

Frankfurt

Atlantic Ocean

Paris

Vienna
AUSTRIA

Munich

Zürich

Bern

SWITZERLAND

SLOVENIA

FRANCE

Geneva

Lyon

Milan

Grenoble

Turin
Genoa

Bologna

A Coruña
Santander

ITALY

ANDORRA

Marseille

Porto

SPAIN

Barcelona

Rome

PORTUGAL

Madrid

Lisbon

Mediterranean Sea

Lagos

Seville

Granada

Málaga

Getting high in the woods. Legally. A drug worth getting hooked on.

It's often said that it's not the destination that counts but the journey. As mountain bikers we instinctively know the truth in that sentiment. Even if you're lucky enough to live right next to some incredible trails (and many of us do), there's still something very rewarding about heading off to a new place to ride some new terrain.

That's where we come in. This is the first true mountain biking guidebook out there. Sure, there are route planners for areas of Cumbria, for XC routes in the Highlands and piste maps for the Alps, but this is the first book to present all that information in one concise volume. The guide is for the daytripper as much as the holiday cyclist: whether you're sneaking in a few pages at work while daydreaming of what to do at the weekend, or whether you're scanning the pages for that well-earned six-month sabbatical, we hope the information contained herein serves the same purpose: where to take your bike to get the best mountain biking experience in Europe.

We've asked friends, pros, photographers, barmen, chalet staff, those who work in the resorts, those who build the trails, magazine editors, newcomers and mountain biking legends. We've tried to show the resorts and trail centres in their true light; we've picked the list carefully after years of riding knowledge, and we've tried to illustrate every resort with good quality photos. In the course of making this book, we've been to some amazing places and hope that the information we have gathered helps you get out there and have more fun on your bike. Which part of the Europe you drop into is up to you, but we do hope this book helps you make some key decisions along the way.

Essentials

Austria and Slovenia

England

France

Germany and Czech Republic

Italy

Scandinavia

Scotland

Spain, Portugal and Andorra

Switzerland

Wales

Cover image
Chamonix
by Seb Rogers

Title page image
Josh Bryceland
by Chris Moran

About the book

It has become increasingly apparent over the past few years that there has been a huge increase in places to ride both in the UK and throughout Europe. Mountain biking is the fastest growing outdoor sport in the UK and it continues to boom as more and more quality facilities are created here and on the continent. It is also apparent just how little information makes it back to the rider, with most returning to the same trail centres and resorts again and again, blissfully unaware of the wealth of resorts out there to explore.

We are at an exciting period right now as more and more ski resorts want a piece of the action and are enlisting the help of professionals and local riders to make them more competitive. Hopefully, this guide will go a long way to opening your eyes as to just how many places there are to ride, and whet your appetite. It should become a regular feature of riders' coffee tables guide, helping them plan many an epic mountain biking holiday.

The resorts and trails have been selected for a number of reasons: their location, their facilities, the town, the views and scenery and ultimately the riding on offer.

We decided to give a double page spread to the resorts that offered a little more in terms of facilities and trails, and single pages to those with limited trails or facilities but which make a great day or weekend visit. For the UK we also produced a small 'Best of the rest' guide which includes some great riding destinations that may be lacking in choice or facilities in comparison to the other featured trails.

We tried to follow a strict system to categorise the resorts and provide perfect continuity but, in the true organic spirit of mountain biking, that soon went out of the window. In its place is a focus on the truly important factors; the riding and the experience the resort will give you. Enjoy.

About the authors

Rowan Sorrell has been riding his whole life and *is* mountain biking. He's been riding in the elite for eight years and for the last six has been on the UCI World Cup. His vast knowledge of the UK scene – especially in his home locale of South Wales – is only matched by his knowledge of the Alpine scene, having spent several summer seasons there. His travels on the competition circuit are well documented through his regular work with *Dirt Magazine* in the UK. Aside from this guidebook, Rowan's main project is Back-on-Track, a company he set up in 2004 with the aim of providing expert consultancy and trail-building skills in the UK. Rowan says his perfect trail is one that is "fun, well designed, and one that makes people want to ride their bikes." He is 27 and lives in Newport.

Left: Rowan Sorrell in his native Wales.
Middle: Chris Moran on a dusty Portuguese trail.
Right: Ben Mondy went on holiday instead of doing the captions for this book and is seriously regretting that decision right now.

Chris Moran has spent most of his adult life in and around the Alps, first as a pro snowboarder throughout the nineties and early noughties, and more recently as an action sports journalists for various international newspapers and magazines. Through his company ACM Writing – and on behalf of Nike 6.0 – he looks after UCI World Junior Champion Josh Bryceland and fellow UCI rider Sam Dale. He has been riding bikes (without stabilisers) since he was five years old, and has a collection of BMX mags going back to the late 1980s. He loves riding out in Lagos, Portugal, and reckons that in the next few years there will be an enormous push by Alpine ski resorts to use mountain biking as the perfect summer sport to balance out their skiing and snowboarding seasons.

Ben Mondy is a partner in ACM Writing with over 10 years of action sports journalism and editing experience. He was a deputy editor for Australia's biggest surfing magazine, *Tracks*, for over five years and since moving to Europe in 2005 has contributed to a wide range of mainstream and niche titles covering his love of various outdoor sports. Since his involvement in Mountain Biking Europe his time on the bike has increased dramatically, as, unfortunately, has his time rolling around the dirt in considerable pain. Not to be deterred, he vows to visit every location in the book, or at least die trying. Given his riding style, we'd bet on the latter.

Acknowledgements

Goradz Strazisar in Kransjka Gora, Sandra Kamper at Semmering, J-Roe at Wagrain, Matej Obu in Maribor, Peter at www.prosurf.si, Stacey at The Track, all at MBR Magazine, Richard Abbot, Luke Webber, the brilliantly named Helena Hospital at the Office du Tourisme in Les Deux Alpes, Alan Milway at the Riders Retreat, Rob Forbes at the Coolbus,

Sebastian Penegault at Tribe Sport, Jason Hodson at Go Montgenèvre, Peter Schmidt at Solid Bikes, Philipe Martin at Todtnau, Tobi Baab and all at the Bikepark Oberammergau, Charlotte Schwartz at radsportakademie.de, Ian Thomas in Italy, Fabio at the Lago Biker, Amelia Dunn at Italian Safaris, Stig Corneer at Kanis, Pirita Mukku from Levi Tourism, Linn Steen at Geilo's Pinkpark, John Ireland in Scotland (go the Gaelic Connection!), Pete Corson, Julie Cartner, All at Rasoulution, the Stream crew (Ben Robinson, Mark Savage, Lucy Epps, James Wilson, Sally Hearn, Alex Cootes, Kiki Karlsson and Olivia Kaye). Andy Heading, Andy Lloyd, Steve Williams, Luis Breitfuss in La Molina, Michael from Switchbacks, Oscar Saiz, Jordi Catellet and Patricia Garcia at Grand Valira, Manel Ibars at Bike La Clau, all at the Flims Tourist Office, Patrick Steib from Lugano, Andreas Cadisch from Lenzerheide, Ferrandes Verena at Kitzbuhel, Clive Davies & all at the Forestry Commission, the dudes at Bikepark Oberammergau – thanks again! Åre Tourism and the amazing crew at BGB (Susie Westwood especially!), Alessandro Modolo, Zeno at Bikepark Tenerife, Bjoern Gramm in Germany, Dominique Bellavarde at Courchevel Tourism, Kathy Sessler, Danny Milner in the UK, Dennis Stadmann in Germany, Ian and Dom at DMR Bikes, Endre Lovaas, the crew at Free Alien, Gary Ewing & Mat Clark, Gary Williamson, Ian Linton, Ischgl Tourism (and the brilliant Sue and Rob Freeman), Lynsey and Becky at Inghams, Jack Beckerson, James Chetwoode, Jamie Rodda, Janet Baxter, Jason Roe from Wagrain Bikepark, Johnny Knoxville & Daniel Ferreira in sunny Portugal, Jorge Canudas, Josh Knox, Kai Crow, Kerry May, Kjell Tore Bjornhaug, all at Kona, Kristian Hendricksson, Kubajsz, all at Livigno Bikepark Mottolino, Louis Rogers, Martin Dalen, Manuel at La Clau Bikepark, Mathius Blix, Neil Cousins, One Planet Adventure, Markus & Peter at Semmering Bikepark, Pete Derret, Pete Tiley, Phil Young, Rene Weinberg, Rob at Esher Shore, Richard Norgate, Scottish Woodlands, Snowdonia Guides, Steve Behr, The Santa Cruz Syndicate, Tiago Santana, Tore Meirik, Jacob Gibbins, Ali and Ash at Trail Addiction, the Bike Academy, Stuart Tee, Neil Cane, Toby and Jim at the Mountainbike Adventure, Anna Jiménez, and last but not least, Walbo wants to say thanks to god and The Inverness Ladies Basketball team.

An extra special thanks to
Nick Bayliss at Royal Racing – you're a legend mate. Dan Milner in Chamonix, France (or in cyberspace at danmilner. com), the super snappers Victor Lucas, James McKnight and Steve Jones, a massive thanks to the organized Chris Ball in Scotland, Christophe Ritzler in Switzerland, the super-helpful Eirik Evjen and Simen Berg in Norway, the amazing Enrico Guala in Italy, Fred Glo in France, Joel Andrade in Germany, Markus Stoeckl and the MS Racing Team in Austria, Rachel Atherton in Wales, Steve Peat, Sam Dale and Josh Bryceland in England – thanks for taking time out of winning the UCI to help us put this together. Stuart Millar at *The Guardian* – thanks for the story and hope to see you, Lachlan and Roxy on the trails very soon! Thanks also to Christie Poulos and Kat MacKenzie at Red Bull, the guys at Dirt (Mike and Billy), Pau and Tomi Misser at Guak, Callum Swift from The Uprising, Sam Reynolds at DMR Bikes and Nike 6.0, Posy Dixon for helping us out of a tight spot on deadline, and those amazing people that sent in shots and info on the more remote trails. Namely, Dugal D Ross, Greg and Gary Williamson, Andrew Denham, Paul England, Richard Norgate, Jimmy Doyle, Rene Weinberg, Allessandro Marengo, Kenneth Smith, Loic Delteil, Jack Beckerson, Dennis Stratmann, Paul Wurzinger, La Raya Creacions, Alicia Anton, Bruce Taylor, Morven Munro and Andy Boyle.

We couldn't have made this possible without:
Rachel Besant for pulling in most of the shots and Matt Barr at ACM for the edits and organising, the crew at Orange bikes, the guys at Cannondale, the dudes at Royal Racing, and all the riders we've met over the years.

Thanks also to all the Footprint crew (Hannah, Patrick, Rob, Zoë and Catherine especially), to editor Alan Murphy for being a cool hand on the tiller, and especially to designer Angus Dawson for making it all look so good and remaining calm in the face of countless last-minute changes.

If there's anyone we've forgotten, huge, huge apologies, and we'll make sure we put you in the re-print. Oh and please send any errors and omissions to: mountainbikingeurope@gmail.com

Rowan, Chris and Ben.

Essentials

Nothing beats the majesty of France. A lone rider in Les Arcs, above Bourg St. Maurice. [WWW.TRAILADDICTIONS.COM]

Planning your trip

Even 15 years ago it would have been unimaginable to think of package mountain biking holidays, resorts staying open all summer long, and bike parks, purpose-built trials and northshore being common-place across Europe. But there you go – progression is quick indeed. Those in it from the beginning are starting to reap the rewards. Morzine, Les Gets, and others in the Portes du Soleil are now considered the hub of the European scene, rivaling their counterpart over in Whistler, BC. Other ski resorts in Europe are either trying to play catch up, or are eyeing up the interest in this summer activity with interest. Along with the ski resort crowd, there are a number of smaller hills that have embraced the mountain bike scene. Tenerife, Portugal and Spain are littered with forward-thinking resorts that can see the potential in the sport. In Germany and Austria, smaller resorts with centenary-celebrating funiculars and cablecars are being given a new breathe of life. It's a great time to be into riding bikes, with every year bringing new trails, new bike parks, new equipment to try, and new countries to explore.

The resorts in this book are, to put it mildly, a diverse bunch, reflecting the wildly varied needs of modern riders. While some need a perfect park, great northshore and some decent dirt jumps, others hanker for some nice XC and a great view at the end of their ride. Many love nothing more than a downhill course to attack ten times in one day, while others like to stroll downhill and simply enjoy being in the countryside. Some of us simply yearn for the adventurous travel only immersing yourself in a truly foreign culture can provide. In making our selection, we canvassed as many expert opinions as we could and drew from our own long experience. Some resorts included themselves by dint of their towering reputations, but some rank outsiders made it in simply because we went on holiday there and had an unexpectedly great time.

Above left: A bike, a backpack, and a great vista. What more could you ask for?
Above: European adventure awaits.

Choosing your destination is only one aspect of planning a riding trip, and the sophistication with which the travel industry is starting to get involved in the mountain biking revolution is matched only by the artfulness of the ski industry and follows a similar arc. The early days abound with tales of riders sleeping in cars to get to the goods, or ramming apartments with like-minded friends to keep the cost down during hedonistic early mountain biking trips. In contrast, today you can buy a bespoke luxury mountain biking holiday online and simply turn up with your kit and have your meals cooked for you for. One company advertises itself as being there so you don't have to "pronounce the funny names of the trails, know where to go, know where to stay, or carry any of the snacks". Each approach has its own pros and cons of course, and budget always helps make the final decision.

Packages

In the past, the idea of booking a mountain bike specific package holiday would have seemed a notion plucked from the realms of fantasy. Not any more. Today, several independent companies specialize in both summer and winter programmes, taking advantage of the low cost airlines and offering essential guiding in remote – and beautiful – outposts. We have tried to cover as many of these companies in the book as possible. The advantages of this for the customer are obvious; you're in the hands of passionate people who know and intimately love their local area, and have a direct 'in' to the mainline of resort life. You're also more likely to have more in common with fellow guests. The disadvantages of this approach are twofold: smaller companies are obviously less able than larger ones to keep the prices down and are, as a rule, more expensive than 'stack 'em high, pack 'em in' packages; and then there's the chance that you'll book with a company that is perhaps not quite the slick outfit that's been made out in the advertising or on the internet bulletin boards. It can happen. Word of mouth is probably your greatest ally here, so ask around and do some research.

DIY

For many resorts mountain biking represents a perfect summer complement to their winter skiing and snowboarding trade. Instead of being mothballed, the infrastructure of lifts, apartments, hotels, shops and transfers can simply be left open in the summer. As such, there are some absolutely fantastic deals to be had if you're prepared to surf or to do a bit of phoning round. And the DIY trip is still a classic. Get a group together, dismantle or strap the bikes to the roof of a mate's banger and head for the hills. There's just something liberating about it, especially when you round that last bend before the resort and see the mountain hove into view, preferably under moonlight.

Top: Forest air.
Above left: Bikepark chilling.
Above right: The lesser-spotted cliff-edge wheelie. Not for the faint-hearted.

The camaraderie, the flexibility and – perhaps more persuasively – the cheapness all argue strongly for the DIY approach.

For many groups of young riders, the cost cutting approach is the only feasible way they can get out to another country. The flexibility this approach gives you, both in terms of cost and the weather (if it's pouring with rain you can always move on until you find somewhere more clement), is invaluable. The feeling engendered by a classic road trip cannot easily be dismissed either. On the flipside, it's an approach not obviously suited to families with young children, or trips of a more involved nature. Older riders with large disposable incomes are also likely to feel that their slumming-it days are behind them. Regardless, some of the more out there destinations featured in the guide can only be reached by following the DIY method, so choose you resort accordingly if comfort and convenience are your main motivations.

Either way, good luck in choosing your destination. Whether you're going out for a day trip, a weekend ride, or a full-blown bike-riding holiday, we hope this guide will help you choose where to go. We also hope that when you're there, this book will also be a mine of information. Just keep the mud off it please; it doesn't fare too well under a power wash.

ANDY LLOYD

VICTOR LUCAS

VICTOR LUCAS

How to pack your bag

Sam Dale is 19 and already a veteran of two UCI World Cup tours. Since the age of 15 he has been travelling to National Point series, Maxxis Cup and one-off events around Europe and the UK. He knows the inside of a Ford Transit better than the guy who designed it. Here are his 10 tips to packing your bike away for travel.

"Is my front wheel on properly?"

❶ Number one has to be: get a bike bag off eBay. It should cost you less that £100, and definitely have a hard base and wheels. Without a bike bag some airlines won't let you on.

❷ If you're going to spend money on anything, spend it on a good lightweight pump, a tool kit with good allen keys and some screwdrivers. And get a good pedal spanner.

❸ What do I take apart first? I take the wheels off first, then the handlebars and brake calipers, then the rear mech (the derailleur) and then the pedals. I take my chain off next to stop it hitting the frame, then the brake levers and the gear shifters. It all goes in the bag.

❹ Wrap your pedals in something and put them in your clothing bag, as they can scratch up anything they come into contact with.

❺ Cut some stiff pipe big enough to go in between the hubs to prevent your swing arm and your forks getting squashed. Keep your axle on for the same reason. You'll also want some cable ties for all the brake and gear cables. If you've got loads then just cut them when you take the bike apart and put new ones on when you put it back together.

❻ Put a bit of plastic in between the brake pads just so if the lever gets accidentally squashed, it won't pull the pads together and the pistons won't get pushed out. They're a nightmare to get back in 'cos if there's no air in the brake system you'll have to re-bleed them.

❼ Take your brake rotors off to stop them getting bent, and then put them in a bit of cardboard and tape it up to stop any oil or anything getting in there. If they get contaminated they won't be as effective.

❽ Take a small bottle of oil to lube the chain with. Make sure it's got a tight top on it so it doesn't leak. Then chuck all your pads, protection wear and rain gear in with the bike to give it extra padding. Not your main clothes though - my sharp suits and going out wear are kept away from all that grease and oil!

❾ Let your tyres down.

❿ Last thing to do before you leave the house is check you're not overweight: 32 kg is the max for any one bike bag. You should be able to take in on pretty much all airlines.

"Yeah I thought it felt a bit loose."

10 things to do before you die

❶ Do the Portes du Soleil tour

A visit to the spiritual home of European mountain biking was always going to be top of the list. Do the whole tour, taking in France and Switzerland, and end the day saddle-sore in Morzine sinking a few Mutzig beers on a sun terrace. Perfect.

❷ Go freeriding in Sauze d'Oulx, Italy

It's got perfect XC terrain, a phenomenal downhill track, and a bikepark shaped by the craftsmen at 4 Guimp. What more could you ask for? Oh, yeah, it's probably the most picturesque terrain in the world. It's a must-visit resort.

❸ Soak up some winter sun in Iberia

It's January and you can't feel the brake levers because your hands have frozen up. Don't grin and bear it – get a cheap flight and see what the dusty, hot trails of Lagos, Bubión or Guimarães have to offer.

❹ Ride the World Championships trail in Fort William

In 2007's UCI Mountain Bike World Champs, Sam Hill posted a time of 4 minutes 51 seconds on the incredible DH course in Fort William. The course is pretty much exactly the same today as it was when he laid down that time. See how close you can get to him. And you can do laps on the gondola, meaning you can probably get 10 goes at it in one day.

❺ Hit one of Norway's bikeparks

Never visited Scandinavia? Now you've got a perfect excuse to see what all the fuss is about. Expect super-friendly locals, ridiculously sexy people to chat up, and in Hafjell and Åre some of the most progressive bikeparks in the world.

❻ Book yourself a guided week of trail riding in Chamonix

The French Alpine city is surrounded by undoubtedly the most impressive views in Europe. To get the most out of a trip you'll have to go deep backcountry. To do that, book a guide and head off on some singletrack. Expect the best picnic you've ever had in your life.

❼ Ride the Mega Avalanche in Alpe d'Huez

It's France's equivalent to the Wacky Races: 1000 riders all taking off down a glacier and some of the sketchiest shale known to man. Expect a few grazes, some dusty clothes, and some seriously good times.

❽ Give Golspie's XC route a try

It's probably the best example of UK trail-building to date. See what the future of mountain biking is going to be like today.

❾ Get scared in Verbier

For those with vertigo, Verbier's epic trail The Ultimate, is a perfect nightmare. For everyone else, the challenge of riding in some of the Alps' most beautiful scenery (admittedly with the odd precipice on the side of the trail), is there to be met.

❿ Take a wash in an Italian Lake.

The only thing that beats the splendour and majesty of riding high in Italy's Finale Ligure or Lake Garda region is riding all the way to the water. Put the bike down and wash the dust off with a dip in the drink. The perfect way to cool down.

Six of the best

❶ Málaga, Spain
Year-round sunshine here on the Costa del Sol is attracting more and more travelling riders each year, though it can be uncomfortably hot in midsummer.

❷ Tenerife, Spain
Year-round sunshine in the Canary Islands. Tenerife has always attracted scores of Brits. Now the new bikepark is filling with riders wanting some winter sun.

❸ Lagos, Portugal
A popular surf spot, this sun-drenched little resort has some beautiful coastal scenery and cracking trails.

❹ Bubión, Spain
Clear blue skies and warm sun are the norm here. It's a little cooler here up in the mountains than down at the coast but still August is a no-no due to the scorching sun.

❺ Montgenèvre, France
Located in the southern Alps, Mongenevre enjoys a Mediterranean climate with long warm summers.

❻ Kranjska Gora, Slovenia
The summer season is long, dry and dusty in Kranjska Gora perfect for a nice break from slogging through the mud back home.

❶ Glentress, Scotland
With trails to suit everyone from young children through to experts, Glentress has the full package.

❷ Brechfa, Wales
Lacks the facilities of some of the other trail centres but the riding more than makes up for it.

❸ Golspie, Scotland
There may only be one stacked loop trail here, but what a corker it is.

❹ Laggan, Scotland
Excellent use of natural features to create a more technical and challenging trail than at any other centre in the UK.

❺ Afan Forest, Wales
Great for riders of an intermediate riding level and above. There are over 120 km of trail on offer and some challenging terrain.

❻ Cwmcarn, Wales
Cwmcarn has a strong local riding scene and this is a hugely popular little trail centre. One of the few trails where you can enjoy both downhill and XC trails side by side.

❶ Portes du Soleil, France/Switzerland
The lift range is vast and the number of trails, both official downhill runs and hidden trails, is unrivalled.

❷ Pila, Italy
With incredible runs up at Pila and also linking the resort to Aosta, Pila is a must for the gravity set.

❸ Les Deux Alpes, France
Deux Alpes is probably France's biggest standalone bikepark with a good vertical height loss and loads of trails.

❹ Sauze d'Oulx, Italy
Sublime singletrack, thoughtfully sculpted to suit the trail-riding purists amongst us.

❺ Åre, Sweden
A range of downhill and freeride trails combined with a solid slopestyle area puts Åre right up there as one of the top gravity destination.

❻ Grand Valira, Andorra
Perfect from beginner through to expert, Soldeu's bike park is exactly how they all should be.

❶ Chamonix, France
The terrain around Chamonix is famous the world over and it provides incredible mountain biking with spectacular views.

❷ Lake Garda, Italy
Lake Garda is one of the most stunning and relaxing places to travel with your bike. Finish off your tougher rides with a dip in the clear waters.

❸ Zermatt, Switzerland
The iconic Matterhorn looms over the town and the trails reach some picture-perfect vantage points.

❹ Tenerife, Spain
The trails on Tenerife throw up some incredible vistas around Monte Teide.

❺ Bubión, Spain
The whitewashed traditional villages along are a sight to behold in this unspoilt and beautiful part of the country.

❻ Champéry, Switzerland
The Dents du Midi provide an inspirational backdrop to the trails around Champéry.

Six of the worst

Busiest trails/lifts

❶ Les Gets, France
A hugely popular resort with some great riding but bigger lift queues than anywhere else and congestion on the trails.

❷ Morzine, France
How many people go on holiday to Morzine and just session the Pleney run day after day? This does mean that you will have to queue to get the gondola and there are all abilities on the trail.

❸ Glentress, Scotland
Glentress has more visitors than any other trail centre in the UK and this is evident on the weekends when hitting the red route.

❹ Winterberg, Germany
Winterberg has a great trail set-up on a small hill. The downhill is under two minutes long, which leaves you back in the queue at the lift. At weekends you'll be in a queue on the trail or at the lift.

❺ Llandegla, Wales
A hugely popular trail centre within easy reach of so many large cities is always going to be busy and the main loops here are no exception. Fortunately the trail has many wider areas for passing between singletrack runs.

❻ Cwmcarn, Wales
Both the Twrch trail XC loop and the DH trail can be pretty busy on a sunny weekend, leaving you trailing other riders if you don't get out early. The uplift is booked up weeks in advance for the weekends.

Weather

❶ Fort William, Scotland
The Scottish mountains have a rugged beauty to them, it's just a shame you usually can't see them for the mist and cloud. Fortunately the world-class trails in Fort Bill run just as well in the wet as they do in the dry.

❷ Portes du Soleil, France/Switzerland
The weather in the Portes du Soleil is unpredictable; it can be glorious more often than not but it is not uncommon to hear of two weeks of solid rain in August which renders the trails virtually unrideable.

❸ Laggan, Scotland
Laggan is quite close to Fort William but that extra distance to the east takes the sting out of some of the rain clouds.

❹ Brechfa Forest, Wales
Brechfa forest does receive more rain than most, but the trails have all been built with this in mind so they still run super fast in the wet, though the shale can be slippery.

❺ Willingen, Germany
It can be wet in Bavaria, but Willengen has surfaced its trails so they all run well in the rain.

❻ Golspie, Scotland
Sitting right on the North Sea coast, it is not uncommon to be battling the wind and rain up the trail in Golspie; it only adds to the achievement when you hit the viewpoint at the summit.

Transfers

❶ Kanis, Sweden
Kanis is way out there, with a four-hour transfer to the nearest airport (and an internal flight required to reach that).

❷ Gesundaberget, Sweden
It's 300 km to the nearest airport at Stockholm!

❸ Livigno, Italy
With its weird tunnel, closed valley and 24-km drive from the nearest airport, it is one of the toughest resorts to reach in Europe.

❹ Vallnord, Andorra
It is a three-hour transfer to Vallnord from Barcelona airport. On the plus side it's through great countryside and you can break this up with a stop at La Molina.

❺ Zermatt, Switzerland
It's 244 km from Zermatt to Geneva.

❻ Levi, Finland
Getting to Levi requires an internal flight from Helsinki to Kittila, otherwise you're looking at the rough end of a 13-hour drive.

Strange opening times

❶ Levi, Finland
One day each summer they run the lifts till past midnight so you can ride into the next day.

❷ Bourg St Maurice, France
The funicular from Bourg to Les Arcs runs every half hour from 0730 to 1930 offering some serious ride time.

❸ Prato Nevoso, Italy
On Fridays they open the lifts back up from 1945 to 2100 for some extended play.

❹ Gesundaberget, Sweden
The season here runs from 22 July to 20 August, but this is sure to change as the new trails there become more popular.

❺ Cimone, Italy
Weekends only during June, July and September.

❻ Lac Blanc, France
Only open on weekends and some Mondays.

Riders' tales
Five technique tips and places to try them

Josh Bryceland is the 2007 UCI World Cup Downhill Junior Champion and sponsored by Santa Cruz, The Syndicate, and Nike 6.0. Here are his five tips for better riding and five spots to try them out on...

Drops

Most people lean back heavily. They lift the forks up and hope to land on the back wheel. Really, though, you want to soak up the drop, so if it's about a foot, you try and push the bike into the floor. Ride towards the drop, get over the back wheel and compress into the bike before you've left the ground. As you leave, extend your legs and arms and push the bike into the floor as quick as you can. If it's a bigger drop, compress before the drop like before, then stay in that position with the bike and push the bike to meet the floor. Best place to learn them? I reckon a really good place to try them out is at the skills training centre at Fort William; they've got really good drops of all size.

Cornering

Common mistakes occur when you don't commit or if you brake while you're in the turn. I reckon it's best if you do all the braking before the corner, then just lean in to it, commit, and look as far out of the turn as possible. If you look at the middle of the corner, you're not committing to the turn as much as if your look all the way to the end. Try it, it really works! A place that has good corners is Llandegla in Wales. There's a cross country trail with loads of berms all the way round; it's amazing to lean into it and bank it.

Jumps

In downhill the most common mistake is when people launch off a booter and just pull up on the bars. What you want to do is look for a jump, roll at it a few times, judge the speed and let the jump do the work. Try and land with both wheels at the same time, keep your eye on the landing and try and get your wheels parallel to the landing. I never use my brakes when I'm in the air, but I always have a finger on each brake lever at all times. Cwmcarn is perfect for practising as there's a track with some cool small jumps at the top and they get bigger as you go down.

Braking

A common mistake that people make is locking up the back wheel because they're only using one brake. Remember you should have two levers, and the front brake works just as much if not more than the back brake. So you want to use both evenly. Also try braking as hard and as late as possible. If you just use your back brake you'll simply skid as you come into the corner; if you use both you'll be more in control. A good place to try this out, where there are loads of steep sections, is Hamsterly as it's pretty steep at the bottom so it's all about being good on your brakes.

Save energy and keep focused

A lot of people burn themselves out because they can't save their energy on longer routes like at Fort William. On any downhill course over two minutes long – unless you're incredibly fit – you can't ride the top sections and push on it. If you're riding a really long course and your pedalling, remember to take a really deep breath and save some energy at the bottom because you won't make up on a short pedalling section what you lose if you're tired and bouncing off roots and rocks and getting messed up in the trees. Have a sit down on an easier section, and take some deep breaths. If it's smooth give your hands a quick shake and get back into it! A good place to try this out? Try Pleney in Morzine it's really long, about 4-6 minutes depending on how fast you are, and it's proper knackering.

Top: Josh Bryceland – Stoked to be beside the seaside...

Discipline breakdown

In times past, there was only one type of mountain biking. Typically, it would involve riding your bike at whatever natural terrain and obstacles the land threw at you. One bike did everything. But today, with bike technology and trails design advancing at a breakneck speed, it is almost a different sport and mountain biking itself has diversified into numerous categories and niches with names to match: freeride, northshore, enduro, XC, downhill, slopestyle, dirt, trails and all-mountain. It all sounds very confusing, but in essence the sport can be broken down into three separate areas.

Cross country

The traditional form of riding, and still massive in the UK, thanks in part to an excellent choice of trail centres and a complete lack of uplift facilities. Cross country (XC in abbreviated form) is basically any riding where you're traversing, contouring and climbing and descending hills. It can be a meander through the countryside or be hugely, technically demanding. Indeed, advances in bike technology and rider skills mean that expert XC riders now tackle some outrageously technical routes. Cross country bikes are lightweight so they're easier to climb with, but subsequently they're not as tough as the heavier freeride and downhill bikes. XC riders use a mixture of hardtail bikes (bikes without rear suspension) and, perhaps more commonly these days, full suspension bikes with between 4" and 6" of wheel travel. This enables riders to ride longer and tackle more challenging terrain with added confidence.

Freeride

Freeride is an all-encompassing term and can be defined as anything that involves stunts or man-made obstacles. Northshore (raised wooden ramps), slopestyle (specific area with lots of jumps, drops and obstacles) and dirtjumping all come under the 'freeride' banner. Bikes usually have stronger frames, wheels and brakes. A good freeride trail will feature jumps, wooden frames and wallrides, and be accessed by lifts. They require a mixture of downhill riding skills and plenty of mastery when it comes to getting the bike airborne. Freeride is probably the fastest growing area of the sport in Europe, as most bike parks build wooden obstacles into their trails and have a dedicated slopestyle area.

Downhill

Doing exactly what it says on the tin, downhill attracts the speed junkies. Most ski resorts concentrate on downhill and freeride trails to maximise the use of their lift system. Trails can range from easy beginner routes with banked corners to ultra

Northshore, Enduro, Freeride, XC, Downhill, Hardtail, Singletrack and Slopestyle. What does it all mean?

technical, rocky nightmares that core racers love but leave most riders scratching their head and asking how that guy in front made it look so easy. Downhill bikes are specialist with heavy tyres and really powerful brakes.

One difficulty with these terms is that they change a lot in individual countries. Don't be surprised if you see XC described as freeride or enduro in some resorts, or downhill trails labelled as freeride in others. It really does vary, so use these terms as a general term and make sure you're clear about what it is you're riding before you drop in. One day, we hope each of these terms will be standardized. But until then, we've grouped them into our own preferred definitions even if the resort in question uses them differently.

When you're using our guide, you'll be able to look at the selection of resorts and quickly identify how they rate for each discipline with our discipline overview ratings. Simply look under the title 'The Trails' and you'll see the three disciplines highlighted with a rating for each featured resort. They're also rated on ability levels, so you'll be able to get an idea if they're best for beginner of advanced riders. All going well, you should be left with an overview of how suitable that resort will be for your preferred style of riding and your ability.

Environment

As the popularity of mountain biking continues to increase at a phenomenal rate, the riding community faces new challenges. How does the increased number of riders affect the environment? Who's in charge of making sure that each new trail is safe and not making too much of a impact on the local environment? Who decides the best way of building a trail and keeping riders every standard happy?

Step forward **John Ireland** of the Forestry Commission, one of the unsung heroes of the UK mountain bike scene. John's official title is Visitor Safety Review Co-ordinator for the Forestry Commission, but what this really means is that he spends his time trying to work out the best way of making trails safe for everybody.

What exactly do you do?

We review all guidelines on visitor safety in the Forestry Commission, and mountain biking comes into it because it involves the biggest risks. So we're trying to manage trails, come up with build standards, and basically trying to justify having such a high-risk sport taking place on our land.

How long has the Forestry Commission been involved in this?

About 20 years, but the sport has changed so much recently that we're having to update our approach. So now we're basically trying to provide better places for people to go. And also to inject money into different local economies. Wales is a good example of how mountain biking can add to rural regeneration by bringing people in: they spend money and the local economy benefits.

What would you like to achieve?

Well, I guess we're trying to formalize things a little bit, and come up with some industry standards. And basically ask questions. How do you know a trail designer is competent? Why is it being designed like that? Why are those jumps shaped like that? Where can trails be built? There are a lot of issues, and its difficult to keep everyone happy these days. All mountain bikers would like a trail near their house, built to their own standards, but this isn't possible. It's about quality not quantity, and finding the right balance. Everyone wants to ramp up the game, build the hardest, sickest trail possible, but that only brings in the elite riders who are only a small percentage of the market. Medium trails are better for most people. We look at it as a triangle: the top has to be supported by a broad base in order to promote

progression and allow people to learn. Sure, the tough stuff is the sexy stuff, but where do people learn?

How detrimental to the environment is mountain biking's increased popularity?

Is the environmental impact a worry? It is, in a way. Some areas just aren't suitable, but people also need easy access. Look at the southeast; there are something like four million people around the M4 corridor, so why build something miles away that they'll have to drive to? In that sense we need to do more urban trails, rather than worry about the impact on remote areas. That's part of the bigger strategic view we're looking at. People tend to focus on the trail and don't look at the bigger picture, so we're trying to come up with systems that make people do that.

Any advice for newcomers?

Take your litter home! Sounds trivial but you've no idea how much rubbish is found. If people would think about the impact of their own actions it would make a huge difference. If you hang out at a dirt jump, or a downhill area, the amount of rubbish is amazing (laughs). People don't think about who's going to tidy up their mess. Seems strange to me; you're in a natural environment, after all. Dalby is a good example of this. All the riders complained that when it gets wet, it's different. Well (laughs), unfortunately that's part of riding natural trails. They do change when they get wet, and you need to stay off them because all you're going to do is trash them. People don't really seem to think about things like that. They just think 'I want to ride now'. I would also advise people to wear helmets and pads, for when it goes pear shaped, it really does count.

Take your rubbish home, and wear a helmet for when things go pear-shaped.

RIDERS OF THE WORLD, HERE'S YOUR NEW TOUCHSTONE.

Alpi bike resort

Bardonecchia · Cesana Torinese · Chiomonte · Claviere
Monginevro · Pragelato · Prali · Sauze d'Oulx · Sestriere

A UNIQUE FREERIDE EXPERIENCE.

www.alpibikeresort.com · info@alpibikeresort.com

Rough single track and amazing views.
The Ischgl mountains all over. [VICTOR LUCAS]

Austria & Slovenia

CZECH
REPUBLIC

Horn

Tullner
Plain

Gmünd

Sankt Pölten

Gmünd

Freistadt

Amstetten

Gallneukirchen

Linz

Leonding

Traun

Wels

Ried

Schärding

Passau

Branau
am Inn

Munich

GERMANY

Garmisch-
Partenkirchen

Reutte

Imst

Telfs

Silz

Landeck

Nauders

Kufstein

Hopfgarten

Schwaz

Wattens

Innsbruck

ALPS

Scharankogel
(3497 m) ▲

Ötztaler Alpen

Wildspitze
(3768 m) ▲

Kühtensspitze
(3148 m) ▲

Lechtaler Alpen

Salzburg

Kuchl

Lofen

St Johann
in Tirol

Saalfelden

Mittersill

Kitzbüheler Alpen

Kitzbühel

Bischofshofen

Badgastein

Ötscher
(1893 m) ▲

Kindberg

Hochschwab
(2277 m) ▲

Leoben

Zeltweg

Fahnsdorf

Judenburg

Hoher Nock
(1963 m) ▲

Liezen

Schladming

Niedere Tauern

Tamsweg

Hochtor
(3254 m) ▲

Ankogel
(3246 m) ▲

Sachsenburg

Oberddrauburg

Grossglockner
(3793 m) ▲

Lienz

Brunico

Cortina d'Ampezzo

ITALY

Bolzano

Trento

AUSTRIA

Graz

Leibnitz

Grosser
Speikkogel
(2140 m) ▲

Zirbitzkogel
(2396 m) ▲

Ladinger
Spitz
(2079 m) ▲

Wolfsberg

Völkermarkt

St Veit

Klagenfurt

Villach

Arnoldstein

Bled

Maribor

SLOVENIA

Ljubljana

Lake
Atter

Lake
Traun

Gmunden

Ebensee

Priel
(2515 m) ▲

Brenner Pass

Tuxer Alpen

Zillertaler Alpen

Hochtorn
(3254 m) ▲

↘ 1

↘ 2

↘ 3

↘ 4

↘ 5

↘ 6

↘ 7

↘ 8

↘ 9

↘ 10

↘ Resorts

20 km
20 miles

N

Austria – no shortage of solitude for the rambling XC rider.

Austria is often viewed as one of the old-world stalwarts. Its chalets are picture perfect, its mountains beautiful and lederhosen and cows with bells around their necks are plentiful. In mountain biking terms however it often rates lower than Europe's other Alpine nations, mainly because of the common perception that its neighbours – Switzerland and France in particular – are better geared for mountain bikers.

The reality is that Austria possesses some of the finest mountains for trail riding in the Alps. In addition, many resorts are realising that to attract the new-school clientele, they just need a well set-out park with the full range of gravity-fed trails.

The result is that throughout Austria there is a limitless number of riding options available, from the cutting-edge and well-managed parks at Semmering, Leogang and Wagrain, to the miles of classic singletrack at Ischgl and Zillertal. Another point in its favour is that the trails tend to be woefully underused, meaning you're likely to have the epic scenery and descents all to yourself. Austria has other attractions too. In comparison to Switzerland, it is cheap, its nightlife is unpretentious and it is gaining a great après ski and bike reputation. In fact, resorts like Ischgl have rebranded themselves with massive outdoor concerts, loads of nightclubs and and an emphasis on raging nocturnal activities. In addition, the transport systems are brilliant, road access to other European cities is easy and most of the population speak English fluently. And while we perhaps wouldn't recommend it to the hardcore vegetarian (the local cuisine is aimed fairly and squarely at carnivores) for any rider looking for a serious alternative destination, Austria should be at the top of the European wish-list.

Overview

VICTOR LUCAS

MAYRHOFEN TOURISM

MAYRHOFEN TOURISM

ISCHGL TOURISM

Clockwise from top left:
1. Careful son, you'll leave a skidmark.
3. Prost!!

2. The love ride. A classic.
4. Haven't I seen those shorts somewhere before?

Both Austria and Slovenia seem to slip under the radar when it comes to listing the top places to ride in Europe, which is surprising when you take into account the beautiful scenery and variety of riding now on offer. Austria has charm with its picture-perfect meadows, alpine forests, mountain huts and traditional chalets. Slovenia wins points for its good climate, friendly people and value for money. Austria in particular offers great variety, with resorts such as Wagrain and Leogang developing the fun freeride side of the sport and in other resorts in the nearby Tryol region you will find epic natural mountain riding away

from the manmade stunts and obstacles. Slovenia meanwhile concentrates on the bike park side of things more so than its XC. Most of the listed XC tours involve more dirt roads than singletrack, but there are plenty of good singletracks to find if you are willing to explore, or even better, take on a guide.

Conditions

Many of the trails in Austria and Slovenia are found below the tree line. This means you get some great ground to ride on which can be soft and loamy at its best, dusty and hard packed after prolonged hot spells, or wet and muddy after periods of wet weather. Trails cutting through the woods also throw up their fair share of roots, which you'll either love or hate, whilst beginner trails have them removed. The weather systems here come in from all sides and, like much of the Alps, in any two-week period you may experience 30°C plus temperatures and heavy thunderstorms with cooler periods.

The scene

Austria's scene has always been some way behind many of the other European countries, but it is emerging now, together with the growth of its parks and resorts. The riders enjoy miles of flowing trails away from the crowds; in fact it must be baffling to the Austrians as to why their trails are so quiet.

The industry

The industry in Austria is minimal. The most famous bike company is KTM, huge off-road motorbike producers, who have developed some of the top enduro and MX bikes over the last few years. Their foray into mountain bikes has not made it into many other countries as of yet, but the bikes are well specced, popular in the country and are being raced internationally by the race team. The main bike magazine in Austria is *Mountainbike Revue*.

Q&A with the experts

Markus Stoeckl is 34 and has been riding since 1992. He is the current mountain bike speed world record holder, is sponsored by Red Bull, and owns the MS Intense Factory Racing team, sponsors of such luminaries as Matti Lehikoinen. They have a fantastic website at ms-racing.at, including rider-cam action and mpegs of downhill courses around Europe.

You've got friends visiting for just one weekend and they can go anywhere in Austria. Name the one place you'd definitely have to take them.

MS That's really hard to say. First of all I would go to Semmering, because there's a good lift and a nice track and it's not too heavy. Well, if you go fast it's getting heavy, but pretty much everyone can ride this course. But Leogang, and one in Graz called Schoeckl are also pretty good. So I would take them to one of those three.

Which trail centre or resort has the best party scene or the best after riding activities?

MS In Austria there are good parties everywhere! I guess it depends on the season. In the summer I would go to the Semmering or maybe Graz again. Graz is a good party town because for Austria it's quite big and it's full of students. And Vienna is about thirty minutes from Semmering.

Where did you learn to ride, and where would you send beginners to ride?

MS I learned in Kitzbühel on normal gravel roads like 15 years ago. Right now I would say Semmering has the best beginner set up. So I would send them there.

In your opinion, which is the best downhill track in Austria?

MS I would say over the DH in Semmering and Schladming. Those two are the ones I go to most.

Where's the best place to avoid pedalling uphill? Where has the best uplifts? Would you avoid anywhere?

MS There's a big freeride scene in Innsbruck without lifts, so that's nice for trail riding and it's quiet. But it's definitely all pedalling!

Semmering – it gets the thumbs up from Markus.

Ischgl

Old fashioned, glitzy resort, where designer outlets, fur coats and a serious mountain co-exist quite happily.

ISCHGL TOURISM

ISCHGL

↘1 The trails

- **Cross country** Excellent/beginner to advanced
- **Downhill** Fair/intermediate
- **Freeride** Poor/beginner
- **Uplift** 6 lifts open to bikers in the summer providing a combination of gondolas and chair lifts, most are high speed
- **Pros** A huge area with lots of trails; XC paradise; quiet trails
- **Cons** No built freeride or downhill trails; expensive

Ischgl has remained a well-kept secret to most yet is an area with a wide range of mountain bike trails definitely leaning towards XC and trail riding. When there are six lifts taking you to 2800 m, you're always going to get some good descents. The area known as the Silvretta Bike Arena is one of the largest riding areas in the Alps with over 1000 km of trails for every skill level and it is where Hans Rey spends a lot of time riding some of the finest trails in the Alps.

Cross country

The area is superbly equipped for XC and trail riding with a plethora of marked trails

① OPENING TIMES

Lifts all open 27 Jun and close 21 Sep; operating hours are 0900 to 1700

⑤ RESORT PRICES

3-day pass: €32.50; Week pass: €43.50

① DIRECTORY

Tourist Office: T+43 5444 5266
Website: ischgl.com

and the option to hire a GPS from the resort to enable you to follow some of the 30+ GPS loops. What is generally popular is to mix the lifts with climbing under pedal power to maximise your time in the mountains. There are also plenty of companies offering guiding around the Tyrol area, so contact the tourist office to find a guide that will suit your needs.

Easy An easier day's itinerary would be to head out on the trail through the rugged Velill Valley. You can opt to take a detour along one of the old smuggler paths into Switzerland, thus capping off a fantastic panoramic ride.

Difficult Probably the hardest ride to undertake would be the longest stage of the Ischgl Ironbike. At 79 km this is the route that the professionals battle it out for in the annual competition. It is marked out from mid-June allowing any rider who fancies themselves to give it a go.

Downhill

Riders looking for designed downhill courses should look elsewhere, but riders

who enjoy good natural singletrack trails could do far worse than Ischgl. With six lifts, no queues, and descending from

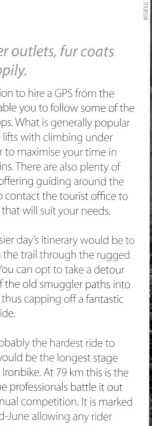

ISCHGL TOURISM

Austria & Slovenia Ischgl

Practicalities ⬤🚲💧♿

Ischgl is a quaint mountain village in the Paznaun Valley in the Tyrol. The town has largely gone unnoticed by mountain bikers, but it has some extensive riding on offer with 6 lifts serving riders. Trail riders will relish riding around this old fashioned, super-efficient resort. It's a marvellously friendly place where the lifts run smoothly, the mountains are great and the après riding scene, despite the resort's small size, is what the town is perhaps most famous for. The nearest airport is Innsbruck, about an hour's drive away.

Sleeping *The Engadin* (engadin. ischgl.com) is a reasonable boarding house at €50 a night. The 4-star *Hotel Solaria* is quintessentially Austrian and has a spa in the basement (solaria.at)

Eating Try the *Ischgler Einkehr* pub in the village for cheap eats. The on-hill *Panorama* is also reasonable. Slightly pricier options are the *Salz und Pfeffer* and the *Steakhouse* at the *Hotel Grillalm*.

Bars and clubs Try the Guinness at the *Golden Eagle*, before following everybody else in the immediate area to the *Trofana Arena*, the hugely over-sized nightclub in the *Trofana Royal Hotel* basement. Ischgl also hosts nights by the famous *Pacha* club.

Bike shop Try *Sport Salner* (T+43 5444 5262) in the village.

Internet café Most hotels are wireless enabled. The *Silvretta Center* also has internet terminals and laptop points.

Bike map available? Bike maps outlining the many tours on offer are available free from the tourist office.

2800 m you can clock in some serious vertical descent over a day's riding.

Freeride

There are no freeride trails or stunts, except for a small skills area but this is aimed more towards the trail riders.

Top: XC paradise.
Above: If only they gave free tea away too it'd be uplift heaven.
Opposite page: A sweet reward awaits all that hard work.

ISCHGL TOURISM

The Lowdown

Locals do... Use the whole of the Silvretta Arena, linking all 6 cablecars; there are loads of trails to find.

Locals don't... Use GPS, they know this area like the back of their hand. You don't, so run the GPS.

Don't miss... Taking the lift up to the highest station at 2800 m where you get an impressive panorama and some great descending.

Remember to avoid... Turning up with a full on downhill rig, you may look a little out of place.

Kitzbühel

⅏2 The trails

- **ⓧⓒ Cross country** Good/beginner to advanced
- **ⓓⓗ Downhill** Fair to good/ intermediate to Advanced
- **ⓕⓡ Freeride** Poor/beginner to intermediate
- **ⓐ Uplift** There are 6 lifts open to riders
- **✔ Pros** Miles and miles of unspoilt trail riding; great place to ride XC; good facilities for young kids with practice trails and coaching available
- **✖ Cons** No downhill courses; freeride is very limited

An emerging mountain bike scene with a wealth of singletrack at a place best known for the scariest downhill ski race on the World Cup circuit.

You can almost hear the yodelling.

Tricky sections take your eyes off the view.

The Tyrol region of Austria is known for its great trails riding in beautiful surroundings. The region has not taken to downhill and freeride as much as other areas, but the range of lifts available to bikers means that going down is never going to be a problem. The area is best suited to those with trail bikes who enjoy putting in some miles, which opens up endless possibilities.

Cross country

There are around 750 km of cycling trails in the area, as well as many tours using gravel and dirt roads. There's still a hefty whack of quality singletrack here, ranging from open alpine meadows to dense, dark and technical wooded trails. The option is always there to save your legs and use some of the lifts available to get more miles under your belt each day. The

Practicalities ⬛🚲🚡

The medieval town of Kitzbühel is perhaps the definitive Austrian resort with its thigh-slapping nightlife, an older client base, and locals who wouldn't look out of place on the set of National Lampoon's Austrian Vacation. Kitzbühel prides itself on the title 'The best of the Alps'; a big claim, and a little ambitious, even given that it is an interesting town set amongst beautiful surroundings with great hills. Mountain biking is still being developed here and Kitzbühel is working to improve its facilities to riders with each summer season.

Sleeping Being a large ski resort the town offers a wide range of accommodation from €25 a night upwards. *Hotel Seebichl* (T+43 5356 62525) offers a great package with lockable bike garages, tools and a bike repair stand, a drying room and guiding for their guests. *The Mountain Edge* (mountainedge.co.uk) is a British company offering guided mountain bike holidays which takes some of the guesswork out.

Eating For traditional good value food try the *Huberbrau* in the town centre. *Hotel zur Tenne* does Austrian tradition with a twist; *Gallo* in the centre is the place for Italian food, or go all out with a sushi at *Ecco*.

Bars and clubs The *Londoner*, *Jimmy's*, *Flannigans* and *Ursprung* are undoubtedly where you'll end up hanging out.

Bike shop There are plenty of bike shops in the town. *Radsport Stanger* (T+43 5356 62549) have knowledgeable staff who can give you tips on the trails and also have rental GPS units available.

Internet café There are several net cafés in the town. Try *Internet Café Kitzbühel* (T+43 664 4971204) or *Kitz* video internet cafe (T+43 5356 72427).

Bike map available? You can purchase comprehensive bike maps from the tourist office for €3.

The Lowdown

Locals do... Have a cool beer in *Desperados* or *Flannigans* after a long ride.

Locals don't... Ride freeride here, they head over to nearby Leogang for that.

Don't miss... Getting on the best trails by arranging a guide with the tourist office or try staying with *The Mountain Edge*.

Remember to avoid... Bringing your downhill bike and kit. Mid travel bikes with trail helmets and gear are the order of the day.

trails are very much quieter here than some other regions, but offer plenty to trail riders. You can also rent a GPS unit to access even more trails and concentrate on the riding rather than the map, or arrange for a guide for the day from the tourist office.

Easy Take the low level Sonnberg Runde, a 10-km loop with much of it on road.

Difficult Try the 32-km Torsee loop: with 1200 m vertical climbing it will sort the men from the boys. Expect a ride time of around four hours.

Downhill
While there remains a lack of downhill courses, the choice of six lifts opens up a whole range of trails to those only interested in clocking up the vertical feet whilst descending.

Freeride
While the area features some small freeride areas with a drop zone, trials section, 4x course, dual slalom and dirt jumps, there is not enough to keep the keen freerider entertained. It does however provide an excellent little extra to the trail riders and downhillers at the end of the day looking for somewhere to play. There is also a practice *parcours* which is designed to help younger children learn how to handle their bikes and ride off road.

ⓘ OPENING TIMES
The Hornbahn lift opens on 17 May; the rest of the lifts open in Jun; all lifts close at the end of Sep; operating hours are 0830 to 1700

ⓢ RESORT PRICES
Day pass: €26; Season pass: €120

ⓓ DIRECTORY
Tourist Office: T+43 5356 777
Medical Centre: T+43 5356 601
Website: en.summer.kitzbuehel.com

Austria & Slovenia Kitzbühel

More love riding. Perfect.

KITZBÜHEL TOURISM

Leogang

A tiny yet forward thinking resort, Leogang has worked hard to put itself on the map as one of the best freeride spots in Europe.

LEOGANG

↘3 The trails

XC Cross country Fair/intermediate to advanced

DH Downhill Fair to good/intermediate to advanced

FR Freeride Good/intermediate to advanced

Uplift The Leogang lift serves the bikepark

Pros A good set up with something for everyone; excellent facilities for young kids with trails and coaching to suit

Cons Maybe won't challenge the elite

Leogang is one of Kona's first bikeparks and they have been working together now for some years to make this place one of the standout resorts in Europe. Whilst it doesn't have the variety of, say, the Portes de Soleil, the trails are well

ⓘ OPENING TIMES

The park opens at weekends until 19 Jun, when it opens every day till 14 Sep, from 0900 till 1745

Ⓢ RESORT PRICES

Day pass: €29; Season pass: €194

ⓘ DIRECTORY

Leoganger Bergbahnen:
T+43 6583 8219
Website: leogangerbergbahnen.at/en/wwwbikeparkcom/

Below: Full speed wood action.
Bottom: More banks than the London Business District.

thought out and generally the facilities are improving year on year. The trails are all below the treeline, so it's soil and trees and roots which can be quite slick in the wet. Now that it has joined nearby resorts on the Austrian Gravity ticket it has seen more and more riders visiting.

Cross country

There are a number of cross country tours running out from Leogang and you can arrange to have a guide take you out onto the trails or pick up a map and guide yourself. Call into the bikeshop; whichever you decide they can arrange a guide or supply you with a trail map. It is possible to ride right the way over to Saalbach and Hinterglemm and take in some of the trails in their bike park before returning to Leogang.

Austrian northshore.

Easy If you're not too confident it is well worth taking in one or more of the skill schools on offer and taking a guided ride that will help bring the newly acquired skills into play.

Difficult Head out on the long tour into Saalbach and back.

Downhill

The Speedstar is the main downhill run in Leogang and contains a whole variety of surfaces, from off cambers and roots to berms and jumps. The rest of your

Austria & Slovenia Leogang

Practicalities ⊕⊘⊘

Surrounded by impressive mountains the small, pretty town of Leogang is set in a scenic location between Zell am See and St Johann, about an hour's drive from the nearest airport in Salzburg. Leogang provides a good set up for all types of riders and its laid-back atmosphere offers a more relaxing experience than the queues and crowds of some of the better-known resorts. In addition it's a real treat to find a town with a home-from-home feeling, a function of its small size and traditional homely accommodation.

Sleeping The *Alm Hotel Forsthofalm* (T+43 6583 8545) is ideally located for the bike park and is one of the official mountain bike hotels in the town. Or try the *Sinnlehenhof Apartment* (T+43 6583 8438) an eco-friendly farm in a peaceful location for the perfect quiet riding break.

Eating Why not try out some traditional Austrian cuisine served in a rustic dining room on the sun terrace of the *Reideralm* (T+43 6583

7342) whilst taking in the views of the Leoganger area? Or on the hill, try the *Stocklalm Alpine Restaurant* (T+43 6583 8255) serving hearty meals to walkers and riders.

Bars and clubs The town is pretty small, quiet and laid-back when it comes to partying in the winter, so in the summer Leogang is positively horizontal! There are a few bars and restaurants to grab a few drinks in, but don't expect to be partying till 6 in the morning here.

Bike shop The Bikepark bikeshop is located at the Leogang cablecar station and hires Kona bikes as well as having a good stock and carrying out most repairs.

Internet café Some hotels have Wi-Fi, although availability is not as widespread as in some resorts.

Bike map available? There are bike maps available from the tourist information office and from the Leogang lift station.

Luis Lacondeguy backflipping over the park.

Austria & Slovenia Leogang

time will be spent playing on the many easy but fun freeride descents such as the Flying Gangster run. Some of the toughest lines in the woods contain huge roots and are great sections.

Freeride

Leogang has loads for the budding freerider, with the long downhill-style flying Gangstar course made up of berms, tabletops, step ups, bridges and wooded singletrack over 2 km long. Then you've got the biker X or 4X course at the bottom of the run. This is 350 m long and you can race your mates down this side by side, with the benefit of a permanent start gate. Leogang is perhaps

known for its dirt jumps where the Braun 26 trix comp has been hosted for the past couple of years and where the first ever double backflip was pulled in competition. There is also a northshore area and notably a kids learning zone or mini bike park for young children.

Easy Take the flying gangster run from the top of the hill. It is packed with obstacles on its course down the hill.

Difficult For the confident jumpers, the large trails are not to be missed.

The Lowdown

Locals do... Session the large dirt jumps/trails at the bottom of the hill; ride short travel or hardtail bikes.

Locals don't... Ride in the wet, as it can be pretty dicey.

Don't miss... Heading out to watch the 26 trix at Leogang when the world's best freeriders battle it out on the trails.

Remember to avoid... Trail blazing, it won't be tolerated here.

Saalbach Hinterglemm

A forward thinking resort that hosts a huge freeride comp every summer.

SAALBACH HINTERGLEMM

↘4 The trails

- **XC Cross country** Good/beginner to advanced
- **DH Downhill** Fair to good/intermediate
- **FR Freeride** Good/intermediate to advanced
- **Uplift** There are 5 lifts open to take bikers to the top
- **Pros** Compact riding area; covers all three disciplines of riding really well
- **Cons** Can get quite cut up in the wet; much of the XC made up from wide tracks and roads and not true singletrack

Saalbach northshore drop. No endos.

SAALBACH TOURISM

Practicalities

The municipality of Saalbach Hinterglemm consists of two small towns, Saalbach and Hinterglemm, located in the Pinzgau region in the Saalbach Valley. The area is well known for its skiing and is one of Austria's premier ski resorts; this is something that the resort wants to convert into similar success and recognition in the summer season with their bike park and trails. Saalbach is a big, but pleasant, traditional Austrian village. Hinterglemm has no real centre.

Sleeping The *Alpenhotel Saalbach* (T+43 6541 66660) is well set up to cater for bikers having a bike garage with tools and some regular tours led by the hotel. Likewise *Bikehotel Conrad* (T+43 6541 6351) run daily guided tours and operates a workshop.

Eating Even the most committed food-lovers will have difficulty sampling all the restaurants in the area as there are 68 in total. The à-la-carte *Heurigenstube* restaurant at the *Hotel Salzburg* offers five-course dinners. *Bobby's Pub*, next to the Tunnel snowboard shop, is low on style but strong on atmosphere and always busy with all kinds of games including bowling, billiards, darts, table football, and computer games.

Bars and clubs Well known for its winter après ski, Saalbach Hinterglemm is much quieter in the summer, but there are still plenty of places to drink and unwind off the bike. There's dancing at the *Pub* and the *Zum Turn*, an old jail next to the church and cemetery, with a small, classy but rather pricey bar. The *Arena Disco* has live music and special promotion nights.

Bike shop The *Bike'n'Soul* shop at the *Bike Hotel Condor* (T+43 6541 6351) hire out bikes and has a well equipped workshop with local riders who can give you invaluable tips of where to ride.

Internet café Most of the hotels in the town offer either web workstations or Wi-Fi connections.

Bike map available? There are bike maps available from the tourist information centre and also from the *Bike'n'Soul* bike shop.

The mountains making up the Saalbach-Hinterglem resort make for some great mountain biking, and that's before you take in the many trails that are being created to cater for the more extreme sides of the sport. With 200 km of marked tours and five lifts open to bikes, there's a lot to explore in Saalbach and it does perhaps more so than others cater for all the different disciplines of mountain biking. The ground here is very alpine and green and most of the trails are through the trees, which means dirt and roots, so it's fantastic in the dry, but muddy and testing in the wet.

Top: Saalbach singletrack through the brush.
Above left: You'll be stumped for words.
Above right: Check out the park!

most famous for its freeride course in Hinterglemm, where a huge pro invite freeride comp is held each year with some massive lines and obstacles. There is also an indoor park with dirt jumps, ramps and a foam pit to dial in the tricks and a blue trail on the mountain that is perfect to develop skills.

Easy Spend your time perfecting technique on the blue line which starts out very easy and gets progressively harder towards the end.

Difficult Try the Freeride red line from the top of the mountain into the Evil Eye northshore trail at the bottom.

Cross country

There are around 200 km of marked trails in the immediate area with tours heading out much further also possible for the fittest enthusiasts. The area has also set out many GPS tours that can be downloaded from home or by calling into the *Bike'n'Soul* shop. This allows you to get on with the important business of riding and not worry about getting lost. The tours are all marked out as blue, red or black which equates to easy, intermediate or hard and there are also bike huts on the mountains which carry basic tools and repair stands and sell refreshments.

Downhill

The downhill on offer in Saalbach Hinterglemm takes a twist on the more traditional racetrack downhill courses. The built trails are really blurring the boundaries between true downhill and freeride and with technical singletrack, northshore sections and jumps all thrown into the mix, it makes for fun riding, especially for those who are comfortable in the air. Having said that, there are still plenty of options to ride the natural path style descents down the mountain from any of the five lifts.

Freeride

There's plenty to keep all the freeriders happy at Saalbach Hinterglemm. The Adidas freeride courses have multiple stunts and technical riding throughout and include the Evil Eye northshore trail at the bottom. The area is perhaps

The Lowdown

Locals do... Ride the indoor ramps and dirt jumps till 2200 dialling the lines and tricks; have some sneaky trails tucked away that they may or may not show you.

Locals don't... Ride the northshore trail in the wet.

Don't miss... A visit during the Adidas slopestyle competition, which usually runs on the first weekend of Aug.

Remember to avoid... Booking your own accommodation too far out of town.

ⓘ OPENING TIMES

The resort is open to riders from 26 May to 21 Oct: daily 0900-1630

ⓢ RESORT PRICES

Day pass: €28.50; Season pass: €190

ⓓ DIRECTORY

Tourist information:
T+43 6541 680068
Website: saalbach.com

Austria & Slovenia Saalbach Hinterglemm

Schladming

Regular host for the UCI World Cup for both cross country and downhill.

SCHLADMING

◹5   The trails

- **XC Cross country** Fair/intermediate to advanced
- **DH Downhill** Fair to good/acdvanced
- **FR Freeride** Poor/n/a
- **↗ Uplift** The main Planai lift can take you to the middle station or to the top of the hill
- **✔ Pros** A true downhill course with all the best elements; other things to do in the area to keep you busy
- **✘ Cons** Very limited options for riding other than the Planai downhill bikepark

Schladming has gained quite a reputation through hosting the UCI World Cup for the past five years. It has become synonymous with the elite of the sport and it's fair to say that the area is not suited to novices. The trails are mostly wooded and as such the soil retains some moisture making for great loamy conditions and roots aplenty. It is clear that the area and terrain could offer a lot more than they currently

ⓘ OPENING TIMES

The summer season runs from 1 Jun through to the 30 Sep; daily from 0900 to 1700

Ⓢ RESORT PRICES

Day pass: €18.70; Season pass: €78

ⓘ DIRECTORY

Tourist information: T+43 3687 22777
Website: planai.at

Practicalities 🍴🚲♨

The town of Schladming is an old mining town in the Styria region of Austria. The ski resort has become popular and there are now plenty of restaurants and bars to entertain the town's buoyant tourist industry. The town has a nice traditional feel and doesn't seem too overdeveloped, yet still offers plenty in the way of amenities. The nearest airport is Graz.

Sleeping There are plenty of large hotels and smaller chalet style apartments to stay in the town, try *Apartments Schutter* for a budget option, or the *Posthotel Schladming*, which is very centrally located in the town.

Eating *Marias Mexican* is a great place to eat with excellent food. Alternatively try the *Alte Post* in the centre of town, which has a more varied menu.

Bars and clubs *Marias Mexican* has a chilled out feel and good music once the food has been served. The main nightclub in the town is found in the basement of *Clubhotel Rossl* and is your usual Euro cheesy disco with poles and neon lights, so great fun after a few tequilas at Marias.

Bike shop The bike shop is called *2 rad Knauss* (T+43 3687 23124) and has a full workshop to carry out repairs after the battering the bikes take on the hill.

Internet café There is an internet café at the town post office and most of the hotels offer Wi-Fi connections.

Bike map available? There are bike maps available from the tourist information office and from the Planai lift station for free.

Austria & Slovenia Schladming

do, but experienced downhillers will always be drawn to the town to ride the infamous course.

Cross country
Strangely, despite hosting the world cup cross country on the Planai hill for several years, there are no waymarked routes on the hill. The tours in the area tend to be mainly on roads so the only way to ride good trails here is to explore or meet up with a local rider.

Downhill
The Planai course is infamous for its speed, steepness and technical wooded sections. The racecourse only runs from the middle station as well. From the top it is a very long run that will have your

brakes boiling and your arms pumped solid. Only really suited to experienced riders, as there are no truly easy runs despite what the tourist office may tell you.

Easy There are no easy routes, but there are easier options down the hill. Follow the signs that mark out the easier routes.

Difficult Take the main downhill course complete with the technical wooded sections that test even the world's best riders.

Freeride
There is no freeride on the Planai.

The Lowdown

Locals do... Break the hill up into sections, otherwise you'll burn yourself out; hit the outdoor pool when it's hot to relax and catch some sun.

Locals don't... Run anything other than full on downhill tyres; always ride bikes – the Dachstein Glacier offers summer ski and riding.

Don't miss... A go down the 7-km downhill go-kart run in the town. Just take your own lid, as the hire ones aren't much better than an ice cream container.

Remember to avoid... The whole area, if you are not proficient at riding technical trails.

Top right: Uplift. Tea not included.
Above right: The hills are alive with the sound of accordion.
Opposite page: Some think yellow rims are a bit Schladminging.

Semmering

MARTIN STEIGER/BIKEPARK SEMMERING

SEMMERING

⬊6 The trails

- **XC Cross Country** Fair/intermediate
- **DH Downhill** Good/beginner to intermediate
- **FR Freeride** Excellent/beginner to advanced
- **⑦ Uplift** A gondola carries riders and bikes to the top of the trails
- **✔ Pros** Trails are maintained daily; good beginners park; easy location to visit being only 1 hr from Graz and Vienna
- **✖ Cons** Not so great for XC; perhaps not enough trails to sustain a long stay

A great little bikepark that has set out to build something fun for beginners and pros alike.

The Bikepark Zauberg opened in 2006 and now contains several routes. It is developing each year with new runs. It is a modest sized hill and the team there have focused on an accessible park that can be used by families and beginners as well as having some more testing obstacles for more experienced riders. The hill is wooded with open piste sections and the ground can cut up in the wet.

Cross country

While the Bikepark is all about the gravity-assisted side of the sport, the family route

① OPENING TIMES

The bikepark season runs daily from Jun to Sep: 0900-1800

ⓢ RESORT PRICES

Day pass: €20.50; season pass: €185

① DIRECTORY

Tourist Office: bikeparksemmering.at

The Lowdown

Locals do... Have a good scene and all hang out at the park on weekends, and party into the night.

Locals don't... All have perfect bikes. Some of the local shredders' bikes are nailed.

Don't miss... If you're still learning the ropes, book a day with the instructors who can help you learn to tackle the obstacles in the park.

Remember to avoid... If it has been very wet. Although the trails are better maintained than most, it can be quite mucky after heavy storms.

descends gently and is rideable on even the most race-orientated XC bike. There are several XC tours through the area in rolling wooded alpine countryside and routes are available from the tourist office.

Downhill

There is a downhill racetrack in the bike park that is technical and has hosted the Austrian Championships; the rest of the park is gentler with more freeride obstacles that are all lift-fed making it plenty of fun on a downhill bike.

Freeride

The park has plenty of freeride obstacles, a northshore route with flowing wooden raised sections, berms and drops. Half way up the hill there is a slopestyle course ideal for intermediate riders and finally the freeride route running from the top of the hill. The trails are generally for all abilities although there are no big stunts to challenge experienced riders.

Easy Warm up with the family route, a real gentle trail down the hill, before tackling the freeride trails opting for the smaller drops and banks until your confidence is up to tackle the harder lines.

Difficult The downhill course contains the more technical steep sections of trail and your ability in the air can be tested on the slopestyle course and the northshore park.

Practicalities 🛏🍴🔧

Semmering bikepark bears the same name as both the ski resort and the pass it is located on. The pass is the most important connection between lower Austria and Styria. Semmering is one of Austria's smaller resorts, leaving you with little else to do but get on with the pressing issue of riding. That's not to say there aren't sufficient amenities; there are all the usual resort services and plenty of places to stay and relax, just don't expect a lively summer in the town. The closest airport is the Austrian capital of Vienna only 90 km away making it perfect for long weekend breaks.

Sleeping The Bikepark have set up plenty of bike deals with the hotels in the town; try the *Hotel Alpenhof* (T+43 2664 21194) complete with bike garage, or the *Sonnwendhof* (T+43 2664 20087) which offers a good bike package.

Eating With a range of bars, restaurants and mountain inns, there is some choice about where you splash your cash. When riding, the *Zauberbar* at the lift station is a great place to grab some food. In the evening, try *Gasthof Berghof* or *Liechtensteinhaus*, for regional specialities.

Bars and clubs Again the *Zauberbar* is a good place to grab a few beers after a day in the park, and later in the night stays open as a discotheque.

Bike shop There is a bike shop next to the lift station that hires out good quality bikes and carries out repairs.

Internet café The *Panhams Hotel* and *Onkel Fritz* both offer Wi–Fi and internet terminals.

Bike map available? A map is not required for the Bikepark. XC routes can be collected from the tourist office.

Top right: Bikepark overview. A beauty and no mistake.
Above: Wallride tabletop. Sweet.
Opposite page: The northshore crocodile gap is a must.

Wagrain

⬂7 The trails

Ⓧ Cross country Fair to good/ beginner to intermediate

Ⓓ Downhill Good/intermediate to advanced

Ⓕ Freeride Excellent/beginner to advanced

Ⓐ Uplift The Flying Mozart Gondola reaches the mid station in just 5 mins; currently all the trails run from here although there are imminent plans to extend to the top lift station

✔ Pros Great design team behind the park; super quick uplift; progressive park

✘ Cons Not so great for cross country; perhaps not enough trails to sustain a long stay

A berm in sight of the gondola. What a scene.

Bringing a taste of Canada's finest trails to mainland Europe.

Whistler is arguably the world's top bike park and a word constantly used as a reference point for quality trails, so it is great to see some of the brains behind the original development coming over to Europe to set up a park. Whistler has taken many years to become what it is today and Wagrain opened its doors in mid-2006, so it is still developing its trails each year but it has the quality stamp already. There are plans to extend to the top station of the gondola giving a 900 m vertical drop. Outside the park are very gentle routes taking in the panoramic views.

Cross country

There are no XC trails within the park but there are smooth machine-built trails that are perfect for the first timer to enjoy the gravity side of the sport. Outside the park there are limited waymarked routes around the mountains, and not the quality singletrack found in other regions, but the choice is there and there is no extra cost to take the bike on the lifts.

Practicalities 🛏🍴🚴

When Canadian Jason Roe, the founding manager of Whistler Bike Park, upped camp to replicate his success on European soil, it was Wagrain that was finally chosen as the site with the ideal terrain to develop a complete trail network. Wagrain is a tradition-rich vacation spot in the heart of Salzburg's mountainous region that has managed to preserve the beauty of its landscapes and its alpine village charm. The area has a warm ambience and does not feel overdeveloped, despite providing all the comforts that a top-notch resort town can offer. In addition Salzburg airport is only 70 km away.

Sleeping There is plenty of choice when it comes to where to stay, but it's important to make sure they have secure bike storage. The *Tauernhof* (T+43 6457 2311) and *Apart-Pension Panorama* (T+43 6413 8427) both do and are located close to the gondola.

Eating While you're on the hill or after a good days ride hit *Amstadl* (T+43 6413 7444) near the base of the park. *Haar Trog Alm* is a popular restaurant in the town (T+43 6413 7286)

Bars and clubs There are a number of après ski bars, but many are closed and the town on the whole is much quieter in the summer. For all your euro pop fun, head for *Disco Tenne*.

Bike shop *Sport Factory* (T+43 6413 7365) is based at the base of the Flying Mozart Gondola and has a fleet of Trek bikes for hire as well as body armour.

Internet café No café, however many of the hotels offer internet access; either Wi-Fi or through terminals.

Bike map available? Bike park map is posted on their website (mountainbikeparkwagrain.com) and a map of the surrounding XC trails is available available from the Tourist Office at a price of €9.50!

JASON ROE/WAGRAIN BIKEPARK

The Lowdown

Locals do... Ride the top of the monster wall ride; manual off the wood step up on Symphony; end their day at Sarastro with a cold one.

Locals don't... Mind riding when it does rain – although that isn't very often.

Don't miss... Bauernstuberl – typical food from the region.

Remember to avoid... Riding down the hiking trails here, the locals will not be pleased!

Downhill
The bikepark is established around having fun rather than the racier style of downhill trails but there are sections that are in the more traditional roots and rocks downhill vein. But any rider will love riding here.

Freeride
The park is geared up for freeriders with plenty of big berms, tabletops, step ups and drops. There are northshore trails and then more traditional DH style runs. There is a new 320-m slopestyle course being built and at the mid station a skills centre which allows riders to become accustomed to freeriding in a safe environment before you enter the park.

Easy Take the Flying Fox to the mid station and try out your skills in the fun skills centre. Once you have learnt to ride the banked corners, rollers and drops there spend the rest of your day hitting up 'on air' and 'memories'.

Difficult Seek out the black sections of trail such as 'old school' and 'symphony' and try the 'R n B' northshore trail.

Top: Luckily, in Wagrain you can see the wood from the trees.
Above: Softly softly grippy monkey.
Bottom: Another rider denies the pit of doom its victim.

ⓘ OPENING TIMES
The bikepark season runs from 31 May to 23 Sep, daily, and onto 7 Oct at weekends

Ⓢ RESORT PRICES
Day pass: €24; Season pass: €150

ⓘ DIRECTORY
Tourist Office Wagrain: T+43 6413 8448
Website: mountainbikepark-wagrain.com

Austria & Slovenia Wagrain

KAI CROW/WAGRAIN BIKEPARK

STEFAN GRUBER/WAGRAIN BIKEPARK

STEFAN GRUBER/WAGRAIN BIKEPARK

Zillertal

Part of the stunning Tyrol region and a huge area for cross country biking.

ZILLERTAL

↘8 The trails

- **XC Cross country** Excellent/beginner to advanced
- **DH Downhill** Poor to fair/intermediate
- **FR Freeride** Poor/n/a
- **Uplift** There are up to 9 lifts that will carry bikes in the Zillertal valley
- **Pros** Massive area to ride; stunning area with some superb trails
- **Cons** Not suited so well to the unfit; very limited facilities for downhill

The mountains surrounding Mayrhofen are big and imposing and the trails that run along, around and over them, range from gravel roads to technical steep, rocky trails.

ⓘ OPENING TIMES

There are 9 different lifts in the valley open to bikers which all open around the end of May and early Jun; most close between late Sep and early Oct

Ⓢ RESORT PRICES

Day pass: €31; Week pass: €164.50

ⓘ DIRECTORY

Tourist information: T+43 528 56760;
Medical Centre: T+43 528 562550;
Website: mayrhofen.at

This means the riding can be as easy or as tough as you like. As part of a region famed for its fantastic trail riding, the Zillertal valley offers endless trails to the enthusiast XC rider in epic country with stunning backdrops and great panoramas.

Cross country

With over 800 km of trails in the valley there is no shortage of riding. Many tours are marked out and you can rent a GPS unit from the resort to access more routes or bring your own and download the routes at the tourist office. You choose how tough you want the routes to be, both physically and technically, and there is always the option of the many ski lifts that will carry bikes up the valley to ease the burn on the legs. This area is probably best suited to the fitter trail rider who could ride all day for two weeks and hit a different trail every time.

Easy Take one of the many bikeways – essentially gravel alpine roads with gentle gradients – which will get you out into the mountains to sample what the area has to offer.

Below left: Love ride with misty view equals definite plus points.
Below: Riding through a ghost town with a trusty sidekick. No whistling 'The Good, The Bad and The Ugly.'
Bottom: The mighty Hintertux glacier.

MAYRHOFEN TOURISM

MAYRHOFEN TOURISM

The Lowdown

Locals do... Cover some massive distances; have unreasonably strong legs.

Locals don't... Ride downhill or freeride.

Don't miss... An afternoon relaxing at the Erlebnisbad, Mayrhofen's swimming pool, it has a slide and river rapids to tackle on inflatable tubes.

Remember to avoid... Heading out on the tours without tools and spares as you will be out all day.

Above left: Yellow jerseys always go first.
Below left: Now that's an uplift.

Difficult How fit are you? Try the 99-km Geiseljoch tour; with an expected ride time of 10 hours this route requires excellent fitness and technique but will reward you with some great trails and panoramic views.

Downhill

There are no marked downhill routes in the Zillertal valley, however, as with many of the resorts in the Alps, some of the more testing and interesting trails are not constructed downhill trails, but old animal or trading trails. There are eight or so lifts open to bikers in the valley though you should realise that they are spread out along the valley so you will have to cycle or catch the bus between the lift stations.

Freeride

There is no freeride in the Zillertal valley.

Practicalities

The largest town in the Zillertal valley is Mayrhofen, though there are many smaller village resorts along the 30-km valley base such as Gerlos, Lanersbach and Zell. Mayrhofen is one of the premier Austrian resorts through the winter season and is also in close proximity to the Hintertux glacier for year-round snow. The town is lively and modern while managing to maintain some traditional Tyrolean feel. There is everything you might expect from a busy resort and Innsbruck is the nearest airport.

Sleeping Ludwigs (opposite the Scotland Yard pub – ask in the bar for Ludwig, no phone or website and he only speaks German!) for €8-10 per night. For a once in a lifetime experience you must stay at the Hotel Strass (hotelstrass.com), only €70 per night and the most central hotel in town, or else try the Elisabeth Hotel (elisabethhotel.com).

Eating In Mayrhofen, try Mama Mia's for pizza and pasta, Mo's has Tex Mex, or try Café Tirol for authentic Austrian schnitzel. For cheap but filling grub the Sports Bar at the Sport Hotel Strasse works.

Bars and clubs In Mayrhofen, Scotland Yard and The Ice Bar are institutions. You're likely to end up at the Arena and the Speakeasy.

Bike shop Try Hervis (T+43 5285 64045) or Rental bei Kaplenig (T+43 5285 62286) in Mayrhofen, where you can get basic repairs carried out but don't expect a comprehensive stock of all brands for spares. Carry any consumables such as disc pads with you.

Internet café The Tirol Café has computers to use, while the Hotels Strass, Kramerwirt, and Eberhater have wireless for around €4 per hr.

Bike map available? There are bike maps available from the tourist information centres for free.

Kransjka Gora

↘9 The trails

- **Cross Country** Fair to good/ intermediate
- **Downhill** Fair to good/ intermediate
- **Freeride** Good/beginner to intermediate
- **Uplift** A chairlift serves the bikepark and you can arrange for shuttle runs outside the park
- **Pros** Close proximity to Austria and Pohorje bikepark makes this a good multi-trip stop; relaxed atmosphere; beautiful area
- **Cons** Not enough to entertain a long stay in the bikepark; much of the jump and stunt building is quite basic when compared to somewhere like Whistler

A low-key funpark surrounded by beautiful nature makes this a truly relaxing place to take a break with the bike.

There are two very different styles of riding in Kransjka Gora: first there is the bikepark with its man-made runs and

loads of wooden kickers and drops; and secondly there is the natural riding in the stunning area around the resort. By mixing up the park with the natural trails you will get the most out of the riding in the resort. The long warm summer here helps to dry the soil out under the trees, so the trails are generally very dry and dusty.

Cross country

There's a whole range of cross country tours running out from Kransja Gora. The maps available even show a 5-day tour through the Julian Alps. There are plenty of shorter rides nearer the town but most of the marked trails are more in the touring vein than singletrack XC. Contact the bikepark via their website to arrange for guides to show you the trails best suited to your ability.

Downhill

The downhill course hosts a round of the Slovenia Cup and is 2-km long with a 350-m vertical drop. It has various split

Clockwise from top:
1. Wood berm.
2. Plenty of scope to kick up a plume.
3. Bikepark uplift. Nearly a monster truck.
4. Gora launch pad.

ⓘ OPENING TIMES

The Park aims to open the last week of Apr each year, but it is weather dependant and stays open right up until the first week of Nov; opening hours are 0900 to 1700

ⓢ RESORT PRICES

Day pass: €16; Week pass: €85; Season pass: €167

ⓓ DIRECTORY

Tourist office: T+386 4580 9440
Website: bikepark.si

sections so you can choose your level of difficulty, and the main route can be made into more than six separate runs if you join it up with the different freeride lines that run off it. Outside the bikepark there are a number of natural descents which you can shuttle. If you arrange with the bikepark they will organise a shuttle and a guide.

Freeride

The freeride trail at Kranjska Gora runs right from the top of the hill with numerous built stunts ranging from wooden northshore runs and wallrides to dirt doubles and step downs. There are different ability choices throughout its length, but make sure you check the lines before sending it down the trail.

Easy Try riding in the Polygon, a learning zone with different size obstacles in to master the basic skills.

Difficult Head out on the full freeride route and roll down to eye up the different obstacles on your first run, before you try and nail it.

The Lowdown

Locals do... Hit the Evil Eye step down at the end of the trail; have one of the longest riding seasons.

Locals don't... Live in the town, most live in the capital, Ljubjana

Don't miss... A shuttle trip up to the three borders where you can stand in Austria, Italy and Slovenia before riding a great trail back to the valley floor.

Remember to avoid... Riding the obstacles without checking them out first. Some have blind gaps or drops.

Practicalities

The resort town of Kranjska Gora sits in the breathtaking Zgornjesavska Valley in the northwestern corner of Slovenia, near the border with Austria and Italy. The surroundings include the Triglav National Park and the imposing Julian Alps, making this a popular area for outdoor enthusiasts. Add the favourable climate and the inclusion of a bikepark at the resort and you'll see why there has been a recent increase in riders visiting the town.

Sleeping The *Bendanc Apartments* (T+386 3897 6740) are reasonably priced and set up to accommodate bikers.

Eating Why not try out some traditional cuisine at the *Restaurant Iz Krusne Peci* (T+386 4589 2088), or the Pri Martin. *Hotel Kotnik* is a good place to grab a pizza and the *Lipa* Restaurant serves some super fish dishes.

Bars and clubs Head to the bikers' hangout at the English-run *Enka Bar* just behind the tourist office in the centre of town.

Bike shop *The Bikeshop* is found at the lift station and also rents bikes. There is a 30% discount for female rentals to encourage more girls to participate.

Internet café The *Nika Youth Hostel* has internet access, as do many of the hotels in the town.

Bike map available? There are a couple of well produced local trail maps available from most bike shops, hotels and the tourist office which there is a small charge for, although they are aimed primarily at the cross country or touring cyclist. Downhillers and freeriders do not require a map for the bikepark.

Austria & Slovenia Kransjka Gora

WWW.BIKEPARK.SI

Pick your line.

Maribor Pohorje

Maribor has more to it than just the scariest gondola ride in Europe; the trails will get your adrenaline going too.

MARIBOR POHORJE

⬊10 The trails

- **XC Cross Country** Fair to good/intermediate
- **DH Downhill** Good/intermediate to advanced
- **FR Freeride** Poor/intermediate
- **Uplift** The main Pohorje Gondola and the Radvanje chairlift, which combined, takes riders to about 2/3rds up the mountain
- **Pros** One of the classic downhill tracks; good long runs from the top of the hill, with decent sections; no lift queues
- **Cons** XC routes not so well set out; perhaps not enough trails to sustain a long stay

Maribor has been synonymous with the World Cup series since 1999 when it started hosting races and has remained a favourite due to its friendly locals and its great courses. There is never much traffic on the trails, so there are no queues, just plenty of riding down any of the many singletracks that add up to over 4 km. The trails range from forest tracks and pistes to super-technical singletrack and, depending on which trails you go for, you can expect to see plenty of roots and rocks on the more testing trails. It can be quite slick in the wet but on the whole Maribor enjoys a favourable climate, and the potential riding area here is huge with the hill running for 80 km across.

Cross country

There are plenty of paths and singletracks on the Pohorje mountain which can make for some good cross country riding, though most of the marked trails are less interesting as they're on wide paths and roads. The World Cup cross country course is a great example of how good the riding can be but is not marked out. To get the best out of the area you should organize a guide by emailing info.park@sc-pohorje.si, or contacting the tourist office.

Downhill

The GT bikepark is geared around the downhill runs, with the World Cup trail being one of the best downhills on the UCI calendar. Unfortunately this is not an official trail outside of competition so it should not be ridden. Aside from this there is a range of steep technical trails cutting through rooty undulating

ⓘ OPENING TIMES
The bikepark is open Mon to Fri 1200-1800 and Sat and Sun 0900-1800 from Apr to Sep

Ⓢ RESORT PRICES
Day pass: €18; Week pass: €99.10

ⓒ DIRECTORY
Tourism on Pohorje:
T+386 220 8843
Website: pohorje.org

Austria & Slovenia Maribor Pohorje

PHIL YOUNG

woodland and down fast, open pistes. Some are official marked trails and others are unmarked routes used by local riders. Most of the riding is suited to intermediate to advanced riders.

Easy There aren't currently any easy runs in the park; the trails are too steep and rough for beginners.

Above: The infamous rock garden.
Opposite page: Maribor's new 'Wallride Star Mix' was a hit.

Difficult The main run under the gondola is steep and physical. A day on this, broken up with a lunchtime pizza from *La Cantina*, will leave you tired as it's a long run from top to bottom.

Freeride

There are a number of obstacles on the one freeride/downhill style run through the park, with tabletops, hips, drops and a nice wooden step up/step down. But don't be expecting a Whistler-style bike park; the 30 features are all covered in a short period of time and it is the technical riding through the woods that is the bike park's main attraction.

Yet another sunset love ride.

The Lowdown

Locals do... Take long all mountain rides across the Pohorje mountain which runs for 80 km; have secret downhill singletracks around the bikepark.

Locals don't... Disrespect the land owners, as the hill has many different owners.

Don't miss... Taking a peek at the infamous rock garden on the downhill course.

Remember to avoid... Pohorje if you are scared of heights, the gondola is one of the highest around.

Practicalities

The ski resort of Pohorje, set around the Pohorje mountain, is a five-minute drive outside Maribor, the second largest town in Slovenia. Maribor gained town rights in the 13th century, and in the late Middle Ages the town had to protect itself with strong walls to ward off the invading Turkish army. The remains are still well preserved in Lent, the old town by the Drava. Slovenia seceded from the former Yugoslavia in 1991 and modern Maribor is a city developing high-quality tourism. This relies primarily on good wine, good cuisine and the well-preserved streets and squares of the town centre. The cost of living, especially food, is very reasonable and considerably cheaper than France and Austria. There is also an international airport in the town making it an easy destination to reach.

Sleeping There is a campsite at the foot of the mountain for campervans and tents and with a great summer climate, *Camp Pohorje* is a good budget option (T+386 2614 0950) and there are several small hotels and apartments on the banks of Pohorje Mountain. Try *Hotel Arena* (T+386 2614 0950).

Eating The food in Maribor is generally plentiful and very cheap. Next to the gondola is *La Cantina* serving good pasta dishes. 500 m from the gondola is the popular *Pri Lipi*, famous for its chicken dishes.

Bars and clubs Around the bike park and gondola there are a few smaller bars, while in Maribor itself there are lots of clubs, with our pick *Klub KMS* or *Samsara*.

Bike shop There is a bike shop run from the building housing the gondola station at the bottom of the bike park. They rent GT bikes and carry quite a few spares.

Internet café There is an internet café in the main square of the city called *KIT* (T+386 2252 4440).

Bike map available? There is no bike map available at present although it is planned that trail maps will be available soon; contact the resort for the latest update.

England

England: everything from classic single-track to the darkest of downhill sections. Just what you're after. [DAN MILNER]

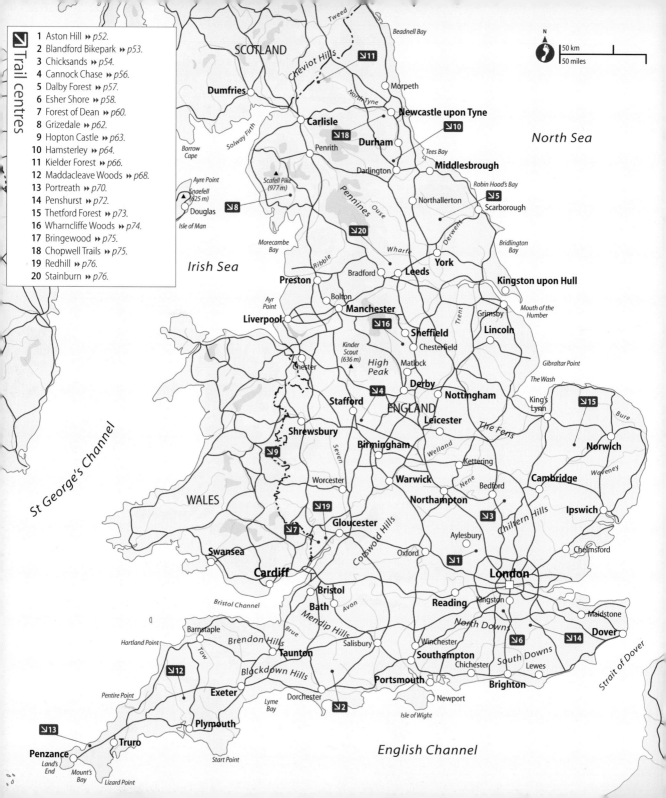

N

50 km
50 miles

SCOTLAND

Tweed

Beadnell Bay

Cheviot Hills

↘11

Morpeth

North Tyne

Dumfries

Newcastle upon Tyne

Carlisle

↘18

Durham

↘10

North Sea

Penrith

Tees Bay

Darlington

Middlesbrough

Borrow Cape

Robin Hood's Bay

Solway Firth

Ayre Point

▲ *Snaefell (625 m)*

Douglas

Isle of Man

▲ *Scafell Pike (977 m)*

↘8

Pennines

Northallerton

↘5

Scarborough

Ouse

Bridlington Bay

Morecambe Bay

↘20

Wharfe

Derwent

Ribble

Bradford

Leeds

York

Irish Sea

Preston

Kingston upon Hull

Ayr Point

Bolton

Manchester

↘16

Mouth of the Humber

Grimsby

Liverpool

Sheffield

Lincoln

Trent

Chesterfield

Gibraltar Point

Chester

Kinder Scout (636 m) ▲

High Peak

Matlock

The Wash

Derby

↘4

ENGLAND

Nottingham

Stafford

King's Lynn

↘15

Bure

Shrewsbury

Leicester

The Fens

↘9

Birmingham

Severn

Norwich

Welland

Woveney

Kettering

Worcester

Warwick

Nene

Bedford

Cambridge

WALES

Northampton

↘3

Ipswich

↘19

Chiltern Hills

Gloucester

Aylesbury

Chelmsford

↘7

Cotswold Hills

Oxford

↘1

Swansea

London

Cardiff

Bristol

Kingston

Maidstone

Bath

Avon

Reading

St George's Channel

Bristol Channel

Brue

Mendip Hills

Dover

↘14

Barnstaple

Brendon Hills

North Downs

Hartland Point

Brendon Hills

Salisbury

Winchester

↘6

South Downs

Lewes

Taw

Taunton

Blackdown Hills

Southampton

Chichester

Brighton

Strait of Dover

↘12

Portsmouth

Pentire Point

Exeter

Lyme Bay

Dorchester

↘2

Newport

Isle of Wight

↘13

Plymouth

Truro

Penzance

Land's End

Start Point

English Channel

Mount's Bay

Lizard Point

Opening up the throttle in a clearing section.

It is perhaps remarkable that England, a country without any sizable mountain ranges, has produced such a strong mountain bike scene and some of the most successful and talented mountain bikers on the planet. This can be traced directly to the passion and spirit of English riders who have carved out many great places to ride, armed with nothing more than a sense of adventure, a few spades and a whole lotta love.

Though overshadowed by the rapid advances of its Celtic neighbours, English mountain biking has made progress, spearheaded by a strong community of riders. Trail centres continue to improve in quantity and quality, complementing the existing great natural and rider-established trails and making England a superb destination for mountain bikers of every standard.

Unlike most other countries, many of England's trails have been developed around the large population centres, allowing them to serve the town's and city's bikers. This gives you the option of staying out in the country, or stopping in some of the great cities of England and sharing a more mixed cultural experience than perhaps a straight out-and-out riding trip. By taking in the sights of London, Manchester, Newcastle and Leeds after a day, or weekend's, ride, you will be enriched both on and off the bike.

In the end though, it's all about the riding and there is an immense amount of that available in England. From the national parks to the ever-multiplying forest centre and rider-created trails there is a huge amount to do in this country and for the adventurous who take to the hills with Ordnance Survey map in hand, the possibilities are endless.

Overview

Many of the riding spots and venues in England have been built and developed by riders themselves, as a response to the lack of good places to ride. Luckily for us, riders generally know what they want and the result of these self-built trails is that many of the better established venues have some great riding to offer which has challenged bikers over the years and is continually bringing new blood into the sport.

Recently however there has been a response from one of the major landowners in the country, the Forestry Commission; this has come as a result of both the neighbouring successes of Wales and Scotland and the perceived benefits of mountain biking tourism.

Another aspect to remember is that mountain bikers do not have open access in England. Throughout the countryside and national parks mountain bikes are restricted to bridleways and public rights of way, whereas the trails in this chapter are all mountain bike specific.

So while England's riders are wise to the trails on offer, the new trail centres, downhill venues and freeride spots have perhaps been overlooked by many riders on the continent.

Conditions

England enjoys a temperate climate, which roughly equates to being not too hot and not too cold. Summer days can be glorious though rarely uncomfortably warm, while winter may bring the occasional snow scatter on hilltops but on the whole with the right clothing and tyres England enjoys a great year round riding season. That's not too say that like the rest of Britain it doesn't see its fair share of rain, and some areas geology may suffer when waterlogged resulting in soft muddy trails. This is where the trail centres do really come into their own as they are constructed to be weather proof, a few splashes of water for sure but still hard packed under tyre. Up on the hills and especially on the moorland areas of the country, riders should be vigilant to the lack of cover and changeable conditions.

The scene

The scene in the UK is huge and England represents the largest sector. From the fluid dirt jump scene around the M25 and south east of England that has spawned some super talented riders to the two time downhill World Series champion Steve Peat from Sheffield in the north, England has repeatedly raised the UK's finest riders in all areas of mountain biking and the scene has always had role models to watch and aspire to. Every weekend there are groups all over England meeting up whether it is to take on an epic ride through the Lake District national park, hit a

Top left: Kenny Smith at Still Woods, Bristol.
Top right: Richard Norgate at Hebdon Bridge.
Middle: Steve Peat teaching the next generation.
Bottom: Andy Waterman on the trail.

fun forest loop, session the dirt jumps or try and beat their mates down the local downhill. What is for sure is that every weekend they will be out there doing what they love. Visitors will soon find themselves acquainted with the local groups and can look to plan ahead their rides by using any of the active mountain bike web forums such as: bikemagic.com, singletrackworld.com and bikeradar for xc, descent-world.co.uk andsoutherndownhill.com for downhill and freeride and trailaddict.co.uk for dirt jumping.

The industry
Around the country are some of the mountain bike powerhouses, such as the beautifully hand-built in Halifax Orange bikes (orangebikes.co.uk) who produce some of the best bikes available. Hope Technology (hopetech.com) are based in Barnoldswick and produce all manner of trick parts for your bikes though they are perhaps best known for their disc brakes. The UK mountain bike magazines also are well known for their quality and coverage and the main publications in England include *Mountain Bike UK*, *Mountain Bike Rider*, *What Mountain Bike*, *Singletrack magazine* and *Dirt magazine*.

England breakdown
While the UK can never compete in terms of uplift with the rest of Europe, it still provides some fantastic destinations to ride your bike. In England we have aimed to show some of the most accessible and high quality places to ride your bike.

The information has been split into three groups (DH, XC and FR) relating to what the trails and/or centre can offer. We've aimed to pick out the best centre based trails, the ones with the best and/or the most riding and facilities on offer (places to eat, sleep and fix your bike) have been afforded the most space. These are England's key destinations. Second to these are the destinations which lack some of the facilities to earn a key destination status, but are nonetheless good.

Q&A with the experts

Steve Peat needs little introduction in the mountain biking world. The three-time World Cup Champion hails from Sheffield and is still the man to beat on the UCI world circuit.

You've got friends visiting for just one weekend and they can go anywhere in England. Name the one place you'd definitely have to take them.

SP Well, for myself it would have to be Wharncliffe Forest in Sheffield, mainly because I've ridden there for 18 years and it has the best technical trails around.

Which trail centre or resort has the best party scene or the best after riding activities?

SP It's England mate, any pub, club or town has loads of life going on! Any day of the week.

Where did you learn to ride, and where would you send beginners to ride?

SP I learnt to ride in Chapeltown Park, Sheffield. I used to follow my brothers around and try and do what they did. i think the best place for beginners to learn is down some local woods or near by trail centers, you get to know the trails then you learn to ride.

In your opinion, which is the best downhill track in England?

SP There are quite a few good tracks around Shropshire. I reckon Bringewood is an old favorite of mine.

Where's the best place to avoid pedalling uphill? Where has the best uplifts? Would you avoid anywhere?

SP Again, Shropshire has a good scene going on, Dave Pearce (Dave Pearce Cycles) does a great job providing downhillers with good uplift services. Hamsterly is a good spot for the northerners too. I don't avoid any place, i just don't have time to visit many.

Where's best for total variety?

SP Read this guide and go try a few places, You'll definitely find the place that suits you best and then keep going back. It's hard to pick one for myself as i am usually in full race mode whenever i go anywhere. My DH bike is made for DH so thats what I do the most.

Aston Hill

ASTON HILL

↘1 The trails

- **XC Cross country** Fair/intermediate
- **DH Downhill** Good/intermediate to advanced
- **FR Freeride** Fair to good/intermediate to advanced
- **Uplift** No uplift
- **Pros** Good transport links; technical trails; quality coaching programme
- **Cons** Difficult to ride in the wet; no uplift

The current tracks were built by Ian Warby over a 10 year period. Ian had a real insight it to what is now a global phenomenon and for years Aston Hill has been one of the only venues to provide for downhill and 4X in the southeast. The soil type here is quite chalky and littered with flint which can make for interesting riding when wet, but the tracks are well maintained, if not manicured, and will test the most proficient of riders. In addition, there are three downhill tracks, a cross country downhill, a 4X track and a 10-km XC loop.

Cross country

The XC loop runs along the outside edge of the wood until it reaches the top of the hill where it meanders through a slightly flatter section, The track is very physical with few places to rest, as well as being technical in places with steep sections, off cambers and roots galore.

Below: A crime scene on Cocaine Alley.
Right: Careful of that flint there, mate.

Practicalities

Aston is in the Chilterns in Buckinghamshire. The mountain bike area is 100 acres of woodland made up mostly of beech and conifer, and has amazing views over the Vale of Aylesbury. In the neighbouring Wendover woods there are more family friendly riding trails for the less adventurous and a number of other activities such as a Go Ape assault course and a nature trail. Aston is one of the very few places in southeast England that has downhill tracks that are over 1½ mins long. It is 40 miles from central London; a 20-min drive from the M25. There are also two train lines within a 20-min ride of the hill, Wendover and Tring.

Sleeping The majority of visitors to the hill just come for the day, but there are loads of B&Bs, hotels and guesthouses within a 10-min drive. For local tourist information you can call Wendover TIC (see Directory).

Eating Try the well-named *Café in the Woods* in the neighbouring Wendover Woods. Wendover and Tring, five mins drive away, both have plenty of place to choose from.

Bars and clubs There are a number of pubs around Wendover, but for clubs your best bet is London.

Bike shops *Mountain Mania* in Tring is a 10-min drive away, they also offer a priority repair service to Aston hill riders and a discount on parts.

Internet café Wendover's library has internet access. Nearby Aylesbury has pubs and cafés with Wi-Fi.

Bike map available? No trail map.

Downhill

The three downhill tracks are all of similar length and make the best use of the gradient and terrain. The black run is the oldest and has received design input from Rob Warner. There is a steep shoot on the track which is pure chalk and has been given the name Cocaine Alley. The other two tracks are equally as technical with a mixture of jumps, drops, berms and off cambers.

Freeride

Built on chalk, the 4X track is almost unrideable when wet but bakes hard and rides very quick in the dry. It features the usual doubles, rollers and tables as well as a road gap. There are plans to surface the track when funds become available.

Locals do...

Session the road gap on the 4X.

Locals don't…

Ride without protection. The flint here is very sharp and can slice your knees and elbows open.

ⓘ OPENING TIMES

Tue and Thu 1800-2100; Weekends and Bank Holidays only 0900-1700

Ⓢ RESORT PRICES

Day pass: £5; yearly membership available on request

ⓘ DIRECTORY

Tourist Office: T+44 (0)1296-696759
Bikepark: rideastonhill.co.uk

Blandford Bikepark

ⓘ OPENING TIMES

The trails are open all day but the uplift runs from 1000 to 1700

$ RESORT PRICES

£3 per day and £20 per day for uplifts

ⓘ DIRECTORY

UK Bike Park: T+44 (0)7881-571069, ukbikepark.com

BLANDFORD BIKEPARK

↘2 The trails

- **XC Cross country** Poor/intermediate
- **DH Downhill** Good/beginner to intermediate
- **FR Freeride** Good/beginner to intermediate
- **↗ Uplift** Uplifts arranged on certain weekends, book early to get a space. See ukbikepark.com for more details
- **✓ Pros** Good progressive ride venue for novice/intermediate riders; good use of the land area; ideal day trip or weekend overnight venue
- **✗ Cons** Limited space on the uplifts; you can exhaust the riding after a couple of days

Definitely a hill rather than a mountain, but the crew here have set about making the most of the modest altitude by cramming it with lines and options over the four main downhill routes. If you manage to book into one of the very popular uplift days you can link up the various different sections and hit a different route each time. The park is ideal for novice to intermediate riders as all the features have chicken lines for building up confidence. Expert or advanced riders may find that there is not much here to challenge them but the park is constantly evolving new lines of all sizes.

Cross country

This is not an XC venue as it has no cross country trails. However, due to its multiple size obstacles it is well suited to the XC rider looking to develop their downhill or freeride handling.

Downhill

There are four main downhill runs and plenty of singletrack sections. Plus all the freeride obstacles are equally fun to incorporate into your downhill day.

Freeride

The park is a popular freeride venue and it heavily leans towards this style of riding. In the park there are various ladder drops, gaps, a mini A-line style trail made up of tabletops and berms, plenty of small to medium jumps, and northshore features.

Locals do...

Book very early to get on the uplift days.

Locals don't...

Mind showing you around the trails.

Below left: Moving shot.
Below right: Moooving outfit.
Bottom: Moving bikes.

JAMES CHETWOODE

Practicalities ◖🏍🛏

The park, now named UK Bike Park, but more commonly known as Blandford Freeride Park, is located at the top of Okeford Hill near Shillington in Dorset. Shillington itself is a very small village with a couple of corner shops and some traditional pubs, so enough to make you comfortable for an overnight stay. The current size and nature of the park makes it a good weekend venue, but you are unlikely to stop for more than one night at a time.

Sleeping *Pennhills Farm* (T+44 (0)1258-860491) is actually located at the bottom of the freeride park so you couldn't be in a more convenient location and they are more than used to looking after mountain bikers.

Eating *The Crown* (T+44 (0)1462-711667) in Shillington is a friendly pub serving good food and beers.

Bars and clubs No nightlife to talk of really, so for evening drinks head to the pubs in Shillington.

Bike shop *Bikelab* (T+44 (0)1202-330011) is found in Poole, only a short drive away from the park and they have a well stocked shop and good workshop.

Internet café *Cyberlink Café* (T+44 (0)1258- 459157) in Blandford has three terminals to access from.

Bike map available? There are trail maps onsite and also jpegs on the ukbikepark website.

England Blandford Bikepark

Chicksands

Beautifully sculpted jumps, smooth sandy trails, and an easy push up at one of the UK's top freeride venues.

CHICKSANDS

✕3 The trails

- **XC Cross country** Poor to fair/ beginner to intermediate
- **DH Downhill** Poor/beginner
- **FR Freeride** Excellent/beginner to advanced
- **Uplift** No uplift
- **Pros** Progressive venue, riders can learn a lot each time they visit
- **Cons** Limited facilities for non XC riders

Chicksands is a block of Forestry Commission land where a hugely popular freeride area has been developed. The area is continually changing with both more challenging and easy lines being created to allow all riders to enjoy the site. The soil in this area is perfect for riding bikes all year round and made for building all manner of jumps and berms. Like surrounding riding areas such as Woburn Sands the soil is a mix of sand and clay that drains well and sticks together to shape transitions and landings.

ⓘ OPENING TIMES

The trails are open 365 days a year

🅢 RESORT PRICES

It costs £5 per day to ride on weekends and is currently free to ride in the week

ⓘ DIRECTORY

Bedford Tourist Info: T+44 (0)1234-215226; bedsfattrax.org

Below: Drop in.
Bottom: Turn on.
Opposite page: Tune out.

DANNY MILNER

DANNY MILNER

Cross country

A trip to Chicksands to purely ride XC would leave you disappointed. Despite there being a blue and red cross country route, they are both less than 4 km. But if these are combined with the jumps and berms of the freeride area there's plenty of fun to be had.

Downhill

Although there's a short downhill track, the runs here are short so it would be crazy to come here solely for this. However, any downhiller would have great fun on the obstacles provided in the freeride area.

Freeride

Chicksands is essentially a freeride hotspot with riders travelling from all around the south of England to ride here. With a good scene and plenty of riding to try out, there's something for everyone. From the tabletops and dirt jump lines, through the dual slalom to the national standard 4X track and freeride course made up of ladderdrops, step ups and northshore obstacles.

The Lowdown

Locals do... Warm up on the tabletops and smaller six-pack jumps before moving onto the bigger sets; ride the bombholes – a network of short trails through a series of interconnected bomb holes.

Locals don't... Ride without paying the fee for the day – it keeps this site running.

Don't miss... Racing your mates down the dual slalom and 4X tracks as a bit of friendly competition never hurt anyone.

Remember to avoid... Casing a landing and not fixing it up. You may have paid your £5, but trail etiquette costs nothing.

Practicalities

Formerly most associated for being an RAF base during the Second World War, Chicksands is a small village in the area that contains some great freeride trails. Just 9 miles down the road is Bedford, a larger town that has more to accommodate weary riders after a day thrashing the trails. Centrally located between London, Oxford and Cambridge, Bedford is a lively cosmopolitan town with a rich heritage. It has a fine riverside setting on the banks of the River Great Ouse and a range of large retail chains and smaller niche shops.

Sleeping Try the *Embankment* hotel (T+44 (0)1234-248920) situated on the river-bank and overlooking the Victorian suspension bridge. Also *De Pary's Guest House* (T+44 (0)123-261982) with an area for bikes and just a couple of minutes walk from the town centre.

Eating For great Italian food try *Villa Rosa* (T+44 (0)1234-269259), a good option in a town known for its large and vibrant Italian community. For some pub food try the *Dew Drop Inn* (T+44 (0)1525-840096).

Bars and clubs Bedford has a number of clubs, bars and varied entertainment venues hosting all kinds of nights and events. Both *Enigma* and *Esquire* cater for more alternative types of music, there's probably somewhere for most tastes in this town.

Bike shop *Michaels Cycles* (T+44 (0)1234-6352937) are in Bedford and carry some mountain bike brands and will be able to repair most mountain bike problems.

Internet café The *Studi Lounge* (T+44 (0)1234-346870) is a late night internet cafe open till 2300 through the week.

Bike map available? There is no bike map for the trails as the area is small and it is not necessary.

England Chicksands

DANNY MILNER

Cannock Chase

CANNOCK CHASE

▼4 The trails

- **⊗ Cross country** Good/beginner to intermediate
- **⊕ Downhill** Fair/beginner to intermediate
- **⊕ Freeride** Poor/beginner
- **⊘ Uplift** There is no uplift
- **✔ Pros** Good family riding and novice/intermediate mountain bike area; lots of good unmarked singletrack, great for weekend stopover
- **✘ Cons** Hills not big enough for the downhill purist; not enough riding to sustain a week break

Chase trails have developed in an area that doesn't have 'mountains' for mountain biking but it does have some nice hills set in the Area of Outstanding Beauty. It is a pleasant place to go for a gentle ride and get away from it all, and that's before you stumble onto the many miles of classic woodland riding. Chase trails attract many riders from Birmingham and other Midlands towns and the trail network now consists of a number of official and many unofficial trails to meet this demand.

Cross country

Follow the Dog is the first place to head to for riders new to the forest. The 7-mile waymarked trail is the ideal introduction

ⓘ OPENING TIMES

The trails are open 365 days a year and you can ride them any time

ⓢ RESORT PRICES

All trails are free

ⓘ DIRECTORY

Stafford Tourist Information Centre: T+44 (0)1785-619619, chasetrails.co.uk

Giving chase in Cannock. Geddit?

to the extensive singletrack and trails. Graded as a red trail it's perfect for intermediate riders who will find their own challenges in the dicey pebbled trails, boardwalk, log rides and snaking singletrack. A second main waymarked loop is due to open at the end of 2008. Once you've cut your teeth on 'The Dog' it's time to pick up the map or catch up with local riders to explore the larger area and sample some of the fantastic hidden trails which crisscross this 26 sq mile area. For families and novice riders there are a network of green graded leisure trails to follow all of which start at the main trail head at Birches Valley forest centre.

Downhill

There is a wide range of DH trails at Stile Cop Bike Park. These range from wide, fast machine-built trails to tight and more technical singletracks. There are two main downhill tracks: one machine-built trail graded red; the other (graded black) a more natural hand-built affair with more roots and features to challenge riders.

Freeride

Freeride is pretty much limited to sessioning the downhill trails and blasting around the singletracks. Riders looking to be the next Darren Berrecloth should probably look elsewhere.

Locals do...

Get involved with building the trails as well as riding them.

Practicalities ⊟⬛⧄⬤

Cannock lends its name to the famous Chase – 26 sq miles designated as an Area of Outstanding Natural Beauty that includes an array of important and unusual wildlife. It is a collection of beautiful woodlands with some sections 600 years old. The town will provide you with a place to overnight before heading north up into the Chase to take in the many trails that have developed there.

Sleeping Try the *Oak Farm Hotel* (T+44 (0)8704-784319) located close to the M6, or for budget accommodation the *Premier Inn* (T+44 (0)8717-162718).

Eating The *Birches Valley Forest* visitor centre has a café which provides hot and cold drinks and snacks. Cannock offers everything you'd expect from a decent-sized commuter town. Try *Fans Cantonese Restaurant* (T+44 (0)1543-502080).

Bars and clubs There are a number of pubs to try including the *Newhall Farm Inn* (T+44 (0)1543-278466).

Bike shop Bike hire is available from *Swinnerton Cycles Forest Centre* (T+44 (0)1889-575170) they are also a repair centre, carry a range of spares and stock some popular mountain bike brands.

Internet café There is no internet café in Cannock but you could try the library on T+44 (0)1543-510365.

Bike map available? There are bike maps available from the *Birches Valley Forest Visitor* centre.

Locals don't...

Ride carelessly on the many popular routes shared with walker and horseriders.

Dalby Forest

DALBY FOREST

↘5 The trails

- **XC Cross country** Good/intermediate
- **DH Downhill** Poor/n/a
- **FR Freeride** Poor to fair/beginner to intermediate
- **Uplift** No uplift
- **Pros** Great location on the edge of the Yorkshire moors
- **Cons** Limited amounts of riding

The north of the forest sits on an upland plateu while the southern parts of the forest are split up into a number of valleys creating a 'Rigg and Dale' landscape formed in the Ice Age and shaped by its people from the Bronze Age to the present day. The riding on offer in Dalby is, as at most of the Forestry Commission centres, focused on sustainable XC trails. There is a family blue route and a red route that combines black sections. Also in a disused quarry you will find the Dalby Pace bikepark.

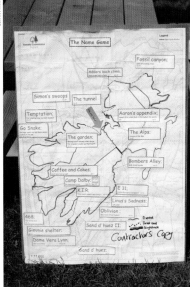

You could be here.

Cross country

The red/black route, at 15 miles long, is made up almost entirely of singletrack. The black sections loop off the red trail and rejoin every few miles or so. With tight, steep sections and plenty of roots and rocks thrown in for good measure, it should have plenty to keep most riders interested. Riders can also head over to the bike park and test out their skills.

Downhill

There is no downhill in Dalby Forest.

Freeride

The Dalby Pace bikepark is quite small and not very well laid out but worth a look while you're there. It has northshore balance obstacles and jumps in a old disused quarry and is located 7 km from the visitor centre and linked by trail.

Locals do…

Link in rides using bridleways to the wider surrounding areas.

Locals don't…

Ride the corkscrew in the quarry too fast as the berm will send you straight into the wall!

ⓘ OPENING TIMES

The trails are open 365 days a year; visitor centre open 0930-1630

ⓢ RESORT PRICES

Access to the forest is free on a bike; to access the visitor centre via the forest drive by car costs £7

ⓓ DIRECTORY

The Purple Mountain Bike Centre & Café: T+44 (0)1751-460011, forestry.gov.uk/england-cycling

Practicalities

Located on the southern edge of the Yorkshire Moors, Dalby Forest is one of the latest Forestry Commission sites to build mountain bike specific trails. The Dalby Forest Visitor Centre, where the trails start, is about 1½ miles from the entrance to the forest. The nearest village of any size is that of Thornton-le-Dale, one of the prettiest in North Yorkshire. This is a great place to access not only Dalby Forest, but also the North Yorkshire Moors.

Sleeping Try *Warrington Guest House* in Thornton-le-Dale (T+44 (0)1751-475028) or for some luxury living in the forest hire one of the wooden cabins set in stunning locations in nearby Cropton; call *Forest Holidays* (T+44 (0)1751-417510).

Eating There is a cafe on site at the *Purple Mountain Bike Centre* (T+44 (0)1751-400011), or for restaurant dining you could try the *Brandysnap Bistro* (T+44 (0)1751-474732) in Thornton-le-Dale.

Bars and clubs You're not going to find any late night bars or clubs around Dalby Forest but the local pubs are hospitable and relaxing. Try *The New Inn* (T+44 (0)1751-474226).

Bike shop The *Purple Mountain Bike Centre* (T+44 (0)1751-400011) offers bike hire, repairs and spares.

Internet café There's no internet café in the immediate vicinity of Dalby Forest. In nearby Malton is the *Theatre Internet Café* (T+44 (0)1653-696563), a cafe, bistro, delicatessen and internet cafe all in one so you can enjoy good food whilst surfing the web.

Bike map available? There are trail maps and info available from the forest visitor centre.

Esher Shore

ESHER SHORE

◢6 The trails

- **⊗ Cross country** Poor/n/a
- **⊕ Downhill** Poor/n/a
- **⊕ Freeride** Good to excellent / beginner to advanced
- **⊘ Uplift** No uplift required
- **⊘ Pros** Unique, well-worked park in the UK
- **⊗ Cons** Depending on whether northshore is your thing, you'll either love it or hate it

Northshore at Esher Shore, even though the coast is a good 50 miles away.

Practicalities ⊞⊘⊘

Esher Shore is in a tiny 3-acre venue right by Sandown racecourse. The town of Esher is located in leafy Surrey and is primarily a dormitory town for commuters to London, but it does serve as a comfortable overnight base for Esher Shore and it has excellent transport links into central London.

Sleeping *Pine Tree Cottage* (T+44 (0)20-8398 8848) and *Lilac Cottage* (T+44 (0)20-8398 7546) are both found in Esher and offer reasonably priced B&B accommodation.

Eating The *Conservatory Restaurant* (T+44 (0)1372-470957) can be found on Winterdown Road and provides a great getaway to enjoy a social meal.

Bars and clubs There are a number of pubs in Esher, try the *Wheatsheaf* (T+44 (0)1372-464014). For clubs Kingston-upon-Thames is not far away and has a vibrant nightlife with a large student population.

Bike shop *Freeborn Bikes* (T+44 (0)1372-476969) are found in Esher; they have a good range of stock and a good workshop. They also are a sponsor of the Esher Shore Park.

Internet café There are no internet cafés in Esher but the town library has some terminals that can be accessed with a day membership.

Bike map available? No need as it's only 3 acres.

Esher shore is perhaps the UK's only dedicated northshore park. The park is only 3 acres but the trails weave back and forth and the low speed nature of the northshore obstacles mean that every last inch of ground is utilised in this unique development. The trails are graded blue or red with the blue lines aimed at encouraging beginners into riding the northshore obstacles whereas the red lines are increasingly technical.

Cross country
There is no XC at Esher, but it can be an interesting diversion from the norm to spend a day riding the intricate and well made wooden trails here.

Downhill
There is no downhill at Esher and the nature of the obstacles isn't suited to big downhill bikes.

Freeride
For those that like northshore and trials type skills riding, there is plenty here to keep you going all day with lots of varied lines and new stunts built all the time. The website gives a great pictorial breakdown. Check out at eshershore.com/shore_park.htm

Locals do…
All help out with the construction and development of the park.

Locals don't…
Ride the wood in the wet, you'd be asking for trouble.

ⓘ OPENING TIMES
Mon-Sat 1000-1800, Sun and Bank Holidays 1100-1600

⊗ RESORT PRICES
£10 yearly membership is mandatory, £5 per day session

⊕ DIRECTORY
Freeborn Bike shop at Esher Shore: T+44 (0)1372-476969; eshershore.com

Riders' tales
Safety must-haves by John Ireland (Forestry Commission)

Step 1: Before you go, prepare

→ Make sure your bike is well serviced and up to the trails you plan to ride.

→ Always wear a good quality helmet, gloves, elbow and knee protection. Wear suitable eyewear and clothing suitable for prevailing conditions.

→ Carry a small tool kit and essential spares, and take food and drinks;

→ Study trail route signage at car parks and carry a trail/OS map with you.

→ For your own safety, please note any trail diversions or closures.

→ Ensure you have the necessary fitness and experience for your route choice.

→ If you need to update your skills and confidence, get some lessons.

→ Carry a small first aid kit and several foil blankets.

→ Carry a whistle for emergencies, as mobile phones may not have a signal. The distress signal is six whistle blasts (or torch flashes), at 60-second intervals.

Step 2: Expect and anticipate

→ Anticipate the effects of weather. Dry conditions make tracks dusty and loose. Wet conditions lead to mud – both lead to slip hazards!

→ Anticipate other users and beware of vehicles.

→ Take care at track junctions or crossing points.

→ Expect that on longer routes you will head into remote sections that may be some distance from the car park.

→ Work within the group's capabilities and progress at the speed of the slowest rider.

Step 3: Here I am

→ Be aware of where you are at all times.

→ Use trail or Ordnance Survey maps and keep be aware of landmarks identified on these.

→ Look out for emergency information posts on some of the more remote routes.

Step 4: Always stop to help others

→ Always offer to help someone if they appear lost or in trouble. Having someone to talk to can help a lot.

Step 5: Protect yourself and others

→ If you come across an accident don't put yourself or others in danger;

→ Assess the situation and immediate area, and warn other users to avoid further accident.

→ Protect yourself and the casualty.

Step 6: Provide First Aid if you can

→ Stay calm – assess the casualty and decide what to do;

→ Remember ABC (Airway, Breathing, Circulation – signs of life, blood loss);

→ Be aware of spinal injuries and control any bleeding with pressure and elevation;

→ Make casualty warm and comfortable and place unconscious casualties in the recovery position if possible.

Step 7: Yell and tell

→ Consider options for safe return to trailhead or send for/call for help;

→ For calling and before you phone 999:

→ Write down the location and telephone number you are using;

→ Ask for Police (Mountain Rescue) before Ambulance if not in easy reach of a route suitable for an ambulance.

→ Ask for Ambulance if in easy reach of a route suitable for an ambulance;

→ If it's not possible to send for or call for help, use the international distress signal to attract attention (six whistle blasts/torch flashes repeated every minute).

Josh Bryceland stoked he put that helmet on. Gutted about the elbow pads though.

Forest of Dean

Super DIY ride venue with XC, downhill and freeride trails all found in the woods near Coleford.

FOREST OF DEAN

↘7 The trails

- Ⓧⓒ **Cross country** Good/beginner to intermediate
- ⓓⓗ **Downhill** Good/intermediate
- ⓕⓡ **Freeride** Fair/beginner to intermediate
- ⓐ **Uplift** No formal uplift but public roads run through the wood and it can be shuttled very easily with your own vehicles
- ✔ **Pros** Super family riding area, with expansive flat routes; fun short trails – lots of good singletrack; great place for XC riders to sample downhill as the courses are not too technical
- ✖ **Cons** Lots of roads to cross; not the same variety for expert riders found in some other regions

The topography of the Forest of Dean is such that it is perfect for mountain biking. The hills are never too steep going up or down and the myriad singletracks throughout this 110-ha ancient woodland have a great flow for trail riding. It also has, perhaps by default rather than careful planning, catered for all three of the major mountain bike groups. The Forest of Dean is one of the best places for easy family rides due do its multiple flat surfaced trails through the woods. These are complemented by the number of technical singletracks and downhill runs that can be linked into a hell of a day's riding.

Cross country

There is a 5-km built trail by the FODCA which runs from the cycle centre and is graded red. But the Forest of Dean is

The Lowdown

Locals do... Ride up to the dips and play up there before riding one of the many descents back towards the centre; use this as a great night riding spot as there are plenty of trails that are kind to night riders.

Locals don't... Always ride up the hills – you can shuttle it; forget to pay and display – the money will benefit the cycle facilities.

Don't miss... A run of the classic downhill which can be ridden on any of today's suspension trail bikes.

Remember to avoid... Some of the features and jumps are badly built so check before you ride.

littered with trails that weave and dissect their way through the woods. Many technical runs have been cut in by local riders and there are plenty of low level cycle paths for simply getting out and about in the woods with the family.

Easy The Forest of Dean is one of the better set up venues for family rides. Bring your own or hire some bikes from the pedal a bike away centre and head out on the low level cycle trail which follows former railways for an 11-mile route which you could expect to finish in the region of two hours.

Difficult Head out from the centre onto the FODCA short trail. On finishing this you can loop up the hill to take in the downhill route and explore some of the many unmarked trails in the area, riding up and down the hill as many times as your body will let you. When all but done head onto the coal tips and try out some of the banks.

ANDY LLOYD

Left: Table Top of Dean.
Opposite page: Pinning it through the forest.

Downhill

Although the downhill course at the Forest of Dean is not officially recognised and waymarked, it has been in existence and hosting races since back in 1996, and is still a great ride. What the Forest of Dean lacks in vertical drop it makes up for in variety and ease of sectioning. This makes it is easy to shuttle on the public road, another reason why it has remained a popular place to ride downhill, despite the bigger hills of Wales being only one hour away.

Freeride

The Forest of Dean is also a reasonable spot for freeriders; not only do the downhills offer a fun spot to session with some jumps and technical lines, but there are quite a few features dotted around the forest built by riders. Near the cycle centre there are some old coal tips with a range of different sized jumps and steep banks to conquer. Up the road you will find the dips a prime play spot with a number of bowls with drops, small jumps and a small set of trails. More suited to beginner to intermediate.

Practicalities

Coleford, the nearest town to the cycle centre in the Forest of Dean, is one with a rich history. First recorded in the 1200's when it was in part of the royal hunting forest, it is well worth taking the town walk to explore its historical buildings. It was here that Robert Mushet invented the process of making steel in the 1800's; steel that later found its way onto the tracks and trails around the forest under the control of many a mountain biker. Now you'll find a range of the latest titanium, carbon and aluminium full suspension bikes tearing up the singletracks around the cycle centre.

Sleeping For B&B try *Allary House* (T+44 (0)1594-835206) or *Lower Perrygrove Farm* (T+44 (0)1594-833187). There are plenty of camping and caravanning sites in the Forest of Dean; try *Bracelands* (T+44 (0)131-3146505). There are plenty of cottages and buildings that can be hired for self-catering groups such as *Stank Farm* (T+44 (0)1594-832203).

Eating The *Cannop Cycle Centre* in the Forest offers a place to get snacks, coffee and tea. Coleford has some pubs serving food, and a few restaurants. For a hearty meal try *The Ostrich Inn* (T+44 (0)1594-833260) or if you're treating yourself, *The Bluebell Restaurant* (T+44 (0)1594-832424).

Bars and clubs There are a number of pubs to relax in after a day on the trails. Try out the *Butchers Arms* (T+44 (0)1594-834313) or a short drive down the hill from Coleford is the *Saracens Head Inn* (T+44 (0)1600-890435) with an excellent location on the riverbank of the river Wye.

Bike shop The *Pedal a Bike Away Centre* (T+44 (0)1594-860065) carry out repairs, stock basic spares and hire very basic mountain bikes for all ages. They also hire tandems, trailers for kids 4-8 years old, and two-kid trailers. Included in the hire charge are waterproofs, puncture repair and basic toolkits, locks, stuffsacks, carriers and route maps. Note these are suitable for the easier family trails only.

Internet café There are no internet cafés, but you could try Coleford's library which has several computers.

Bike map available? There are bike maps available from the cycle centre but many of the more challenging trails are unmarked.

England Forest of Dean

ⓘ **OPENING TIMES**

The trails are open 365 days a year and you can ride them any time

Ⓢ **RESORT PRICES**

All trails are free the car park is pay and display

ⓘ **DIRECTORY**

Pedal a Bike away Cycle Centre: T+44 (0)1594-860026;

Coleford Tourist Information centre: T+44 (0)1594-812338;

Website: pedalabikeaway.com

Grizedale

GRIZEDALE
🔽8 The trails

- **XC Cross country** Good to excellent/ intermediate to advanced
- **DH Downhill** Poor/intermediate to advanced
- **FR Freeride** Poor/beginner to advanced
- **Uplift** No uplift
- **Pros** Beautiful national park site; huge amount of XC riding for those prepared to map read
- **Cons** Many other users in the park; no DH or freeride areas; boardwalk section on North Face trail lethal when wet

Staying in Ambleside there are two main types of riding you can access. Firstly you have the Grizedale Forest Park and secondly you are on the doorstep of the Lake District National Park, which has some of the best riding in the UK. What is worth noting though is that much of the terrain on offer in the national park is out of bounds to bikers and when riding on the Bridleways you will be sharing the trails with horses and walkers in a very popular area.

Cross country

The North Face trail in Grizedale Forest is a 16-km loop starting from the Visitor Centre that contains nine sections of sinuous singletrack trail. Throughout the trail you will encounter viewpoints and have to tackle leg-burning climbs, but after every climb there is a reward in the shape of a flowing descent. There is a yearly event, the Grizedale Challenge, that takes in some great riding around the

ⓘ OPENING TIMES
Trails open all day every day but may be closed for forest operations; check website below

$ RESORT PRICES
All trails are free

ⓘ DIRECTORY
Ambleside Tourist Information: T+44 (0)1539-432582; **Forestry Commission:** forestry.gov.uk/england-cycling

Left: Streamer! **Right:** Braking through the bracken.

area so if you're in the area at that time you should take part. See gmbc.co.uk for information. The riding in the national park is second to none; grab an OS map and get out there.

Downhill
There are no downhill courses in Grizedale or the lakes.

Freeride
There are no freeride obstacles in the area.

Locals do...
Make the most of the bikes only North Face trail; pick up the Cross Lakes shuttle at Bowness to Grizedale (7 miles), then after a day's riding, catch the boat from ferry house: T+44 (0)1539-445161.

Locals don't...
Hang about; the style of trail and the hills soon develop fitness and speed.

Practicalities 🍴🚲♻️

Grizedale forest is in the heart of the Lake District. The nearest town, Ambleside, has a long history, predating the Roman invasion and surviving a Viking invasion. Nowadays the only invasion is from tourists who enjoy the town and its perfect setting. Mountain biking is still a relatively new pastime as the area is better known for its rock climbing and upland walking.

Sleeping For B&B accommodation in the town try *Lyndale Guest House* (T+44 (0)1539-434244). For a self-catering cottage try *Gale House Cottage* (T+44 (0)1539-432321) which sleeps up to 6 people.

Eating Grizedale tea room at the Forest Visitor centre offers some light snacks and hot and cold drinks. In Ambleside try *Fellwalkers Café* or the *Log House Restaurant*.

Bars and clubs No clubs, but plenty of quality pubs selling real ales and a cosy setting to while away some time. Try the *Unicorn Inn* (T+44 (0)1539-33216) and if you drink too much there you can always stay the night as they also offer B&B.

Bike shop *Grizedale Mountain Bikes* (T+44 (0)1229-860335) stock some leading brands for hire and sales and also carry out any repairs you may need.

Internet café No.

Bike map available? Yes, from the Forest Visitor Centre.

Hopton Castle

CHRIS MORAN

HOPTON CASTLE

↘9 The trails

⊗ Cross country Fair to good/ beginner to intermediate

⊕ Downhill Good/intermediate

⊕ Freeride Poor/beginner to advanced

⊘ Uplift There are uplifts usually one weekend a month; see pearcecycles.co.uk for more info

✔ Pros A wide range of challenging trails

✘ Cons Some riders will struggle with the roots especially in wet conditions

The trails in Hopton Woods are varied, from gentle and smooth family trails to the highly technical downhill courses. The courses are all within the conifer plantation wood and as a result the more technical trails are strewn with roots and stumps. With three cross country trails and three downhill routes the wood is a fun place to ride that can cater for beginners through to experts. The ground bakes hard in the summer, but can be quite greasy when wet.

Cross country

The routes around Hopton are well waymarked and offer some very short flat rides for novices and kids through to the red route with some tough climbs and

Top: Shanksy's uplift.   **Bottom:** The sweet reward for pushing.

PAUL ENGLAND

switchbacks. Experienced cross country riders will enjoy the more challenging black downhill trails. The gradient here allows cross country bikes to be comfortable on the downhills.

Downhill

The downhills at Hopton are known for their tight turns and having loads of roots; it's a great place to perfect your bike handling and is regularly used by some of England's best riders as a training ground. The hill is not very steep so it is quite easy to section the trails here.

Freeride

There are no trails for freeriders but the downhill routes do contain various small jumps.

Locals do...

Ride cross country mixed in with some of the downhill courses to provide a fun, challenging loop.

Locals don't...

Ride on their own without a phone as you are far from the nearest houses or help.

Practicalities ⊜⊘⊘

Hopton Woods lies amongst the south Shropshire Hills, a designated area of outstanding natural beauty. It has been a feature on the UK mountain bike calendar as a race and training venue for many years. The nearest village is Hopton Castle which includes the castle ruins. It is a small country village and does not offer any accommodation or amenities; you will have to look to the nearby town of Craven Arms with the incredibly well preserved Stokesay Castle, the best example of a 13th-century fortified manor house in England.

Sleeping Take in *Stokesay Castle* during your stay at the *Castle View B&B*, T+44 (0)1588-673712. Also B&B at *Hopton House*, T+44 (0)1547-530885.

Eating The *Craven Arms Hotel* offers a 'biker brunch' on Saturdays and also have a daily carvery, and the *Engine and Tender Inn* serves traditional home cooked food.

Bars and clubs No clubs but try the family run *Sun Inn*, serving award-winning local ales.

Bike shop *Fort Royal Mountain Bikes* are found in *Craven Arms* (T+44 (0)1588-673500) and are well stocked with expert staff so will be able to provide for most XC and DH bikes.

Internet café *Craven Arms Community Centre* (T+44 (0)1588-672847) offer free internet use.

Bike map available? Yes, waterproof trail maps are available from the secret hills discovery centre in *Craven Arms* for £1.

England | Hopton Castle

ⓘ OPENING TIMES

Trails open every day of the year but areas of the forest can be closed due to operations

⑤ RESORT PRICES

All trails are free

ⓘ DIRECTORY

Tourist Board: shropshiretourism.co.uk

Hamsterley

The forest centre has been developing over the years and now is a mainstay for cross country, downhill and freeride riding in the northeast of England.

HAMSTERLEY

⬂10 The trails

- **Cross country** Good/beginner to advanced
- **Downhill** Good/beginner to advanced
- **Freeride** Fair to good/beginner to advanced
- **Uplift** Has been suspended for the time being; check descendhamsterley.co.uk for updates
- **Pros** Hamsterley can offer something for most riders; good club and scene at the trails
- **Cons** Hills rather than mountains; can be quite muddy on the unsurfaced trails in winter

The Lowdown

Locals do... Get involved with the trail building in the forest too.

Locals don't... Dodge out of buying a day permit on the DH or 4X – you'll ruin it for everyone else.

Don't miss... The 4X trail – one of only a few national standard tracks in the UK.

Remember to avoid... The old NPS Downhill track which is quite flat. It does make a great XC route though.

Practicalities ⬛🍴☕

The nearest town of any size is Durham although there are smaller villages nearby, such as Hamsterley, Witton-le Wear, Wolsingham and Bishop Aukland. Durham is full of cafés, galleries, hotels and independent shops. Don't miss the 'best cathedral on planet earth' in the words of travel writer Bill Bryson. Whether you locate yourself in Durham itself, with all its amenities and attractions, stay out in the quiet country villages around Hamsterley Forest; the riding around the area will keep you entertained.

Sleeping For B&B close to the forest try the *Dale End* (T+44 (0)1388-488091) in Hamsterley, or *Mayland Farm Cottage* (T+44 (0)1388-718237). In Durham try the *Kings Lodge Hotel* (T+44 (0)1913-709977)

Eating Snacks and meals are available at the visitor centre during opening hours. Two local pubs offering meals to hungry bikers near the trails are the *Cross Keys* (T+44 (0)1388-488457)

in Hamsterley and the *Moorecock Inn* (T+44 (0)1833-650395) in Egglestone.

Bars and clubs The country pubs around the forest are great for whiling away an evening, but for those looking for something a little livelier Durham doesn't have much choice when it comes to clubbing. Try the *Fishtank* which has varied alternative nights from rock to drum and bass. For a good night take a trip to the cities of Leeds or Newcastle which both offer much more in the way of nightlife.

Bike shop *Wood N Wheels* is a small shop based on site at Hamsterley (T+44 (0)1388-488222); they offer cycle hire and repairs for many brands.

Internet café Try *Intercafe* (T+44 (0)1207-238000) in Durham or the *Connect Café* (T+44 (0)1914-691899).

Bike map available? There are trail maps available from the Forest Drive Visitor Centre.

GARY EWING

The trails can be accessed by cycling into the forest or by paying £3 to drive your vehicle into the forest drive where the visitor centre is found and all the trails start and finish. It's a simple set up with all the gravity trails (downhill, 4X, duel and dirt jumps) located together on one side of the hill. The XC trails run out into the forest from here also with green, blue, red and black trails to suit all riders. The easier ones are surfaced while the red and black trails are made up of more natural terrain involving plenty of roots and can be quite slick when wet.

Cross country

Hamsterley has the full house, with green and blue family and beginner trails and red and black trails for the more experienced riders. There is also a trailquest course which is essentially orienteering on bikes and will take you right out to the corners of the forest on easy going tracks and a skills loop for rider development.

Easy The trail quest is a non-technical ride to get groups out into the forest, but if you are looking for some real riding it's not until the red route that you will find singletrack; at 10 miles it's a fairly easy ride if you take your time. Brush up your skills on The Loop a 1-mile skills training loop with plenty of features to learn the basics.

Difficult For XC riders, head out on the red loop and after a quick break follow it up with the shorter but more technical

black loop which is a refreshing change from the hardcored trails found at many centres. This is a more rugged, raw and rooty affair.

Downhill

Hamsterley is one of the few venues offering official downhill trails in the north of England. There is one main run with plenty of split sections offering different styles, from rock gardens, to technical singletrack, wide open berms and jumps. There is usually a good scene on weekends and holidays with plenty of local riders sessioning the track.

Freeride

With a duel track, a 4X track and a set of dirt jumps, Hamsterley has enough to keep most riders who like to get airborne busy. The 4X trail is of a national standard having hosted several rounds of the NPS 4X series.

ⓘ OPENING TIMES

You can ride the XC trails at any time although the 4X and DH trails cannot be ridden without a membership fee to cover insurance costs

ⓢ RESORT PRICES

XC Trails are free; the forest drive access to the visitor centre and start of trails costs £3 per vehicle; a day pass permit for the DH and 4X costs £5

ⓘ DIRECTORY

Hamsterley Visitor Centre:
T+44 (0)1388-488312
Website: hamsterley-trailblazers.co.uk

Right: The long and winding road downhill.
Below: The view, and not a hamster in sight.
Opposite page: Triple trouble on the trebles.

GARY EWING

MAT CLARK

England Hamsterley

Kielder Forest

KIELDER FOREST

↘11   The trails

- **XC Cross country** Fair to good/ beginner to advanced
- **DH Downhill** Poor/n/a
- **FR Freeride** Poor/n/a
- **⚡ Uplift** No uplift
- **✓ Pros** Huge forest near other trails in northeast
- **✗ Cons** Limited amount of trail for more experienced cyclists

At 250 sq miles Kielder Forest is England's largest wooded area and contains England's largest blanket bog which gives you an idea of the going underfoot. All the trails in the forest have had to be constructed from imported aggregate so that riders don't sink into the soft ground. There are eight trails in total: three are blue, three red, one green and one black. It's worth noting that the black trail is only 1.2 km long, so don't travel here if you are purely looking for a challenging black route. The red routes are quite short also but can be combined to make a longer ride.

Sunset showdown.

DANNY MILNER

Cross country

The waymarked trails and skills loop will cater for most XC riders although there is a limited amount of more challenging riding so best combined with visits to other trails in the area for advanced riders. Plenty of gentle trail riding for kids and beginners

Downhill

There is no downhill in Kielder forest.

Freeride

No freeride at Kielder.

Locals do...

Often ride the up and over section more than once.

Locals don't...

Ride off the marked trails as the ground is soft and easily damaged by bikes.

Practicalities ⬛🍴🚵

Kielder Forest covers a huge area and there are many surrounding towns and villages including Kielder Village, Bellingham, Hexham, Newcastle, Jedburgh and Hawick. Kielder Village is near the Scottish border at the top of Northumberland and has the largest man-made lake in Europe along with the largest forest in England. Newcastle is well known as a vibrant city that mixes the modern with the historic, and can provide a great base with which to explore mountain biking in the northeast of England.

Sleeping The *Twenty Seven B&B* (T+44 (0)1434-250366) is the only B&B in Kielder Village. There's also a youth hostel and a campsite. Newcastle has loads of hotels and guesthouses. *Travelodge* (T+44 (0)8719-846164) provide decent budget accommodation and bikes can be taken into rooms when clean.

Eating The *Anglers Arms* in Kielder Village serves hot meals. The *Dukes Pantry Tearoom* at the Kielder Castle visitor centre is also open on weekends and busy periods.

Bars and clubs In Kielder itself you're limited to the *Anglers Arms*. In Newcastle you could lose yourself all week in different bars and clubs: try the *Salsa Club* on Westgate street.

Bike shop The *Bike Place* in Newcastle (T+44 (0)1654-700411) will look after you for spares and repairs and they also hire bikes out.

Internet café There's no internet café in the immediate vicinity of Kielder Forest so you'll have to look to Newcastle.

Bike map available? There are trail maps and info available from the Kielder Castle Visitor centre.

Riders' tales
Trail etiquette

Sam Reynolds *is 17 years old and part of the DMR team. He counts Kingswood's Kech Trails as home, but can also be found on various dirt jumping sites across Europe, including the Nissan Qashqai tour. Here's Sam's etiquette tips for when turning up to new trails. As Sam says: "follow these simple tips and hopefully you'll be invited back to ride again!"*

1 If possible, before going to the new trails for the first time, try to find out who owns or digs the jumps, and give them a call or drop an email asking if it's ok to come along sometime. If you don't know who that person is, just turn up and generally be polite. When you turn up ask the locals if it's ok to ride, and offer to help dig. You can't have all that fun without helping out a little!

2 Wear a helmet. Besides being sensible, most trails have rules in place not allowing you to ride without one.

3 Take the right bike. Put on slick dirt/street tyres for most trails, knobbly tyres don't go down too well with the builders as they churn it up. A dirt jump bike or bmx are most suited to trails, so don't expect to be allowed to ride on a downhill bike with chunky tyres.

4 Respect the locals. Probably the most important rule of all it to respect the jumps, riders and the land they are on. Try to skid as little as possible and if you do damage the jumps, get a spade and fix it. Before dropping in to your run, make sure no one else is going; cutting out in front of someone is not cool. Litter is also a big one; if anyone dropped litter at my trails they certainly wouldn't be invited back. The cleaner the land, the less likely the jumps are to get knocked down, so the happier the locals will be.

5 Lastly, why not dig your own trails? Find a plot of land, preferably ask the landowner if you can use it, and start building. Seeing your own jumps coming to shape can often be as satisfying as riding them. Also, when you have a few jumps to ride you can invite other riders and they will most likely invite you back to their trails, giving you more and more places to ride. What goes around comes around. So get digging!

Top: Don't get blackballed on the trails.
Bottom: Digging brings its own rewards.

Maddacleave Woods

A recent development in the southwest, an area not famed for its hills or mountain biking, now offers some of the toughest downhilling in the UK.

WWW.JACOBGIBBINS.CO.UK

MADDACLEAVE WOODS

↘12 The trails

- **ⓧⓒ Cross country** Fair to good/intermediate
- **ⓓⓗ Downhill** Excellent/intermediate to advanced
- **ⓕⓡ Freeride** Poor to fair/intermediate to advanced
- **↗ Uplift** Likely to run every weekend and school holidays; contact Dartmoor Cycles for latest information
- **✔ Pros** One of the most technical downhill facilities in the UK; a well-managed facility
- **✘ Cons** Riders looking to get some miles under their belt will have to look elsewhere

The trails are situated on the steep face of the Tamar Valley overlooking Cornwall. The woods are a mixture of plantation and broadleaf and house some spectacular rock formations that jut out imposingly on the severe slope. The trails are cut into this steep slope with three permanent downhill routes; two are aimed at experts with the third more gentle and suitable to ride on an XC bike or hardtail. The rock here makes up a large proportion of the trails features as there are exposed outcrops and loose fragments littering the hill.

Cross country

The third easier downhill route also acts as a short cross country loop as there is a trail to return to the top. The overall distance of this loop is only very short but is packed with interesting features and can be sessioned again and again. There are links from this venue out to other general cycle paths in the Tamar Valley which link many of the heritage sites,

Above: Hipped banks rock!
Left: Berm systems go.

WWW.JACOBGIBBINS.CO.UK

ⓘ OPENING TIMES

The trails are on private land and can only be ridden on open days, weekends and holidays; contact *Dartmoor Cycles* for more information

Ⓢ RESORT PRICES

Prices are not available at the time of going to press; contact *Dartmoor Cycles* for more information

ⓒ DIRECTORY

Dartmoor Cycles: T+44 (0)1822-618178; woodlandriders.co.uk but they are not designed specifically for mountain bikes. There is some excellent XC riding on Dartmoor which is an expansive moorland national park. You should not ride out onto the moor without being prepared, as the weather can change very quickly and it is easy to lose your way. Take a map and compass or GPS and you'll have a great time.

Downhill

This is primarily a downhill venue with three courses that will test all riders' abilities. The black routes should only be attempted by expert downhillers who will love the challenging features on offer from this hill. It is a national standard competition trail though many have commented on it being of international competition difficulty. The third red trail runs down the hill following much gentler gradients and with less technical features is more suitable for riders with less downhill experience.

Easy Ride the easier downhill course learning to ride big switchback berms and pump the rolling terrain, there are also optional small drops and doubles along the route that a keen eye will seek out. Once at the bottom you have the option to ride back up or, if you've booked in, then catch the uplift to the top to do it again.

Difficult For expert riders it will probably take more than a full day's riding to master all the lines and options on the two more technical downhill runs as there are plenty of roots, rock features and a couple of big jumps.

Freeride

There are no stand alone freeride stunts or trails; however some of the harder lines and bigger jumps on the downhill routes will challenge all but the professional freeriders, so a day's riding using the uplifts here should appeal to all freeriders.

A roots manoeuvre.

The Lowdown

Locals do... Use the uplift facility to get the most out of a day on the hill; ride within themselves.

Locals don't... Ride here when it's very wet – the rock can be very slippery; ride on their own.

Don't miss... A run down the novice downhill route as it flows perfectly.

Remember to avoid... It is an old tin mining site, so stick to the marked trails at all times.

Practicalities

Three miles from the Maddacleave Woods mountain bike area is the pretty market town of Tavistock. Tavistock is close to Plymouth, Dartmoor National Park and within reasonable driving distance of many of the southwest's sandy beaches. And while not famed for its hills, the Maddacleave Woods site goes a long way to alter perceptions and attract people to this pleasant, laid-back corner of the country, all but forgotten by mountain bikers until now.

Sleeping Being a popular tourist area there is no shortage of B&B offering somewhere to put your head down either in town or on many of the farmhouses in the area. Try former railway station *Brentor Station* (T+44 (0)1822-810403) or *Sunnymead* (T+44 (0)1822-612801).

Eating If you're looking for a snack or something to keep you going when out at the woods then stock up with pasties from the *Original Pasty House* (T+44 (0)1822-616003); they have 13 different flavours to choose from.

In the evening try *Monterey Jack's* (T+44 (0)1822-612145) for a range of enchiladas and tacos.

Bars and clubs Tavistock has a number of pubs but is more a sleepy country town than a late night party town. Plymouth is not far away with its student population so you can be guaranteed a lively night there. The *Trout and Tipple* (T+44 (0)1822-618886) in Tavistock is a good starting point with cask ales. In Plymouth *Ride*, *Cuba* and *Fuel* are all popular student haunts.

Bike shop *Dartmoor Cycles* (T+44 (0)1822-618178) in Tavistock is the place to go for all servicing, spares and bikes. They also have a great knowledge of the local trails.

Internet café Try *Silver Surfers* in Tavistock (T+44 (0)1822-614201).

Bike map available? Not at present although all trails are shown on the information board at the car park.

England Maddacleave Woods

WWW.JACOBGIBBINS.CO.UK

Portreath

Perfectly matched to the chilled Cornish vibe, the set up here is all about having fun on your bike. As public dirt jumps go in the UK, it doesn't get any better than this.

Top: Gap jump, me haarties!
Bottom: No footer... aaaarrrghh!
Opposite page: X up she blows!

WWW.THE-TRACK.CO.UK

England Portreath

↘13 The trails

- **XC Cross country** Fair/intermediate
- **DH Downhill** Poor/n/a
- **FR Freeride** excellent/beginner to advanced
- **Uplift** None required at the track
- ✔ **Pros** UK's top dirt jump facility; great chilled, friendly atmosphere
- ✘ **Cons** Very specific type of riding; can be quite exposed to wind and rain

The Track in Portreath is essentially a dirt jumper's paradise, heavily leant towards the freeriders or dirt jumpers. What is easy to miss is that for families this is the perfect setting for kids to progress their riding in a safe environment, while there are plenty of scenic trails around the surrounding area. In fact, there is a coast-to-coast trail running from Portreath that is only 11 miles one way. The dirt at the track, as you may expect, is perfect for building and shaping lips and transitions. And don't go thinking that the fun stops when it's dark; with a full floodlight system, large PA music set up and a viewing platform it really is a great social scene every bit as much as a riding one.

Cross country

Whilst the track itself offers nothing to the XC rider other than the opportunity to

ⓘ OPENING TIMES

Opening times vary throughout the seasons; check before travelling: the-track.co.uk

Ⓢ RESORT PRICES

Prices vary; non-members pay around £10 for a full day's riding

ⓓ DIRECTORY

The track: T+44 (0)1209-2110, the-track.co.uk;

Cornwall Tourist Board: cornwalltouristboard.co.uk

progress their riding skills on the beginner jumps, there are coastal paths and trails in country parks that can be cycled to from

the Track. There are very few marked rides so to find the more interesting trails it is be worth hiring a guide. Try *Mobius Trails* (T+44 (0)8456-430630) who will assess your ability and take you on a ride to suit.

Downhill

The track does not offer any downhill riding and Cornwall on the whole is not a good place to ride downhill due to its topography. Any downhiller would do far worse than to spend a few days here on

a hardtail brushing up on their jumping skills. Then for real downhill riding it's about an hour's drive to the Maddacleave Woods downhill trails.

Freeride

A freeride haven, the track offers so many ways to progress your riding skills with multiple lines of dirt jumps for all abilities. In fact there are over a mile of jumps! In order to learn some of the harder tricks there is a 50-sq m Foam Pit with multiple ramp and transfer lines in and a resi ramp to test your tricks before taking them to dirt. Also under construction is a Kona Slopestyle course. The place is constantly evolving so there will always be some new lines to try. Close by in Newquay are Mount Hawke indoor skatepark and Wooden Waves outdoor skatepark.

Easy Start out on the beginner jumps, there is so much here that it is definitely a case of building up slowly to make sure you have mastered what you're riding now before moving onto something much bigger.

Difficult There are plenty of hard lines to try for the more advanced jumper. The only limitation in a place like this is your imagination!

Practicalities ◻●🚴♿

The Track is 2 miles from the sandy beaches of Portreath and Porthtowan, with the summer haven of Newquay only 22 miles away. Where you stay really depends on what you want from your stay; if you're looking to relax in the Cornish country with great beaches then stay locally in Portreath. There are several shops and cafés and the village has a very friendly atmosphere whilst not being over commercialized. On the other hand, you have the heavily developed and lively resort of Newquay nearby, which has everything you would want to keep you entertained day and night. Mind you, it won't be to everyone's taste. Most will combine their riding holiday with some time spent on the beaches, either hitting the surf or chilling with friends or family.

Sleeping *Elm Farm*, T+44 (0)1209-891498 has a campsite and B&B, is very bike friendly and is only a 2-min cycle away. Those looking for the ultimate holiday experience should try *Gwel-an-Mor*, a new 5-star luxurious holiday village which sits high on hills above the Atlantic Ocean.

Eating The Track has the onsite *Snax Shax* to keep you topped up through your day with burgers, bacon and

chips. For a biker's pub meal nearby try the *Basset Arms*, or for a gastronomic delight head for *Tabb's Restaurant* in Truro (but make sure your wallet is fully loaded).

Bars and clubs Portreath has a number of cafés and pubs; Porthtowan has the beachside *Blue Bar* which often has live music. For something more lively, Newquay has a plethora of nightclubs and bars that are swamped in the summer season and can keep you out all night partying.

Bike shop The Track is only three miles from *Bike Chain*, which stocks a wide selection of bikes and accessories. There are also a limited number of Kona hire bikes available from the track at £15 per day.

Internet café Try *Tramways* internet café (T+44 (0)1872-870341) in Truro which also happens to be a MTB hire shop on the low level coast to coast cycle path.

Bike map available? The track facilities do not require maps. There are very easy rides throughout the county that have maps and are suitable for families or relaxing evening rides. Leaflets can be collected from the tourist office.

The Lowdown

Locals do... As you may expect with this on their doorstep, ride amazingly well; fix up any cases

Locals don't... Try and ride the jumps when the sea breeze is strong; respect the laws of gravity

Don't miss... The foam pit will see most people practicing their X-games moves

Remember to avoid... Travelling here in less than perfect weather conditions; call before you leave

WWW.THE-TRACK.CO.UK

Penshurst

PENSHURST

↘14 The trails

- ⓧ **Cross country** Poor to fair/ beginner to intermediate
- ⓓ **Downhill** Fair/beginner
- ⓕ **Freeride** Fair/beginner to intermediate
- ⓩ **Uplift** No uplift
- ✓ **Pros** Good on a hardtail or a suspension bike
- ✗ **Cons** The dirt jumps could be better maintained

Penshurst (or PORC, as it is commonly referred to) is a relatively small area but manages to cram quite a lot in. It is one of the original bike venues in the UK and used to hold lots of downhill races before the real hills were discovered and courses became a lot more technical. That said, it is still a great place to spend a day honing the bike handling skills on the range of short courses and features.

Cross country

A day trip or break at Penshurst purely with the intention of trail riding would leave you a little disappointed: there are some marked out cross country trails, but the area is very small and you would soon exhaust what is on offer. But if you have an open mind and mix it up with the other downhill and freeride tracks (none of them are too steep for an XC bike), you'll have a good time.

ⓘ OPENING TIMES
0900-1800

Ⓢ RESORT PRICES
£4 per day

ⓓ DIRECTORY
PORC: T+44 (0)1892-870136

Practicalities ●●●

The riding area known as PORC is found in Penshurst in Kent, an historic English village where you can expect to see thatched roofs and quaint old cottages nestled around the old town hall and church. It's also within communiting distance of London.

Sleeping *Manor Court Farm B&B* (T+44 (0)1892-740279) and *Well Place Farmhouse B&B* (T+44 (0)1892-870894), both offer comfortable country accommodation in the village.

Eating The *Spotted Dog* serves some great food using locally sourced products.

Bars and clubs No late night bars and clubs but if you're looking for that it may be wise to stop in London itself. In the village there are a few pubs serving good beers and ales. Try the *Leicester Arms* or the *Spotted Dog*.

Bike shop Nearby Tunbridge Wells has a large cycle dealer called *Wildside*, T+44 (0)1892-527069, who stock just about everything you could need.

Internet café *TecNet* café in Tunbridge Wells is open till 1930 and has 12 terminals.

Bike map available? No, but the area is small and well marked out.

Downhill

There are a number of short downhill routes at PORC which will keep you busy for a day; being a small hill it means the runs are short but also that the push back to the top is far easier than some larger steeper venues.

Freeride

There are a few freeride gaps, a fun 4X track and a quarry area full of dirt jumps.

Below right: A crackling gap at PORC.
Below left: Eat my dust.

Locals do...
Have quite rounded bike skills due to the riding here.

Locals don't...
Ride here in the wet, jumps are no fun unless they're dry.

Thetford Forest

⊿15 The trails

- **⊗ Cross country** Good to excellent/ beginner to intermediate
- **⊗ Downhill** Poor/n/a
- **⊗ Freeride** Poor/n/a
- **⊘ Uplift** None required
- **⊘ Pros** Sweet singletrack
- **⊗ Cons** Not much in the way of climbs or descents

One thing that can be said with certainty about East Anglia is that it's pretty damn flat, and Thetford is no exception. The trails do however make the most of the terrain by providing fast flowing routes that keep momentum high. When dry and hardpacked the trails actually run very fast and are best suited to hardtails; when it's wet the trails do cut up somewhat and run a lot slower.

Cross country

A great XC area, the forest regularly hosts a round of the national XC race series and the lack of any big hills or descents means that any loop around this forest can be ridden hard and fast. There are four official waymarked routes from green through

The only 2 m of Downhill for 50 miles.

blue, red and to black. The green and blue are really only of any appeal to young children and leisure cyclists. The red and black routes offer more typical singletrack riding and these can be complemented by the host of unmarked tracks and trails that make up the bulk of the riding for the racecourses. Expect swooping singletrack that snakes its way through the forest over whoops and in and out of bombholes.

Downhill

Don't even think about it.

Freeride

No freeriding in Thetford Forest.

Locals do...

Often run hardtails, they're much quicker here; know how to build good singletrack.

Locals don't...

Have much else to ride.

Practicalities ⊖🚴🚲

Thetford Forest Park is on the border of Norfolk and Suffolk in the heart of Breckland in East Anglia. The nearest town to the forest is Thetford, lying on the edge of the forest. This ancient market town has a rich heritage: Castle Hill is England's tallest Medieval Earthworks, and the Desert Rats Memorial Walk is the site of the training camp of the Desert Rats in 1944 before the D-Day landings.

Sleeping With a secure lock up for bicycles, *The Old Rectory*, T+44 (0)1842-765419, offers B&B just outside the town centre. Also try the *Pink Cottage*, T+44 (0)1842-764564, in the centre of town.

Eating For snacks while on the bike try the *Bakers Oven*; for wholesome evening food try the *Mulburry*. For something different the *Steel River Blues* restaurant is a 55-ft barge specializing in Mediterranean Cuisine.

Bars and clubs Not much choice for bars and clubs, but there are plenty of pubs to sample. If you do feel like throwing some moves down on a super cheesy dancefloor then you could try *Club Ice*.

Bike shop *Bike Art*, T+44 (0)1842-810090, are located at Thetford Forest and offer bike hire as well as repairs.

Internet café There are no internet cafés in Thetford but the town's library has web access.

Bike map available? Trail maps are available from the *Bike Art* shop.

Wharncliffe Woods

WHARNCLIFFE WOODS

↘16 The trails

- **Cross country** Good/ intermediate to advanced
- **Downhill** Good/intermediate to advanced
- **Freeride** Fair/beginner to advanced
- **Uplift** None
- **Pros** Fantastic technical downhill and trail riding
- **Cons** The push back to the top

You may be thinking why ride in Wharncliffe when the expansive Peak District National Park is only a stone's throw away? True, the riding in the park is great for all day trail rides, but what Wharncliffe offers is technical singletrack riding that few places in the UK can rival. The woods have some steep slopes that are interlaced with downhill trails and the XC routes reach out to the furthermost fringes of the wood. Wharncliffe is also renowned for its landscape, with large rocky outcrops and plenty of rock features in the trails.

Cross country

The woods are riddled with singletracks that have been adopted and created by mountain bikers over the years. The WRC are working on a new 16 km red graded loop with black technical options that will suit most intermediate riders, but the woods contain trails to challenge the best bike handlers.

Downhill

There are loads of unofficial downhill trails throughout this wood and now the Wharncliffe Riders Collective (WRC) are working to manage these trails, looking after erosion and meaning that everyone should be able to enjoy these trails for years to come. The rocky trails range from fast and fun to tight and super technical, and if they've proved such a successful training ground for Steve Peat there must be something about them.

Freeride

There are no freeride trails or stunts as such, but many of the downhill routes contain technical rock drops and rock gardens whose technical nature will keep riders trying again and again to perfect.

Locals do...

Run heavy duty tyres and tubes to cope with the rocks; float over the rocks, not ride through them.

Locals don't...

Ride without padding on – rocks hurt.

ⓘ OPENING TIMES
The wood is open at all times

ⓢ RESORT PRICES
Riding and access to the woods is free

ⓘ DIRECTORY
South Yorkshire Tourist Information: T+44 (0)1142-211900

Practicalities ⏸🚲♻

Wharncliffe sits just 5 miles north of the city of Sheffield, home to some of the UK's most talented riders such as Will Longden and Steve Peat, a testament to the rugged riding found in the area. Sheffield has plenty to offer in terms of entertainment and culture; it's one of the largest cities in England, with a thriving student population. Part of the Peak District National Park lies within the city boundary, and with its 170 ha of woodlands it has more trees per person than any city in Europe. Wharncliffe Woods is just one of these and one that provides a great challenging place to mountain bike in the north of England.

Sleeping Sheffield has plenty of options when it comes to places to stay and things to do. Try the *Old Crown Inn* (T+44 (0)7807-065738) for reasonably priced B&B in the heart of the city centre.

Eating Try *Taste* on Ecclesall Road for a contemporary feel or for a good tapas bar head to *Cubana* on Trippit Lane.

Bars and clubs Head for Division Street and West Street in the city for an excellent mix of places to drink. Or try the *Forum* on Devonshire Street.

Bike shop *Langsett Cycles* (T+44 (0)1142-348191) is one of the longest established bike shops in business, starting out in 1915. *Je James* Sheffield store (T+44 (0)1142-923103) will also stock many parts and new bikes.

Internet café Try *Havana* (T+44 (0)1142-495452), a relaxed affair, with spacious surroundings.

Bike map available? There are no physical trail maps available for Wharncliffe although some websites have produced their own on line maps, try disfunktional-dirt.org.uk/wrc/maps.html.

STEVE BEHR

Sheffield nerves of steel.

Best of the rest

CHRIS MORAN

England Best of the rest

DOWNHILL/XC

↘17 Bringewood

- **Number of runs** Two main tracks that have been used over the years for downhill races, also a number of unmarked XC routes through the wood
- **Uplift** Not regular; check website below for organized uplift days
- **More info** pearcecycles.co.uk

Used to be a mainstay in the UK national series calendar for both downhill and cross country and now the trails are used for local races and by many of the riders in Shropshire and across the midlands. Good trails with lots of whoops and technical turns that are fun to ride; suitable for intermediate to advanced riders. Very slippery after heavy rain

Above right: Country life – you'll never put a better bit of sunset on your knife.
Below right: There's a quid in that pond. Finders keepers.
Below: Kenny Smith taking it off the ground.

PETE TILEY

VICTOR LUCAS

XC/FREERIDE

↘18 Chopwell Trails

- **Ability range** Trails range from easy through to a black technical run, with effort minimal due to the individual trails very short lengths
- **More info** visitnorth eastengland.com/mtb

Trails built by a local group of enthusiast mountain bikers who had to overcome many restrictions before they could claim these woods for building. What they have achieved are four short but fun and intensive trails that will interest and challenge cross country and novice freeriders with the technical and fast singletrack.

STEVE BEHR

ANDY LLOYD

Clockwise from top left:
1. Skiiiiid. **2.** Northshore chicken wire. **3.** Cleared forest traffic jam. **4.** Woodland leap. **5.** Knee's eye view.

STEVE BEHR

England Best of the rest

4X

↘19 Redhill 4X

- ⊕ **Ability range** Caters for everyone; the track is entirely rollable with some bigger pro lines
- ↔ **Length** 350 m
- ⓘ **More info** redhillextreme.co.uk

The Redhill extreme site is a great 4x facility with a track that has hosted the 4x national championships and also is progressive to learn on. There is an uplift vehicle as well and various tabletops and jumps on the site for playing on too.

XC

↘20 Stainburn

- ⊕ **Ability range** Very high on the main boulder trail. Due to the range of XC trails it fitness required ranges from intermediate on the Norwood edge trail to high on the Black routes
- ↔ **Length** Trails are short, around 4 km
- ⓘ **More info** singletraction.org.uk

The Stainburn trails have been gaining an increasing reputation as some of the best built and most challenging out there. It's definitely a case of quality over quantity but that just adds to the fun of the riding here as it encourages riders to try over and over again to clean sections as they don't have to worry about the 50 km that they still have to ride!

France

Mer du Glace – France is in a league of its own when it comes to majestic views.

[DANMILNER.COM]

Marne-la-Vállée

CHALONS-sur-Marne

METZ

Langres Plateau

Meuse

Lorraine Plateau

Nancy

St.-Nicolas
Lunéville

Haguenau

Vosges

Strasbourg

GERMANY

Saal

Sens

Troyes

Montagis

Sancerrois Hills

Barrois Plateau

Chaumont

Meuse

Epinal

Moselle

Colmar

Rhine

Auxerre

Langres

FRANCE

Grand Ballon (1423 m) ⬇8

Avallon

Saône

Lorraine Plateau

Vesoul

Mulhouse

Alsace Plain

Loire

Yonne

De la Marche Plateau

Nevers

Langres Mts.

Dijon

Saône

Belfort

Basel

ZÜRICH

Besançon

Doubs

Bourgogne

Moulins

Millevaches Plateau

Charolles

Châlon-sur-Sâone

Revermont

BERN

Dolen

SWITZERLAND

Vichy

Allier

Beaujolais Mountains

Mâcon

Jura

Ain

⬇12

Lausanne

Lake Geneva

Clermont-Ferrand

Bourg-en-Besse

Geneva

⬇14 ⬇2 ⬇5

⬇10 ⬇4

Martigny

Grand Colombier (1531 m)

Annecy

LYON

Villeurbanne

⬇7

Mt. Blanc (4808 m)

Courmayeur

St. Chamond

Chambéry

⬇3

Isère

Thournon sur-Rhone

⬇6

⬇16

Vercors

⬇1 ⬇18

Charbonnel Point (3752 m)

MILAN

Valence

Grenoble

Frejus Tunnel

ITALY

Oulx

Montelimar

⬇9

Mt. Pelvoux (3914 m)

Briançon

⬇13

Turin

Pelvoux Range

Cottian Alps

Alpes du Dauphine

Embrun

⬇19

⬇11 ⬇15

⬇17

Mt. Pelat (3502 m)

N

30 km
30 miles

VICTOR LUCAS

Alpe d'Huez has shale aplenty.

Over the recent years France has been recognised as the place to go mountain biking. It is a reputation earned by its huge mountains, its laissez-faire attitude to danger and the fact that is was one of the first places to open up its lifts to the crowds of eager riders. The Portes du Soleil has been fundamental in bringing about the recent changes throughout Europe and creating the mountain biking summer season, and it remains a firm favourite for many Brits. As a result, Morzine has the largest seasonaire community in the Alps and many of the world's fastest racers have used it as their summer base over the years.

But the Portes du Soleil is not the whole story. France is also full of unspoilt resorts with groomed, quiet trails, and while the country is a little behind some of its European counterparts in terms of building expansive and progressive bikeparks, the French really haven't had to. With plenty of vertical metres at their disposal, it is the classic trail and singletrack that attracts riders here.

Off the trail, too, France is a tantalizing prospect. There are few countries to rival the French when it comes to pride in their culture, particularly in the kitchen. Our Gallic cousins will never concede that any other country could rival their fish and meat dishes, garnished with rich sauces and accompanied by more fine wines than you can shake a corkscrew at.

Overview

What can't be said about the mountain biking on offer in this, our closest EU neighbour? Without a shadow of a doubt it receives the most visitors from our shores each summer in search of the endless ski lifts, singletrack and sunny trails. This concentration of riders has typically been focused around Morzine and Les Gets and though this still remains one of the best destinations for the racer heads amongst us, the more casual rider looking for a fun holiday with their mates now has plenty more choice throughout the rest of the country with resorts such as Les Deux Alpes, Les Arcs and Chamonix all offering miles and miles of superb singletrack for both XC and descending.

With great access to the resorts from flights to Nice, Geneva, Lyon and Grenoble, all the resorts can be reached with ease and many holidays start on the bike the same day you fly. Alternatively, for longer breaks a drive down opens up a wealth of opportunity with so many of the resorts easily strung together into one glorious summer holiday.

The landscapes can be striking, the food is, well, French, and the mountain bike scene on the whole is growing each year. The beauty of France is that you can pick and choose the best resorts to suit your style of riding and so on the whole, it's easy to understand why France remains for many the hot ticket of summer mountain biking.

Conditions

The Alps can prove a little bit of a lottery when it comes to the weather and trail conditions. While it is true to say that the southern resorts of Montgenèvre, Les Orres, Pra Loup, Val d'Allos and Valloire benefit from a pleasant Mediterranean climate with

Top: Lac Blanc Bikepark's power wash.
Above left: Portes du Soleil salad lunch.   Above right: Courchevel BBQ in full swing.

almost exclusively bright blue skies and clear sunshine through the summer months, the same cannot be said of the resorts further north.

The mountain weather can be a little unpredictable, with localized thunderstorms and bands of heavy rainfall. There are no hard and fast rules as to when is the best time of the year to visit these resorts, but on the whole the summers are usually fine. Just be warned that it is not unheard of for people to endure a whole two weeks of rainfall during their holiday, so pack for hot sun and torrential rain: it's best to be prepared.

Anyone suffering poor weather would be very unlucky, but should be warned that the trails can become very slick and difficult to ride in the wet, so again it is best to pack winter mud tyres and summer hardpack ones.

The scene

Les Gets and Morzine have built up a massive scene over the years with loads of riders returning year after year, and due to the number of seasonaires and holiday companies, there are bikes all over these towns. Elsewhere in France the vibe is more relaxed and there are core groups of riders in the know who religiously return for the amazing singletrack around resorts such as Chamonix, Les Arcs and Les Orres. One race which has created a whole sub-scene in its own right is the awesome Mega Avalanche at Alpe d'Huez. It's a must-do, once-in-a-lifetime

Below left: Chamonix again, this time the view from Brévent.
Below right: Straightlining Alpe d'Huez.

Q&A with the experts

*French legend **Fred Glo** is the organiser of the Enduro series and owns the Tribe Sport Group (tribesportgroup.com)*

You've got friends visiting for just one weekend and they can go anywhere in France. Name the one place you'd definitely have to take them.

FG Not easy to answer, but I love all-mountain rides on natural single tracks and sunshine so I will have to say Val d'Allos.

Which trail centre or resort has the best party scene or the best after riding activities?

FG There are too much English guys in Morzine-Les Gets! So it has to be Les Deux Alpes where there's more chance to meet girls.

Where did you learn to ride, and where would you send beginners to ride?

FG Metabief. There are nice tracks and a good school with Greg Noce managing it.

Where's the best place for views, sunsets, or just total rustic charm?

FG Valloire is a very nice traditional village, and so is Val d'Allos. The views around the Galibier are amazing but Chamonix and the Mt Blanc are probably the most 'scenic' in France.

In your opinion, which is the best downhill track in France?

FG Everybody says Venosc in Les 2 Alpes is our A Line... it's fun for sure but as a pure DH track I prefer Montgenèvre.

Where's the best place to avoid pedalling uphill? Where has the best uplifts? Would you avoid anywhere?

FG Almost all the ski resorts are well equipped with the lift in France. If you've the chance to get to the top of Alpe d'Huez and the glacier this will be the start of an incredible and long downhill for sure!

Where's best for total variety?

FG Valloire is a good combination of classic rides and great scenery. As a gravity bike park resort though, I would say Les 2 Alpes is number one.

event where some 2,000 riders have a mass race down the mountain from the glacier to the valley floor. This has kick-started the hugely popular enduro DH series around many of the resorts featured here where you can ride in the same format but on a slightly smaller scale. See enduro-series.fr

The industry

France was perhaps most famous for its world dominating team of Sunn Chipie. Sunn all but disappeared for a period until recently but they have made a strong comeback with some great bikes in their range.

France also houses one of the most respected suspension technicians in the world, Olivier Bossard, whose eagerly awaited range of new rear shocks and suspension forks designed from his Toulouse base have just hit the top end of the market.

Mavic are a huge brand and major player in the mtb industry and their name is still the brand associated with true build quality when it comes to mountain bike rims. Lining the Mavic rims there is the choice of Hutchinson or Michelin tyres. Michelin have spent years developing their range of excellent tyres for all disciplines and you won't go far wrong with these.

France breakdown

The resorts featured in France are those that have decent mountain biking during the summer months. We have tried to identify the resorts which are quieter for those looking to get away from the crowds on unspoilt trails, those that are hot spots, and of course some of the hidden gems such as La Clusaz. Many of the resorts have more than enough trails to keep you happy for a week – Les Gets, Morzine, Les Arcs, Les Deux Alpes and Alpe d'Huez. Others such as Lac Blanc or Métabief would make a great weekend break.

Portes du Soleil

The vast Portes du Soleil is undoubtedly the best known mountain biking area in Europe, with loads of trails and lifts open to riders through the summer season. The area comprises 12 resorts, including Les Gets, Morzine, Avoriaz, Châtel, Morgins and Champéry. All are great places to ride in their own right, and when you throw them all together on the same lift pass you've got some bike trip.

There's a real sense of adventure and freedom in travelling from one valley to the next using the lifts and then shredding down the other side. This ability to cover large areas of ground with minimum effort has really opened people's eyes to just how much fun mountain biking can be in the Alps.

Most riders tend to base themselves in the French resorts of Les Gets and Morzine, and both towns are packed out with British riders throughout the summer. From here you can experience some epic days heading out through the Portes du Soleil into Switzerland and back: it's not unheard of for downhillers to clock up 60 km plus in a day's riding. There is a range of trails to suit all levels, from beginners to experts, and the resorts are now finally investing in the sport and expanding the trail network further. The PassPortes de Soleil XC trail is a fantastic waymarked route that takes you over 60 km around the area, and if you're legs become tired you can simply hop on a lift.

The only down side to coming here is its popularity. It is not uncommon to be stood in lift queues for long periods in Les Gets and Morzine, and the sheer volume of riders causes constant braking bumps which can become wheel-swallowingly big on the steeper trails. This can be avoided by heading out to Avoriaz, Morgins and Champéry where it is much quieter.

Another problem riders have to deal with in the region is the unpredictable weather. On the whole it is pretty good but when

Top left: The BBC badger-cam was set off – yet again – by some bloody mountain bikers. David Attenborough went ballistic.
Top right: A fish's-eye-view of the PDS.
Above: Three wise men. There's gold, frankincense and myrrh in those backpacks. It's a contemporary re-make.

DANMILNER.COM

it rains, it pours; sometimes continuously for a week or more. The riding here suddenly becomes a whole lot more technical as these tracks are very difficult in the wet, so it's a good idea to bring spike tyres with you. But don't let a bit of unpredictable weather put you off. This is one of the best places to mountain bike in the world; you'll meet plenty of likeminded people and experience some of the best riding of your life.

Right: Bootiful. **Far right:** A sign.

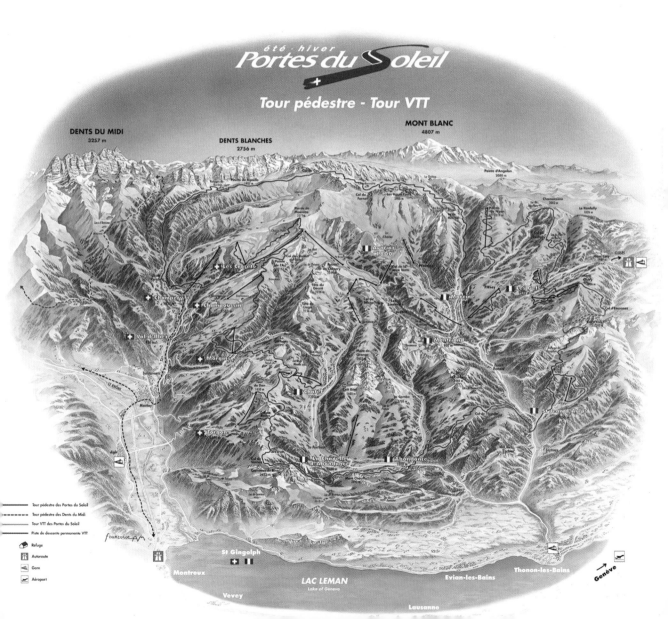

Alpe d'Huez

Home of the world-renowned Mega Avalanche.

ALPE D'HUEZ

↘1 The trails

- **XC Cross country** Very good/ beginner to advanced
- **DH Downhill** Excellent/beginner to advanced
- **FR Freeride** Poor/intermediate
- **Uplift** 5 lifts running in Alpe d'Huez, plus a further 2 linking the nearest resorts below
- **Pros** Plenty of trails; close to Les Deux Alpes
- **Cons** Poor for freeride

The resort sits high up on the plateau and all the riding above the resort is above the treeline as you head up towards the Sarenne Glacier. As you head up, the landscape changes from green mountain

The Lowdown

Locals do... Head out and ride the longer descents over the day.

Locals don't... Session the shorter downhills.

Don't miss... The Mega Avalanche! 1400 competitors take on the mountain in a mass start race beginning on the glacier before passing through Alpes d'Huez at its midway point and onto the valley floor to finish.

Remember to avoid... The glacier after a lot of riders have been down, unless you like sliding down on your head. Make sure you only ride it after it has been piste bashed.

Clockwise from top: **1.** Take your strongest brake lever.
3. That's mist caused by burning brake fluid.

2. Emerald-green lakes await.
4. The Mega Avalanche course in full effect.

pastures to a lunar moonscape of exposed rock and scree. In great contrast the riding from Alpe d'Huez down to the lower resorts is often through forest and gives a good mix of terrain. Alpe d'Huez is very close to Les Deux Alpes, making this a great place to stay and ride a whole heap of trails during your stay.

Recently the resorts have come together and anyone whose purchases a 6-day or longer lift pass can ride in the other resort for one day for free.

Cross country

There are 60 km of XC trails around the Alpe d'Huez resort over nine marked trails that are graded to suit each ability. The stronger riders may want to link across to Les Deux Alpes and access a further mass of trails. For most abilities though there is more than enough around the resort with the benefit of being able to use the lifts when tired.

Downhill

Alpe d'Huez has become one of the most famous downhill venues in Europe, purely down to the success of the Mega. However even without the Mega's success there are not many resorts where you can rack up so many vertical feet descent is a single day. On one descent alone, an 8500+ft vertical drop is possible! The sprint avalanche course in Oz en

Oisans is also widely regarded as one of the most technical and best tracks in Europe. Add to this is the other two permanent DH trails and the six marked downhill routes and there is plenty for the DH enthusiast.

Easy Take the Grand Rousses cablecar and jump out after the first stretch. This will lead you onto the beginner downhill run, which, once you have come to grips with, leads you up the mountain onto the DMC car. This will take you down an intermediate DH route that links back into the lower stretch.

Difficult No one can visit Alpe d'Huez and not take on the Mega route. The fastest racers have won this event in 55 minutes, but a more realistic time for most is around 1½ to 2 hours.

Freeride

There is a small bikepark with some ramps and drops found behind the DMC lift, but this really is more of a token gesture. If you're looking for some freeride trails and a decent park, head up to Les Deux Alpes for the day.

The bikepark is so laid-back you could almost drop off.

ALPE D'HUEZ TOURISM

ⓘ OPENING TIMES

Lifts are open from 28 Jun to 31 Aug

🅢 RESORT PRICES

Day pass: €17; Week pass: €67

🅞 DIRECTORY

Tourist Office: T+33 476-114444
Website: alpedhuez.com

Practicalities ⬤🅐🅑

Alpe d'Huez offers some of the very best 'big mountain' terrain and riding in the Alps. The resort has become infamous due to the hugely popular Mega Avalanche event. This extravaganza features a whole week of descending around the resort before the main event mass start race. The runs here are located on a mountain pasture, the setting for perhaps the most famous ascent of the Tour de France, a long climb from the valley up to the resort taking in all 21 hairpins. While the resort itself is not particularly inspiring, its surroundings most certainly are.

Sleeping Alpe d'Huez has a roaring winter season so there are plenty of apartments and hotels to choose from in the much quieter summer months. Shopping around will guarantee you get a good deal, however for starters try the *Alpe Privilège* (T+33 4-7611 3839) who have some great offers. Also *Agence Petit* (T+33 4-7680 6548) who offer studio apartments for groups of 3 to 10.

Eating You're certainly not going to go hungry in Alpe d'Huez with the wide

range of quality restaurants on offer. *Au Bleu Noir* is a good call with a range of crêpes as well as raclette and tartiflette and an à la carte menu. For a quick bite during the day's riding, head to the *Alaska* pizzeria.

Bars and clubs While summer is certainly a lot quieter than the winter season, there are still a few bars that pick up during peak times and if you head to the resort during Mega week, then the whole place is pretty lively. If you're looking for the late-night experience, then head for *L'igloo* which has the obligatory Ibiza foam party on certain weekends.

Bike shop *Nevada Sports* (T+33 4-7680 6561) and *Huez Sports* (T+33 4-7680 6342) both hire mountain bikes and stock a decent range of spares for most bikes. *Rocky Sports* probably have the best equipped workshop in the resort.

Internet café *L'Agua* and *l'Olympe* both have several terminals and Wi-Fi access.

Bike map available? Free trail maps for the whole region are available from the lift stations.

Avoriaz

Like Marmite, you will either love or hate the crazy architecture of this purpose-built resort perched on the top of huge cliffs.

AVORIAZ

↘2 The trails

- **Cross country** Good/moderate to advanced
- **Downhill** Excellent/intermediate to advanced
- **Freeride** Fair to good/moderate to advanced
- **Uplift** A large cablecar into town, a chairlift into town and easy access to all the 24 chairlifts of the region
- **Pros** A developing resort willing to add to its trail network each year; great for young kids with its riding school and skills area; perfect for families looking for a quieter stop in the Portes du Soleil
- **Cons** The town is not really developed at the moment for British clientele so most stay in the neighbouring resorts and take the lifts to Avoriaz for the riding

Avoriaz sits above Morzine and has valleys that fall away on either side of it, giving access to some amazing tracks and

① OPENING TIMES

Lifts open at 0900; the Prodains lift runs till 1730-1800

⑤ RESORT PRICES

Day pass: €16; Week pass: €64; Season pass: €128
(These prices are for the full Portes du Soleil region which covers over 6 resorts in 2 countries)

① DIRECTORY

Tourist Office: info@avoriaz.com
Website: avoriaz.com

incredible views. Many of the trails are fairly rocky and bed in very well making them great in all weathers. There are three downhill tracks that run from Avoriaz down to the Linderets village and this area is being developed as the Linderets Bike Park with more being added constantly. There are also numerous cross country tracks that run from Linderets up towards the Point de Mossettes and around the high ridges to finish above the town of Avoriaz (for the adventurous and fit- as the climb is tough. If you are feeling lazy you can choose to take the chairlift!). The town has a bike school for children and beginners as well as many guides to show you the most suitable tracks. In addition, the Prodains lift and the Mossettes express lifts running either side of the town two valleys are readily accessible. As well as this, the Chatel bike Park is accessed from Linderets (it is not actually in Chatel itself) so there is a huge variety of trails on the doorstep of this town.

Cross country

For the adventurous explorers and keen cross country riders this is an ideal place to start from. Look for the climbs and loops that run high into the surrounding mountains which have some of the

best unridden trails. The Col de Pic a Talon, Col de Fornet, Col de Coutis and Ressachaux Mountain are all in close proximity to Avoriaz and will reward those willing to follow the map and put in the effort. For the less adventurous or less fit, there are many more scenic and relaxing paths that can take you across and down to Morzine, to the beautiful Montriond Lake, or around and down from Mossettes on the well-ridden GR 5 trail.

The Lowdown

Locals do... Get the Prodains lift to access more trails and Morzine's nightlife.

Locals don't... Head into Switzerland after 1500 and risk getting stranded.

Don't miss... The Passportes du Soleil; the inaugural *Roof Top Slope Style* event (13-15 July), a track carved out of the roof tops of the hotels which attracts the world's top riders.

Remember to avoid... Getting stranded far into Switzerland, it is a big climb back out of the valley without a chairlift.

France
Avoriaz

Downhill

The French National Downhill series visits annually and the course starts from Avoriaz and runs down to the village of Linderets. This hill is being developed yearly and the track has been added to and caters for all abilities in the newly named Linderets Bikepark. From the bottom of these tracks a chairlift takes you up to the top of the Châtel Bikepark with its 9-10 tracks. Add to this a short downhill roll to the tracks in Morzine and the Prodains lift, accessed tracks and you have a ridiculous amount of riding on your doorstep.

Easy Take the easier route down to Les Linderets and then the lift up to Pré-la-Joux where you have a whole range of easier trails to ride.

Difficult Try the French National downhill course from Avoriaz to Les Linderets, definitely one of the most technical trails in the area.

Freeride

The Linderets Bikepark has numerous tracks that are being added to with various 'Modules' and bridges, thus catering for the freeriders out there. Also the Châtel Bikepark, accessed from just below Avoriaz, will take care of all your freeriding needs with many tracks, graded for abilities and offering something for everyone, even up to the very experienced.

Below: The Indiana Jones Trail. The rolling ball is just out of shot.
Opposite page left: Sweet, sweet chairlift. How I love thee.
Opposite page right: I remember when all this was just fields. Yesterday.

DANMILNER.COM

Practicalities

The town of Avoriaz is a purpose-built ski resort and linked to the town of Morzine. Avoriaz sits at 1700 m, and in the winter is a bustling, car-free town. Located within easy reach of Geneva, it is very accessible for visitors from all over Europe. In the summer the town is much quieter, attracting mainly French families. It is steadily growing and adding many new tracks to its local area, to the point where some riders are now basing themselves in Morzine, looking for a quieter town.

Sleeping *Maeava* are the largest agency offering apartments in Avoriaz with many properties on their books. With the town being quieter in the summer, it means you can find some good deals.

Eating *La Falaise* (T+33 450-741048) is perhaps the only pizza restaurant in the world on top a 300 m cliff, or for those suffering vertigo try *Le Chalet d' Avoriaz*.

Bars and clubs Avoriaz is pretty quiet in summer months, so for partying head down to Morzine. Alternatively, if you want to grab a drink try *Shooters*, *Le Tavaillon* or *Pub Le Choucas*.

Bike shop *Intersport* has basic spares, but for more technical support or spares head to *DERT* in Morzine.

Internet café The tourist office and the bowling alley both have web terminals.

Bike map available? Yes, good free trail maps for the whole region are available from the lift stations.

France Avoriaz

Bourg St Maurice/Les Arcs

Les Arcs has remained one of France's best kept secrets.

BOURG ST MAURICE/LES ARCS

↘3 The trails

- ⓍⒸ **Cross country** Excellent/ beginner to advanced
- ⒹⒽ **Downhill** Excellent/beginner to advanced
- ⒻⓇ **Freeride** Poor/intermediate
- 🄰 **Uplift** Funicular from Bourg to Arc 1600 and numerous chairs and gondolas accessing the trails on the mountain and linking the 3 mountain resorts
- ✓ **Pros** Great trails; quiet and in great condition
- ✗ **Cons** Poor for freeride

Les Arc has a lot to offer the mountain biker; there are more than enough trails to keep you interested for a whole summer, never mind a week's holiday. One thing in particular that makes Les Arcs stand out is the amount of vertical drop available; from the highest lift to the valley floor gives you nearly 2 vertical km to play with. This allows for descents lasting up to an hour and also explains why a lot

ⓘ OPENING TIMES

The funicular itself runs every half hour from 0730 until 1930; the lifts generally open from the start of Jul until the end of Aug

$ RESORT PRICES

1 day: €21; 1 week: €65

ⓘ DIRECTORY

Tourist Office: T+33 479-070492
Hospital: T+33 479-417979
Taxi/Airport Transfers:
T+33 632-192962; coolbus.co.uk

Clockwise from top:
1. Amazing sunset straight on.　2. Rock stack photo op.　3. Let it roll, let it roll.
4. Singletrack traverse.　5. Another pleasant valley Sunday.

of people have been using the area as a warm up for the Mega Avalanche. Above the treeline everything is very open and rocky with a good mixture of fast and slower technical trails. Below the treeline the trails tend to be a bit more loamy with some steeper sections to contend with. Whilst there is a variety of trail difficulties available it is certainly towards the harder end of the spectrum where Les Arcs excels. The forests below 1800 m, running from below Arc 2000 all the way round to Peisey, is littered with trails that criss-cross each other allowing for many variations.

The Lowdown

Locals do... Time it so they get the last funicular ride up and take the bus up to arc 1800 giving one big final descent and meaning you can ride until 2000.

Locals don't... Wake up early, the trails are deserted before noon.

Don't miss... La Varda trail. This requires a bit of a pushing or uphill to reach but is well worth it as it is a dictionary definition of the word epic; be prepared for one of the longest sections of technical riding that you are ever likely to ride.

Remember to avoid... Riding without spare tubes, the ground is rocky here.

Cross country

There are plenty of great technical cross country rides throughout the valley and up around the Les Arcs resorts. Some are mapped many aren't, which adds value to having a guide. For an out and out XC break try the *Bike Village* (bikevillage.co.uk) in nearby Landry who have great trail knowledge.

Downhill

There are so many good downhill trails, and mostly natural routes, so a guide is best to make the most of your time here;

try Rob at the *Coolbus* or *Velo-City* (rob@thecoolbus.co.uk). With two purpose-built downhills and countless trails through the forests, many finish further up or down the valley and may require a pedal to get back to the funicular but are more than worth it.

Easy The two downhill courses found at Arc 1800 and 2000 are both pretty easy to ride and good fun to get to grips with the area before trying the steeper and more technical natural trails.

Difficult Take the great black eight trail, which runs approximately from the top of the funicular to the bottom. The uplift takes 10 minutes and departs every half hour. This gives you 20 minutes to get down the 800 m of vertical descent in time for the next lift which is feasible but not easy!

Freeride

If there is an area that is slightly lacking in Les Arcs it would be the small amount of man-made stuff available. There is plenty of scope for development of this but at the time of writing Les Arcs show very little interest in putting any effort into it. Fortunately, the resort more than makes up for this with its extensive quality singletrack.

Practicalities

As with a lot of French resorts, Les Arcs is split up into several different villages. Bourg St Maurice sits lower in the valley at an altitude of 850 m. Arc 1600 is directly above Bourg, then, as you traverse the mountain south from here you come to Arc 1800 followed by Peisey/Vallandry. Arc 1950 and 2000 are situated in the next valley to the east. During the summer months Bourg is the busiest town. There is always something going on and the high street and surrounding bars are generally pretty busy.

Sleeping The cheapest place to stay in town geared up to cater for mountain bikers is *Velo-City* (velo-city.net). Their apartment in the Bourg high street is right in the thick of it, yet still only a 2-min pedal from the ski lift. Prices here start from €18 a night for this cheap and cheerful accommodation and you can arrange for them to show you around the trails as well. *Hot Marmot* (hotmarmot.com) offer a step up from this with prices of €45 a night B&B or €55 half board. Their huge chalet sleeps 16-20 people and has a large workshop, two large lounges and a garden complete with barbecue, mini-ramp and trampoline! Two companies offering bike packages are *Trail Addiction* and *Bike village* who both offer guiding.

Eating There are many good restaurants in Bourg and Arc 1800 covering the full spectrum of dining experiences. In Bourg the best fast food experience to be had is the local kebab shop on the main road through town just after the Tonneau roundabout. The Turkish owner's Bo Selecta! impersonations add an extra element of entertainment! Opposite here you will find the *Petit St Bernard* which has an excellent €16 set menu, and just a bit further back, the *Montagnole* which probably serve up the best food in town. For food on the go, the goats cheese and honey paninis in Arc 1800 are pretty special.

Bars and clubs For boozy nights, again the two best options are Bourg or Arc 1800. In Bourg the *Bar Central* (aka *Spot Bar*) is a long standing favourite with the local seasonaires and the owner Christian is not shy about pouring some eye-watering home brew spirits down your neck. *Bazoom*, just opposite the train station is another good hangout and frequently has bands and DJs on. The *Tonneau* is also a favourite largely due to its extensive outdoor seating which is ideal for an afternoon beer in the sun. After midnight head to the unfortunately named *L'Impasse* for an unparalleled nightclub experience. Arc 1800's *Chez Boubou* is a very friendly

place with an extensive list of shots on offer. The bowling alley is another good option but for later on head to the *Apocalypse* nightclub. Just make sure you visit the cash machine before you go in.

Bike shop In Bourg the only option for bike spares is *Intersport*. Luckily they do carry a surprising amount of stock and you can usually pick up what you need there. For a more specialist shop go up to Arc 1600. The shop in the courtyard has a lot of downhill specific parts and bikes. They also hire out Commencal bikes and have a good range available, complete with body armour and full-face helmets.

Internet café There are few internet cafés dotted about but the easiest one to find is probably the one next door to the *Indochine* restaurant on the main road through Bourg. *McDonalds* also has free Wi-Fi if you have a laptop with you.

Bike map available? Lift tickets and bike maps are available from the funicular station in Bourg. Be aware that the bike map only shows a fraction of the trails in the area so it could be worth picking up a small scale map from one of the bookshops in town.

Chamonix

Sublime singletracks surround this world-famous resort.

CHAMONIX

◢4 The trails

- ⓍⒸ **Cross country** Excellent/ intermediate to advanced
- ⒹⒽ **Downhill** Good/intermediate to advanced
- Ⓕⓡ **Freeride** Poor/intermediate
- ⓩ **Uplift** There are several gondolas and chairlifts in Chamonix, Vallorcine and Le Tour; all cater for mountain bikers
- ✔ **Pros** Vibrant town centre; great trails in a stunning setting
- ✖ **Cons** More hikers than anywhere else in the Alps and hikers and bikers don't mix so well on the trails

Chamonix really does have some classic singletrack with steep rocky sections and flowing silky traverses. It is the Brévent and Flégère side of the valley that features the most trails, as the Aiguille Du Midi does not cater for bikes. Further up the valley

Below: Weaving through the avalanche barriers in Le Tour.
Bottom: The Aiguille du Dru in all its sunset glory.

DANMILNER.COM

CHRIS MORAN

The Lowdown

Locals do... Know the best backcountry trails away from all the tourists.

Locals don't... Eat in the pricey mountain restaurants.

Don't miss... A trip to the top of the Aiguille du Midi for breathtaking views of Mt Blanc and the Chamonix valley.

Remember to avoid... Some of the hiking trails are closed to bikers during peak summer season.

Le Tour and Vallorcine also have numerous trails that can all be interlinked on longer rides or sessioned for the downhillers. Chamonix is also a highly popular walking destination, so it is best to come right at the start or at the very end of the season when the trails are quieter.

Cross country

There are copious amounts of singletrack to take in both in the Chamonix valley and riding out and beyond. To get the most out of a cross country stay in the town we would recommend you join

up with a good guide so all your time is spent heading the right direction. *MBMB* are one of the best for XC holidays.

Easy Take the Charamillon télécabine from Le Tour. Follow the signs to the Col des Posettes (1997 m). At the col turn right on the 4WD track that heads up to the Col de Balme. It is easily recognisable by the stone Alpine restaurant in the centre of the col. A great place for hot chocolate and shelter, an hour from Le Tour.

Practicalities ⊙🍴🚲

Situated at the base of Mt Blanc – Western Europe's highest mountain, at 4807m – Chamonix is arguably the world's most famous mountain resort. However, it's actually very different from the typical notion of a resort, in that it's a self-contained 'proper' town with thousands of inhabitants. There are a number of populated areas that come under the Chamonix banner, but two main focal points are Chamonix itself and the satellite town of Argentière, 10 km further up the valley.

Sleeping Depending on the type of riding you will be doing in the town it may be better for you to take a package deal which includes guiding to the best trails. *MBMB* have some of the best

trail knowledge of the area (mbmb. co.uk). If you are descending most of the time and want to do your own thing try the *Apartment Les Alpes* (T+44 020-73710527).

Eating *Mojos* (T+33 450-891226) in Chamonix town square is a good choice for snacks. *Grand Central* (T+33 450-535609, directly opposite *McDonalds*) is also very popular, with home-made cakes and excellent fresh juices and smoothies. For a top class meal try *Le Délice* (T+33 450-915206) in Les Houches, or *Munchie* (T+33 450-534541) in the Rue du Moulin.

Bars and clubs *The Jekyll* does a great pint of Guinness and also serves

excellent food. *MBC* brews its own beer, and often puts on live music. *Goophy* (also an excellent restaurant) and *Elevation* next door are both very popular. *Le Garage* is Chamonix's main after-hours drinking den.

Bike shop The *Legend Bike and Board* shop stocks plenty of good brands and is located near to the Aiguille du Midi lift. They also hire a range of bikes.

Internet café *Le Bureau*, on edge of the river on the Rue du Moulins.

Bike map available? There are free trail maps for the valley available from the lift stations.

France Chamonix

Difficult From Les Praz take the La Flégère cablecar to the top (1877 m). From here the views of the Mer de Glace and the Grande Jorasses are incredible. From the station take the 4x4 track on the immediate left outside the station. This is another steep track through the trees to the valley floor. It is a one-hour descent from the station.

Downhill

Some of the singletrack descents down the Brévent mountain are superb. Fast, flowing and technical enough to keep you on your toes. Further up the valley Le Tour has opened a downhill course on the open slopes which is pretty fast. Not to be missed for the more experienced riders is the new mega long downhill into Vallorcine which clings to the steep face of the hill for around 7-8 minutes.

Freeride

There are no freeride trails in Chamonix.

Left: Riding in the sunset under the Aiguille du Midi.
Above: The craziest uplift in the world.
Right: A well-earned rest overlooking the Mer du Glace.

① OPENING TIMES
The lifts open the 2nd week of Jun and close at the end of Sep

⑤ RESORT PRICES
Day pass: €20; Week pass: €80

ⓘ DIRECTORY
Tourist Office: T+33 450-530024
Medical Centre: T+33 450-558055
Taxi: T+33 450-531914
Website: chamonix.com

Châtel

CHÂTEL

↘5 The trails

- **XC Cross country** Fair to good/ beginner to advanced
- **DH Downhill** Excellent/beginner to intermediate
- **FR Freeride** Excellent/intermediate
- **Uplift** 1 gondola in Châtel, 2 chairlifts in Pré-la-Joux and access to the rest of the Portes du Soleil
- **Pros** Great bikepark with lots of fun trails; nice welcoming resort
- **Cons** All but experts will struggle when it has been very wet

The quieter side of the Portes du Soleil, now hosting some killer new trails.

Châtel is an impressive setting, with some great views to accompany the trails once you get up the mountain from the Super Châtel gondola. The terrain is a mixture of pistes and woods and most of the ground is quite earthy. This equates to hardpack when it is dry and slick and muddy after heavy rains. There is a trail crew that maintain the bikepark so on the whole the trails stay in pretty good condition and Châtel are investing in a future of mountain biking in their resorts with an already good infrastructure set to improve.

Cross country

While there are no specific XC routes in the bikepark, many of the easier blue runs are pretty straight forward and good fun to hit a few times. Heading further afield you can either utilize the Pré-la-Joux lift and drop into the Linderets Valley or head up to Morgins and round the Portes du Soileil that way. The Passportes du Soleil can be picked up from Châtel for an epic day in the saddle and there are plenty of hiking routes to follow.

Practicalities ⬛🚲🏔

Châtel is a more traditional mountain village with many working farms still in the area that add to its Alpine charm. Luckily Châtel still has the modern infrastructure and facilities required for today's tourists. The main riding area is found just up the valley at Pré-la-Joux where a free bus service shuttles riders and bikes up and back during the day. Châtel is definitely the place to stay as Pré-la-Joux is very quiet and a little remote, while Châtel has a pleasant summer vibe with a beautiful lake and lots of open-air restaurants to relax in.

Sleeping Most of the accommodation in Châtel is in medium-sized traditional Alpine hotels. Our pick of the bunch is the *Belalp* or the *Hotel Choucas,* both located right near the Super Châtel gondola and near the bus pick up point.

Eating When you spend your days up at Pré-la-Joux you will find yourself enjoying food on the sun terrace at *La Perdrix Blanche*. Back in Châtel proper,

Chez Jojo is a great crêperie and *La Flambée Pizzeria* is popular amongst the locals; always a good sign.

Bars and clubs Châtel enjoys a steady influx of tourists through the year with many families and walkers staying in the town during the summer months. The bars and clubs are never really lively here though and it has a more relaxed social vibe about the place. *Le Tunnel* or *L'Avalanche* are the bars to best soak up the good vibes.

Bike shop There are a few bike shops offering hire in Châtel although none are very well stocked when it comes to spares and clothing. For the basics try *Intersport*.

Internet café There is a terminal available at the tourist office.

Bike map available? Well laid-out and free trail maps for the whole region are available from the lift stations.

DANMILNER.COM

Downhill

The two downhill routes on Super Châtel are great fun, comprising an easier flowing blue run and the steep and technical black run for experts which has some great sections. Up at Pres la Joux there are over 10 runs to hit from green through to black and they have been well designed to offer increasing challenges as you work up the gradients right through to the steep and technical black routes.

Freeride

At the base of the downhill routes on Super Châtel there is a somewhat tired 4X course that is fun to end your DH run with. Mind you it is easily conquered and there is a wealth of freeride up at Pres la Joux, from northshore trails to an extreme and steep slopestyle course. The only criticism would be that the obstacles seem to step from beginner and intermediate straight to the lines on the slopestyle which are mostly pro lines.

Easy Try out the purple shore trails in the bikepark accessed from the blue route, most of the lines are simple enough with some harder ones you can opt in or out of.

Difficult Head across the Serpentine trail until you reach the start of the black Che Nada trail which is a mix of freeride skills and downhill control. Expect drops, jumps, narrow northshore and super steep downhill chutes.

DANMILNER.COM

Above: Play follow-the-leader on the trails.
Below: Or check out your run from the chairlift!

France Châtel

ⓘ OPENING TIMES

The lifts are open from the 29 Jun to 2 Sep and operate between 0900 and 1700

Ⓢ RESORT PRICES

Day pass: €15; Week pass: €60; Season pass: €120

Ⓒ DIRECTORY

Tourist Office: T+04 5073 2244
Website: chatel.com

The Lowdown

Locals do... Book into the Passportes du Soleil at the start of July, a massive fun MTB event.

Locals don't... Miss the bus back from Pré-la-Joux. It's a long ride.

Don't miss... The Fantasticable at the top of Pré-la-Joux, a huge zip ride which fires you across the valley from mountain to mountain at over 50 mph.

Remember to avoid... The mountain style course, unless you have the minerals and skills to back it up.

Courchevel

COURCHEVEL

◢6 The trails

- **⊗ Cross country** Excellent/beginner to advanced
- **⊗ Downhill** Good/beginner to intermediate
- **⊗ Freeride** Poor/intermediate
- **⊘ Uplift** 3 main lifts running in Courchevel with others throughout the wider Three Valleys area
- **⊘ Pros** Enormous area; great for families and beginners
- **⊗ Cons** Riders with heavy downhill bikes won't be able to make the most of the area

The largest of the Three Valleys resorts, Courchevel offers some expansive terrain and its glitzy winter reputation has kept most of the mountain bike crowd away... until recently.

Why Courchevel isn't up there in the ranks with the other top French resorts is something of a mystery. Its reputation may lead you to believe that it's little more than a fashion parade for the French elite, but when it comes to the mountains, nothing could be further from the truth. From mellow beginner trails slopes to funparks, to beautifully kept high-speed doubletrack, this place has it all. It offers a greater variety of terrain than its Trois Vallées counterparts, including open and steep trails and an abundance of good forest runs.

Cross country
With pedal power at your disposal, summer does not pose the same

ⓘ OPENING TIMES
Lifts are open from 4 Jul to 29 Aug; 0930-1645

⑤ RESORT PRICES
Day pass: €15; Week pass: €40

ⓒ DIRECTORY
Tourist Office: T+33 479-080029
Medical Centre: T+33 479-083213
Taxi: T+33 479-082346
Website: courchevel.com

COURCHEVEL TOURISME/PATRICK PACHOD

CHRIS MORAN

COURCHEVEL 1650

Practicalities 🛏🍴🚲

Courchevel is made up of several widely spaced out populated centres at differing altitudes, each with their own distinct character. This ranges from chic 1850 with its preponderance of fur coats and wealthy Parisians to the low key and homely feel of La Tania and Les Praz at 1300 m and 1400 m respectively. Though 1850 is the most central in terms of lift access, many people prefer the vibe of 1650 or La Tania, the latter having seen huge development over the past few years. Plus it means you can end your day with a longer descent.

Sleeping If you're on a tight budget go for B&B at the 2-star *Edelweiss Hotel* (courchevel-edelweiss.com), or if cost isn't much of an issue, then *Le Seizena* (T+33 479-014646) is worth a look. Both are in 1650. Alternatively *Pleisure* (pleisure.co.uk) offer a variety of chalet accommodation around the valley.

Eating For snacks on the go, try *S'no Limit* in 1850's *Place du Forum*. *Petit Savoyard* (T+33 479 082744) in 1650 is great for traditional fare.

Bars and clubs The *Bubble Bar* or *Rocky's Bar* in 1650 for après and evening drinks, after which you can head to *The Space Bar* till 0400. If you're after a suitably chic late-night establishment, try 1850's *Le Kalico*.

Bike shop In 1650 head to *Gilbert Sports* (T+33 479-081646) which has XC and DH bikes for hire and a decent workshop.

Internet café *Cybercafé* in 1850 and *Bubble Bar* in 1650.

Bike map available? Well laid out and free trail maps for the whole region are available from the lift stations.

France Courchevel

Above: Perfect singletrack.
Above right: Courchevel 1650. 1650 m above sea-level.
Opposite page: Stopping to check out the view near the Saulire.

problems as winter in the Three Valleys where the spread-out locations of the resorts can be a pain. In the summer it is simply a means of getting in more great

The Lowdown

Locals do... Hang out in 1650 – it's the more down to earth option.

Locals don't... Ride big rigs, all the downhills can be tackled on a 6" trail bike which allows more variety in their riding.

Don't miss... The Three Valleys tour on the 6 July, an 80-km ride using the lifts and trails of all Three Valley resorts.

Remember to avoid... As with any of the Three Valleys resorts, here getting stuck in one of the other valleys after the lifts close is an expensive mistake.

trails between stops. There is a marked 117-km trail around all three resorts plus there are over 10 routes around Courchevel ranging from very easy to difficult.

Easy Les Ecureuils is a gentle starter XC loop with just 300 ft of climbing over its 6 km length.

Difficult It has to be the Three Valleys 117-km itinerary. Riders will obviously have to be fit and strong to complete this loop that takes in some superb views and reaches parts of the valleys you would otherwise never see.

Downhill
One event that will appeal to all downhillers is the Free Bike event on 5 July which takes in 20 km of descending in one day and allows you to find some of the best trails in the area without the effort of hunting them down. This is a great way to begin a week here, and with the Free Raid Three Valleys on the Sunday you will become familiar with your surroundings and can enjoy the great terrain on offer the rest of your time in Courchevel.

Freeride
There are no freeride features or trails in Courchevel.

La Clusaz

↘7 The trails

- ⓧⓒ **Cross country** Very good/ beginner to advanced
- ⓓⓗ **Downhill** Good to excellent/ intermediate to advanced
- ⓕⓡ **Freeride** Poor to fair/intermediate
- ⓐ **Uplift** There are now 6 lifts open through the summer to riders in the Aravis resorts
- ✅ **Pros** Very near Geneva airport; beautiful, unspoilt French village
- ❌ **Cons** Relatively short season; may be too quiet for those looking for nightlife

While La Clusaz is viewed as the poorer cousin of the higher resorts nearby during the winter months, the wooded slopes and mellower gradients are perfect for mountain biking and the resort has

A great little resort with a very French feel, within spitting distance of Geneva airport.

gained almost a cult following amongst those in the know, who head there for the quiet unspoilt trails and peace away from the nearby mega resorts. The resort has taken pride in building this reputation with a crew working every day on the trails to maintain the quality and variety.

Cross country

The XC trails spread out from La Clusaz to the surrounding resorts of Le Grand-Bornand, St Jean de Sixt and Manigod, offering in total some 22 intermediate and advanced trails and 14 very mellow family routes, making this a perfect resort for the family with trails to suit all abilities and ages.

ⓘ **OPENING TIMES**

Lifts open on 28 Jun and close on 31 Aug

ⓢ **RESORT PRICES**

Day pass: €13; Week pass: €60; Season pass: €120

ⓒ **DIRECTORY**

Tourist Office: T+33 450-326500
Medical Centre: T+33 450-024022
Taxi Number: T+33 663-513258
Website: laclusaz.com

Downhill

The downhills in La Clusaz are superb, open and fast without the heavy braking bumps of the busier resorts. The runs will suit intermediate riders and above with three runs to choose from and the longest trail, the Crêt du Loup, can be linked into the new four cross track. There are more runs in the resort of St Jean de Sixt just down the road.

Gangs of pirate sheep are a problem. They'll strip your Maxxis off you in seconds.

CHRIS MORAN

Easy Take La Greneche trail from the Crêt du Merle chairlift it winds down through the forest and across the pistes back down to the lift station.

Difficult Try out La Ferriaz trail. Take the Beauregard Gondola to the start and then rip back down the 3.3-km descent with berms, jumps and northshore sections.

Freeride

The resort may not have a bikepark like some, but it has built many of the obstacles that you may find in one into its descents with jumps, big berms, bridges and northshore all incorporated in some of the downhills. There is also the new four cross trail at the foot of the Crêt du Loup. Ultimately though, those looking for out-and-out freeride spots should look elsewhere, but if you enjoy your trail riding with your stunts then you'll enjoy yourself in La Clusaz.

"Leg it! The sheep are behind us!"

The Lowdown

Locals do... Take day trips to nearby Annecy, possibly one of the most stunning towns in France; have frequent days riding at other nearby resorts, such as Morzine, Chamonix and Les Gets.

Locals don't... Always choose to speak to you in English.

Don't miss... A night out rounded off with a dance above the river on the glass dancefloor at the *L'Ecluse* nightclub – a strange yet compelling experience!

Remember to avoid... If your French is appalling. At least make sure you know the basic phrases.

Practicalities ◉⌁◎

La Clusaz mightn't seem an obvious choice for inclusion in this book, but where else in France can you get away from the bustle and experience an unspoilt French mountain town, all merely an hour's drive from Geneva airport? The town is both pretty and unassuming. It's long been the preserve of the French and thus retains a very French feel. You won't find much in the way of rowdy nightlife, but this is one resort that has got its mountain bike trails right, unlike some of the bigger and better known French resorts. La Clusaz is part of the wider Aravis area which contains a further three small resorts and is a superb area to ride.

Sleeping The 3-star *Hotel Beauregard* (hotel-beauregard.fr) is very central and has its own excellent restaurant, along with a jacuzzi, sauna, steam room and an 18-m swimming pool. The 2-star *Hôtel Les Sapins* (T+33 450-633333) is also well situated.

Eating *La Calèche* (T+33 450-024260) or *Au Cochon des Neiges* (T+33 450-026262) for traditional Savoyarde cuisine. *La Bergerie* (T+33 450-026340) serves pizzas and local specialities, and though it's a bit cheaper the food is still excellent.

Bars and clubs Popular bars include *Le Pressoir*, *Les Caves du Paccaly* and *Le Grenier* – the latter two frequently put on live music and DJs. *L'Ecluse* is the town's nightclub, replete with glass dancefloor over the river.

Bike shop There are a few ski shops in the town that are now stocking and hiring bikes as well as carrying out repairs.

Internet café You can get online at *Arvimedia* (T+33 450-323805) and *Service Académie* (T+33 450-326589).

Bike map available? A trail map is available from the tourist office for €2 and maps out the 120 km of XC tours.

Lac Blanc

A fun bikepark that makes the perfect long weekend break from the UK.

LAC BLANC

↘8 The trails

- **Cross country** Fair to good/ beginner to intermediate
- **Downhill** Fair to good/ intermediate
- **Freeride** Good/beginner to intermediate
- **Uplift** There is an efficient 4-man chairlift up to the top of the bikepark
- **Pros** Perfect weekend break destination; fun bikepark trails; not too hard; long season
- **Cons** Not open through the week; trails run slower when wet

WWW.LACBLANC-BIKEPARK.COM

The rustic gap sees a lot of supermen.

The park in Lac Blanc is how you'd imagine a park in the UK would be if there were good ski lifts in operation. With just 300 m to play with, much less than some of the other resorts in the Alps, it has been used well with plenty of fun on the way down; which is what any good bikepark should be all about. In addition, the terrain is not too steep and can be ridden on a hardtail by the more skilful, though a freeride or mid-travel trail bike is ideal.

Cross country

There are 250 km of FCC approved trails in the area surrounding the park, so although the park itself does not have

any XC itineraries there is plenty of trail riding to do. It's entirely possible to

Practicalities ⬤🚲⚙

Lac Blanc is in Alsace, in northeastern France. Unlike some of the other resorts covered, this ski resort is hardly even a minor blip on the winter ski map and its trade is nearly all from the local area. However, the resort has been wise and spent a lot of time working together with local riders to create a great little bikepark with plenty of trails. It's a gem that will keep riders grinning as it is the perfect long weekend break. The nearby towns of Orbey and Kaysersberg both offer a place to stay and access to the park.

Sleeping The *Au Bon Repos* in Orbey (T+33 389-712192) and *Hôtel Les Terrasses du Lac Blanc* (T+33 389-471017) both offer a good base from which to head to the trails. There are also numerous campsites near the lifts, such as the *Birches Farm* (T+33 389-712273).

Eating There are restaurants at the top and bottom of the trails. *Auberge du Vallon* is at the bottom of the trails, while *Auberge Des Crêtes* is found at the top. Both offer a varied menu to keep you fuelled during riding hours. In the evening, try the tasty home-made meals served at the *Ferme Auberge Pre Bracot* (T+33 389-712529).

Bars and clubs There are no clubs in the valley and on the whole the area is very quiet.

Bike shop There is a bike hire store at the base of the trails and the ski lift which stocks a good range of bike brands including Scott and Commencal.

Internet café There is no internet café at the station or in the valley.

Bike map available? A trail map is for sale in the tourist office and covers some of the 250 km of FCC approved trails in the region. The bikepark is easily navigated without the need for a map.

Freeride

There are two freeride trails through the park; these are graded black and red. They feature plenty of wooden obstacles, raised platforms, kickers and drops into natural downslopes and gap jumps. There is a good mix between the wooden obstacles and natural loamy and rooty ground making these pretty rounded and fun routes to ride. At the bottom of the slopes there is a four cross course, a small slopestyle and dirt jump area and also a trials arena for those with suitable bikes.

extend your stay to a week, especially if you have a bike that is capable of the fun descents and putting in some miles. You will need to buy the trail map from the tourist office or lift station for these routes outside the park.

Downhill

There are two downhill trails in the park; one is graded black and the other red. The gradients in the park are not very steep, so most riders will be able to pick their way slowly down either, while more experienced riders will love riding this natural terrain. The ground is still quite loamy due to the low numbers of riders hitting the trails meaning which means you can really carve the turns.

Easy Take the red trail from 1200 m back down the mountain. This is a gentler trail that doesn't have any nasty surprises.

Difficult Follow the expert black route with plenty of drops, off-cambers, roots and rocks; it is a more testing line for riders with some previous downhill experience.

The Lowdown

Locals do... Get involved in the building and development of the park; end up with pretty good handling skills as a result.

Locals don't... All ride fancy expensive rigs; you will see plenty of riders shredding on battered bikes.

Don't miss... The inauguration weekend of 16/17 July when all the riders from the surrounding area group together. There is a great vibe about the park with everyone riding together and egging each other on.

Remember to avoid... If having a whole lot of fun on your bike is not your thing!

Top: A fire took the rest of the chalet but left a perfect wallride.
Above right: The 'Free Pastis' sign drew quite a crowd.
Bottom right: Getting twisted in the woods.

France Lac Blanc

Les Deux Alpes

DAMILNER.COM

LES DEUX ALPES

↘9 The trails

- **Cross country** Good/beginner to advanced
- **Downhill** Good to excellent/ beginner to intermediate
- **Freeride** Good to excellent/ beginner to advanced
- **Uplift** There are 6 lifts open to bikers that link the various ride areas and resorts
- **Pros** Great park; large, wide open area
- **Cons** Lack of tree runs

As its name suggests, Les Deux Alpes consists of two distinct mountains on either side of the valley. Each is well serviced by lifts, with the bulk of the rideable terrain on the side accessed by the speedy Jandri Express gondola. The overall riding area is massive, and though it's largely open and lacking in trees, there's a good variety of terrain to suit most levels of rider. The resort is notable for its progressive attitude to the trails and its bikepark, and each summer the place transforms itself into one of the main European focal points for trail riding, with more and more events hosted here each year.

ⓘ OPENING TIMES

The lifts open from 14 Jun to 30 Aug; timetable depends on the lift running but most of the time from 0930-1900

$ RESORT PRICES

Day pass: €19; Week pass: €94; Season pass: €259

ⓘ DIRECTORY

Tourist Office: T+33 476-792200
Medical Centre: T+33 476-792003
Taxi Number: T+33 476-800697
Website: les2alpes.com

'Has one of the best trail offers in the Alps and plenty of events to watch or ride in through the summer.'

Cross country

The resort has made a solid effort to really make mountain biking a success in Les Deux Alpes. It is an effort that has paid off with 15 cross country itineraries providing more than enough to fill a one- or two-week break here. And if that isn't enough, there are a further 16 downhill itineraries which can be ridden on most trail bikes.

Downhill

Les Deux Alpes hosted a round of the World Cup about five years back where the UK's Steve Peat wiped the floor with everyone by six seconds, and now you can ride the same course, as well as another 17 descending trails. It is this variety and quality that make it one of the most popular French stops.

Easy The Pied Moutet trail, graded blue is a great way to break yourself into the riding in Les Deux Alpes.

Difficult The Venosc trail is a fun ride with jumps and even finished down through some woods. It's not too challenging but will get you into the swing of things before taking on the expert-only Thuit trail.

Practicalities ⬛🚲♿

Located in the Oisans area in the southern French Alps, Les Deux Alpes is a fairly large town strung out along the length of a narrow valley. Though it isn't the prettiest of resorts, its magnificent and unusual setting gives the place a certain charm. Only 5 years ago the resort used to be like a ghost town through the summer, but the huge amount of work and investment they have put into creating a strong summer package is paying off with riders from all over Europe now coming to stay here.

Sleeping Les Deux Alpes has a daunting range of hotels, B&B and self-catering accommodation to navigate. Most accommodation can be booked through the resort's central reservations service. The resort also offer some great mountain bike packages based on 6 people sharing an apartment for the week with a 6-day mountain bike pass from just €152. See 2alpes-vtt.com/hebergement.htm.

Eating The pasta dishes and set menus at *La Spaghetteria* (T+33 476-790577) are excellent value, and it has a great buffet salad bar. Also try *Thai Alloi* (T+33 618-583924) *Smokey Joe's* (T+33 476-792897) does good value pub food (till 2300) and a cracking English breakfast. Ditto *The Red Frog* (T+33 476-792897).

Bars and clubs *Smokey Joe's* is the main hangout, and it's right next to the main lift area for easy après ride. Also check out *The Red Frog* at the Venosc end of town, and *Smithy's* in Venosc. For late nights it's the *Avalanche* and *Brésilien* all the way.

Bike shop There are plenty of shops throughout the resort at 1650 that hire XC, freeride and downhill bikes. Try *CH Sports* (T+33 476-792236).

Internet café *Smokey Joe's* has several terminals.

Bike map available? There are trail maps available at the lift station and most of the trails are well signed.

The Lowdown

Locals do... Know the best ways to link the riding areas and get the most vertical metres in a day.

Locals don't... Ride the jump trails on windy days that has a gusty wind, they'll stick to the singletrails.

Don't miss... The Freeraid classic event on the second weekend of June every year; it covers nearly all the trails in the area over two days. You'll get loads of quality trail under your belt if you do this.

Remember to avoid... If you like slower techy riding in the trees, as Les Deux Alpes is nearly all in the open.

Freeride

Many of the downhill itineraries feature jumps and drops and the resort has just added a new trail called the Serre Palas which aims to emulate the legendary A-line trail in Whistler, so expect plenty of airtime. The bikepark is of a high standard and has been put together with some thought; often lacking at other ski resorts. There are lines that will challenge advanced riders and for 2008 the park has added some easier lines to allow beginners and novices to start to learn the skills.

Above left: Two victims about to succumb to the Bikes Of Death.
Above: Bikes Of Death DH course. No pads allowed.
Opposite page: Classic moonscape terrain.

Les Gets

Perhaps the most famous of all bike resorts in Europe, this small French Alpine town has been hosting mountain bikers longer than most.

Dropping in to one of the hottest spots in Europe.

LES GETS

↘10 The trails

- **⊗ Cross country** Very good/ beginner to advanced
- **⊕ Downhill** Excellent/beginner to intermediate
- **⊕ Freeride** Fair/intermediate
- **⊘ Uplift** 2 gondolas and 2 chairlifts in town to access the immediate trails, and over 24 lifts in the region
- **⊘ Pros** A reputation as a bike mecca; in the centre of the massive Portes du Soleil region with access to over 30 lifts and 6 villages all with their own trails and tracks
- **⊗ Cons** Can be a victim of its own success, with larger lift queues and busy trails; bikepark on Mt Chery, could be great, but is poor

Les Gets is very well known among mountain bike circles as one of the

ⓘ OPENING TIMES

Lifts open at 0900 and Les Chavannes lift runs all the way through to 1730-1800

⑤ RESORT PRICES

Day pass: €16; Week pass: €64; Season pass: €128
(NB These prices are for the full Portes du Soleil region)

ⓞ DIRECTORY

Tourist Office:
lesgets@lesgets.com
Website: lesgets.com

premier destinations in Europe, a title which it has earned through its good lift access and great terrain but can also be largely attributed to being part of the wider Portes du Soleil region. Buy a lift pass here and it will allow you to ride in any of the other resorts in the region with a total of 24 lifts open.

Cross country

There are numerous routes around Les Gets that are not only great loops but offer amazing views and singletrack. One of these heads up the Chavannes and around past the Col de Joux-Plane (a famous Tour de France climb) and over to the Chappelle de Jacquicourt, a small shrine at the top of the mountain. On the way you can stop for amazing views of Mont Blanc, before heading down some flowing singletrack back into town.

Downhill

There are downhill courses on each side of Les Gets valley. The Chavannes boasts the Grass Track downhill course that flows over many jumps and berms from the very top of the lift. Half way down this you can peel onto another track known locally as the Gulley Run which is continually being added to with bridges and drops and snakes its way down the river valley. On the opposite side of the valley the Mont Chéry gondola takes you up to a long downhill track that is very physical.

Easy Take the Chavannes lift up to the top and enjoy flowing down the straight forward but fun grassy track. Just try and stay off the brakes.

The Lowdown

Locals do... All get on and are a very laid-back and friendly bunch considering they are some of Europe's fastest racers.

Locals don't... Ride these trails without paying them the respect they deserve. Bikes need to be well set up and maintained and protection is advised.

Don't miss... The Passportes du Soleil at the start of July, a huge mountain bike festival; the Tour de France often visits and is an incredible sight.

Remember to avoid... If you like the trails to yourself.

The mellower side of the Portes du Soleil.

Difficult Take on the infamous Gully Run on the Chavannes side; with copious amounts of roots and rocks this run has been sessioned by riders for years.

Freeride

There is a dedicated Kona bikepark on the Mont Chéry side of Les Gets with jumps, rhythm sections, drops, ladders and bridges all dedicated to bikers.

Though this park is poorly laid out and lacks any real direction, there are some obstacles that riders will find fun to master. Also the Chavannes Gully Run has incorporated numerous ladders and bridges to keep the track flowing, giving a good crossover track.

Practicalities ⬛🚲🚲

The town of Les Gets is close to Geneva which makes it very easy to reach from the UK and all over Europe. It has developed from a small Savoyarde farming town and is now very family orientated in the winter with a newly updated centre with many shops, cafés and bars and a relaxed but vibrant atmosphere. The town has two main lifts that access different sides of the valley and their different tracks and trails. It also links to neighbouring Morzine and the whole of the sprawling Portes du Soleil region. The town has grown in its stature since its hosting of World Cup downhill events and the Mountain Bike World Championships in 2004. It is this commitment to mountain biking that has given the area its reputation.

Sleeping As one of the most popular resorts in Europe there is plenty of choice in the town, although we have found the *Riders Retreat* (riders-retreat.co.uk) to be one of the best. The Retreat boasts one of the biggest properties in Les Gets, run by avid mountain bikers. It provides a newly converted property with some of the best-equipped accommodation in its large chalet including a huge garage downstairs for bike storage, a workshop and pressure washer for maintaining the bikes.

Eating There are lots of traditional Savoyarde restaurants in town that offer good value meals and all centrally located around the main street. Try out the *Le Flambeau* or *La Grande Ourse*. For a quick fix during riding there are burger bars close to each lift station but beware, they get very busy at lunch time.

Bars and clubs The first bar people think of is *The Boomerang*, a mountain bike bar that plays videos and attracts many of the riders. Near by is the *Irish Bar* and *Bar Bowling*, each offering a good atmosphere. If it is late drinking/partying you want, head over to *Club Igloo* for late-night antics.

Bike shop There are numerous, well equipped bike shops in town, but if you want the best servicing and parts, head to *Evasion*. With good bike rental, loads of parts, from those you need to those you want, and a large workshop, this is an ideal place to go.

Internet café There are numerous internet cafés in town. *The Boomerang* has internet access as does the tourist office.

Bike map available? Well laid out and free trail maps for the whole region are available from the lift stations.

Les Orres

With 900 m of easily accessible vertical drop, Les Orres is a classic under-the-radar destination.

Les Orres is in a prime location with great gradients for mountain biking. The resort has remained another somewhat guarded secret by the locals. The French national series has been coming here for its XC and DH events, but not many other people have picked up on this hill which has an easy 900 m of vertical descent possible on each run.

Cross country

The resort has concentrated its efforts around the lift accessed trails providing many gentler blue and green routes down. So the best XC trails are found by taking the hiking maps and following

LES ORRES

↘11 The trails

- **Cross country** Fair/beginner to intermediate
- **Downhill** Good/beginner to intermediate
- **Freeride** Fair/intermediate
- **Uplift** 2 chairlifts are open to bikes carrying riders up to 2550 m
- **Pros** Beautiful location; great gradients for bikes, not too steep; 300 days of sunshine per year
- **Cons** Still developing; not a great number of trails

Above left: Tundra.
Right: Washboard solo coming up.
Below: "You did tighten my front wheel nuts right?"
Opposite page: The forest is littered with sweet gaps.

The Lowdown

Locals do... Have this place to themselves.

Locals don't... Thank their lucky stars that they have the place to themselves as the trails are still buff and smooth.

Don't miss... The northshore trails have been well put together with lines that will be fun for intermediate riders.

Remember to avoid... Sticking to just the resort and town. Montgenèvre is within easy reach.

Practicalities 🔊🚲🚲

Les Orres in the Haute Alpes is one of the most southerly French resorts, and enjoys more consistent good weather through the summer months. The town is also near to Montgenèvre, making these two resorts perfect to combine during a riding break. The resort has a tranquil feel to it, being surrounded by small mountain hamlets where people have worked the land for hundreds of years. Even the inclusion of the obligatory high-rise apartment blocks and hotels around the lift base does little to spoil the ambience.

Sleeping Head either for the larger hotels and apartment surrounding the lift station or look around the periphery of this small town and find yourself some perfect mountain chalets. *Hotel L'Ancolie* is literally at the end of the trails at the lift station whereas *Chalet Tomi* will give you a more peaceful location for larger groups of 10 to 15. The resort also offer some all inclusive riding deals with lift passes and accommodation, so check the website for the latest offers.

Eating *La Marmotte* is in the centre of town, it is one of the best restaurants and is very popular with the locals and tourists. They serve a range of excellent local dishes, at reasonable prices and the atmosphere is warm and friendly. A great place to grab lunch or a quick bite after riding is the *Pizzeria la Dolce Vita*, located at Hodoul square. The *Sandwhicherie Chez JP*, also on Hodoul square, is another great place to go and have a light meal for lunch.

Bars and clubs *Les Caves* in the centre of town is one of the best bars and a great place to go and party the night away.

Bike shop Not much choice when it comes to bike shops in Les Orres. Head to *Intersport* which offers all kinds of bike for hire and have a decent workshop for repairs.

Internet café Head to the tourist info office by the main lift station.

Bike map available? There is a simple bike map available from the lift station and the tourist office.

some of the contouring walks. With fewer riders and walkers in Les Orres, most people are cool with bikers using these trails, but be aware that you are sharing the trail.

Downhill
In two relatively short lifts you can climb 900 m giving a nice long black run to take you all the way back down to 1650 from 2550 m. There is also a red trail heading down on a gentler grade from the top which can be linked into the four cross course or the northshore area. There are currently four trails in the park, one of each gradient.

Easy The 'Tu Crois que le Jeux' trail is an easy run down the lower slopes of Les Orres, suitable for beginners.

Difficult Follow the tougher Les Crêtes black trail from the top of the second lift, it is an 8-km long trail dropping 880 m along its length.

Freeride
The bike park contains some well-built northshore areas of differing difficulties, a four cross line and various drops, gaps and wallrides spread along the trails. There is a small dirt jump area with small and medium sized trails.

ⓘ OPENING TIMES
Lifts open at the end of Jul and close on 31 Aug: 1000-1700

💲 RESORT PRICES
Day pass: €14; 1-week pass: €35

⚙ DIRECTORY
Tourist Office: T+33 4-9246 5131
Medical Centre: T+33 4-9246 5405
Website: vars.com

Métabief

MÉTABIEF

↘12 The trails

- **Cross country** Good/beginner to advanced
- **Downhill** Good/beginner to advanced
- **Freeride** Fair/intermediate to advanced
- **Uplift** The main uplift for the trails is the Métabief chairlift
- **Pros** Good exposed rocky technical routes; easier routes also provided; very quiet
- **Cons** Very quiet

While Métabief is set in the rolling hills and does not have the scale of some

A quiet country town with some wicked trails ranging from easy through to advanced on the slick white bedrock.

of the other French resorts it does have some superb and technical trails in a quiet area where you can just get on with the riding with 500-m vertical descent to play with.

Cross country

There are a few mapped out tours which are predominantly descending with some short sharp climbs and flatter traversing sections. That is of course if you opt for

The Lowdown

Locals do... Take their karaoke seriously.

Locals don't... Ride the steepest trails after heavy rain as the rock gets very slick.

Don't miss... The speed trap, it brings out the competitive beast in everyone.

Remember to avoid... The black freeride trails if you're not a competent rider, especially if wet.

Below: Uphill comp.
Bottom: "Slurp."

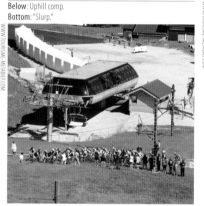

WWW.TOURISME-METABIEF.COM

WWW.TOURISME-METABIEF.COM

WWW.TOURISME-METABIEF.COM

Focused on the win.

the lift to the top; if not then the rides are far more challenging. The four routes are graded green, blue, red and black. A further 150 km of routes are available in the area, but you will need to buy a map for these.

Easy Take the trots view point trail a short 5½ km ride graded green with easy gradients suited to families or novice riders.

Difficult Head up the Eastie trail; this route is graded black with steeper descents and climbs. It is a short ride, but way more challenging.

Downhill

The classic downhill run here is great fun; it's graded red with a pretty high overall speed. There is even a speed trap on the fastest stretch so you can see your maximum velocity. Now there are three new trails, from green through to black, completing Métabief's offer to all abilities.

Freeride

There are three freeride routes on the hill which are more technically challenging than the downhill courses as the two black runs are steep and over rocky and often slippy ground. The red route contains more man-made obstacles but ultimately these are more technical terrain trails than stunt-packed freeride routes.

Practicalities ▣🚲🚠

Métabief is located 75 km south of Besançon, 20 km south of Pontarlier and is just 5 km north west of the Swiss border, with Geneva airport only 90 km away making it an easy destination to reach. This small and quiet town feels more rural than many of the larger ski resorts. Métabief has made real efforts to make mountain biking a popular pastime here, an effort which has paid off with some great trails on its rocky terrain.

Sleeping It is a small town so accommodation is limited, but so are overall visitor numbers so you shouldn't have any problems booking in. Try the *Hotel-Etoile Des Neiges* (T+33 381-491121).

Eating The restaurants in the village serve beautiful traditional dishes and other more familiar dishes for those who prefer to stick to what they know. Try *L'Excuse* or *Le Chamois* for a wide variety of dishes.

Bars and clubs Métabief is far from a party town, however if you head down the hill to the bottom of the main road through the town you will find the discotheque, with karaoke bar.

Bike shop There are several bike shops in the town all offering bike hire. *Adrenaline Point* (T+33 381-490883) is probably the best equipped with a good workshop and hires bikes to suit all disciplines.

Internet Cafe *L'Excuse* offers Wi-Fi access.

Bike map available? There are trail maps available from the lift station and tourist office.

France Métabief

A mellow afternoon taking in the view.

ⓘ **OPENING TIMES**

The trails and lifts are open daily from 23 Jun to 31 Aug

Ⓢ **RESORT PRICES**

1-day pass: €15; 1 Season pass: €100

Ⓓ **DIRECTORY**

Tourist Office: T+33 381-491381
Lift Company (Orex): T+33 381-492000
Website: Metabief-montdor.com

Montgenèvre

MONTGENÈVRE

↘13 The trails

Ⓧ Cross country Good/beginner to advanced

Ⓓ Downhill Good/beginner to advanced

Ⓕ Freeride Fair/beginner to intermediate

Ⓤ Uplift There are 2 gondolas and 2 4-man chair lifts which work on alternate days; they take you from resort level (1860 m) to the top (2540 m)

Ⓟ Pros 12 signposted circuits and many more off piste; spectacular views; great altitude training

Ⓧ Cons A quieter resort with not a great deal of nightlife

On the mountains there are many trails leading to different areas for all levels of cyclist. Jumps have been installed all over the mountains which are just waiting to be tested by those out there who think they are good enough! The terrain is varied with courses taking in open grassy pistes and meadows, rock, dirt, dust, rooty wooded sections and also cutting

① OPENING TIMES

7 Jul to 2 Sep

Ⓢ RESORT PRICES

Day pass: €14; Week pass €45

① DIRECTORY

Tourist Information Office:
T+33 492-215253
Lift pass office: T+33 492-219173
Medical centre: T+33 492-219120
Go Montgenevre accommodation but local English information:
T+33 688-358473
Taxi (English): T+33 607-067998

Below: Compression dedication.
Bottom left: Gondola uplift right above the DH track.
Bottom right: The Northshore ain't bad either!

Sat on the French Italian border, Montgenèvre offers great riding at altitude for all levels.

through rivers. Every level of rider will be comfortable in this resort with graded runs from green to black and it is a great place to learn with local instructors.

There are two gondolas and chairlifts that operate alternately through the summer to get riders up to the 2500 m. They carry bikes as well as people and take you above the treeline to the bare beauty of the mountains, part of which is a world heritage protected geological site. Both sides of the mountains, from Mount Janus to Mount Chaberton, can be used.

Cross country

Whilst in Montgenèvre, you have the choice of many routes to explore in the resort and also in the surrounding terrain where you can follow in the tracks of Le Tour. You can cross borders and have a day riding in Italy or a day up the unspoilt Vallée de la Clarée, following the winding river to Chalets de Laval where you can experience the waterfalls and the charm of the high valley. The resort has track supervisors who are there to look after you and make sure that the tracks are safe.

Downhill

Montgenèvre often hosts international competitions and recently hosted the French national downhill championships which shows its downhill pedigree.

Easy Take the Chalmettes gondola up and ride along to the observatoire chairlift. Take this chairlift up and cycle

The Lowdown

Locals do... Hit the local karting circuit or quad biking after a good day in the saddle.

Locals don't... Mess up their lift opening days. With alternating gondolas – you have to get your days right!

Don't miss... French Cycling Cup finals in downhill, freeride and cross country on 23/24 August. Competitors from all over the world.

Remember to avoid... Riding without a trail map, you need it to get the most out of the resort and also to know which lifts are open on which days.

Practicalities ⬛🚲🔧

Montgenèvre could be described as one of the original Alpine ski resorts. Just a few hundred metres from the Italian border. Montgenèvre celebrated its 100th year as a ski resort in 2007 and is one of the oldest in the area, if not the world. Two times winner of the regional towns and village award, Montgenèvre is in beautiful bloom in the summer, vibrant with different colours of flowers.

Sleeping As a result of its experience as a ski resort Montgenèvre has a variety of accommodation to offer, from 2-person studios available for the weekend to 14-person chalets. *Go Montgenèvre* is the only UK-based company based in the resort all year round specializes in organising accommodation and other trip requirements (bike hire, transfers, catering, lift passes, etc). Their site, go-montgenevre.com, gives a range of accommodation for all budgets including: *Chalet Banino*, an apartment for 4, *Appt La Crèche*, a 6-person apartment and *Luxury Chalet*, a top end accommodation with 6 bedrooms.

Eating Being on the Italian border the resort has a great selection of French or Italian restaurants. Favourites in the town include *Pizzeria Kilt* and *Clavière*, with a great atmosphere and great food; *Le Refuge* boasts excellent quality French cuisine which is reasonably priced, and *La Crepouse* is a favourite lunchtime crêpe house.

Bars and clubs Try *Le Chaberton* with good local brews and live music through the season, or *Le Graal*, with its sunny terrace and sports TVs.

Bike shops The *Snowbox* shop carries out service and repairs and also rents out all levels of bike. Alternatively, *Horizon Tout Terrain* in the centre offers cycle hire plus cycle school from €15 per day.

Internet café *Le Graal* burger bar has free Wi-Fi access or paid terminal access.

Bike map available? Bike maps are available from the tourist office, the lift pass offices and many of the local bars. A more comprehensive guide with suggested itineraries is available from the Tourist Information Office for €5.

along the top of the ridge before descending down through the bowl (the source of the River Durance) back to the resort. There are beginner obstacles on the way down to test your skill.

Difficult Take the Chalmettes Gondola up and cycle down to the Rocher chairlift D'Aigle. Take this to the top and cycle around Le Collet Vert (2510 m) past Le Chenaillet (2650 m) and onto the Fort Janus (2565 m). You can head straight down from the top taking in the two bike parks and all their jumps on the way.

Freeride

Most of the trails are XC tours or more technical downhill runs but the resort had been working hard to make fun skills zones and bikepark areas so now there are more freeride areas appearing each year with wooden kickers, drops and northshore balance pieces. Suitable for freeride beginners.

Morzine

Part of Europe's best known mountain bike region of the Portes du Soleil, which encompasses six towns and spans France and Switzerland.

France Morzine

MORZINE

⬂14 The trails

- **ⓍⒸ Cross country** Very good/beginner to advanced
- **ⒹⒽ Downhill** Excellent/intermediate to advanced
- **ⒻⓇ Freeride** Fair/intermediate
- **⑦ Uplift** 2 gondolas and a chairlift in town to access the immediate trails, and over 24 in the region
- **✓ Pros** Europe's best known mountain bike resort; in the centre of the massive Portes du Soleil region with access to over 30 lifts and 6 villages all with their own trails and tracks
- **✗ Cons** Many riders come to Morzine and simply session the Pleney lift meaning the course is both busy and hammered with huge braking bumps

---

Morzine is in the heart of the Portes du Soleil region and not only offers great trails in the town itself, but also chairlift access

ⓘ OPENING TIMES

Lifts open at 0900 and Le Pleney lift runs all the way to 1800

Ⓢ RESORT PRICES

Day pass: €16; Week pass €64; Season pass: €128
(NB These prices are for the full Portes du Soleil region)

ⓘ DIRECTORY

Tourist Office:
info@morzine-avoriaz.com
Website: morzine.com

---

to all the other areas in the region. There is the legendary Pleney downhill course that starts and finishes at the Pleney cable car, with another downhill trail in the same area due this summer. A more leisurely track runs through the woods on the same side of the hill and there are numerous singletracks that weave down the hillside. Heading off in the other direction is the Super Morzine lift, with more variety of trails, from singletrack to fire road to 4x4 tracks, plus access to all the trails in Switzerland. They cater for a wide range of

A leisurely cruise through the forest.

DANMILNER.COM

---

abilities. For more man-made tracks and freeride tracks, the chairlift allows access to Les Gets and Avoriaz/Châtel offering another wide range of trails.

Cross country

There are many routes that head from the town and either offer lift-assisted cross country, or will let you ride off into the less populated and ridden areas. The Valley de la Manche, the Plateau de Nyon and also the Joux Plane are all great areas of singletrack and cross country riding, often away from the main hub of riders. Be warned that there are many long climbs if you don't take the lifts, but the downs more than make up for it!

Downhill

The Pleney downhill track is the main course in Morzine, and is due to be added to this summer with another track. Along with this are numerous singletracks on both sides of the valley. Although not all marked on the maps they are easily found and offer a variety of riding for all abilities.

Easy The Pleney trail is not really an easy beginners route but there are alternate lines around most of the steeper sections so most riders with some previous experience will be able to ride the trail.

Difficult Due to the high concentration of some of the world's fastest riders based here you will find some very steep technical rides only suitable for experts tucked away in the woods to the sides of the main runs.

Freeride

With no freeride in Morzine itself you will have to look to the nearby resorts in the Portes de Soleil. For true freeride tracks with bridges (Passerelles), ladder drops etc, the best place to head is over toward Linderets (the other side of the Super Morzine lift) for the Châtel Bikepark (though not based in Châtel itself). It offers nearly 10 tracks with all sorts of challenges.

Practicalities ●🏍️🔄

Located about an hour's drive from Geneva, Morzine is easily accessible and the town has 2 main lifts that access the whole of the sprawling Portes du Soleil region. The town boasts numerous bike shops, restaurants and bars. The area attracts many professional riders and teams and there is always a good atmosphere in town.

Sleeping *Riders Retreat* (riders-retreat. co.uk) has grown as a company in this resort and is run by avid mountain bikers. It provides some of the best equipped accommodation in town in its 2 chalets: *The Barn* and *Chalet Alpin*; each one with a large garage for bike storage and also jacuzzi, broadband internet and satellite TV, making them a lovely place to be when you get back from riding.

Eating There are lots of traditional Savoyarde restaurants in town that offer good value meals. A firm favourite is *L'Etale* in the centre of town, try the local *tartiflette*. If you want a quick fix of a hearty burger the legendary *Burger Bar* at the bottom of the Pleney lift is always filled with riders and often a great place to watch the world go by. At the other end of the spectrum try *Le Clin D'Oeil* or *Le Chaumade* for the best food around.

Bars and clubs The first bar people think of is *The Cavern*, an English-run bar that stays open until 0200. Just a few steps away is the *Buddha Bar*, a common gathering ground for after-riding and night time activities. Often bike videos are played in these bars so you can get motivated for the following day! If it's an Irish pub you are after, down at the other end of town is *Dixie Bar*, where live football is shown. Legendary in Morzine is *Bar Robinsons* where many mountain bikers can be found passed out after a couple of *mutzigs* on top of a hard day's riding. There are 2 nightclubs staying open till 0500 for those who want to party hard.

Bike shop There are numerous, well equipped bike shops in town, but if you want the best servicing and parts, head to *DERT*. Run by keen riders and with a World Cup mechanic there, you're sure to get your bike fixed whatever the problem.

Internet café There are numerous internet cafes in town: *Monty's Café*, The *Rhodos Bar*, *The Ridge Hotel* and also internet can be accessed via the tourist office.

Bike map available? There are well laid out free trail maps for the whole region, available from the lift stations.

France Morzine

Pra Loup

Where the old boys battle it out every year.

PRA LOUP

↘15 The trails

- **XC Cross country** Fair/intermediate
- **DH Downhill** Good/beginner to intermediate
- **FR Freeride** Fair to good/beginner to intermediate
- **Uplift** 2 cablecars take riders to the top of the trails.
- **Pros** Great summer climate; quiet trails; near to several other mtb resorts
- **Cons** A lack of signed XC trails around the bike park area; in its own right perhaps Pra Loup does not have the variety of trails for stays of a week or longer

Pra Loup's proximity to Val d'Allos, as well as Les Orres and Montgenèvre, really does open up some great possibilities in this southern region of the French Alps. The trails in Pra Loup are nearly always dry and deep in dust due to the good climate.

Cross country

The resort has little in the way of mapped XC routes compared to some of its competitors, but there are some nice singletracks through the woods following the hiking paths which no one seem to mind bikers using. This may be largely attributed to the relative lack of people who currently use the trails. The world masters cross country event is held at Pra Loup in a circuit that comprises pistes and wooded singletrack.

Downhill

The resort hosted the French championships back in 2001 down a classic course with open flat-out piste

"I wonder if there are any dusty right hander berms around here?"

"Ah yes, there are."

sections and steep technical wooded runs. You can ride the same route now with a couple of the hardest bits cut out and also the course that is currently used for the masters world championships.

Easy Try the classic old-school downhill of the French champs, which is quite fast but pretty easy to ride for beginners.

Difficult The current trail used for the masters' champions is a more challenging track taking a more direct line with plenty of off-cambers and short technical wooded sections.

Freeride

The bikepark in Pra Loup accessed from the Clappiers cablecar at Pra Loup 1600

Practicalities

Pra Loup sits on a plateau overlooking the Ubaye valley. It is a peaceful valley that enjoys the clear and warm sunny climate of the Mediterranean with the freshness that comes with the altitude. High up on the surrounding peaks the graceful ibex can be spotted grazing between the rocks. The resort is split into two towns; Pra Loup 1500 or Les Molanes and 1600. It is best to stay in 1600, especially during the quieter summer months, as it is the busier of the two with more facilities, though they are only 2 km apart.

Sleeping Although created during the building boom of the 1960s, Pra Loup has retained much of its heritage and Alpine feel. *Auberge de Pra Loup* is in a great location near to the cable-car and is a pleasant family run hotel. Similarly *L'Harricana* also in Pra Loup 1600 is in a quiet location with a restaurant.

Eating *L'Artichoutte* is found at the bottom of the main runs so is a great

location to eat during the day while watching the riders finishing off their runs. *Le Croq'loup* is also a good place to grab a bruschetta or crêpe during the day. In the evening *L'Harricana* is frequented by locals and tourists looking for wholesome traditional food.

Bars and clubs The town is very quiet through the summer months so you won't be clubbing through the night, but *Le Grays* bar is the place to head for a few drinks in the evening.

Bike shop *Verdier Sports* is the shop in Pra Loup 1600 found right near the cablecar with both XC and DH and freeride bikes available for hire.

Internet café Most of the larger hotels have Wi-Fi connection and the hall of the tourist office has free Wi-Fi.

Bike map available? There is a trail map available from the tourist office.

The Lowdown

Locals do... Know how to handle a bike in the deep dust bowls that form on the open piste turns.

Locals don't... Mind showing you some of the more secret trails if you're polite and respectful.

Don't miss... The Masters World Championships in both DH and XC take place in Pra Loup and are a pretty big and fun event.

Remember to avoid... Following your riding buddies too closely through the bike park or one of the see-saws will have you off.

France Pra Loup

is designed by French sporting legend Jean-Michel Bayle and has some good lines throughout. It is graded from beginner through to expert with lots of northshore linking short sections of trail, jumps, gaps, drops and see-saws.

Top: Bubbles with bikeracks. So rad.
Above left: Forest Speedway riding at its best.
Above right: A rare double skid shot.
Bottom: Forest technicality. Eyes on the wood.

ⓘ OPENING TIMES

Lifts open on 5 Jul and close on 31 Aug

ⓢ RESORT PRICES

Day pass: €12.80; 1-week pass: €54

ⓒ DIRECTORY

Tourist Office: T+33 492 841004
Website: praloup.com

Tignes

High-altitude rocky trails and a park with facilities for all abilities.

France Tignes

TIGNES

↘16 The trails

- **⊗ Cross country** Good/intermediate
- **⊗ Downhill** Good/beginner to advanced
- **⊗ Freeride** Good/intermediate to advanced
- **⊘ Uplift** 2 lifts: 1 gondola on Troviere and a detachable chairlift on the Palafour side of the valley; free bus linking Tignes Des Boisses with Tignes Le Lac
- **✓ Pros** Close to Les Arcs, Pila and Courcheval; good graded trails; will suit riders with rounded skills
- **✗ Cons** Quite barren in places; riders may get bored if they are here for a long time without visiting nearby resorts

Being well above the tree line means that most of the trails in Tignes are wide open and rocky. All of the new trails in the bike park have been manmade over the last two years, a task for which Tignes enrolled the help of Dr Love himself, Karim Amour, one of the French mountain bike elite. The two lifts that open for bikes during the summer access opposite sides of the Tignes bowl. The Toviere side offers gondola access to three downhill tracks and two cross country trails, with the top of the trails at 2700 m. The Palafour side has chairlift access to two downhill tracks and four cross country trails

Cross country

With six enduro trails mapped out and built in the bikepark there is plenty to keep you busy on these fun routes

TIGNES TOURISM

Pronounced 'teen' but it's an old, bearded mountain with rugged views to match.

ⓘ OPENING TIMES

The park opens on 1 Jul and closes on 31 Aug; it runs Fri-Wed, 1000 to 1630

$ RESORT PRICES

1-day pass: €16.50; Week pass: €41; Season pass: €105

◐ DIRECTORY

Tourist Office:
T+33 479-400440; tignes.net
Bikepark contact:
bikepark@tignes.net
Medical Centre:
T+33 479-065964
Taxi/Airport Transfers:
T+33 632-192962; coolbus.co.uk

The Lowdown

Locals do... Nail the massive natural bowled wallride up in the freeride area of the mountain.

Locals don't... Ride down the trails forbidden to mountain bikers and risk losing the bikepark.

Don't miss... Take a guided day out riding a trails motorbike on amazing terrain and with awesome backdrops. Hired from *Evolution 2* who will provide everything you need including expert guidance and tutoring on route.

Remember to avoid... Being lazy and missing the bus up to Le Lac as it is a three-hour wait between the first and second bus.

which are predominantly descent with some climbs to traverse out to the periphery of the Tignes bowl. The best of the cross country trails is the Rocky Trails which is over 7 km, the majority of which is downhill. There is also the possibility to ride offroad all the way

Top: Cornering with the Grand Motte in the distance.
Bottom: Contemplating the classic 'Moses' lake crossing.
Take all the speed you can.

down to Bourg St Maurice from where you can access Les Arcs by ski lift. Be warned though; you would have a long return ride or you need to arrange to be collected.

Downhill

The two easier downhill tracks of the Troviere run down to Val Claret and are both really good fun with easy jumps and berms spread over 3-4 km. The two harder trails are pretty unrelenting and steep, meaning there is little opportunity to let the bike run. On the opposite side both the downhill tracks are relatively easy and mellow with the easiest stretching to 5½ km. There are other secret trails to seek out around the Tignes bowl.

Easy Take the mellow 'gunpowder' downhill down from the top of the Troviere lift which drops you back down to Tignes Val Claret. You'll have to spin across to Tignes Le Lac to pick up the Troviere lift again.

Difficult Take the Troviere lift from Tignes Le Lac and then take the Gypsy downhill

route from the top. Halfway down you can leave the trail to take the Black Metal tougher downhill route which will have your rotors burning as it is steep all the way back down to Le Lac.

Freeride

There is a good freeride area halfway down the red run with some fun features including an excellent step up

that you can hit at any speed and a 360° wallride. The slopestyle area features boxes of all sizes, a dirt spine, wallrides and drops. At the bottom of the Toviere side you will also find a 4X track and dirt jump area.

Practicalities ⬛🍴♻

Situated at the very top end of the Tarentaise valley, Tignes is a famous winter resort and, along with its neighbour, Val d'Isère, makes up the vast Espace Killy ski area. Tignes is made up of four distinct areas with most of the summer action occurring in the highest villages of Le Lac and Val Claret. Both of these sit in a large natural bowl at about 2100 m. The treeline is around 1800 m so the landscape up here is rather stark and this is not really enhanced by the slightly council estate look to the architecture.

Tignes Les Boisses and Les Brevieres are both much more attractive, being made up of more traditionally built chalets nestled amongst the trees, but there is only one cross country trail running down to here. For those who would rather stay in the more attractive surroundings of Les Boisses there is a free bus to take you up to Le Lac with your bike. Fly into Geneva, Lyon or Grenoble airports and get transferred to the resort with the Coolbus serving Tignes and the surrounding resorts. Tignes is a great stop for riders who like to board too with snowboarding on the Tignes Glacier throughout the summer which has a good snow park.

Sleeping Self-catered accommodation to suit most budgets is available through the good people at

tignes.co.uk. They have access to a large number of varied apartments throughout Tignes and can offer some competitive prices due to the relatively low demand during the summer. A very good catered option is the *Hotel Melezes* (mountainsunltd.com). They also have a range of beginner/intermediate bikes for hire and carry a modest selection of spares. *Bazoom* in Val Claret and *Le Vallon Blanc* in Le Lac also hire bikes and have workshop facilities.

Eating The bars and restaurants that open during the summer tend to fluctuate from year to year but two definites are the *Alpaka* and *TC's* in Le Lac. *Bagus* and the *Escale Blanche* are two excellent restaurants that will be open during summer 2008.

Bars and clubs *The Couloir* in Val Claret and the *Loop* in Le Lac have a good selection of drinks and friendly locals.

Bike shop There aren't many places to pick up spares in Tignes so bring any specialist pieces like spare drop outs and brake pads. Try *Le Vallon Blanc* in Le Lac for repairs and spares. The bike park have bikes for hire near the lift station.

Internet café The *Alpaka* in Le Lac has Wi-Fi connection.

Bike map available? The Bikepark trail map is available from both the tourist office and the lift station.

Val d'Allos

A good family and learner resort in beautiful surroundings.

VAL D'ALLOS

↘17 The trails

- **Cross country** Good/beginner to intermediate
- **Downhill** Good/beginner to intermediate
- **Freeride** Poor/beginner
- **Uplift** There is a gondola and 2 chair lifts serving the trails in Val d'Allos
- **Pros** Good family and beginner resort; great climate and beautiful surroundings
- **Cons** The marked XC trails only total up to 44 km; no challenge for experienced downhillers or freeriders

You're pretty much guaranteed blue skies and sunshine in Val d'Allos and there's a wealth of good singletrack around the resort. It really is a good all-round spot. A 5 or 6" trail bike is perfect here as it allows you to pedal out to some of the trails that run around the valley and still ride the descents with confidence.

Cross country

There are a number of marked trails running out from 1400 and 1800 which can be ridden between the town, or use the lifts to access 1800 and start the loops from there. The marked vtt routes are all quite short though and intermediate riders and above will soon have them covered. Then it's time to look at the more expansive hiking trails which more experienced riders will love. Unfortunately any routes within the national park are out of bounds; this includes the great trail to the beautiful Lac d'Allos, but we recommend you hike this one day. Some of the walking paths have very exposed drops and cliffs.

Downhill

With eight downhill routes there is enough riding in Val d'Allos to make this a good beginners and family resort. From the summit of Le Gros Tapi, at 2371 m, all the way back down to 1400 m, is just under 100 m of descending, which

ⓘ OPENING TIMES
Lifts open on 28 Jun to 31 Aug; 0930-1630

$ RESORT PRICES
Day pass: €13

ⓘ DIRECTORY
Tourist Office: T+33 492-830281
Medical Centre: T+33 492-830316
Website: valdallos.com

R PALOMBA/ VAL D'ALLOS TOURISM

R PALOMBA/VAL D'ALLOS TOURISM

Above: "Go!"
Opposite page: Could there be a more pleasing XC route?

The Lowdown

Locals do... Enter the Tribe 10,000 competition, usually held on the last weekend of June, the popular downhill enduro event at the resort; ride some of the walking routes around the resort.

Locals don't... Ride in the national park.

Don't miss... A hike up to the highest lake in the Alps, Lac d'Allos which is stunning.

Remember to avoid... Riding your bike on the trails in the national park area.

Practicalities 🍽🚲🚠

Val d'Allos is split into three smaller Alpine villages or resorts, known as 1400, 1500 and 1800. 1800 is the more established purpose-built resort with the usual hotels and amenities, while 1400 is a beautiful traditional Alpine village with far more character. For a mountain biking break, you will benefit from basing yourself at this lower village, and with good lift access up to the trails you can finish your ride with a longer descent back down to the village and enjoy a slightly more cultured experience. The mountain resort borders the edge of the Mercantour National Park and is in a very stunning part of the southern Alps, with the nearest airport, Nice, just 120 km.

Sleeping While sleeping options and bed numbers are more plentiful in the higher resort of 1800, it is the smaller village of 1400 which will provide a better base for mountain biking and to enjoy the swimming lake by the river Verdon. Try either the *Hôtel Plein Soleil* or the *Hôtel Beau Site*, both of which offer a range of different rates from room only to fully catered.

Eating *Le Croustet* and *Le Dahut* in 1400 and 1800 respectively are both convenient stops for quick eats during your riding day. In the evening the *Hôtel Beau Site* has a decent restaurant on site. For a wider choice of evening restaurants it's best to pop up to 1800.

Bars and clubs If après riding is as essential as your actual riding then Val d'Allos will have little to satisfy your needs. The resort is a popular family break amongst the French but there is virtually no nightlife during the summer months.

Bike shop *Lantelme Sports* in 1800 is the main shop in the resort but is still quite limited when it comes to spares. *Au Petit Allossard Sport* in 1400 may be able to help you with basic tools and spares.

Internet café *Sucré Salé* in 1400 is a small web cafe with a range of snacks and drinks. They have terminals to use as well as a Wi-Fi connection.

Bike map available? There are trail maps available from the tourist office and lift station for both XC and DH marked itineraries. For more adventurous and experienced XC riders, you should pick up the hiking guides.

is as much as you can expect at any of the bigger Alpine resorts. None of the trails are very difficult and the resort is a good place to learn downhill mountain biking primarily on open pisted slopes and get to grips with bike control skills without the braking bumps, queues and intimidation of faster riders at some of the more popular resorts.

Easy Take the Bertrand chairlift to 1916 m and you have a choice of three blue trails which are all pretty easy to get going on. For total novices there is the Champons green route, otherwise plump for La Verte.

Difficult Take the Télésiège up to the top of Gros Tapi (at 2371 m) where you can take the Gros Tapi trail right the way back down to 1500 m. Even this trail is not too technical and is fun on a good trail bike.

Freeride
There are no freeride obstacles built in Val d'Allos.

Valloire

A quiet and unspoilt resort tucked away in the golden valley.

VALLOIRE

↘18 The trails

- **Cross country** Good/beginner to advanced
- **Downhill** Good/beginner to advanced
- **Freeride** Fair/beginner to intermediate
- **Uplift** The main gondola in Valloire services the mountain bike trails
- **Pros** Beautiful, unspoilt French resort; very quiet and peaceful on and off the trails
- **Cons** Relatively short season; may be too quiet for those looking for nightlife

Valloire is a relatively modest set up, but provides something for most riders to keep them excited. Apart from the black descent most of the trails are relatively mellow and good fun for most abilities to ride. The area is well marked out and mapped allowing you to pick and choose your trails and get on with the riding. All in all there is around 150 km of trail in the Valloire resort surrounding area, most of it XC, single and doubletrack.

ⓘ OPENING TIMES

Lifts open at the end of Jun and close on 31 Aug: 0930-1630

ⓢ RESORT PRICES

Day pass: €12

ⓘ DIRECTORY

Tourist Office: T+33 479-590396
Taxi: T+33 479-590021
Website: valloire.net

Reaping the benefits of unknown trails and empty lifts.

Cross country

The four XC itineraries are labelled as enduro routes at Valloire, and they can be ridden with or without lift assistance. These enduro/XC routes are ideal for less serious XC riders who enjoy trail riding but aren't too concerned with clocking up serious mileage. Once these have been ridden there are the freeride zones and the easier downhill routes which can all be tackled by intermediate trail riders. More experienced cross country riders will look to the wider region using the hiking and biking map for sale at the tourist office which marks out some more technical singletrack trails.

Downhill

With 700 m vertical descent to play with, the resort have designed and built three permanent marked and managed downhill courses: two gentler descents and a more difficult one designed by one of France's most consistent World Cup racers over the past 10 years, Michael Pascal. This route has a good mix of technicality and high speed.

Easy Take the gondola up from Valloire 1430 m and pick up the granges descent from the top, a more mellow introduction to riding.

The Lowdown

Locals do... Tackle the gnarly rock garden on the Pascal trail with flair.

Locals don't... Run thin sidewalled tyres; freeride or downhill tyres are the order of the day here.

Don't miss... The enduro series when it visits the resort usually in early August.

Remember to avoid... The black route if you are not experienced as it has been designed by a professional downhiller.

Practicalities

Located in the Savoie region of the northern Alps and at the foot of the famous Galliber Pass, Valloire is a pretty resort made up of 17 traditional hamlets nestled in the 'Golden Valley'. Built around a 17th-century baroque church, Valloire has retained the charm and authenticity of days gone by and is a warm and friendly place to stay. The nearest airports are Chambery and Grenoble, both just over 100 km away.

Sleeping Those looking to plan their trip on a budget or just enjoy the mountain air can book into *Sainte Thècle Campsite* (T+33 479-833011) or alternatively look to the many chalets and apartments that are available in the resort. Try *Chalet Les Mésanges* (T+33 479-590381) a chalet that sleeps six with storage.

Eating Valloire has a superb variety of little cafés and restaurants to while away the days and evenings. Try *Le Poutre* or *La Trappeur* for good evening meals. While out on the bike you can get snacks and takeaway food from the *Sucrée Salée Crêperie*.

Bars and clubs While Valloire has a good après ski reputation it is a lot, lot quieter during the summer months. The 1300 inhabitants keep the numerous bars ticking over though and there is no shortage of places to sink a quiet few before the next day on the bike. Try *Le Centre* for some drinks before heading onto *Le Mast'Rock*, the only live music venue in the resort with gigs on selected nights. Or go and hit the bowling lanes at *Le Mafayo*.

Bike shop *Magnin Sport* (T+33 479-590355) hire out mountain bikes but probably your best bet in the resort is *Val d'Aurea Sport* who hire out Scott and Kona bikes and have a decent workshop for repairs and spares.

Internet café The town library has a multimedia room where you can access the internet.

Bike map available? A trail map showing the main downhill itineraries is available for free from the tourist office, a further XC guide map with all the hiking and riding trails in the area is available for €6 also from the tourist office.

Difficult From the top of the same lift you can also take the black graded Michael Pascal trail with a more direct line back down the mountain.

Freeride

Valloire has a small freeride area with four short trails made up of northshore, jumps, berms and other obstacles. These are suited to beginner to intermediate riders who should be able to conquer most of the features after a few days riding. The rest of the time can be spent playing on the descents and enduro trails.

Gorge -ous.

Vars

↘19 The trails

- **Cross country** Good/ beginner to intermediate
- **Downhill** Good/intermediate
- **Freeride** Poor/intermediate
- **Uplift** 1 gondola and 3 chairlifts operate in the Vars area during the summer season
- **Pros** Ride a virtually unchanged World Cup downhill course; well marked FCC XC routes
- **Cons** Bikepark a little disappointing; will benefit from additional trails

The FCC (French Federation for Cycling) have been working on establishing and signing more and more trails throughout the country and Vars is one of the resorts to benefit from this with some 100 km of marked XC trails recognised by the federation. Offering wide gravel roads and paths for family rides through to

A quiet resort set in the high mountains close to the Italian Border, Vars is a perfect resort as part of a multi-trip tour.

The Lowdown

Locals do... All look forward to the Enduro France series coming to town when they get to race down all their favourite trails with their mates and hundreds of other competitors.

Locals don't... Have any attitude; they are happy to see new riders on the trails and will often show you around the trails.

Don't miss... The long Var Spray trail, it takes you through some stunning countryside along its length.

Remember to avoid... Timing this badly and missing the shuttle bus which runs just three times a week.

Top: The Ming Dynasty DH Course is a winner.
Bottom: A picture of Vars with some flowers in it. This could get confusing.

slightly more challenging singletracks for enthusiasts, Vars is starting to build a reasonable offer for summer biking.

Cross country

The main XC routes around Vars are all shown on the map available from the tourist office and marked on the ground as well. The riding here is not so technical as some of the Alpine resorts, but is fun and in a great open environment. The Var Spray trail is a popular ride with a long 32 km descent through forests and open

ground that can be started from the top of the Mayt lift. You will need a return lift which is organized three times a week. Ask in the tourist office for the days of the return shuttle bus and give it a go.

Downhill

Vars was brought to the media attention when it hosted a round of the UCI World Cup here way back in 2001. The track was typical of much of the riding here; wide open, fast and, although not technically challenging due to the

ⓘ OPENING TIMES
Lifts open at the end of Jul and close on 31 Aug; 1000-1700

Ⓢ RESORT PRICES
Day pass: €14; 1 Week pass: €35

ⓘ DIRECTORY
Tourist Office: T+33 492-465131
Medical Centre: T+33 492-465405
Website: vars.com

features, the speed makes everything much harder. Since 2001 Vars has almost become forgotten outside of France, but the track is still open to ride along with amendments to its route to make it a little more flowing and fun with some drops added. There are a further six descents labelled as freeride descents which are just more playful and mellow downhills.

Easy You really should do the 32-km Vard Embrun descent; it is not particularly technical and can be ridden by anyone, with rest stops on the way.

Difficult The Christian Taillefer-designed downhill course is a traditional race course, fast with some technical sections. Steve Peat won here back in 2001.

Freeride

As with many resorts these days Vars has a small bikepark area with a small slopestyle area. The pieces don't flow together too well and riders looking for a freeride destination in its own right should definitely look elsewhere. Riders happy to hit the downhill trails and play on some of the wallrides, drops and jumps at the end of a run will enjoy the park.

Practicalities ●⬤⬤

Situated between Dauphiné, Provence and Italy, Vars is in a great location, right in the heart of the high Alps yet benefiting from the clear blue skies and mildness of a Mediterranean climate. The surrounding mountains, with summits of over 3000 m, provide the backdrop to the resort and its four villages. The heart of the resort is the modern village of Les Claux which is then surrounded by the old traditional villages of Saint Marie, Saint Catherine and the oldest, Saint Marcellin. It is this set up that makes Vars an interesting town with the modern amenities of Les Claux, the pastoral way of life still very much present in Sainte Catherine and the old stone and wood buildings of Sainte Marcellin. The scale of the whole resort is very low key with just 600 inhabitants between the four villages.

Sleeping With four villages to choose from and a range of sleeping accommodation we recommend you contact the tourist office who will book somewhere that meets your needs. That said, *Le Serre de Jaume* (T+33 492-466131) in the old town of Sainte Marcellin is a good choice.

Eating In the centre of the resort you will find *L'Arlequin* which make a mean pizza, or along the same lines but with a slightly broader menu is *La Passerelle*, opposite the gondola station. During the day keep your energy levels topped up at *La Tavola Calda* who make good sandwiches and panini.

Bars and clubs While choice of places and the number of people to party with is pretty limited in the summer, the locals are sociable and friendly around the bars and you may even rouse them enough to crank open *Le Lynx* discotheque.

Bike shop *Carretta Sport* (T+33 492-465246) and *Planète Montagne* (T+33 492-465441) both offer bikes for hire, have a servicing workshop and will carry out repairs on your bike if you should need it.

Internet café There is no internet cafe in the resort but the tourist office has a Wi-Fi connection if you have a laptop or suitable palm-held device.

Bike map available? A trail map is available from the tourist office for €1.80 and shows all the major trails around the resort.

Germany & Czech Republic

A solidly-built berm, 100 kg of bike and downhill muscle, and a disposable camera. Guess which one won? [JOEL ANDRADE]

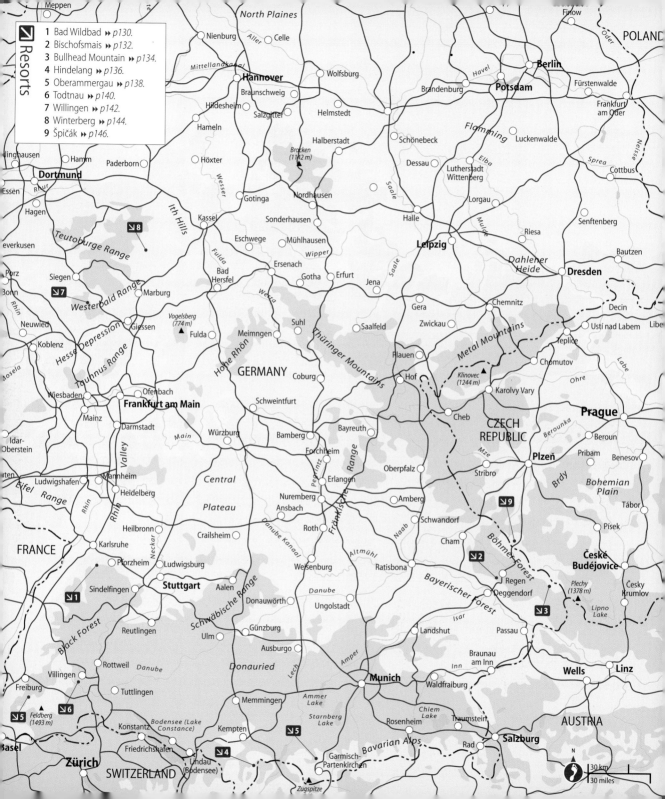

Winterberg weekends are proper popular.

Germany has the highest population of all the EU nations, is the world's largest exporter of goods and has the third highest GDP. It's an impressive CV, for a country that also manages to retain huge swathes of ancient forests and luscious green rolling hills. The countryside does not seem at all dissimilar to the UK – hills and small rounded mountains as opposed to the jagged peaks of the Alps – but Germany has worked out that you don't need huge mountains to have heaps of fun on your bike and has developed lots of smaller bikeparks using short lifts so that you can spend most of your time doing what matters; riding your bike.

Getting around couldn't be easier, with efficient public transport and the high-speed autobahns an absolute godsend. It constantly makes you wonder why other countries don't follow suit.

In the neighbouring Czech Republic the riding scene is not as well developed but it is improving, with an increase in size and choice of resorts and parks to ride. We have picked the one with the most potential and predict, with the immense growth of parks like Winterberg in Germany, both countries are going to see more and more international visitors over the coming years.

Overview

In mountain bike terms, Germany is often viewed unfavourably to its neighbouring Alpine countries such as Switzerland, Austria and France. However, this is set to change, due to its forward-thinking bikepark set ups and strong mountain bike scene. Germany lends itself to a great drive and ride holiday, for although it's a big country, the autobahns allow for speedy travel and the various bikeparks combine to make a great couple of weeks. The food and beer is good, the countryside interesting and there is a pretty good availability of parts and spares around the shops. A long travel trail bike would make the perfect companion for a trip to Germany, while hardtails are great for spinning the miles out on the singletrack. Long travel downhill bikes are not really necessary, a trail bike will allow you to keep your options open and enjoy most of what Germany has to offer.

Conditions

Most of Germany has a temperate climate in which humid westerly winds predominate. The climate is moderated by the North Atlantic Drift, a northern extension of the Gulf Stream. Mountain biking in Germany is comparative to the UK; it is a very green country and much of it features rolling hills and mountains with the added bonus of ski lifts. The trails are generally very earthy and can cut up quite a bit when it is wet. On the flip side, during the bike season Germany can experience very hot weather with maximum temperatures exceeding 30°C.

The scene

Germany has carved itself out a very healthy scene and one that has remained almost untouched by the masses. While hordes of riders flock to the big mountains and multiple lifts available in the French resorts, Germany has set about making as much as they can from their smaller and more manageable hills. The result is a whole range of bikeparks and resorts that are all about having fun on your bike, and which lean heavily towards the freeride aspect of the sport. Don't be fooled into thinking that there is a lack of XC trail riding though as there are some cracking trails along the valleys and through the forests.

The industry

Germany has a name synonymous with high build quality; Volkswagen, Audi and Mercedes all hold an association with quality engineering. The bike companies here are doing their utmost to maintain this tag of innovation and quality, with perhaps the best example being Nicolai, whose progressive

Above: Gapping the Wildbad.
Below: Cornering through the forest at Bad Wildbad.

Q&A with the experts

*Although originally from Portugal, **Joel Andrade** has become one of Germany's most prolific freelance mountain bike photographers, working for the two main magazines* Mountain Bike Riders *and* Freeride. *His shots can be found at the site:* joelandrade.com

You've got friends visiting for just one weekend and they can go anywhere in Germany. Name the one place you'd definitely have to take them.

JA I would prefer to go to Bischopfsmais, to the Bikepark Geisskopf, because it's got everything: northshore, downhill, freeride, dirtjumps. It's the best place for just one weekend.

Which trail centre or resort has the best party scene or the best after-riding activities?

JA Ooh, that's a tricky question. I would say Oberammergau. I think there's some barbecue and it's pretty cool there. They're definitely very friendly.

Where did you learn to ride, and where would you send beginners to ride?

JA I learned to ride in Bad Wildbad, which is probably Germany's most technical place; lots of rocky stuff. I think it's a good place to learn so I would send them there. A bit of tough love because if you can ride there you can ride anywhere!

In your opinion, which is the best downhill track in Germany?

JA For me it's Todtnau. It's a really fast technical track and it's long. Most tracks in Germany are one and a half to two minutes long, and I think Todtnau is around three and a half minutes. It's technical and you need lots of strength. For the arms its really tough.

Where's the best place to avoid pedalling uphill? Where has the best uplifts? Would you avoid anywhere?

JA If you hate pedalling? There's nowhere in Germany that doesn't have a lift. Bad Wildbad has the train which is really nice. I guess if you wanted to avoid somewhere it might be in Todtnau: there are a few problems because there's a rollercoaster so you have to wait sometimes for a gap to go down when it's good weather.

designs have opened many eyes. Add to this Solid bike and Rotwild and you have a healthy choice. Tyre giants Continental produce some great trail tyres and Schwalbe have some of the market leading XC race tyres. For years Magura have led the way with their hydraulic rim brakes, and although nowadays you are only likely to see them adorning trials riders bikes, their disc brakes are widespread among the specifications of the mainstream brands.

There is also a strengthening publishing scene, with the most popular magazine being *Bike-Magazine* followed by *Freeride-Germany* and *Mountain Bike*. Between them, they have the scene well covered.

Germany and Czech Republic breakdown

In Germany we have concentrated on the funparks or bikeparks and most of these have a double page spread due to the facilities on offer. Any resorts with only a single page are great places to go and ride but do not have the variety or depth of riding to sustain a week's break. The scene in Germany has dictated the focus of the chapter, though we emphasise that almost all the resorts have some great singletracks contouring through the area. The Czech Republic is some way behind the established German parks and this is reflected in the chapter, but the featured resort is working to build on its summer bike seasons.

Bad Wildbad

Some of the most technical downhill tracks in Europe.

BAD WILDBAD

↘1 The trails

- **XC Cross country** Poor/beginner to intermediate
- **DH Downhill** Excellent/advanced
- **FR Freeride** Fair/beginner to intermediate
- **Uplift** A funicular serves the 2 downhill trails and a towlift operates in the small bikepark area
- **Pros** Great downhill courses; good beginner's freeride park
- **Cons** The freeride descents; downhills are not suitable for beginners

The terrain here is rugged and the trails reflect this with their technical nature. Once again it is a case of making the most of the hill here at Bad Wildbad as there is not a massive vertical drop but the hill has a couple of gravity trails offering options for the downhillers a small, fun bike park and plenty of cross country around the area.

ⓘ OPENING TIMES

The season runs from Apr to the start of Nov and the opening hours are from 1000 to 1800

Ⓢ RESORT PRICES

Day pass: €18 (funicular), €12 (lift); Season pass: €269

ⓓ DIRECTORY

Tourist Office: T+49 708-110280
Website: bad-wildbad.de;
northwave-bikepark-bad-wildbad.de

Germany & Czech Republic   Bad Wildbad

Top: The rock garden in full effect.
Above: Rockery heaven with little coming loose.

Practicalities 🏨🚲🚲

Bad Wildbad is a spa town of some 11,000 inhabitants in the heart of the Black Forest. The town mixes the urban flair of its centre with its rural location and accommodates many tourists looking to revitalise in the thermal waters and the Black Forest air. The Spa towns are all about pampering yourself and any rider who has spent a hard day on the hill will have no shortage of places to unwind in the town.

Sleeping There are plenty of hotels and apartments to stay in but if travelling in a group why not rent a house out. Try the vacation home *Sommerberg* (T+49 7041-6856) or for a hotel try the *Weingartner* (T+49 7081-1706) with web access. *Guesthouse Schmidt* is found right at the top of the downhill tracks and has a secure bike lock up.

Eating Try the Black Forest schnapps with your local speciality meals at the *Gastatte Skihutte* (T+49 7081-2506) or for pasta try the *Pizzeria Rialto* (T+49 7081-2135).

Bars and clubs Bad Wildbad is a very quiet town and has no nightlife at all.

Bike shop *Bikers Paradise* is the bike shop found at the park and is well stocked to keep you on the trails.

Internet café There is no internet café in Bad Wildbad.

Bike map available? All the routes in the bike park are well marked and signposted.

Cross country

The bikepark itself is set up for the downhill and freeride routes but there are XC trails heading out from the park area. If you call into Bikers Paradise they will point you in the right direction.

Downhill

The downhill courses are renowned for their boulder-strewn technical runs. The IXS trail is the more difficult of the two, with some great corners, fast sections and rocks galore. The second route is easier but still just as fun. These are hard and technical downhill courses and suited to advanced riders.

Easy There are no easy trails in Bad Wildbad. Start out with the easier – but not very easy – Number 2 trail.

Difficult The IXS trail will test all your skills and line choice is important, as you will soon learn.

Freeride

The freeride trails in Bad Wildbad are truly terrible and the term freeride is a little misleading for what is essentially an old path. The small bikepark area operated by the tow lift is a lot better though with a fun 4X trail, a dual slalom track, a short northshore run and some beginners jumps. There is nothing worthy of a trip in its own right here as it is the downhill routes that people will travel to ride but the dual and 4X runs are fun to ride with your mates.

The Lowdown

Locals do... Ride in pads; there is nowhere soft to land on the downhills.

Locals don't... Rush; the pace is very laid-back about town.

Don't miss... The highly technical IXS course.

Remember to avoid... Losing your grip on the tow lift or you'll be rolling back down to the queue at the bottom.

BAD WILDBAD TOURISM

Germany & Czech Republic Bad Wildbad

Above left: Snaking section.
Above: There is a proper chairlift too, so easy on the press-ups just yet.

Bischofsmais

↘2 The trails

- **XC Cross country** Poor/beginner
- **DH Downhill** Fair/intermediate
- **FR Freeride** Good to excellent/ beginner to advanced
- **Uplift** There is a chairlift to the top of the trails
- ✔ **Pros** Good varied freeride park; new developments each year
- ✘ **Cons** Some of the jumps will be a bit short for fast riders; lack of XC provision

The trails in the bikepark run almost entirely through the woods alongside the pistes. They are steep in places but on the whole are on a reasonable gradient. There is a mix of the traditional natural descents with all their technical features and the new-school, smoother runs with berms and jumps. The park leans heavily towards this element of riding, but is trying to maintain its traditional style trails alongside.

Cross country

Unfortunately there is no provision for cross country at Bikepark Geiskopf, but there are many miles of marked bike trails through the Bavarian forest, suitable for the less experienced rider.

ⓘ OPENING TIMES

The season runs from May to Oct and the operating hours are 0915-1645

ⓢ RESORT PRICES

Day pass: €23

ⓓ DIRECTORY

Tourist Office: T+49 9920-903247
Website: bikepark.net

Germany's jack-of-all-trades, with cool trails through the Black Forest, some good downhill and dirtjumps, and the Bikepark Geisskopf: amazing purpose-built riding.

Germany & Czech Republic Bischofsmais

Downhill

The downhill courses are a mix of the Willingen-style, man-made trails with lots of jumps and more traditional old-school trails with dirt and roots. The trail has options to take either style along its length.

Practicalities 🎿🚲🍴🔧

Bischofsmais lies between 700 and 1100 m in the Bavarian forest area. Although tourism is a relatively recent arrival to this rural community, it now accommodates up to 350,000 visitors per year. The big attraction is that the lifts are quick and efficient meaning you can spend all your time on your bike and not in queues at the lift stations.

Sleeping *Pension Christl* (T+49 9920-1266) is a guesthouse with a range of room sizes and also has Wi-Fi. Alternatively *Ferienwohnung Kuhbeck* (T+49 9920-1374) is a holiday flat available to rent.

Eating The *Forest Inn* (T+49 9920-245) serves hearty meals with warm Bavarian hospitality and cool beers; or try the *Geibkopfhutte* (T+49 9920-336) on the slopes.

Bars and clubs There is no nightlife in the town; there are pubs and inns to have a few drinks after riding, but the lack of late-night bars and clubs means you'll be in bed nice and early.

Bike shop *MTB Zone* (T+49 9920-903135) is a bike shop with workshop that also rent out bikes.

Internet café No, but most hotels are equipped with Wi-Fi.

Bike map available? All the routes in the bike-park are well marked and signposted.

Freeride

There are a number of trails in the park: from the Freeride trail, which is essentially a mellow downhill course with jumps, to the northshore Evil Eye trails and You Go First containing some tall and technical northshore features. The lower slopes feature the two biker cross trails, the dual slalom and the small dirt area and learning areas.

Easy Take the Freeride trail, which is rideable to beginners, unless it has been very wet, as the roots can be slick.

Difficult You go first is only for the most proficient riders, with great balance required.

The Lowdown

Locals do... Plan to build a German 'A' line at the park.

Locals don't... Ride the Evil Eye trails when it's wet as they are lethal.

Don't miss... Taking full advantage of the Bikepark. Incredible facilities.

Remember to avoid... If XC is your thing. The only trails are for beginners

Opposite top: Amazing rock sections...
Opposite bottom: ...Perfect jumps...
Below: ...The ultimate bikepark. What more could you want?

JOEL ANDRADE

Germany & Czech Republic Bischofsmais

Bullhead Mountain

↘3 The trails

- **ⓍⒸ Cross country** Fair/ intermediate
- **ⒹⒽ Downhill** Good/beginner
- **ⒻⓇ Freeride** Good/beginner
- **⑦ Uplift** There is a relatively modern 2-man chairlift to transports riders to the top of the trails
- **✓ Pros** A good beginners or novices trail
- **✗ Cons** Only one gravity trail; too mellow for experienced riders

The terrain here is a very stony soil with plenty of larger rocks, which makes the trails on what is a relatively small hill much more interesting. With a vertical drop of just 250 m, this is more comparable to a hill in South Wales or the Scottish Borders and as such, the trails are well suited to beginners. They all follow mellow gradients and the features are generally not too big. Overall, there isn't enough here to

BODEN GRAMM

justify a standalone trip, but with an all mountain bike you could enjoy both the XC and DH on offer.

Cross country
Using the recommended map you can follow some nice long trails through the surrounding area outside the park. The ones marked H are particularly technical and well suited to all mountain bikes.

Downhill
There is just one shared downhill and freeride route: at just over 2 km long,

The Lowdown

Locals do... Run downhill tyres for protection on the rocky ground.

Locals don't... Have to queue for their uplift; the park is pretty quiet most of the time.

Don't miss... Having a run down the toboggan run and hitting it brakeless.

Remember to avoid... Running your tyres too soft – you'll spend most of your time repairing punctures.

ⓘ OPENING TIMES
Open May to Oct: 0930 to 1700

Ⓢ RESORT PRICES
Day pass: €19.50; Season pass: €190

ⓒ DIRECTORY
Website: fichtlride.de

it takes most people around 4 to 5 minutes. The upper rocky sections are more challenging and the trail becomes gentler and easier as you work your way down. Overall this is a good introductory trail for downhill or freeride.

Freeride
The downhill route has plenty of small drops, log rides and jumps built in along its length that you can progress to and conquer. Again it is good as a beginner's introduction to riding drops and jumps mixed with some mellow downhill. The lift is quite quick and the trails are very quiet.

Above and below: Philipp Fella.

BODEN GRAMM

Practicalities 🏠🍴🚲🚠

Bullhead Mountain is found on Ox's Head in Fichtelgebirge. Confusing? Well, a little; the hill is actually called Ox Head and the Bullhead part came more recently as it was viewed as a more modern name that sounded better to bikers. So Bullhead Mountain Bikepark it is, located at the ski lift Ochsenkopf south, in Fleckl, in Bavaria. Fleckl is 2½ hours from Munich or Frankfurt airports.

Sleeping It's got to be *Bullhead House* (T+49 9277-975379). It is kitted out to accommodate bikers with comfy rooms and bike storage. There is also camping nearby, at Fichtelsee.

Eating Again, *Bullhead House* is the perfect place to eat offering both evening meals and snacks through the day and only a stone's throw away from the trails.

Bike shop There is no bikeshop at the park so bring basic spares and tools.

Internet café No internet access, so leave the laptop at home.

Bike map available? A good trail map is available for some XC rides in the area it is called Fichtelgebirge and the Stone Forest. The hiking trails on here are well suited to mountain bikes.

Riders' tales
Five best MTB films

Callum Swift is an up and coming UK film maker behind the new DVD release 'The Uprising'. Check out www.theuprisingfilm.com for more info. Here he gives us his review of the best ever mountain bike films.

Best film ever

CS 'Earthed 1'. It really captures the spirit of the sport, with plenty of flat out riding by all the top pros. The soundtrack fits perfectly with the riding and the shots done on a super 8 camera give it a nice retro feel. Check out Sam Hill and Nathan Rennie rocking to Led Zeppelin or when all the Iron Horse lads style it up over the bridge in Bromont.

One for the scenics

CS It's got to be 'Roam'. There's the stunning cinematography; it's shot on film with beautiful settings, the best riders, the best locations, big film crew, great sountrack....what more could you want? It really makes you want to ride your bike whenever you watch it. Check the bit in Morocco; such a unique location. Or where Jordy Lunn jumps the river gap in Moab. And don't get me started on the cable cam in Whistler with Darren Berreclough through all the northshore.

Best downhill film

CS 'Between the Tape'. It's got incredible cinematography and editing. Clay Porter's documentary style is interesting and the gladiatorial voiceover adds drama to the whole thing. The rider sections are all amazing, especially the Athertons section with some amazing cable cam shots. The best shot is of Sam Hill coming into the finish of the World Champs: Clay manages to track him through the crowd perfectly and it looks insane.

Best for watching again and again

CS 'Illusionary Lines'. The soundtrack is superb and the split screen race shots with the timer running are an interesting addition. Check out Kovarik ripping up Scoul during the opening credits with his typical destroyer style. Some of his whips are insane.

Best for showcasing Europe

CS 'Earthed 3'. I had to include this for a guide to riding in Europe! It covers the World Cups brilliantly and has some awesome rider sections and a good soundtrack. The Mega Avalanche section is a must see for anyone wanting to do the event. When someone crashes on the singletrack of the Megavalanche the camera follows his bike from a helicopter as it tumbles about a kilometre down the mountain. Pretty bad news.

Hindelang

HINDELANG TOURISM

HINDELANG

↘4 The trails

- **Ⓧ Cross country** Fair to good/intermediate
- **Ⓓ Downhill** Fair/beginner
- **Ⓕ Freeride** Fair to good/beginner to intermediate
- **Ⓐ Uplift** There is a 6-man gondola to the top of the mountain
- **Ⓟ Pros** A good beginners and intermediates venue; very quiet trails
- **Ⓒ Cons** Experienced riders will struggle to find any challenge here; rough around the edges

Hindelang's bikepark does not have the glossy finish of many. It is a more rickety affair, with just the basics in place, but anyone who enjoys the rush of gravity will still have plenty of fun. The XC riding

Considered the 'shanty town' of bikeparks, but don't be put off; beginners will still find this a great place to ride and develop their skills.

through the area is very good and GPS is recommended to get the most enjoyment due to the fact that most of the map instructions are in German.

Cross country

There is some great backcountry riding through the Hindelang area. The bikepark does not have any signed XC trails, but the surroundings have some great singletrack, which has been put together into 20 tours and is available as a trail map for €10. Or you can pick up a GPS or get GPS routes from the *Sport Waibel* shop.

Downhill

There are no out-and-out downhill routes in Hindeland, the trails are really

① OPENING TIMES

The bikepark opens in May and closes in Oct; opening hours are 0900-1630

⑤ RESORT PRICES

Day pass: €18.50

⑥ DIRECTORY

Tourist Office: T+49 8324-8920
Website: bikepark-hindelang.de; bad-hindelang.info

a hybrid between freeride and downhill due to the rough natural paths they follow and the built stunts included along the route. They will suit riders interested in downhill but not the racers, as they are not particularly steep or fast.

Freeride

The freeride trails are almost like tame downhill tracks with built features. They are not super-smooth, groomed BMX affairs, but instead have rocks, roots and breaking bumps. They also use a lot of mountain paths but have wooden drops and doubles incorporated into them. The northshore trail has the usual skinnies, ladders and drops and the dirt jump trail is suited to beginners to intermediates.

Easy Take the easier yellow trail down the hill. It is 3.3 km long and on a steady gradient.

Difficult Try out the black route, with numerous wooden step-downs of various sizes to choose from.

The Lowdown

Locals do... Still wear a lot of lycra.

Locals don't... Really ride downhill in the traditional sense. Everyone here is a trail cruiser rather than a racer.

Don't miss... The view from the top of the lift is refreshing, as it overlooks the lush green surroundings.

Remember to avoid... The dirt jump trail jumps are quite short, poorly constructed and usually in need of maintenance.

Practicalities

The town of Bad Hindelang in Bavaria is the main tourism focus in the local region, and with good reason. It's a charming, traditional town and super laid-back. There are the usual restaurants, accommodation and entertainment in the town, which is also well situated for sun lovers. The riding in the area is split between the gravity trails in the bikepark and the XC backcountry riding through the surrounding forests and valleys.

Sleeping *Haus Wineberger* (T+49 8324-330) and *Gastehaus Wiedmann* (T+49 8324-2198) are both found in the town and are used to having riders stay and have bike lock ups.

Eating *Restaurant Kaminstrube* (T+49 8324-973846) is one of many serving traditional Bavarian dishes. For the obligatory pizzeria try *Taormina* (+49 8324-472).

Bars and clubs This is a sleepy traditional town with no nightlife.

Bike shop There are a couple of bike shops in the town, *Sport Waibel* (T+49 8324-2528) has a workshop and limited spares.

Internet café There are no internet cafés listed for Bad Hindelang but many hotels offer Wi-Fi; check when you book.

Bike map available? A map is not required for the bikepark due to the signed layout. XC maps are available from the tourist office and GPS from *Sport Waibel*.

Right: Now THAT is a rock garden. Without the garden.
Opposite page: Nice kicker.

Germany & Czech Republic Hindelang

Oberammergau

↘5 The trails

- ⓧⓒ **Cross country** Poor to fair/ beginner to intermediate
- ⓓⓗ **Downhill** Good/beginner to intermediate
- ⓕⓡ **Freeride** Good/beginner to intermediate
- ⓩ **Uplift** 1 chairlift, 1 T-bar for the bikepark
- ✓ **Pros** Riding in a beautiful landscape; friendly people, mostly English speaking; beautiful restaurant on top of the mountain where the trails of the bikepark start
- ✗ **Cons** Muddy conditions first day after rain

The mountain at Oberammergau is not massive and the trails at the park have been well designed to maximise the descent. Contouring down the hill they are fast and interesting as opposed to being more direct, steep and scary. As such, the park is perfect for beginners

The Lowdown

Locals do... Head to the bikepark during the week if possible to ride quieter trails and chill around the BBQ at the lift station on the weekends.

Locals don't... Use the same trails as the hikers (well, most of the time anyway).

Don't miss... A visit to the castles, the public swimming pool, Wellenberg and, of course, a Bavarian beer.

Remember to avoid... Never go on longer XC rides in the mountains without perfect equipment.

This little-known German park has steadily been adding to its roster of trails and garnering a reputation as a great fun spot to ride.

Above left: Beam-balancing in the clearing.   **Above right**: A quick pipe session.
Below: Night-time wall ride session. A tyre-thread from going OTT.

OPENING TIMES

Summer season 1 May to 15 Oct;
1 May to 5 Jul only weekends except
the local holidays; from 5 Jul daily
0900-1645

RESORT PRICES

Day ticket: €19.90; Half day: €13.90;
Season ticket: €298

DIRECTORY

Tourist office: T+49 8822-92310
Taxi: T+49 8822-94294
Website: ammergauer-alpen.de;
bikepark-oberammergau.de/

---

but probably be left wanting more challenging steeper runs after a few days.

Freeride

The park is really a freeride venue with descending trails made up from wooden berms and wallrides, drops, and narrow, slower balance beams. There is usually a choice between smaller and medium sized drops and obstacles. There is also a four cross course serviced by a separate tow lift. There are riding technique lessons available at the bikepark which can be booked in advance or when you arrive.

Top right: Bike lift arty tree shot.
Bottom right: Pushing back to the northshore start.

---

through to intermediate downhillers and freeriders. The XC riding involves taking a map out and investigating the many singletracks in the area. The terrain is predominantly under forest cover, with earthy soils that are great to ride when dry, although many parts of the bikepark have been surfaced to allow them to ride well in all weathers.

Cross country

Each Friday at 1300 there is a guided XC ride meeting at the tourist office. The remainder of the time you will need to grab a map from the tourist office and head out on the singletracks through the forests.

Easy Meet up with the guided ride on the Friday for an interesting but not too physical tour of the local trails.

Difficult Try out the silent path through the forests and meadows to Linderhof Castle

Downhill

The park has a few downhill runs that follow gentle but fun gradients and contain some rooty sections and small northshore features suitable for beginner riders through to intermediates. Advanced riders will still enjoy the trails

Practicalities ▢✦●

Oberammergau, in Bavaria in the south of Germany, is 100 km from Munich, and next to Ludwig's two castles, Linderhof and Neuschwanstein. The town is world famous for the 'Passion Play', a religious piece recently made into a feature film of the same name. The town is also famous for its wood carving tradition, and on the old houses around the town you can find many painted facades. Its location in the thick of Bavaria's forests make it a great location for mountain biking.

Sleeping There is a *Youth Hostel* (jugendherberge.de/jh/bayern/oberammergau) in town which is perfect for those on a budget. *Pension Klieber* (zimmer-oberammergau.de), offers a great place to rest and keep your energy levels up. Those looking for a luxury stay should try the 4-star *Hotel Maximilian* (maximilian-oberammergau.de).

Eating The Mexican *El Puente* (elpuente-oberammergau.de)

is a great place to grab tortillas and enchiladas at lunch or after a hard day on the trails. *Restaurant Mühlbartl* (restaurant-muehlbartl. de) and *Gasthaus Zur Rose* (hotel-oberammergau.de) both offer more traditional dishes and are located near the centre of the town.

Bars and clubs The town is quieter in the summer months with mainly families visiting. If you're looking for a few beers in the evening head for *Kino Café* (kinocafe-ogau.de) or back to *El Puente*.

Bike shops *Radsport Lang* (radlang. de) rents out traditional XC bikes while the *Bikepark Rental Station* just rents out freeride and DH bikes.

Internet café There is internet access at the *Hotel Alte Post* (ogau.de).

Bike map available? At the tourist office.

Todtnau

Germany's original bikepark.

TODTNAU

↘6   The trails

XC Cross country Fair to good/ intermediate

DH Downhill Good/intermediate to advanced

FR Freeride Fair to good/ intermediate to advanced

Uplift There is a new chairlift to take you to the top of the trails

Pros Long runs for Germany; DH trail is a must for enthusiasts

Cons The park itself is not set up for cross country riders; freeride trail disappointing

Todtnau is the oldest bikepark in Germany, but that doesn't mean it is outdated. It wasn't until the Maxxis international series came and hosted a race here in 2003 that the place gained some recognition overseas but it was soon labelled by some of the pros racing there as one of their favourite courses, and rightly so. The bikepark has one of the biggest vertical drops in Germany and recent problems with the owners hiking up their prices have been ironed out and put Todtnau back on track.

The Lowdown

Locals do... Compare their times on the DH to the course record set by Fabian Barel at 3 minutes 17 seconds.

Locals don't... Beat it!

Don't miss... The highly acclaimed downhill course.

Remember to avoid... If you are a freeride fan.

Cross country

There are 20 tours marked out on the available maps around the surrounding area, though it should be noted that only two start from Todtnau. To access the others you will either have to ride further to the nearby villages, or if you have a car drive to the start points. There are also GPS tours available from the tourist office.

Easy Take the Knopflesbrunnen loop starting from the town centre; it is a 17-km ride.

Difficult Take the 45.2-km Hochkopfregion tour that contours around the region covering some good distance in the surrounding areas.

Downhill

The downhill course at Todtnau features stacks of perfect corners and steep technical wooded sections as well as plenty of fast open straights on the piste, which is largely why it has been so popular over so many years amongst riders.

Freeride

There is one trail called the Wildride, which is a mellower machine-built downhill with some rollers and berms which is quite fun for beginners but there is not enough there to sustain a visit. The downhill and XC is the main attraction here.

Practicalities ⚫⚡🌀

Todtnau is located on the river Wiese in the heart of the southern Black Forest. It is a small but well equipped town in lush surroundings. The town was one of Germany's first ski resorts, but has not suffered from mass development and retains an authentic feel, with all you need close at hand. The closest airport is Basel although Zürich, a little further away, schedules more international flights.

Sleeping The budget *Harry Apartments* (T+49 7671-1467) are not too far from the trails and from €18 a night are perfect for those on a budget. There's a wide choice of hotels such as the *Waldeck* (T+49 7671-999930).

Eating In Todtnau you can expect to find plenty of cafés and restaurants serving traditional German food. Try the *Gastof zum Baren* or if you must go with something more familiar, then *Bella Italia* is a popular Italian.

Bars and clubs Head to *Andy's Pfeffermhule*, a biker bar just down from the lift station and a popular haunt with all of Andy's biker memorabilia decorating the bar.

Bike shop There is a bike shop and Kona Groove centre at the bikepark, where you can also hire bikes.

Internet café There are no internet cafe's listed for Todtnau, but most hotels offer Wi-Fi; check when you book.

Bike map Available? A map is not required for the bike park due to the signed layout. XC maps are available from the tourist office.

Below: Shake it like a tail feather.

JAMES MCKNIGHT

ⓘ OPENING TIMES

The bikepark opens in Apr and closes in Oct; opening hours are 0930-1700

🅢 RESORT PRICES

Day pass: €29

🅓 DIRECTORY

Tourist Office: T+49 7671-96969
Website: todtnaur-ferienland.de; mtb-fun-park.de

Willingen

↘7 The trails

- **Cross country** Good/beginner to intermediate
- **Downhill** Good/intermediate to advanced
- **Freeride** Fair to good/intermediate to advanced
- **Uplift** Willingen have just installed a new 6-man gondola.
- **Pros** Challenging gravity trails; great region for cross country
- **Cons** Used to be the slow chairlift but it's since been replaced

The hill at Willingen is no bigger than many hills in England, Scotland and Wales, but the chairlift and the few runs that run from the top of the hill mean that there is no shortage of fun to be had in this stunted ski area. The yearly bike festival is a huge event here and the whole town goes bike mad, with spectators lining the courses for the events held on the former World Cup slopes. And although it can be damp in the summer, the trails hold up well in the wet making them all weather runs.

① OPENING TIMES

The bikepark is open all year, weather permitting, but obviously being a ski resort expect it to be closed in winter months; 0900-1700

⑤ RESORT PRICES

Day pass: €24.50; Week pass €123; Season pass: €300

① DIRECTORY

Tourist Office: T+49 5632-401180
Website: willengen.com; bike-willengen.de; bike-arena.de

Home to downhill racing's biggest jumps.

Top: The crowd willingen him on. <Ahem>.
Above right: Whoops section.

Above left: Race day banners.
Opposite page: Rootsy bank.

Cross country

Willingen has hosted rounds of the World Cup cross country and the area is quite good for XC. The trails and routes heading out from the town through the Sauerland region are expansive. With downloadable GPS tracklogs you can set about exploring this luscious region. See the bike-arena.de website for the entire trail and route information.

Downhill

The downhill course was built for the UCI World Cup in 2005 and has hosted two rounds over the subsequent years. It was unique on the circuit, being almost 100% man-made; with huge jumps and boulder fields it can be rolled down without too much bother, but to hit the fast lines requires some special skills.

Easy Any rider with previous downhill experience will be able to roll most of the trail.

Difficult Try hitting some of the many gaps and jumps on the racing line, only for the experienced.

Freeride

Willingen's freeride trail is well suited to less experienced or skilled riders with plenty of smooth flowing trail and berms, tabletops and small drops. It is all rollable, with chicken lines that will suit beginners also. The four cross trail here is another track constructed for the World Cup and it features some fast straights

including one huge 50-ft gap jump, big berms and plenty of rollable jumps. There is also a small training trail at the foot of the hill much like a small BMX track it is good for practising the skills required on the trails, as well as being great for young kids.

Practicalities ▢🚲🔧

The town of Willingen is tucked well away in the hills, some 80 km from the city of Kassel. It is a modest-sized town which hosts a massive bike festival each year with up to 35,000 people visiting during the weekend. The town has a modern feel, although more traditional style chalets can be found around the suburbs.

Sleeping *Bike Hotel Schroeder* (T+49 5632-6444) has secure bike storage and can arrange to take you out with guides on the many trails in the area. Alternatively try *Sonnenhof Willingen* (T+49 5632-968900) who are also well set up to accommodate bikes.

Eating A good German restaurant is the *Manor Sitter Bach* (T+49 5632-96940). For international and Mediterranean dishes try *Le Petit* (T+49 5632-6439).

Bars and clubs The *Principal* pub is a popular watering hole and the *S'lift* nightclub will keep you partying through the night with their motto of 'good times'.

Bike shop *Didis Bike Shop* (T+49 5632-966688); *Sports Wilke* (T+49 5632-6443).

Internet café No cafés. Most hotels equipped with Wi-Fi.

Bike map available? A trail map and GPS routes are downloadable from the bike-arena.de site and covers the whole Sauerland area.

The Lowdown

Locals do... Drink like fish; the beer festivals are a sight to behold.

Locals don't... Clear many of the jumps on the trails as they are built to such a high pro-class standard.

Don't miss... Will anyone nail the big scary hip up in the woods on the downhill course? Make sure you take a look if they are.

Remember to avoid... If you're not prepared for some Steiner clinking and thigh slapping.

DENNIS STADTMANN

Winterberg

WINTERBERG

↘8 The trails

- **Cross country** Fair to good/beginner to intermediate
- **Downhill** Good/intermediate to advanced
- **Freeride** Excellent/beginner to advanced
- **Uplift** There is a 2-person chairlift to take you to the top of the trails
- **Pros** Excellently maintained trails; great for all abilities with a learning area to develop skills before heading down the trails
- **Cons** Not set up for cross country riders

JOEL ANDRADE

The Winterberg region has suffered poor winter snowfalls over the past years and they have really taken to developing their summer season with loads of bike trails and features crammed into the small hill. It is a great example of bigger being not necessarily better, as a well set-up and looked-after set of trails on a shorter hill with a quick turnaround time means more time on the bike.

The Lowdown

Locals do... Rip it up; with all the progressive trails the younger riders are rippers.

Locals don't... Ride without suitable helmets and armour. You are not allowed to ride the trails without them.

Don't miss... Try and time your visit with the IXS Dirt Masters held here yearly; it is one of the biggest events in Germany.

Remember to avoid... Weekends and holidays can be very busy in the park, so if you don't like queuing then head over during the week.

JOEL ANDRADE

Germany's most popular freeride park, Winterberg is a busy little resort with some great trails and ripping locals.
139

Top: The bikepark is pretty tech. **Above**: Plenty of interest on the DH course too.

Compression finish line.

ⓘ **OPENING TIMES**

Opens in May and closes in Oct; Mon to Fri 1000-1800 and Sat and Sun 0900-1800

Ⓢ **RESORT PRICES**

Day pass: €24.50; Week pass €123; Season pass: €300

ⓘ **DIRECTORY**

Tourist Office: info@winterberg.de
Website: winterberg.de; bikepark-winterberg.de

Cross country

There are no routes in the Winterberg bikepark itself but the trails and routes heading out from the town through the Sauerland region are expansive. With downloadable GPS tracklogs you can set about exploring this luscious region. See the bike-arena.de website for the entire trail and route information.

Downhill

The bikepark only has one true downhill course, made up with rock gardens, drops, jumps and plenty of drifty turns. All the other routes are gravity fed and any rider who likes pushing themselves will have plenty to do.

Freeride

Winterberg has it all for freeriders, with a free cross course (think of a giant downhill biker x trail) and a northshore trail running from the top to the bottom of the hill. Then there is the fun ride trail, with all manner of road gaps, step ups, berms and wallrides as well as a 4X track and the slopestyle course, which is almost a mini version of Whistler's Boneyard.

Easy Start out on the parcours practice area. It contains all manner of jumps, drops and northshore.

Difficult There's plenty to test you here. The more confident will be nailing the road gaps on the fun ride descents and playing on the slopestyle course.

Practicalities 📖⚡🚲

The town of Winterberg is in the Sauerland area, a heavily forested and sparsely inhabited hilly region where tourism has become increasingly important. Many steps have been taken to ensure that tourists continue to visit the region, including the planned reintroduction of European bison in the area, and also the development of some excellent summer riding facilities. The chocolate- box town has many traditional shops and cafés to explore and its tourism is built around Winterberg as a gateway to the great outdoors. It is worth noting that the town is quite spread out and you may have a short cycle to the lifts. The nearest airport is Cologne.

Sleeping Why not spoil yourself at the *Dorint Resort & Spa* (T+49 2981-8970) with a wellness suite and indoor pool. There is also a go-kart track on site that will keep all the speed junkies entertained. If you want to be on the doorstep of the bikepark, try the *Central Hotel* on the main street.

Eating Relax at the *Ruhrquellenhutte* mountain restaurant which is not far from the trails. This is a great place to unwind at the end of the day. If you want to take a break or try some local specialities, head for the *Haus Herrloch Restaurant* located beneath the huge St Georges ski jump.

Bars and clubs Where would you be without your obligatory Irish bar? For a drop of the black stuff head to *Black Water*. You have a choice of 3 clubs – *Tenne* with its 3 floors, *Alpenrausch* and the *Raidon* – which serve over 100 types of beer between them.

Bike shop Bikes can be hired from the bikepark and they also have a small workshop for repairs.

Internet café There are no internet cafés listed for Winterberg, but many hotels offer Wi-Fi so check when you book.

Bike map available? A map is not required for the bikepark due to the signed layout.

Špičák

ŠPIČÁK

↘9 The trails

- **XC Cross country** Fair/beginner to intermediate
- **DH Downhill** Fair/intermediate to advanced
- **FR Freeride** Fair to good/intermediate
- **Uplift** There is a chairlift to the top of the trails
- **Pros** A good start for a bikepark that is sure to become popular as it grows
- **Cons** Not much variety at the park yet

A developing Kona bikepark in the Czech Republic.

The Špičák bikepark was only opened in June 2007. It has limited trails at the moment, but has already been very popular within the country due to its fun and not-too-difficult trail. It is perfect for the intermediate rider, as none of the drops or jumps are big, but there are plenty of features to keep it fun and interesting. The trail crew are working hard to bring more trails to the park and after a period working with the guys in Whistler we're sure any new additions will be up to standard.

Cross country

There are waymarked cross country trails around the area though any XC riders will find themselves on the lift and enjoying the freeride trail due to its low difficulty level.

Practicalities 🍴🛏🔧

The Špičák bikepark is at the Špičák ski resort, only 5 km east of the German border. The resort is also relatively close to Prague. Having only opened its doors in 2007, it is still early days, but it has proved very popular and as the park develops and creates new trails that popularity will continue to grow.

Sleeping Staying up at the resort near the lift and right next to the trails you have the choice of three lodges. The *Hanicka* and *Blazenka* lodges are the best suited to riders and can be booked through the parks website.

Eating The sport area Špičák is a small operation and there is not much choice of facilities. You can choose to go half board with the Lodges or alternatively eat at the restaurant at the lift station. You have a choice between traditional meat and potato dishes and other European dishes such as pasta.

Bars and clubs Those looking for lively entertainment at night should take an overnight excursion to Prague as there is no nightlife in the resort.

Bike shop Kona bikes can be hired from the bikepark and they also have a small workshop for repairs.

Internet café There is no internet café in Špičák.

Bike map available? A map is not required for the bikepark. Due to the signed layout the XC trails are waymarked.

The Lowdown

Locals do... Respect the rules and stick to the marked trails as there is a lot of ecological opposition to the park.

Locals don't... Build their own trails here as there are many issues stopping them. They session the park's trails.

Don't miss... Book your kids into the bike school to progress their handling skills.

Remember to avoid... Riding closed trails.

Top right: A berm-ease cat.
Right: More wallride madness.
Below: High-speed wallrides rock.
Opposite page: Bikepark audience.

Downhill

A black run course is currently under construction and will be an out-and-out downhill route with natural features; all the built stunts will be kept to the freeride course.

Freeride

The freeride trail is 2.3 km long and of a medium difficulty but with options around most of the obstacles so all riders will be able to ride down the trail; it features, wallrides, drops, tabletops, step-downs and see-saws. There is a dirt jump area, again of a medium difficulty, at the bottom of the trail and also a skills area for learners and young children to ride.

Easy Riding the freeride trail itself is easy enough and you can build up to the different drops and features on the trail.

Difficult Try out the harder features; can you stick to the wallride all the way around, drop the bigger step-downs and clear the tables?

Germany & Czech Republic Špičák

ⓘ OPENING TIMES

14 Jun to 14 Sep; 0900-1800

ⓢ RESORT PRICES

Day pass: 380 CK

ⓘ DIRECTORY

Bike Park: T+42 376-397167
Website: spicak.cz/english/leto_bikepark.htm

The Wile E Coyote route near Lake Garda.
Just before the dynamite section.
[DANMILNER.COM]

AUSTRIA

SWITZERLAND

Laax
Chur

Brenner Pass

To Bolzano

Venosta

Martigny

Simplon
Tunnel

Zermatt

Domodossola

St Moritz

Ortles
(3905 m)

FRANCE

Matterhorn
(3738 m)

Mount Rosa
(4634 m)

Pennine Alps

Mt Blanc
(4808 m)

Lugano

Pernina
(4049 m)

Chiavenno

Cevedale
(3757 m)

Trento

10

Aosta

Lake
Maggiore

Lake
Como

Orobie Alps

Gran
Paradiso
(4061 m)

6

Varese

Como

Lake
Iseo

4

Frejus
Tunnel

1

Novara

Milan

Bergamo

Brescia

Lake
Garda

Verona

Susa Valley

Turin

Asti

ITALY

Ticino

Oglio

Bardonecchia

9

Po

Piacenza

Sestriere

Alessandria

Taro

Viso
(3841 m)

Po

Tortona

Cottian Alps

Tanaro

Maggiorasca
(1799 m)

Cuneo

7

Genoa

Succiso
(2017 m)

Appennino Modenese

Maritime Alps

Savona

Finale Ligure

3

Western Riviera

Gulf of
Génova

La Spezia

Apuane Alps

Cimone
(2165 m)

FRANCE

Eastern Riviera

2

San Remo

Ligurian
Sea

Nice

MONACO

8

Florence

N · 20 km · 20 miles

	Resorts	
	1	Bardonecchia ▸ p154.
	2	Cimone ▸ p156.
	3	Finale Ligure ▸ p158.
	4	Lake Garda ▸ p160.
	5	Livigno ▸ p162.
	6	Pila ▸ p164.
	7	Prato Nevoso ▸ p166.
	8	San Remo ▸ p168.
	9	Sauze d'Oulx ▸ p170.
	10	Val di Fassa ▸ p172.

FINALE LIGURE TOURISM

San Remo descent.

Italy

When it comes to Italy it is almost impossible to define the typical resort. In mountain biking terms the country is deeply divided. The resorts on the eastern side – The Dolomite Region – are so different to those on the western end of the Alps as to feel almost like different countries. And if those two regions weren't contrasting enough, you can add into this the glitzier romance and warmer climate of the coastal region bordering France. There is an enormous variety of riding, taking in trails that wind through the hills and mountains, vineyards and groves, with views of lakes, villages and epic mountainscapes.

With this pedigree it is no surprise then that in the mid- to late-nineties Italy had two tracks on the Grundig World Cup series, at Cortina and Nevegal, and was at the forefront of technical downhill racetracks. The boom of resorts in France, such as Les Gets and Morzine, coupled with similar resorts all over Europe embracing bikeparks, left Italy somewhat in its wake as the country failed to capitalize on the huge interest in mountain biking. It is only in the last five or so years that the Italian resorts have started to catch up, investing in the infrastructure that the terrain demands. These days anyone bold enough to go against the grain and try somewhere new could do far worse than planning their riding holiday in Italy. The terrain is amazing, the weather good, there are spectacular views; it is also relatively inexpensive and it doesn't suffer from big lift queues. Oh, and we don't even have to mention the superb food and wine. What else do you need?

Overview

With the Dolomites in the northeast, the Alps to the northwest and the Appenines all the way down the middle of the country, there is plenty of trail riding to be found throughout Italy.

The country's recent history has cycling embedded in the national culture and a typical Sunday morning sees hundreds of cyclists on the roads. Unfortunately this heritage of road cycling has probably hindered the development of mountain biking when compared to the rest of Europe. What Italy does boast is classic singletrack surrounded by amazing scenery and the recently developed bikeparks are, rightfully, embracing this, rather than constructing downhill-only resorts.

Bring a mid to long travel trail bike set up to deal with the rocky terrain, and handle well on the downs, while giving you the capability of gradually climbing your way up and you'll be in trail heaven. Indeed, Lake Garda is regarded by many as one of the best spots in the world, with its technical singletrack in outstanding countryside.

While you could come to Italy and ride your bike pretty much anywhere, if you are looking for bikeparks and uplifts, then you should be looking to the north of the country. If XC is your game then the lower (than the Alps or Dolomites) Appenines are perfect, with many of the peaks just over the 1000 m mark. Most of these routes you'll have to organize yourself and italybikehotels.it is a good place to start if this is what you fancy. Elsewhere in Italy there are waymarked trails, looked after by Club Alpino Italiano (cai.it.), the national organization. Unfortunately, there is no equivalent of Ordnance Survey in Italy, making it rather difficult to find detailed maps. This makes the use of guides even more useful in Italy. As an example check out skeddadle.co.uk who organize guided tours in the Umbria region.

Conditions

Italy has a varied climate, especially in the mountains. Some areas have good year-round riding conditions such as the San Remo/Argentina valley and Lake Garda, making them excellent winter or early season options. The area around Liguria benefits from the Mediterranean climate, also making it a good spot when the mountain bikepark resorts are still under snow. In contrast areas to the east of the Appenines are more humid during the summer months, which can make XC riding hard work.

Most of the bikeparks are found in the north and this part of the country generally enjoys sunny days in slightly cooler temperatures than those found down at the coast.

Clockwise from top left: 1. Bikepark heaven.
3. Berm heaven.
2. Coffee heaven.
4. Thigh burn hell!

As in all mountain areas, don't be fooled by the glorious sunshine: storms can move in quickly and you should always be prepared when in the mountains; this is especially important if you are likely to be far from your base. Some of the longer rocky trails can become quite hard work when wet and slippery, especially for novice or beginner riders.

The trail and ground conditions are also reasonably varied throughout Italy; the majority of the riding is on rocky terrain, especially in the slightly more exposed locations such as Finale Ligure and around Lake Garda. Most of the bikeparks featured here have a light covering of soil over a rocky underbed, which gives a great variety of conditions on each trail. Towards the end of the summer deep piles of dust and dust-covered rocks 'liven up' the trails.

The scene

The mountain bike scene in Italy is fairly big, but it is heavily biased towards XC riding with large groups and clubs in abundance in most towns. Lightweight XC bikes are the order of the day. The downhill scene has been rather stagnant since the early days of Corrado Herin and Giovanna Bonazzi riding their Sintesi and Ancillotti bikes in the Grundig World Cup races. Things are on the up, however, with the development of bikeparks, and advances in bikes making the previously technical trails more accessible to a wider range of riders.

The XC race scene is strong at local, regional and national level with plenty of riders religiously putting the miles in during the week to be race ready. Regional level DH races suffer somewhat with poor quality tracks, though the national series is contested on more serious tracks with 2007 seeing the return of Cortina on the calendar.

Freeride is becoming more popular and illegal north shore sections are sprouting in the hills in most areas. Many of the new bikeparks have been designed and built by a small company called 4Guimp and the these guys really are helping to shape the future of Italian riding and bikeparks, mixing natural trails with man-made features.

Big events in Italy include the 24-hour Finale Ligure and the annual Single Speed Championships. 2008 sees the MTB World Championships held in Commezadura after it hosted the European championships in recent years.

The industry
The Italian bike industry is huge, with such legendary brands as Colnago and Pinarello. The mountain bike industry, is slightly smaller, with Bianchi probably the biggest brand, although others such as FRM and Extralite offer serious components for the XC riders. Marzocchi are consistently one of the big players in the suspension fork market and now produce rear shocks from their Bologna HQ.

The DH scene is dominated by Ancillotti, with many of the fastest privateers aboard the hand-made Tomaso DHP as well as supporting some of the top Italian racers. Sintesi no longer produce a DH bike, but still produce a large range of other bikes. MDE bikes based in Piemonte may be less well known but, like Ancillotti, produce bikes hand made by passionate riders and people passionate about bikes.

Other big players in the Italian industry cross over from one of the other favourite national pastimes, motorbikes, with Dainese, Alpine Stars, Axo and UFO all producing DH clothing.

Q&A with the experts

Enrico Guala was an Italian National Trial rider 1983-1992 and came 4th in the World Championship in 1989 as well as being several-time Italian Champion. He opened his first bike shop in 1992, worked with different companies (Santa Cruz, Seven Cycles, Magura, IBIS) and organised XC-DH and 24H events (24hfinale.com). He started 4 Guimp, a company that designs and constructs bike parks for resorts in Italy and abroad with partner Andrea Balli, a former World Cup downhiller, in 2006.

You've got friends visiting for just one weekend and they can go anywhere in Italy. Name the one place you'd definitely have to take them.

EG For sure it's the place I'm at right now; Sauze d'Oulx. It's such an amazing place. This part of Italy is made up of the eight Olympic villages plus the French Montgenèvre and, together with the central government, they are putting a huge amount of investment into mountain biking. As part of that project, we're designing the bikeparks and helping them make something really special here. The land is just so perfect too. I was saying that yesterday; we didn't need to move the dirt around too much, we're just sculpting it, you know? It's already such a perfect shape.

Which trail centre or resort has the best party scene or the best after riding activities?

EG That would be Finale Ligure. It's been such a good spot for mountain biking for so long. They have the history, it's such a beautiful place and there's of course the incredible sea view. You'll definitely have a good time there and there's lots to do. And there is a huge mountain bike community too.

Where did you learn to ride, and where would you send beginners to ride?

EG I learned in Genoa, and my first bike was in about 1984. I was a country boy you could say! I think to start mountain biking in summertime I would recommend Bardonecchia: perfect for beginners with lots of easy trails and nice summer activities for families.

In your opinion, which is the best downhill track in Italy?

EG Oh, the best downhill track is in Pila where the World Cup was three or four years ago. We also have the Val di Sole track which is going to host the World Championships in a week or so, but I haven't had chance to ride the new course there yet.

Where's the best place to avoid pedalling uphill? Where has the best uplifts? Would you avoid anywhere?

EG All the places we have been talking about have lifts or shuttle services, it is up to the rider to choose his or her daily ride. I mean, everyone can avoid peddling up if they do not want to. But you need some exercise to deserve a good plate of homemade pasta, don't you?

Bardonecchia

Bardonecchia has a good mix of trails that are fun to ride with a good uplift making a great intermediate ability resort.

BARDONECCHIA

↘1 The trails

- **Ⓧ Cross country** Fair/beginner to intermediate
- **Ⓓ Downhill** Good/beginner to intermediate
- **Ⓕ Freeride** Good/beginner to intermediate.
- **Ⓤ Uplift** 2 chairlifts and 1 gondola runs during the summer giving access to a wide area of trails
- **✓ Pros** Good lift access to a large area with a good variety of trails; kids' area and bikes make a good option for those travelling with a family
- **✗ Cons** Trails in the park are not challenging for experienced riders

With three lifts serving the area, the beauty of Bardonecchia is that it allows bikes to get out into a wider area and make much more of the trails, rather than the one lift often opened to bikes in most resorts. Those looking to head further afield and who don't mind a bit of climbing can take in some long rides, while the downhillers will be happy hopping on and off the lifts. The main DH runs are pretty gentle, but there are more technical paths and tracks on the hills.

Cross country

Cross country riders are reasonably well catered for here, but maybe the one thing lacking is waymarked loops as all the marked trails are pretty much all downhill. This means that if you are looking for long

ⓘ **OPENING TIMES**
Lifts are open Jun to Sep; daily 0900 to 1750

Ⓢ **RESORT PRICES**
1-day pass: €12; 6-day pass: €48; Season pass: €97

Ⓘ **DIRECTORY**
Lift Centre: T+39 01229-9137
Ambulance: T+118
Doctors: T+39 01229-9037
Taxi: T+39 01229-01333
Website: bardonecchiabike.com

climbs you'll have to find your own way up. There is still plenty on offer though as the length of the trails provides you with a decent amount of riding, although these trails are to cater for a wide range of ability riders.

Downhill

If downhill is what you are after, there are five or so black routes that have good service from the lifts. The trails are predominantly man-made with banked corners and small kickers. These trails can be linked up with the various red runs giving good riding from top to bottom.

Easy Take the red graded routes which are more man made with bermed turns and small jumps.

Difficult The black routes have some steep sections which will challenge you more than the mellow red routes.

Freeride

Linking up the red and black runs can give you some excellent and long downhills, some of which you'll need do a little climbing or traversing to get to. In this regard a freeride bike will be ideal, giving you a large number of trails that you can access. There are northshore areas with a variety of obstacles progressing in difficulty for you to build up to.

FREE ALIEN

SIMON.CITTATI.COM

The Lowdown

Locals do... Cope with the altitude better than the tourists; it's 2800 m at the top of the trails.

Locals don't... Ride at midday; you'll find them all in the cafés soaking up the sun.

Don't miss... Bardonecchia Bike Festival, a freeride festival soon after the opening of the lifts which declares the season well and truly open.

Remember to avoid... Straying from the marked mountain bike trails.

Practicalities ⬛🚴🚠

Ruled by, variously, the Romans, the French and now the Italians, Bardonecchia has always been strategically important. Today, the town itself is quite small, but it is very well equipped for tourism with hotels, residences, bars and restaurants all within a small radius that can comfortably be walked. Located at 1300 m in the Italian Alps, about 90 km from Turin, Bardonecchia is the intersection point of four valleys. This location makes it perfect for a mountain bike resort as the access into the four valleys gives a huge area in which you can ride.

Sleeping There are two campsites in Bardonecchia; *Camping Bokki* (T+39 01229-9893) and *Camping Pian del Colle* (T+39 01229-01452). Both are located on Pian del Colle. Check out *Da Valerio e Maite*, Via Orti 2 (T+39 01229-02664) a B&B that is a good cheap option. Hotels are in abundance here; just click on the hotels link from the website (bardonecchiabike.com) for a comprehensive list.

Eating The typical local cuisine here is more French than what you'd expect in Italy. In the town there are plenty of restaurants and you'd be hard pressed not to find something you fancy just by walking around.

Bars and clubs The customary Irish pub is located in via Des Geneys, but again the town here offers plenty of choice, and it's all within walking distance in the small town centre.

Bike shop Kona now sponsor the bikepark and thus a large range of hire bikes is available at the bottom of the lift. There is also a supply of the essentials and tools at the shop (T+39 01229-6559). Alternatively there is the *Planet Mountain* (T+39 01229-07753) which stocks all your needs.

Internet café *IT Bardonecchia* in the town centre has 2 terminals.

Bike map available? Maps are available from the tourist office and lift stations. A PDF version is also available to download from the website (bardonecchiabike.com).

SIMON.CITTATI.COM

Italy Bardonecchia

FREE ALIEN

FREE ALIEN

Top: Beautiful townscape.
Above: "And a wax finish, too, if you don't mind."
Bottom left: "Weeeeee..."
Bottom right: "Yeeehaaa!"
Opposite page: "Buttercups? You're having a laugh. They're chrysanthemums I'm telling you."

Cimone

Cross country and descending trails all lift assisted in the heart of the Appinino Modenese.

CIMONE

☑2 The trails

- **XC Cross country** Good/beginner to advanced
- **DH Downhill** Fair to good/intermediate
- **FR Freeride** Fair/beginner to intermediate
- **🚠 Uplift** Chairlifts in Sestola and Montecreto; chairlift at Lago della Ninfa; cablecar from Passo del Lupo to Pian Cavallaro; shuttle bus from Pian del Falco to Passo del Lupo
- **✔ Pros** Good access to trails directly from the lower lifts in Sestola and Montecreto; excellent singletrack suitable for all ability levels; cross country trails cover a wide variety of terrain, from open sections on higher slopes to tight singletrack in the wooded areas lower down
- **✘ Cons** Lacking in man-made north-shore style sections or jumps to test more experienced riders

"Are we in the heart of the Appinino Modenese?" "Si."

The whole of Monte Cimone is littered with trails to ride and by using the lifts and shuttles you are able to cover a large area relatively easily by connecting up trails. Riders on downhill bikes are really restricted to the area directly above Sestola and Montecreto up to Pian Cavallaro where the cablecar stops. Cross country bike riders, however, can explore a much greater area descending down to Fanano or Riolunato.

Cross country

There are several cross country loops which are marked on the trail map. There is enough variety to satisfy everyone from beginner to expert here; the length and altitude gain of each loop is indicated on the map, making it easy to choose a trail suitable for your fitness level. Technically the cross country is suitable for all ability levels with sections that will be a challenge for beginners and yet experts can still have a load of fun on.

Obviously, just because the trails are marked as loops it doesn't mean you have to ride the whole loop; with a bit of planning and studying the trail map you can chop and change between trails linking up with freeride sections and the uplift facilities.

Italy Cimone

The Lowdown

Locals do... Remember that the main lifts shut for lunch so go up to the highest slopes on the last lift for a long downhill back to the lower lift in time for it to reopen.

Locals don't... Always stop for lunch. If you head to the Lago della Ninfa for lunch at the refuge you can make use of the chairlift there which remains open.

Don't miss... The annual Funky Day marks the opening of the lifts for the season with free food and drink for everyone. This is usually the first weekend in June and sees riders come from far and wide with a great atmosphere and a laid-back day's riding.

Remember to avoid... Self-catering for your entire stay. The food in this region is not to be missed.

Easy From Sestola take the number 4 trail, a 20-km loop with 500 m of vertical ascent.

Difficult If you are on an all-mountain bike then try out the freeride descent number 64 which drops you down near Montecreto after a 7-km descent.

Downhill

There are two downhill tracks in Sestola which run underneath the main lift; these are where they hold a round of the national series each year. The old track, which was used up until 2004, is barely ridden now but is still good fun to ride; it is tight and quite steep and will have your discs glowing into the turns. Expect a heavy dose of arm pump by the time you reach the bottom.

The newer course is all natural, like the old course, but takes a slightly more

Practicalities ●🚲🌿

Monte Cimone is situated in the heart of the Appinino Modenese on the Emilia Romagna and Tuscany border. There are 2 towns based on the side of Cimone that are linked to the network of MTB trails via ski lifts. The town of Sestola is overlooked by the 'Fortezza', a castle which dates back to AD735. Sestola is a traditional town with its shops and restaurants along the main drag. The main tourism here is the winter ski industry, although the short ski season in recent years has led to the extended summer season. Montecreto is a little more hidden, nestled under its dense beech and fir woods and feels slightly more cut off than Sestola. The ski lift in Montecreto is slightly out of the town but this is remedied by the quality of the singletrack. This returns you back to the lift and makes it a good option.

Sleeping *Residence Margherita* in Montecreto is a good low-price option with breakfast included in the price and cooking facilities in the rooms, giving you the option of cooking in the evenings. There is also a bike storage area.

Eating Take a walk along the main street in Sestola and you'll find restaurants serving traditional local food. The local specialties are *tigelle* and *gnoccho fritto* which make an excellent starter. Depending on the season fresh mushrooms, truffles, wild boar and hare are likely to be served.

Bars and clubs Neither Sestola nor Montecreto could be recommended for nightlife, the *Gosling* Irish pub in Sestola being the only real night spot.

Bike shop There are 2 bike shops in Sestola, the shop below the lift station being well equipped with the essential heavy duty tyres and innertubes. Commencal bikes are also available to hire. *Dimensione Nature* in Fanano is also well stocked and the staff are very knowledgeable regarding local trails, bike set up, etc. They have Kona freeride and downhill bikes available for hire, plus a shuttle service can be provided taking you up to Pian del Falco. This means you can end the day with a long ride back down to Fanano off the mountain.

Internet café No internet café, so leave the computers at home.

Bike map available? There is a map of all the designated MTB trails available in the lift stations.

meandering path down the hill, traversing the ski piste a few times with more technical rooty sections with a few rocks thrown in under the trees either side of the piste. The courses are quite short with a fast time being around two minutes.

Freeride

Probably the best trails to ride on Cimone are signed as freeride trails. Basically they are all natural singletracks, with the only entirely man-made trail being the freeride course in Sestola with bermed corners, tabletops and drops. The trails marked red are suitable for all abilities while the blue are probably tame for intermediate riders. The black routes, especially those in Montecreto, are very technical natural trails and really for expert level riders.

Italy Cimone

Finale Ligure

Great all-year-round Mediterranean climate on some classic rocky Italian singletracks.

FINALE LIGURE

↘3 The trails

- **XC Cross country** Good/intermediate to advanced
- **DH Downhill** Good/beginner to advanced
- **FR Freeride** Poor to fair/beginner to advanced
- **Uplift** Uplifts in vans or shuttle buses can be arranged via private companies; see Finale freeride and rivierabike.co.uk
- **Pros** Amazing natural singletrack; rocks all the way; good conditions; all-year-round climate
- **Cons** No ski lift so have to arrange uplifts; organizing your own group is best as you can end up in a group of slower (or faster) riders

The terrain here is challenging yet fun. There aren't many trails that most

ⓘ OPENING TIMES

You can ride most of the trails year round although you should contact the websites listed below for information on uplifts

$ RESORT PRICES

Finale Freeride offer a day's uplifts for €35 per day per person

ⓘ DIRECTORY

Tourist office: T+39 019-681019
Taxi: T+39 019-692461
Website: justridefinale.com; freeridefinale.com

Hot, dusty singletrack with fantastic views. Perfect.

riders couldn't ride but it's how you ride them that will change with riders' abilities. A lot of the routes here are old hunter's trails and they make for superb mountain biking. The corners are never too tight and often banked so you can maintain rhythm and flow. This is a great place to bring a 6" travel bike and just enjoy the terrain either riding XC up and down or shuttling the place and riding the countless descents with a local guide.

Cross country

These are fantastic 100% natural trails, technical and rocky singletracks which wind down the mountainsides to sea level. Cross country riders can ride loops climbing up to the trail heads. The rocky natural trails also make for technical climbs and the riding in Finale is probably not suited to beginners.

Downhill

Riders will love hitting the trails at speed. Generally the guides in the area are good riders and if guiding a group of DH riders they will ride accordingly once they have established fitness/skill levels.

The Lowdown

Locals do... Send someone on ahead on the trail to make sure it is clear of hikers, animals or fallen trees.

Locals don't... Drop litter on the trails; ride flat out – unless they know it's clear up ahead.

Don't miss... The Finale Ligure festival, a 24-hour bike race and festival around some great trails that can be taken as easily or as seriously as you wish.

Remember to avoid... Being stuck at sea level with a DH bike and no uplift!

The trails certainly don't make a DH bike a necessity; all the trails are rideable, albeit at a slower pace on an XC bike. A mid travel bike is probably the ideal choice for slicing up the singletrack, with slightly more relaxed geometry and just enough travel to make sure you can last a full day.

DANMILNER.COM

Practicalities 🍴🚴🔧

The province of Liguria sits right on the Mediterranean Sea and carries you right up into the Maritime Alps. Finale Ligure is roughly halfway between Genoa and the French border on the Riviera di Pontente. Finale, like many of the towns in Liguria, still has many of its medieval buildings, although the main development of the town was in the late 1920s. Narrow streets, alleyways and medieval walls are a pleasant reminder of it's history. Finalborgo is the original centre, on the river Pora, while Finale Pia is based on the seafront. Finale Pia is on the eastern side, towards Genoa.

Much like Lake Garda, this is no Whistler-style bikepark, rather a place of outstanding natural beauty whose mountains are riddled with singletrack, with the bonus of leading all the way down from the mountain tops to the beaches. It is these beaches that are one of the many attractions to Finale, making this another good location for those with interests other than purely riding bikes; the rock climbing here is well known, there are plenty of architectural attractions and the walking is endless.

Sleeping *Hotel Florenz* on via Celesia 1 in Finale Ligure offers bike storage, lock up, workshop, bike wash, an 'athletes' breakfast, MTB guides and uplift on request/booking. Night rides are available for suitably skilled riders. *Hotel Medusa*, Lungomare di via Concezione, is also popular with mountain bikers, offering secure bike storage, a workshop and providing routes for mtb riders and roadies. They also have 2 qualified guides. *Just Ride Finale* offer a bed and bike package from €47 a night and shuttles to the trails.

Eating *La Tavernetta*, in via Cristoforo Colombo 37, is a typical local trattoria serving real Italian food.

Bars and clubs *Finalborgo* is the place where you will find quieter bars and enotecas. Towards the beach there are more developed areas with livelier nightime entertainment.

Bike shop At the *Outdoor Café* (T+39 019-680564), on the piazza in Finalborgo, you can rent full-suspension Kona bikes. The café doubles as Italy's headquarters of the International Mountain Bicycling Association (imba.com). Outside the café, you'll find a mechanic for on-the-go tune-ups.

Internet café Many of the hotels here have internet access, otherwise there is an internet point at *Studio Lomax Compuvideo* in via San Pietro, 30 (T+39 019-680101).

Bike map available? No map is available but: *Alp, Cartoguida del Finalese*, 1:25.000, reading is recommended for your own trails.

Easy Try out the sweeping gully trail called 'Madonna della Guardia' which runs from the village of Melogno to Calice. Though not a true beginners' route most riders will have no problems.

Difficult Try the Varigotti Downhill, one of the more challenging trails in the area with a looser riding surface.

Freeride
There are no freeride-specific trails as all the descents are natural routes. So riders looking for lines with multiple berms, jumps and man-made features should look elsewhere. On the other hand, those who just love shredding on their bike down good trails will love this place.

There is a tiny man-made bikepark which is really designed to teach young kids the basic skills, but most novice riders will enjoy rolling around it.

Left: First one to the sea wins a dunking.
Above: "Chaaaaarge!"

Lake Garda

▲4 The trails

- **⊕ Cross country** Excellent/ intermediate to advanced
- **⊕ Downhill** Fair to good/ intermediate
- **⊕ Freeride** Poor/beginner
- **⊘ Uplift** Malcesine cablecar; shuttle services from most shops, or check mtb.ongarda.com
- **⊘ Pros** Endless flowing singletrack; excellent climate
- **⊗ Cons** Limited, expensive uplifts – shuttles have to be booked; Malcesine cablecar only takes bikes at set times

With the trails starting at over 2000 m and the lake at 65 m, this is one hell of a vertical drop. Any run here contains a great variety of terrain due to their sheer length: with exposed ridges, dry, dusty soil, large rock slabs, tunnels, trees and loose rock all the way down to what is one of the world's famous beauty spots.

Identified by many in the know as the world's best riding. A big statement and luckily one that doesn't seem too far fetched.

Cross country

The cross country riding here is really for riders who have a good base level of fitness, even if they are experienced and technically proficient. Long uphills are the order of the day. Beginners are likely to struggle on the long climbs and

Above: Spirito de biko.
Below: "Fancy a coffee in the next village?" "Si."

The Lowdown

Locals do... Relax at *Mecki's* after a day in the mountains; get up early to get the first lift on the Malcesine cablecar in the morning; take a camelback with tools and tubes to make sure you can enjoy the full length of the downhills.

Locals don't... Go flat out from the start and get arm pump with 40 minutes of downhill to go; pull massive skids in front of groups of German ramblers.

Don't miss... The legendary 601 trail from Monte Altissimo to Torbole.

Remember to avoid... German bank holidays.

descents. Because there is no bikepark as such it is back to the traditional methods and you'll have to get the map out. This is relatively easy as there are plenty of trails on the map, all of which are open to bikes. It would be worth consulting one of the bike shops first for suggestions and to benefit from local knowledge. Check the trails on lagobiker.it; these can be downloaded in pdf form but you will still need a map.

Easy Head up Monte Brione, the small hill between Riva del Garda and Torbole; it's a great warm up short ride with a stunning vantage point looking out over the lake from the old fort at the summit. From there you can follow the trail back down some fast sections to the bottom.

Difficult Take the classic 601 trail from Mte Altissimo. You can either climb up to the top on a long and hard XC loop or utilize the gondola and enjoy the 20-km descent to Torbole.

Downhill

There are no downhill courses at Lake Garda, but don't let that put you off bringing a DH bike along, though a 6" or 7" trail bike is probably best. Arrange an uplift at any one of the shops or get on the cablecar at Malcesine and you'll be

Practicalities 🍴🚲🏨

Lake Garda, the largest of Italy's lakes, lies just south of the Alps, surrounded on three sides by mountains. Based on the northern edge of Lake Garda are three areas – Riva del Garda, Torbole and Malcesine – which serve as a good base for mountain biking. Busy periods can see these towns full of German-speaking tourists as its proximity and motorway links to Austria and Germany make it a popular holiday location. To the south of the lake is the Roman spa town of Sirmione with its sulphur baths. Beaches around the lake and the watersports available also make this a destination suitable for those travelling with non-biking friends or family.

Sleeping Finding accommodation is not hard; try the excellent and very bike friendly *Hotel Santoni* (http://santoni.hotelsingarda.com) with a secure bike lock up, bike wash and great knowledge of the trails. Also in Torbole, *Mecki's Bike Shop* provide low cost accommodation next door; a perfect location as most days invariably finish at the bar and bike shop.

Eating There are plenty of restaurants in Torbole and Riva del Garda to cater for all the German tourists. Most of these serve a mix of standard Italian food, a few German plates and US-style meals. That's not to say that you won't get a high quality meal here. Well worth the drive is the *Al Commercio* (T+39 0457-211183) in Bardolino on the southern side of the lake below Garda.

Bars and clubs For a drink after riding there's not much that can beat sitting outside *Mecki's Bike & Coffee* with a beer looking at all the bikes, the surrounding mountains and the lake. Later in the evening head to *Winds* bar in Torbole where most people meet up and chill out.

Bike shop *Mecki's Bike & Coffee* (T+39 0464-505191) is as much a place to hang out as a bike shop. The shop is well stocked with components and has a large range of clothing. A bike shuttle service is also available from here. Or you can try *Capentari*, on the main road through Torbole (T+39 0464-505500), another quality bike shop with a lot of useful stock and components. The range of maps on sale here is also good making a visit almost essential. Shuttle buses can also be booked from here.

Internet café *Internet point* (T+39 0464-520724) in Riva Del Garda is the easiest place to check your emails and *Hotel Santoni* has free Wi-Fi.

Bike map available? There is no one specific trail map in Garda so you'll have to buy a standard map and pick the trails out from that. Probably the best maps are from an Austrian company called *Kompass* (kompass.at). These are available at *Carpentari* bike shop in Torbole. Other maps are on sale in most of the shops. Check out naturedynamics.com/index.dhtml for more maps on the area.

able to enjoy some of the best natural downhills you are ever likely to ride! Long technical singletrack is the order of the day here and you'll be picking your way over the rocky ground as the trails run on and on. A map is still required and a little more forward

planning than at specific bikeparks, but it's well worth the effort.

Freeride

Lake Garda is no freeride area really; it's all about the singletrack.

Livigno

Excellent facilities across the board make Livigno one of Italy's premiere biking spots.

LIVIGNO

↘5 The trails

- **Cross country** Excellent/ intermediate to advanced
- **Downhill** Excellent/Kona Groove Approved Downhill Park in centre of town
- **Freeride** Excellent/intermediate to advanced
- **Uplift** There are 2 lifts out of Livigno, the Mottolino and, on the opposite side of the valley, the Carosello 3000, both are bubble cars suitable for mountain bikers
- **Pros** Duty free resort, so plenty of cheap food, drink and fuel; endless quiet singletrack trails; local mountain spa centres for relaxing those tiring muscles
- **Cons** 3-4 hr transfer from an airport, but once you get there it's well worth the journey

Livigno was home to the 2005 MTB World Championships, 2004 MTB World Cup and the annual Transalp cycle races. Many famous cycling legends have lived

Above: Riding on a wall, heading for the soil, That's Livigno alright.
Below: That's Livigno alright.

and trained in the area, including Lance Armstrong, Marco Pantani, Hans Rey and Paula Pezzo.

With over 1500 km of amazing singletrack covering an area of over 10,000 sq km and the Kona Groove Approved Downhill Park, Livigno is a strong contender for any summer break. The trails take you out to remote, high exposed Alpine singletrail, through technical forest switchbacks and over mountain passes. On the Livigno side, the trails tend to be less rocky, through forests and high mountain paths, while on the Swiss side the terrain is a lot rockier.

There are plenty of trails to choose from but you will need help from a taxi or guide to make the most of your day's riding. This is especially the case if you don't fancy another two mountain passes to get you back to the town as many of the classic rides are linear. To get the most out of your visit, it's worth contacting British mountainbike company Italiansafaris, who can guide and advise you on the best trails in the area, and they can help you with accommodation, transfers and anything else you need to know about the area!

Cross country

All the cross country trails have been specially prepared for mountain bikers and are free from ramblers! Expect long days, big climbs and endless descents from 3100 m down to 400 m on fast flowing singletrack.

The Lowdown

Locals do... Drink coffee and local wine from a café terrace while watching other Italians shopping.

Locals don't... Rush about or forget to drink coffee or enjoy a good drink.

Don't miss... The Alta Rezia 20,000 Freeride Safari, pioneered by Hans Rey and Thomas Frischknecht. Find out about it through italiansafaris.com.

Remember to avoid... Endless supply of free grappa after dinner in restaurants; hangovers kill the riding!

Downhill

In Livigno there's the Mottolino Kona Groove Approved Downhill Park with a vertical descent of over 500 m. There are a number of freeride tracks packed with banked turns, tables, small doubles and forest sections. The course takes you back to the cablecar station and the *Tea dal Vidal* bar for a refreshing beer.

Easy Follow the blue signs for the easy route down from the Mottolino mountain to the village, which includes an easy northshore course at the top

ⓘ OPENING TIMES

Mottolino (Kona Groove Approved Downhill Park): 14-15 Jun; 21 Jun-21 Sep (daily); 27-28 Sep
Carosello 3000: 21 Jun-21 Sep (daily)

ⓢ RESORT PRICES

Day pass: €20; 5-day pass: €50; Season pass: €20

ⓘ DIRECTORY

Tourist office: T+39 0342-996379
Hospital: T+39 0342-978107
Taxi: T+39 335-217850
Website: livigno.com

for learners. En route there's also a section to the side of the main run which has jumps starting from small and increasing in size to build you confidence and skill.

Difficult There are red and black routes down the mountain; these take you over tabletops and small doubles. As the route descends down banked turns it takes you in the long forest section of drops and northshore sections.

Freeride

There's a must-do freeride tour, the Alta Rezia 20,000 m, pioneered by Hans Rey and Thomas Frischknecht. This takes you from 3100 m down to 400 m and is achievable if you commit to staying around for 5 days riding. The tour takes you on exposed trails under glaciers, before finding your own route down to the *rifugio*, where you rest your head. Check out the film 'Alta Rezia Freeride', available from Italiansafaris. This is

technical trail freeriding as opposed to built stunts and jumps.

"Ciao, pet."

Practicalities ⬛🍴🚲

Livigno, at altitude 1815 m is known as 'Little Tibet' due to its setting in the remote Valtellina Valley. The town is spread out, but easy to get around on foot or by bike. It's an old Alpine mountain village, set amongst the spectacular and wild mountains of the Stelvio National Park in the Italian Alps. Bordered on three sides by Switzerland, Livigno's neighbouring resorts are St Moritz, Poschiavo and Bormio. Collectively this area is known as the Alta Rezia.

Since the time of Napoleon, Livigno has had the privilege of being a tax free and independent province of Italy. Today, duty free shops abound, selling all sorts of luxury goods, electrical items, wines and alcohol. This makes for a favourable and cheap destination to spend a summer, with prices in bars, hotels and restaurants normally far cheaper than equivalent resorts in Europe. Livigno is relatively easy to reach via Milan, Bergamo, Zürich and Innsbruck airports, though there is a 3-4 hr transfer.

Sleeping There are plenty of hotels of all grades and self-catering apartments available throughout the summer, but avoid the second and third weeks in

August, when all the Italians take their holidays at the same time! The 4-star *Hotel Bivio* has really friendly staff, delicious food, rustic Alpine interior, its own wellness centre and a bar/club in the basement. The 3-star *Hotel Piccolo Tibet* offers bed and breakfast, and for half board head to *Mario's* restaurant which is right next door.

Eating The warm hospitality of the local residents and the intimacy of the valley are complemented by the many excellent bars, cafés and restaurants in the village. Local cuisine includes the renowned specialties of tarragon polenta, pizzocherie pasta, mountain mushrooms and wild game dishes such as venison. The local wines of the neighbouring Valtellina produce some of Northern Italy's most sought after red wines, including Sassella and Sforzato, and the local home-made grappa blended with rosemary and mountain berries. We recommend you try the *Hotel Bivio* with excellent local cuisine in the middle of town, or the *Bait dal Ghet*, also in the centre, which has cheap local dishes and is popular with the locals.

Bars and clubs Livigno's isolated position doesn't stop it from being

a lively mountain community and the *Kuhstall Pub* in the *Hotel Bivio* basement is open till late with a DJ. Alternatively try *My Coffee*, a vibrant, modern cocktail bar. You're sure to find yourself in the conveniently located *Tea del Vidal* bar found at the bottom of the Downhill park.

Bike shop There are some very good bike shops in the town. *Arcobaleno Sport* has really friendly staff also speak English, can get anything for you and sell good clothing too. Italiansafaris also rent out good mountain bikes while *DeeFox* is very friendly, have English-speaking staff, plenty of Freeride clothing, a mechanic and rent bikes.

Internet café *Engadina Bar* located in the western part of the town near the church. Remember though you need a passport as ID to use it; approximately €1 for 10 mins. Most hotels have internet access, and some have wireless connection.

Bike map available? You can buy a map from all bike shops, newsagents and hotels. Some hotels have GPS routes marked for downloading – you can do this from altarezia.eu.

Italy Livigno

Pila

Pila is a great riding spot, with a range of trails and the awesome Pila to Aosta 8-km run.

PILA

⬊6 The trails

- **XC Cross country** Good/beginner to intermediate
- **DH Downhill** Excellent/beginner to advanced
- **FR Freeride** Fair/beginner to intermediate
- **Uplift** Chamole chairlift from Pila 1785 m to 2311 m; cablecar from Aosta to Pila
- **Pros** Excellent gravity trails; Pila-Aosta freeride
- **Cons** Pila is cut off from the town, so be prepared to spend the whole day up on the mountain

Pila is a great example of a successful, interesting and challenging bikepark. The trails have mostly been built or cleared by hand and are natural technical singletracks. They are labelled as freeride runs, but really are more in the way of downhill runs. The World Cup DH sees a little more built berms and jumps, but a

Above left: "What drop? Waaaaaaaah!".
Above right: Follow-meadow-leader.
Below: The 'Fun' conveyer belt.

① OPENING TIMES

The lifts open at the end of Jun and close on the 2nd week of Sep; from 0845-1700

⑤ RESORT PRICES

Day pass: €15.50; Week pass: €62; Season pass: €140

① DIRECTORY

Tourist office: T+39 0165-236627
Hospital: T+39 0165-5431
Taxi: T+39 0165-262010
Website: pila.it

healthy proportion of it remains technical wooded natural trail. Although it's been inexpensive to create, it has potential for further building and, when combined with the long Pila to Aosta descent, it makes a great riding destination.

Cross country

Twelve routes are waymarked – aimed more towards the beginner – and all use the ski lift for the uphill part. More experienced cross country riders would be perfectly happy on the freeride marked trails but if technical climbs are what you are looking for then consult the bike shop for their local knowledge.

Downhill

Pila was host to a round of the World Cup Downhill series in 2006, and therefore boasts a world cup standard DH. It was designed and built by Italian legend Corrado Herin and is a good example of a fast technical track. Beginners to downhill riding will enjoy the track as most of the hard sections have easy lines around them and the sections that are marked as black have red alternatives. Experienced riders will be able to push themselves, hitting the fast lines through the rocks, trying to nail the tight berms and make it cleanly through the black sections. Either deep dust or rain can make one notorious section a challenge for any rider. Downhill bike riders are not restricted to the marked DH track as the freeride trails are all really great natural DH runs.

Easy Take the route labelled freeride 4; this is one of the more mellow runs down the hill but still real good fun.

Difficult Take the black-graded World Cup trail from the top of the chairlift. It is pretty rideable to most; only a couple of tougher sections have alternative lines. Decent riders will soon have all the fast lines down.

Hook on, sit down, have a cappuccino.

Freeride

Freeride in Pila consists mainly of steady downhill singletrack that has the odd drop thrown in for good measure and a few small jumps in the woods. All the trails are good fun and riders of all abilities can spend a few days riding here, mixing the downhill and freeride trails.

One of the highlights of Pila is the Pila to Aosta freeride. This is an 11-km downhill singletrack which takes you back down to the bottom of the valley to the lift station in Aosta. Be wary though as halfway down there is a strange drop area which seems a little out of place considering the largest is more than big enough for all but advanced level riders. Connecting the downhill or one of the freeride trails from the top lift with this trail can give you a downhill run with a height loss of over 2300 m.

Practicalities ▣ ✎ ◔

Pila is a small resort in the shadows of Gran Paradiso, above the town of Aosta. Although a busy ski resort during winter, it is very quiet during the summer and you should really look for accommodation in the town of Aosta, capital of the region, of which Val d'Aosta is the smallest in Italy and also one of the wealthiest. The area has a mixed history having formerly been part of France, with the locals speaking a dialect more similar to French than Italian. If you don't speak any Italian, French is widely spoken and understood. The town is situated on the main through road up to the Mt Blanc (Monte Bianco for Italians) and Petit Sant Bernard tunnels, which makes it ideal if you plan on riding in other areas such as Chamonix, Verbier and Les Arcs. The nearest airports are Geneva and Turin.

Sleeping *Hotel Milleluci*, located slightly out of the town, is a place where you can soak up the remainder of the day's sun by the pool looking out to the mountain opposite and then relax in the sauna and jacuzzi after a day's riding. They also have a campsite if you're on a budget.

Eating Take a walk along via de Tillier in the evening and you'll find a wide choice of restaurants, even if they are a little touristy. During the day you can eat at the restaurants at the bottom of the DH course in Pila. Try the fresh pork roast which is cooked out on the terraces of the restaurants.

Bars and clubs The *Sweet Rock Café* in via Piccolo San Bernardo has a well stocked bar and is a good place to meet in the evening, the restaurant also serves American style food.

Bike shop There is a shop based in Pila at the lift station which stocks all the tools you may need in any emergency and the staff are friendly and helpful. Hire bikes are also available with a choice ranging from Commencal supreme DH to 24" wheel hardtails (T+39 3047-411 0227). A wider variety of stock is available at the shop behind the main lift station in Aosta.

Internet café Aosta has many internet cafés and facilities, so take your pick.

Bike map available? Bike maps can be collected at the lift stations. Three separate maps are available covering the bikepark, the downhill/freeride tracks and the Pila to Aosta freeride. These maps are also available in pdf format online at pila.it. Cross country trails are also mapped.

The Lowdown

Locals do... Style up the step-up jumps on the DH track.

Locals don't... Get stuck in Aosta when the lift shuts for lunch.

Don't miss... Finishing the day with the Pila-Aosta freeride.

Remember to avoid... Parking in Pila, as you won't be able to finish with the Aosta freeride trail.

Italy Pila

Prato Nevoso

Another fine example of northern Italy's thriving bikepark scene.

PRATO NEVOSO

↘7 The trails

- **XC Cross country** Good/beginner to advanced
- **DH Downhill** Good/beginner to advanced
- **FR Freeride** Good/beginner to advanced
- **Uplift** 2 chairlifts take you from the main village directly to the trails
- **Pros** A lot of riding in a compact area; well designed and thought-out trails; a very well organized bike resort
- **Cons** Still relatively new and quite a small resort

Cross country

Cross country riders have some good loops to choose from with distances varying from 7 km to 52 km, catering for all fitness levels. More experienced riders will also be quite happy on the freeride trails. Junction and Let's Dance are perfect freeride trails that can be ridden on XC bikes by riders of all levels.

Downhill

There is a specific DH course in the bike park. Wide, open and fast is the order

① OPENING TIMES

Lifts are open 0830-1230 and 1330-1700; also Fri 1945-2100

⑤ RESORT PRICES

Day pass: €16; Week pass: €95; Season pass: €170

① DIRECTORY

Tourist Office: pratonevoso.com

The northshore roman sling-shot about to send another victim to Croatia.

of the day here. Technically, the course is enough to challenge everyone, with some steep sections and only advanced level riders will be smoothly hitting the downslopes of the jumps. Beginners will probably be better off on other trails as the trail only really flows if you have a good combo of speed and rhythm.

Freeride

A number of the trails here are signed as freeride and offer an excellent variety of terrain. There are short northshore style sections which complement the natural features of the mountains, linking up sections and creating obstacles that otherwise would be unrideable, which give the trails a real flow. Unlike the stop-start nature of some northshore trails, these really add to the quality and enjoyment of your riding. On the rocks is the trail that exemplifies this. Situated under the lower lift is the bike park which has some small drops and wallrides to play on, but nothing too challenging. There is also a dirt jump section, a pump track and a funbox. On Friday nights these sections can all be ridden during the after-hours opening. For those of you also are working on perfecting your backflips, there is a foam pit too.

Easy Check out the On the rocks trail with ladders linking the boulders on the hill – a refreshing take on northshore.

Difficult Most of the trails drop you into the bikepark at the foot of the slope with its wallrides, jumps and drops. Once you have a couple of lines dialled you'll soon be hitting them on every run.

"Wahooo!"

The Lowdown

Locals do... Remember that Friday nights is late opening on the lower slopes.

Locals don't... Ride without their hydration packs.

Don't miss... Prato Nevoso is near enough to other riding spots like San Remo and Finale Ligure, giving you a perfect excuse for a trip round the local area and into France at La Peille.

Remember to avoid... Following riders to closely as the dust cloud from the dry trails will soon stop you.

Practicalities

Prato Nevoso is a small resort above the Mediterranean coast, close to both Finale Ligure and San Remo, meaning this a great place to stay and travel to the other riding areas. Everything you'll need you can find in the village, making it almost like a self-contained made-for-mountain biking unit. Built as a resort in the 1960s, its location is perfect with great access mainly by road. The village itself is at 1480 m and the ski lift runs right from your doorstep. Bike Land is a proper bikepark, typical of modern resort towns with the runs being directly above the village and directly accessed by the lifts.

Sleeping *Residence Stalle Lunghe*, situated next to the lift, is the obvious choice and also provides safe bike storage. The *Stalle* also has a restaurant serving typical local foods along with more international dishes. Prato Nevoso also has a large area for those staying in tents, vans or campers, or those wishing to make it a stop on a road trip.

Eating/Bars and clubs Being a small resort village you're not exactly overwhelmed with choices, leaving you eating, drinking and dancing at the *Stalle*. Maybe even sleeping there too!

Bike shop At the base of the chairlift there is a bike shop which should cover all your usual requirements. Hire bikes are available here with a good selection of Commencal bikes from XC hardtails to the World Cup downhill standard supreme DH. Full-face helmets and body armour can also be hired if necessary.

Internet café An internet connection is available in the tourist office for a small charge.

Bike map available? A map of the bike park is available at the lift station and also in the tourist office.

San Remo

Lying on the French-Italian border, San Remo is a great base to enjoy the fantastic riding and the sights along the Riviera.

Sweet singletrack.

Great views.

↘8 The trails

- **Cross country** Good to excellent/ intermediate to advanced
- **Downhill** Excellent/intermediate to advanced
- **Freeride** Poor to fair/intermediate
- **Uplift** Uplifts in vans or shuttle buses can be arranged via private companies, see argentinabike.com
- **Pros** Great climate; lots to see and do apart from the riding; great riding
- **Cons** No ski lift, having to arrange uplifts

With so many trails around the immediate area, San Remo is a great place to base yourself, whether you decide to stay in the city and ride the local routes, or head across to the Côte d'Azur to sample some of the equally great trails there. You can expect dry and exposed rocky trails through shrub-covered ground and lush wooded areas. This is a great place to trail ride or put in some winter downhill training.

Cross country

A network of 2000 km of specially equipped itineraries for mountain biking has been created within this cross-border region of France and Italy. Most trails are of a reasonable technicality due to the geology and terrain of the region, so not suited to beginners. The scenery and views are second to none and it is a truly great experience to ride

Practicalities ⌨🍴🚲

San Remo lies on the western Ligurian coast, and is known as 'The Pearl of the Riviera of the flowers'. Unsurprisingly then its main export is flowers, cultivated on its hills in the luxuriant botanical gardens. The year-round mild climate and low rainfall that help grow flowers also make great conditions for riding. There is a wealth of singletrack to explore and being only a short drive from the Côte d'Azur, with the cities of Monaco, Nice and Cannes, and a shed load more quality riding in the vicinity, this is a must-do trip when the weather is miserable back home.

Sleeping The *Nyala Bike Hotel* (T+39 0184-667668) in San Remo is well geared up to cater for all riders' needs, with a safe storage area for bikes and a laundry service for your sports clothes so you can keep your kit looking and smelling fresh. Or why not try renting out one of the apartments on the sea front at the *Residence Dei Due Porti*; they can be let from just €35 per person per night at emmeti.it/welcome/liguria/rivierafiori/sanremo/alberghi/porti/prezzi.uk.html.

Eating As you may expect from a traditional Italian city on the coast, there is a wealth of choice when it comes to eating out and you'd struggle to find a bad meal; try *Le Cupole* on via Roma 1 for a typical local trattoria, or the *Trattoria Del Ponte* on via S Antonio 5.

Bars and clubs Most of San Remo's cafés and bars liven up in the evening, and if you're looking for a nightclub then head down to the *Skybar* disco. If you're really wanting to live the high life while on the Riviera, then it has to be a trip to the *San Remo Casino* to try your luck.

Bike shop The *Nyala* Bike Hotel has some special deals set up with the bike shops in the city and can offer you discounts.

Internet café The *Nyala Bike Hotel* contains Wi-Fi in all rooms.

Bike map available? There is not a specific bike map of the area, but there are numerous websites offering downloadable routes and also GPS tracklogs so you only have to worry about the riding; sanremoguide.it is one of the best.

The Lowdown

Locals do... Hold some impressive silverware.

Locals don't... Tend to ride midday in the summer as it can get really hot. Early morning starts are the norm.

Don't miss... Heading over to ride in nearby Côte d'Azur, taking in Monaco, Nice and Cannes and, of course, Finale Ligure along the coast in Italy.

Remember to avoid... Being left mid-ride without enough water.

the small town of San Romolo where they have many mountain road rallies around the fantastic windy mountain roads. This is a serious trail over rocks from top to bottom with some steeper switchback sections. New trails have been added to the area and you'll need a vehicle for any uplifts. Into France and you have the proving ground of two multi world champions who live only a short distance from the Peille track. Add to this the old-school Grundig classic course of Cap D'ail overlooking Monaco and you are starting to build a picture of a quality year-round riding area. You can uplift in your own van but we recommend the service of the Argentina Bike uplift which can shuttle you and show you to the best runs.

Misty forests.

overlooking the sea and finishing up at the beaches to cool down and unwind after a hard day on the trails. With so many trails to choose from, covering a large area, we would recommend you use a local guide; Fabrizio Marani has amassed a wealth of trail knowledge (sanremobikescursion.com).

Downhill

San Remo is world renowned for its descent which starts 16 km from San Remo from Mont Bignone and ends in

Easy None of the runs here are easy; this is a spot for more experienced riders.

Difficult The downhill track that finishes in San Romolo is a gem; hit it again and again but make sure you have a well-maintained bike – it's a killer.

Freeride

Similarly to Finale Ligure, there are no specific freeride trails but any free-spirited rider will love the technical riding in this area. Just don't head here

expecting gaps and kickers galore; this is natural riding at its best.

ⓘ OPENING TIMES

You can ride the trails year round

Ⓢ RESORT PRICES

Argentina Bike offer uplifts; contact them at info@argentinabike.com

ⓘ DIRECTORY

Tourist Office: turismoinliguria.it
XC Guiding: sanremobikescursion.com

Italy San Remo

And a view of the Riviera. What a holiday.

Sauze d'Oulx

↘9 The trails

XC Cross country Fair/beginner to advanced

DH Downhill Good/beginner to intermediate

FR Freeride Good/beginner to intermediate

⊘ Uplift In Sauze 2 lifts take you up from the village, the majority of the trails start at the top of the first lift; there are 2 further lifts being adapted for bikes to link Sauze to Sestriere

✓ Pros Good quick access to the trails from the town; great riding in small area

✗ Cons No DH course and no XC trails in the bikepark

The trails here are beautifully sculpted, utilising predominantly natural terrain but with man-made features to enhance flow, maintain rhythm and link the sections. Floaty jumps and northshore

Beautiful flowing trails on mellow gradients make this a fun spot for all riders from beginners to pros.

sections are used to exploit the natural terrain to the fullest. There are currently plans to link this resort by lift to nearby Sestriere for the 2008 season, thus opening up more trails. The gradients are all fairly gentle so you won't be hauling on the brakes and pumping up your arms while still maintaining a good fast speed down the mountain.

Cross country

XC riders should take a look at the local website (sauzemtb.it), click on 'cartine & itinerari' for a couple of suggested loops. The bikepark does not have any specific cross country loops, although any mountain bike fan will love riding the trails in the bikepark which can be comfortably ridden on an XC bike.

The Lowdown

Locals do... Get to the top as the lifts shut for lunch then descend down to La Capannina to fuel up, before continuing down just in time for the lifts to open.

Locals don't... Ride so much XC here as the Sauze trails are so much fun they just session them.

Don't miss... September Fest, a small scale bike festival with a trade exhibition area. Basically a meeting of like-minded people towards the end of the bikepark season.

Remember to avoid... Straying off the marked routes in the bikepark; they have been designed to maximise the use of the terrain.

Downhill

There is no specific DH course in Sauze. A long travel DH bike may be overkill for the trails, but despite this you'll still have a blast as they are all downhill, fast and

WWW.SAUZEFREERIDE.NET

Above: Stopping to check out the view.
Below left: Sunset ride down, chairlift ride up. Sweet.
Below right: "Are the trees leaning or is it me?"
Opposite page: Mountain biking perfection.

flowing. You will love the trails even if they aren't the gnarliest in the world.

Freeride

There is a freeride area at the base of the Sportinia lift and various obstacles are well placed around the park on the trails. All the trails here could be tagged as freeride, due to the fact that they are natural downhills that have had man-made features constructed to help the flow and throw in a little air time.

Easy Take the Karamel trail from the first lift. This is a flowing, well-crafted run which even includes a 360° berm around a crater.

Difficult Take the Sportinia Express trail and halfway down peel off onto the Black Gruiz section, a 1 ½-km black graded steep, rocky and technical affair.

Practicalities 🖥️⚡🔋

Sauze d'Oulx is another resort located in the Piemonte region of the Italian Alps. Sauze d'Oulx itself is quite a small resort, but it has a large number of bars and restaurants it's a favourite destination for skiers from nearby Turin. The resort is well established with a tourist industry dating back to the early 1900s. In the 2006 Winter Olympics it hosted freestyle skiing events.

Mountain biking is a more recent development, but has been fully embraced by the community and this shows in the investment that has been made in the new bikepark. The area from Montgenèvre through Sestriere down to Sauze is known as the Vialattea (or the Milky Way in English); these are linked for skiing, so hopefully the bikepark will extend into the neighbouring villages before too long. In the meantime there's still plenty to enjoy in Sauze.

Sleeping *Hotel Gran Baita* is first choice for mountain bikers as it is based only metres from both the town centre and the ski lifts. The hotel also has a restaurant/bar and a sauna. *La Capannina* is a very different option based up on the mountain, meaning you can get up in the morning and start the day with

a downhill. Freeride lessons are also available here making this a good place if you are with family or in a mixed ability group. The *Orso Bianco* is another good choice in Sportinia, at the top of the chairlift from Sauze.

Eating As with most of Italy the local food here is fantastic and the residents take pride in providing the tourists with high-quality food, try out *La Fontaine Le Pecore Nere*, on via Assietta 40, or alternatively the *Old Inn Via Colle Bourget*, on 26 La Capannina, is a great place to eat during the day.

Bars and clubs There's the usual ski resort Irish bar at *Paddy McGinty's Pub*, on via Clotes 18, or go upmarket at the *Moncrons Cocktail Bar*, on via Monfol 8.

Bike shop *Besson Sport* in Sauze have freeride bikes available to hire and can also supply you with body armour if required. Basic spares are also kept in stock.

Internet café Look for *S@ms* internet café on Piazza Assietta 4 in the town.

Bike map available? Bike map available online at sauzefreeride.net and from the tourist office.

Val di Fassa

A small, new bikepark set amidst spectacular scenery with some fun trails overlooked by the steep signature limestone peaks of the Dolomites.

RALF BRUNEL/PHOTO ARCHIVE APT VAL DI FASSA

VAL DI FASSA

↘10 The trails

- **Cross country** Fair/intermediate to advanced
- **Downhill** Fair to good/beginner to intermediate
- **Freeride** Fair to good/beginner to intermediate
- **Uplift** 2 ski lifts take you up the mountain from Canazei
- **Pros** Amazing mountain vistas; quiet trails with perfect loamy soil in the wooded sections
- **Cons** Small number of trails; currently the only way back down to the lift is via a black run, so not good for beginners who would have to roll down the road

The bikepark itself only contains a couple of trails, but they have also mapped out a couple of longer tours. Val di Fassa is a fun trip at present but couldn't really sustain more than a long weekend stay. As a stopover as part of a longer trip though, it's great – and it's the incredible scenery that makes the riding that little bit more special.

Cross country

Cross country riders in the area will need to get the map out and find their own routes as there are plenty of trails in the area but these are not part of the bikepark. The park has mapped out a couple of routes you can try, setting out from the bikepark area, but both are longer tours in the region of 60 km so are only really suited to stronger riders. Guided rides on trails to suit your ability are available and can be booked in the bike shop.

Downhill

There are two marked downhills served by the uplifts. Double U, the first, is a higher up trail and not too difficult, making it good fun for riders of all abilities. The trail is 3.7 km long with a height loss of 457 m and includes bermed corners and fast singletrack on the higher slopes before going into the woods and bringing you out at the top of the second downhill, called Electric Line. This trail, which starts at the top of the first lift, is more difficult, being a more natural route. In the woods there are off-camber corners, rocks, roots, drop offs and steeper sections. These two trails can be linked to give you a long downhill with a descent of 900 m. The surface is a lovely loamy soft soil that allows riders to carve lines and drift through fast sections. Great fun. Under construction are another two lines on the lower slopes, which will mean there are easier and harder trail choices and a second line from the top lift giving a lot more variety.

ⓘ OPENING TIMES

The bikepark opens in mid-Jun and closes mid-Sep; 0900 to 1800

Ⓢ RESORT PRICES

Day pass: €16; Week pass: €46; Season pass: €110

ⓘ DIRECTORY

Tourist information: fassa.com; canazei.org
Bikepark: fassabike.com

The Lowdown

Locals do... Link up the two downhills for one long, fast downhill; time it so they get to the top before the lifts shut for lunch and at the end of the day for maximum riding time.

Locals don't... Hurry. There is a very relaxed pace to Val di Fassa.

Don't miss... The 360° panoramas from high up on the hills. Stunning.

Remember to avoid... If you are a complete novice. There is not enough choice here to learn safely.

Easy Take the Double U trail from the top of the mountain. This is a fast and flowing trail that cruises across the open ground. At the end of this you can take the newly built easier line back down to the valley bottom after 900 m of vertical riding.

Difficult The Electric Line is suited to riders who want to push themselves a little more. Although still not particularly technical it does contain a lot more natural challenge with roots, off-cambers and rocks.

Freeride

The two downhills mentioned above are perfect for anyone on freeride bikes. The ground is still quite fresh here and, as the trails do not get the kind of punishment some of the resorts in the French Alps do, they're more forgiving. There is also a northshore area next to the ski lift with all the usual skinnies and drops to keep you entertained at the end of the day or between runs.

Practicalities

Base yourself in Canazei, a well established, popular ski resort in the Dolomties, just northwest of Marmolada, the highest point in the Dolomites at 3343 m. This was the border between Italy and Austria before the First World War and the people here are proud of their German-speaking roots so German is widely spoken and understood.

At the time of writing the park here is new and still developing. It currently only offers a small variation in the way of marked trails, so don't expect a Portes du Soleil-style experience if you do make the trip. A weekend would probably suffice.

Sleeping Try the *Hotel Bellavista*, Streda de Poroi 12, in Canazei. This is a perfect place to relax after riding with a fully equipped wellness centre including sauna, Turkish baths and massages. There is also a good restaurant in the hotel serving local and Italian dishes. For the cheaper option, camp at *Camping Marmolada* for around €8 per person per night. It's close to the ski lift so is ideal location-wise after a long day's riding.

Eating *Ristorante Pizzeria Kamerloy*, on Via Dolomiti 22, and *Osteria La Montanara*, on Streda Dolomites 183, serve up typical local food and stay open late so you can enjoy a late-night drink.

Bars and clubs There are a few bars and clubs in Canazei. In the centre you can find *Speckkeller Pub*, in via Pareda 54, or *Roxy Bar*, in via Roma 52. If you are looking for a club there's *Deodat*, in via Dolomiti 5, which it gets pretty lively on weekends.

Bike shop There are 2 bike shops in Canazei, both of which offer rental bikes and the usual spares: *Northland Ski*, in Streda del Piz 15, and *Detomas*, in Streda Pareda 29.

Internet café *Dot.Com*, in Streda Dolomites 28, offers an ADSL connection, have Skype facility and can also offer translations, which may be useful.

Bike map available? Available in pdf online (fassabike.com/tracciati). The info point, *Fassa Bike*, at the base of the lift also have the bike maps.

Italy Val di Fassa

RALF BRUNEL/PHOTO ARCHIVE APT VAL DI FASSA

Above right: No shortage of cliff drops in the distance then!
Opposite page: Dolomite rock drop.

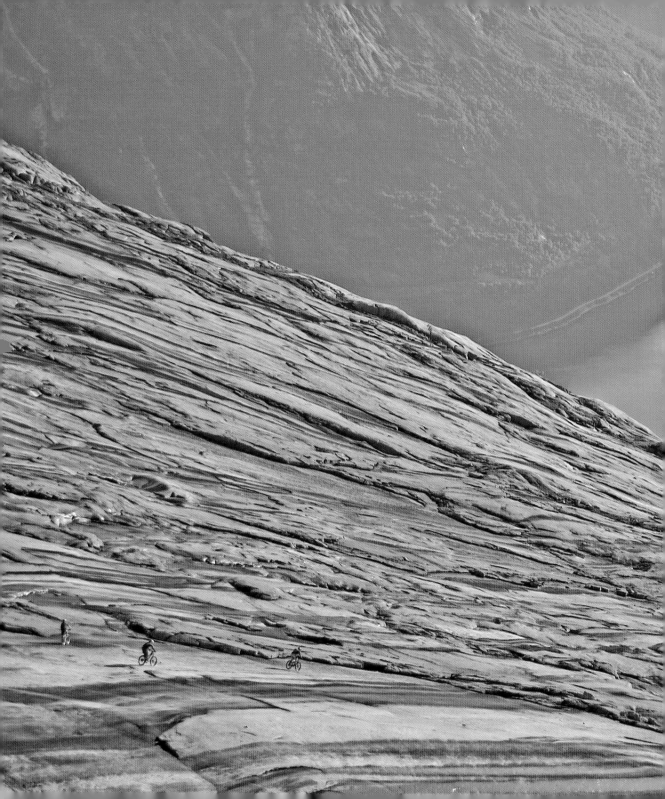

Scandinavia

There are rock gardens, and then there's Norwegian Rock. Staggeringly beautiful descent to the Fjords. [ENDRE LOVAAS]

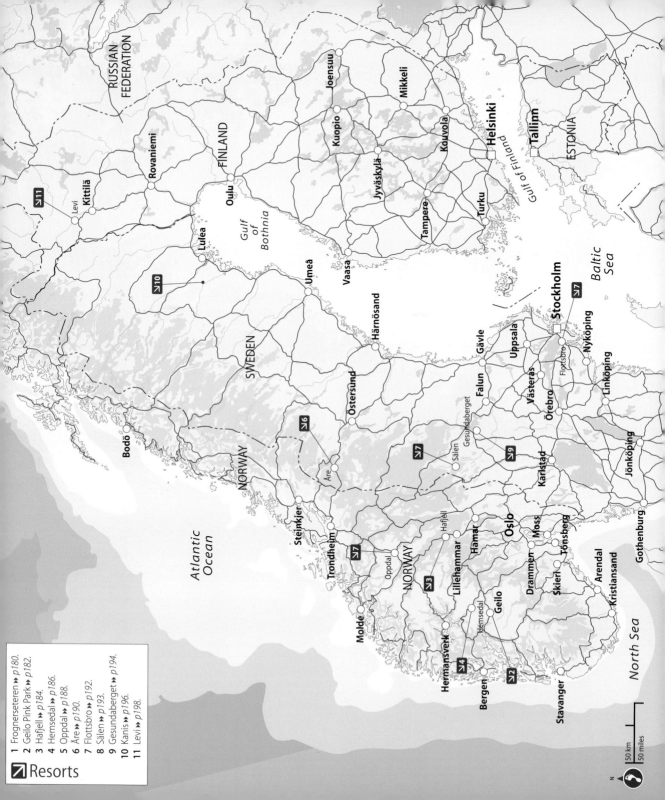

RUSSIAN FEDERATION

FINLAND

Rovaniemi

Kittilä
Levi

↗11

Oulu

Luleå

Gulf of Bothnia

Joensuu

Kuopio

Mikkeli

Kouvola

Helsinki

Tallinn

ESTONIA

Gulf of Finland

Jyväskylä

Tampere

Turku

Vaasa

Umeå

Härnösand

SWEDEN

Östersund

Åre

↗6

Bodö

NORWAY

Stein kjer

Trondheim

↗7

Oppdal

Molde

Atlantic Ocean

Hafjell

↗7

Sälen

Gesundaberget

Falun

Gävle

Uppsala

Stockholm

Flottsbro

Nyköping

↗7

Baltic Sea

Västerås

Örebro

Linköping

Karlstad

↗9

Jönköping

Lillehammar

Hamar

Oslo

Moss

Drammen

Tönsberg

Skien

Gothenburg

Arendal

Kristiansand

↗3

NORWAY

Hermansverk

Hemsedal

Geilo

Bergen

Stavanger

↗4

↗2

North Sea

50 km
50 miles

N

Hafjell wallride. Check the matching shoe/pad combination. Sweet.

Scandinavia's mountains might not be among the highest in Europe, but the Nordic countries have nevertheless carved out quite a niche in Europe's mountain biking scene thanks to some great trail riding over interesting, varied terrain and through beautiful countryside. The Scandinavian success story is proof that you don't really need huge mountains to build great trails. Smaller mountains are easier to manage, lend themselves to great parks and, thanks to shorter lift times, allow riders to mix up their runs.

Scandinavia contains great diversity as well, from the long, deep fjords of Norway, to the virgin wilderness of Sweden's vast parks and Arctic Levi in Finland, the northernmost resort featured in this book. Scandinavians are great outdoors people and know how to enjoy the tranquillity and nature that surrounds them. The more northerly resorts are also the best place to see the Northern Lights, a spectacle everyone should see once in their lifetime.

So look beyond the fact that the mountains are relatively flat and lack the grandeur of the Alps or the Pyrenees. The parks and facilities are great, and in reality it's not as expensive as legend has it. Above all, a trip to Scandinavia offers something of real substance for the visiting rider. If you are passionate about riding and travelling, you'll never regret checking out one of Europe's great riding and experiences.

Overview

ENDRE LOVAAS

Top left: Backflip over the park at Voss. Why not? **Top right:** Hardanger fjord riding.
Bottom left: Those miniature remote-controlled boats are great eh.
Bottom right: "No way is Chuck Norris harder than Sylvester Stallone."

ENDRE LOVAAS

ENDRE LOVAAS

Most people would be hard pushed to name more than two places to go mountain biking in Scandinavia, and in this light is seems as though the Scandinavians have been a little slow on the uptake when it comes to the mountain bike boom. Happily, this couldn't be further from the truth, and the Nordic peninsula is now home to some of the best parks in Europe. They just haven't really shouted about it, so most people won't know that Scandinavia contains a couple of belters in Åre and Hafjell, and numerous other smaller lift stations and resorts that are opening up, or that Flottsbro and Frognersteren are so close to exciting capital cities that they make a perfect weekend destinations.

In addition, Scandinavia is also one of the very best places to ride XC. Sweden's Right of Public Access allows you to ride anywhere in the countryside; and the adventurous can camp there too. It's a similar story in the rest of Scandinavia, with

wide-open spaces and challenging terrain making it perfect for mountain biking.

One thing to bear in mind is that the distances between resorts in Scandinavia are enormous, and it is certainly a lot quicker and easier by air than by road. But a road trip across this vast landscape has a certain appeal, thanks to its combination of amazing vistas and some inspired riding away from the masses: a fitting description o f riding in this part of Europe in general.

Conditions

Scandinavia's climate differs from country to country and north to south as it covers a large area. Norway's average midsummer temperature ranges between 15 and 20°C, making it perfect for riding. Sweden, similarly, is mild and pleasant in midsummer, while even Finland can see summer temperatures up to 20°C. There are no prolonged rainy spells, just occasional summer showers with west Norway receiving the most rainfall. Also remember that in the summer months, the northerly areas of Scandinavia enjoy 24-hour sunlight, adding a further intriguing angle to any trip here.

The scene

Scandinavia has produced strong XC riders on the world scene since the sport began and now has some up and coming talent in both downhill and freeride. It seems that, much like within the winter scene, Scandinavia will continue to develop its freeride side of the sport and become one of the standout areas in Europe. The Åre Mountain Mayhem Festival is already recognized as one of the bigger freeride events and one that always showcases young local groms pulling some ridiculous lines and style for their size and age.

Q&A with the experts

Eirik Evjen is a photographer, filmer and track builder based in Norway. He oversaw the ExtremeSportWeek in Voss in 2005, 2006 and 2007 and regularly works with Fri Flyt magazine (friflyt.no). He is also the online editor for Norway's biggest mountain bike site – utfor.com and recently made a commercial for Hafjell Bikepark along with his friend Christian Magnussen which can be seen at pinkbike.com/video/378/. He has been riding since 2003.

You've got friends visiting for just one weekend and they can go anywhere in Scandinavia. Name the one place you'd definitely have to take them.

EE I would without doubt take them to Hafjell, the best downhill and freeride trails in Norway. The have around 2-3 lifts and a gondola. If my friends are in to dirt jumping (as many of my friends are) it's also the best place as they've brought in Trond Hansen, who was 3rd in the Quasgai total. Hafjell also has a downhill trail (they are hosting The Nordic Championship in downhill this year), but it's not exactly the steepest track around. Saying that, they've made the most from what they've got.

Which trail centre or resort has the best party scene or the best after riding activities?

EE That's a tough one. The best 'one off' party is definitely at the Ekstremsportveko (ekstremsportveko.com) contest at Voss. It's the second biggest extreme sport festival in the world. I've been lucky enough to be the "head of mtb-freeride" there, and it's pretty cool. Voss is a two-hour drive from Pinkpark, so you could go there

and ride and also hit Voss to see the slopestyle contest and join the party. There are good party scenes at all the resorts, but Hemsedal has without doubt the best party scene.

Where did you learn to ride, and where would you send beginners to ride?

EE I learned to ride at my local trails at Frognerseteren. It's a good place for beginners, but the trails are only fixed one or two times a year by voluntary riders. The trails are easy to get to with the tram and cost very little. If you want to try out better trails I would send beginners to Hemsedal or Hafjell. Hemsedal is a little more adjusted for beginners, easier trails, although Hafjell works fine as well because of the chicken runs in all the tricky places in the trails.

In your opinion, which is the best downhill track in Norway?

EE Oppdal in the middle of Norway. It's the steepest and most technical. Oppdal is getting better every month now. The elevation team (the ones in charge of Mayhem Festival at Åre) are building track there right now.

Frognerseteren

Rider-built trails with the joy of a night in Oslo on your doorstep.

FROGNERSETEREN

↘1 The trails

- **⊗ Cross country** Very good/intermediate to advanced
- **⊗ Downhill** Good/intermediate
- **⊗ Freeride** Fair/beginner to intermediate
- **⊗ Uplift** Take Tram #1 from Majorstua to Frognerseteren, ride down the trails to Midtstuen tram station and take the tram back up again
- **✓ Pros** Great easy access location, makes a good city and riding break; easy to combine with a trip to Hafjell
- **✗ Cons** Anything more than a weekend will leave you wanting more

Shale by day, Oslo by night.

ⓘ **OPENING TIMES**

The tram network runs 0800 to 2400

Ⓢ **RESORT PRICES**

Day pass: €5

ⓘ **DIRECTORY**

As this is not a resort, there is no website specifically for the trails; the best place for information about riding in Oslo is the Norwegian forum site utfor.com; it's in Norwegian, but if you create yourself a user and post a thread and ask for advice the members will help out; the site will soon be available in English

There aren't many capital cities that offer downhill riding a few minutes from the centre. Try to imagine that in London! This is no bikepark though as you might think. Instead, the trails here are all built by the local freeriders who have created a strong riding scene in their city. Many of the trails follow or use parts of cross-country ski tracks, and while they are not steep, they are still good fun with a downhill/freeride bike. Most trails are pretty technical with

Kicking up the dust with a couple of mates. What could be better?

Taking the drip after riding the tram.

EIRIK EVJEN

EIRIK EVJEN

EIRIK EVJEN

EIRIK EVJEN

Scandinavia Frognerseteren

a lot of roots and stones. The lower slopes are more earthy and loose with berms, jumps and northshore elements.

Cross country

There is some pretty good XC riding around Frognerseteren, and it's possible to finish your ride right in the centre by heading downhill. In addition, there are countless cross country ski tracks to ride, and many narrow single track lines.

Downhill

The downhill here is fair. There is not a great deal of hill to play with and only so many runs but its a good to ride for the weekend and to get some runs under your belt. The trails have plenty of features but, as they're not very steep, you'll need to work quite hard to keep your speed.

Freeride

The local riders have built different stunts and features into their trails with jumps, berms and drops, as well as some northshore elements. Around Frognerseteren you can also find some dirt jump spots, and the street riding in Oslo is

The Lowdown

Locals do... Welcome visiting riders to their trails and are pretty helpful.

Locals don't... Disrespect the trails. They all put a lot of work into them and there is a trail culture here not dissimilar to that of the dirt jump scene in the UK.

Don't miss... The Frognerseteren Freeride Festival each year around May/June. Go to utfor.com for information about the festival. It's the perfect way to sample the trails and taste the local scene.

Remember to avoid... Hikers. Going down singletracks and steaming past them at 50 kph won't impress anyone.

Practicalities ●●●

The trails at Frognerseteren are just minutes on the tram from the capital Oslo, making this a unique and interesting weekend break or a great riding stop en route to the country's biggest bike park in Hafjell, a further 2-hr drive away. The city has a great location at the head of a fjord surrounded by forested hills. With easy access to the hills and trails and just a 10-min boat ride to take you to the lovely beaches of the Oslo Fjord Islands, it is easy to see why Oslo comes top in many polls as one of the greenest and most enjoyable city environments.

Sleeping There are plenty of hotels around Oslo. Sadly there are none specifically for mountain bikers. For the full range of accommodation on offer in the city to suit all budgets check out visitOslo.com. For a good budget choice try the *Lovisenberg Guest House* (T+47 22-358300) in the centre of the city.

Eating As you may expect from a large city there is everything from fast food to expensive gourmet restaurants. Try out the traditional Norwegian *Dovrehallen* restaurant (T+47 22-172101) or *Kaffistova* (T+47 23-214210) for tasty homemade dishes.

Bars and clubs Oslo has plenty to offer as far as bars and clubs go

meaning those that like to party hard as well as ride hard will be satisfied. You can also expect a more genuine experience that out in some of the ski resorts. Try out *Sikamikanico*, a lively bar and club, or the huge *Smuget* with five areas playing diverse (read: a little strange) different styles of dance music.

Bike shop There are numerous, well equipped bike shops in town. One of the best shops is Bikes and Boards (bab.no) at Grünerløkka near the centre. You could also hook up with other mountain bikers around this store to find all the trails.

Internet café *Arctic Internet Café* (T+47 22-171940) is at the main train station in Oslo centre. There is also an internet café at Majorstua where you take the tram to get up to the top of Frognerseteren.

Bike map available? There is no bike specific map of the trails, though many of the XC routes follow the cross country ski trails and these are mapped. To find most of the trails you have to follow your nose when up at Frognersteren or, even better, meet up with some local riders at the bike shop or organise to meet some riders beforehand using the main rider's forum (see Directory).

pretty good with the added bonus of no security guards or police chasing you away. There are a few good skate parks around the city as well, so if you bring a hardtail there will be loads to keep you busy.

Easy Take the Doseringløypa trail, a fun trail with lots of small berms leading out to some jumps.

Difficult Hook up with some of the locals and get them to take you to some of the bigger ladder drops around the park. They might also show you some of their street spots around the city if you're nice to them.

Geilo PinkPark

GEILO PINKPARK

↘2 **The trails**

- **Cross country** Fair to good/ beginner to intermediate
- **Downhill** Fair/intermediate
- **Freeride** Fair to good/beginner to Intermediate
- **Uplift** There is a chairlift to the top of the trails
- **Pros** Easy to get to, thanks to train stopping at Geilo
- **Cons** Expensive; not the best place if you have an aversion to pink

Whilst Geilo PinkPark is not going to make the executives at Whistler Bikepark lose any sleep, it is a typical family resort with varied, but not extreme, terrain. Although the park is not steep, there are obstacles

Where else in the world can you ride down ramps and boxes painted a bright pink?

① OPENING TIMES

The bikepark is open daily from 23 Jun to 19 Aug and on weekends during Sep; operating hours are from 1000 to 1700

⑤ RESORT PRICES

Day pass: 215 NOK; Season pass: 1200 NOK

① DIRECTORY

Tourist Office: T+47 3209 5900
Medical Centre: T+47 3209 2250
Taxi: T+47 3209 1000
Website: geilo.no

to challenge intermediate riders. Overall, the park is great for beginners and children through to intermediate riders.

Cross country

There is a well-produced guidebook with various routes around the Geilo area. Most of the trails are relatively easy and the book offers various graded rides; the harder routes head up onto shared hiking and biking trails running along the ridgeways overlooking the national park. The ground is quite rocky and drains really well so there are no problems riding here if it has been wet.

Easy Try the Havsdalen Tour, a 5-km loop that offers enough technical challenges to keep it interesting whilst being an easy ride.

Difficult Take the Geilohovda-Urandberget-Tuftelia-Ustedalfjorden Tour, a 13-km route that is scenic and interesting.

Downhill

The downhill Halinkast Trail hosts a round of the Norway Cup each year and is the most challenging of the trails on the hill, featuring technical root sections, kickers and drops.

Freeride

The park is laid out with the HeXe freeride trail running down to the Pink Park slopestyle and the bicycle cross trail. The freeride route is designed to be ridden by everyone so is suitable for less experienced riders and features kickers, tabletops, wallrides and northshore.

Clockwise from far left:
1. Christian Magnussen on the long northshore at 'Hekseløypa'.
2. Christian Magnussen on the wallride in 'Hekseløypa' (Witchtrail).
3. Eirik Evjen
4. Eirik Evjen

Practicalities

Like many of the Scandinavian resorts, Geilo has an almost otherworldly beauty when the light is right. It's one of the oldest winter destinations in Norway and is now turning its hand to mountain biking through the summer with the opening of their PinkPark. It opened its doors in 2005 and is slowly picking up the pace adding to its choice of trails each season. As far as the numbers go, its not the hugest place in our guide, but worth noting that its close proximity to Oslo and Hafjell make for an ideal combination break.

Sleeping Built in 1909 and with a spa and a couple of pools, *Dr Holms* is one of the more traditional hotels in Geilo. If you prefer self-catering to keep the costs down try the *Geilo Apartments* which are within walking distance of the slopes and boast free internet.

Eating Try *Halligstuene* (T+47 3209 5640) for gourmet local specialities or *Peppes Pizza* for an informal alternative. *Sofias Café and Bar* has great cakes and pastries.

Bars and clubs *Lille Blaa* is good for après and has a nightclub for the younger crowd. Another option is the *Recepten Club* in *Dr Holms*'s hotel, although the crowd is a bit older and it can be quite busy during the holidays.

Bike shop There is a bike shop in the bikepark that hires Norco bikes and has a workshop for repairs.

Internet café *Lille Blaa Café* has internet, and so have several of the hotels.

Bike map available? A trail map is not required for the bikepark trails and a well-produced XC tour guide is downloadable from the geilo.no website or can be picked up from the ticket office.

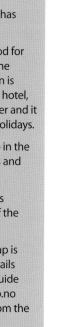

SIMEN BERG/BERGPHOTO.NET

SIMEN BERG/BERGPHOTO.NET

The Lowdown

Locals do... Blast down the Halinkast downhill, and have their lines dialled through the pinkpark.

Locals don't... Ride pink bikes; they clash with the ramps in the slopestyle area.

Don't miss... The after-riding session at the *Recepten Club* should really be experienced for the full Scandinavian drinking experience.

Remember to avoid... Opening a tab behind the bar here; they can be astronomical.

Hafjell

Hafjell, with good reason, has its sights set on achieving recognition as Europe's premier park.

HAFJELL

◢3 The trails

- **◉ Cross country** Good/beginner to intermediate
- **◉ Downhill** Good/intermediate
- **◉ Freeride** Good to excellent/ beginner to advanced
- **◉ Uplift** There is a chairlift and a brand new gondola
- **◉ Pros** Well set-up resort catering for most ability ranges; fun trails; interesting local area and landscapes
- **◉ Cons** It's an expensive place to visit

Hafjell bikepark is Norway's premier resort and with its well-built trails and beautiful scenery it offers an attractive package. The trails here will satisfy all styles of rider, but the park is perhaps more focused on the fun freeride trails. The park has set its

The Lowdown

Locals do... Go out in Lillehammer on Thursdays. It's a big night for local students.

Locals don't... Go out to party before 0100.

Don't miss... Spending some of your time in Lillehammer, which is a beautiful city.

Remember to avoid... Don't travel all the way here and not take in nearby Geilo PinkPark as well.

Above: The wallride – sideways Norwegian style.
Opposite page: Bike jump overlooking the seemingly never-ending forest.

Practicalities ⬤🔧⬤

Lillehammer is a small and cozy town situated near Norway's biggest lake, Mjosa. The city has kept its small-town charm, with small shops and cafés, yet still has all the mod cons of a bigger city. Lillehammer has four alpine resorts within an hour's drive of Hafjell and is the closest, a 15-min drive away.

Sleeping *Nordlia* cabins and apartments offer housing for 6 to 16 people. It's ride in, ride out, located on the north side of the Hafjell Alpine Centre. For apartments, *Gaiastova Hafjelltoppen Apartments* are located 950 m above sea level at the top of Hafjell. A good compromise might be the *Hotel Illsetra*, which has apartments with 2 bedrooms. They serve breakfast, lunch and dinner on request. Contact *Hafjell Booking* for different options, or book online at hafjell.no.

Eating *Restaurant Elgen* is located at the base of the ski area and offers an á la carte menu. For something less formal, try the *Hafjell Hotel* (T+47 6128 5550) which has a nice restaurant and pub.

Bars and clubs *Gaiastova*, at the top of the hill, has a relaxed vibe, while at the base, *Ryk og Reis* has live music and 'a happy vibe'. Then there's the *Brenneriet*, one of the biggest nightclubs in Norway, and the hippest club in Lillehammer.

Bike shop There is a bike hire shop, repair centre and training schools all run from the bikepark.

Internet café There's a wireless connection in the café in the base area. In Lillehammer intself you have internet at *Café Banken*.

Bike map available? A map is not required for the bike park trails due to the well-signed layout. For the back country XC routes see the staff in the bike shop.

ENDRE LOVAAS

the trails. There are easier graded family descents so anyone can enjoy the bike park experience without having to be a pro. The dirt jump trails at the bottom of the hill are of a refreshingly high standard for a public park.

Easy Catch the chair or gondola up the hill and take the family trail down, a very simple route made up from dirt roads and wider trails but with some small features in that will ease beginners into the descending trails.

Difficult Start out with the fun Buldre trail, pure freeride fun with berms, hips, step-ups and table tops. Also try out the downhill trail that will appeal to freeriders and downhillers alike.

sights on being the European equivalent of Whistler bikepark and, while it will need many more trails to rival the global leader, what it has built is of a very similar style and a great start for what is one of the more fun places to mountain bike in Europe.

Cross country

There is a cross country route in the park used for the Norwegian XC cup and it makes for a good trail ride. The backcountry riding is outstanding though, over great terrain that offers outstanding views. There are very limited trail maps, though, so you should get route information by talking to the bike shop staff.

Downhill

The main downhill run in Hafjell hosts races each year and is made up of traditional natural technical trail, coupled with a load of new-school wooden features and drops thrown in for good measure. The hill is not particularly steep so allows most people to ride the trail at their own pace.

Freeride

The freeride routes down the mountain in Geilo Hafjell are the bikepark's main focus as it builds up its range of trails each year in its aim to become Europe's premier park. There are all the usual obstacles and the hill is littered with jumps: stepups, step downs, gaps, drops and hips are all present complete with fun wallrides on

ⓘ **OPENING TIMES**

The bikepark opens at the start of Jun and closes at the end of Sep; opening hours are daily from 1000 to 1900

💲 **RESORT PRICES**

Day pass: 225 NOK

ⓘ **DIRECTORY**

Tourist Office: T+47 6128 9800
Medical Centre: T+47 6127 8279
Taxi: T+47 6122 2020
Website: hafjell.no; lillehammer.com

Hemsedal

Norway's most famous winter resort is now turning its hand to building a strong summer season.

Scandinavia Hemsedal

HEMSEDAL

↘4 The trails

- **Cross country** Good to excellent/ beginner to intermediate
- **Downhill** Fair/beginner to intermediate
- **Freeride** Good to excellent/ beginner to advanced
- **Uplift** The 8-seater Hollvin Express is the main lift for the gravity trails
- **Pros** Extremely beautiful part of the world; out of the way backcountry location; great XC area
- **Cons** Bikepark still very young and small; short lift season

The terrain around Hemsedal is predominantly open with beautiful mountains surrounding the town. These mountains make for some great biking and for XC there are trails for all abilities. In 2006 Hemsedal opened its first two purpose-built freeride/gravity trails, perhaps a little misleadingly named the Hemsedal and Skarsnuten Bike Parks (misleading in the

Martin Hjelseth.

ERIK EVJEN

Practicalities

Hemsedal, about 2½ hrs' drive from Oslo, is often called 'The Scandinavian Alps', and for good reason. At an altitude of between 625 and 1920 m the mountains up here are mighty and characteristic, with a distinct alpine feel to them. The town is surrounded by rugged and beautiful mountain landscapes and is close to the majestic Sognefjord, one of the world's longest fjords. The town is busy in the summer with hikers, people on elk safaris and trips to the Sognefjord. Mountain biking is becoming increasingly popular as the town looks to build on its great winter success of recent years: Hemsedal has become synonymous with quality freeriding in the winter months. The new built downhill trails and XC around Hemsedal looks to slowly build the summer season up to the heights of success achieved through its winter.

Sleeping Close to the Hemsedal lifts are the *Alpin Apartments* sleeping from two to 10 people and with various onsite entertainments. Also in the town are the *Haug og Bru-Haug* cabins which are a less expensive alternative for groups of 4 to 6.

Eating The *Experten Sportsbar* (T+47 3205 5410) is a comfortable place to relax and eat during the day or grab a snack between runs. Try out traditional Norwegian dishes at the *Fjellkafeen* (T+47 4157 4092) found in the ski centre.

Bike shop *Norwegian Adventures* (T+47 3206 0003) offer bike rental for easier touring and XC and freeride bikes. They have basic tools but riders travelling with their own bikes would be advised to carry any specialist tools with them.

Internet café *Hemsedal Café* (T+47 3205 5410) offers free internet use as well as a full lunch and takeaway menu.

Bike map available? There are 2 trail maps, one of the bikeparks which is available for free and one of the hiking/biking routes around the town to the various surrounding peaks which costs 95 NOK from the tourist office.

sense that both bikeparks only contain one trail). For the rider who loves to ride in beautiful landscapes and enjoys the freeride descents as well as getting out into the wilderness by pedal power, Hemsedal is a gem.

Cross country

The trail riding in Hemsedal ranges from easy family gravel tracks to technical mountain paths up to the surrounding peaks, and for the more adventurous there are longer overnight trips staying in the many mountain cabins in the area.

There is a bike map with graded trails and you can buy a book from the tourist office with the top 20 hikes in the surrounding mountains some of which make great rides.

Downhill

The downhill courses added in 2006 built in the freeride vein of the sport with plenty of jumps and drops. All quite small, and suited to beginners and intermediate riders; most downhillers will have a blast shredding the lines at speed.

Eirik Evjen.

SIMEN BERG/BERGPHOTO.NET

ⓘ OPENING TIMES

The lifts are open from 23 Jun to
19 Aug; daily from 1000 to 1600

⑤ RESORT PRICES

Day pass: 200 NOK;
Season pass: 1500 NOK

ⓒ DIRECTORY

Hemsedal Tourist Office:
T+47 3205 5030
Hemsedal Skicentre:
T+47 3205 53003 27

The Lowdown

Locals do... Ride from Monday to
Friday.

Locals don't... Mind a good drink; it
can be quite boozy at busy times.

Don't miss... A trip to the nearby
famous Sognefjord.

Remember to avoid... Norway is very
expensive, especially when it comes
to alcohol. Take as much duty free as
you can.

Freeride

The two routes in the bike parks are fun
freeride descents suited to most abilities,
as the features are not too big. The
Skarsnuten line is the more challenging
of the two with bigger jumps. The trails
feature drops, northshore, big bermed
turns and jumps.

Easy Follow the Hemsedal bikepark trail
designed for all abilities and with optional
drops and jumps.

Difficult Pick up the Skarsnuten trail
from the *Skarsnuten Hotel*, an expert line
with bigger more challenging jumps than
the Hemsedal run.

Oppdal

OPPDAL

⛰5 The trails

- **Cross country** Excellent/ intermediate to advanced
- **Downhill** Good to excellent/ intermediate to advanced
- **Freeride** Poor to fair/intermediate
- **Uplift** There is a gondola to the top of the hill
- **Pros** Great for XC riding; good downhill route
- **Cons** Poor for freeride at present; maybe too quiet for some people looking for after-riding entertainment

Norway's best-known downhill venue set in a beautiful area surrounded by a national park.

the tighter wooded runs in the French Alps. There are currently only two official downhill runs off the hill, but there are other trails that can be ridden if you look for them.

ⓘ OPENING TIMES
The gondola is open all week from 9 Jul to 17 Aug and is open on weekends from 23 Jun to 7 Oct; opening hours are 1100-1700

Ⓢ RESORT PRICES
Day pass: 200 NOK; Season pass: 1050 NOK

ⓘ DIRECTORY
Tourist Office: T+47 7240 0470
Oppdal Skicentre: T+47 7240 4480
Medical Centre: T+46 6471 6600
Website: oppdalMTB.com

The area surrounding Oppdal is both scenic and vast with much of the land being above the treeline giving great views out over the valleys below. On the descents the open ground makes for fast intense runs and the climbs and riding are through stunning countryside. Generally the trail riding above the tree-line is steadier, whilst in the trees it is super technical with plenty of roots and rocks to keep you focused on the trail.

Cross country

The XC riding out through the national parks is stunning, taking in lakes, glaciers, wide-open spaces and highly technical wooded sections of trail. The gondola can be used to gain some initial height and save some energy for the rest of the ride. You will need a hiking map to explore the trails around Oppdal, or meet with some local riders. Head to the bike shop to speak to the staff; they are all very knowledgeable on the local routes.

Downhill

The mountain regularly hosts Norwegian downhill races and has a good variety of terrain though most of the hill is open and quite fast, a nice change to some of

An Oppdal or Downdal, just stay clear of the dreaded Sidewaysdal.

TORE MJØRK

Easy Take the route labelled freeride, which is a gentler run down from the gondola station with less severe gradients. While still being a fun downhill route, it will ease you in until you feel confident to tackle the steeper trail.

Difficult Take the international-standard downhill route with its mix of wide-open fast sections, rocks and drops. You'll need a good day of runs to nail them and get up to speed.

Freeride

Oppdal does not have much for the budding freerider as most of the downhill trails difficulty is due to the natural features, rocks and speed that you ride them, not the built features found in some riding areas.

Terje Hovden.

TORE MEIRIK

The Lowdown

Locals do... Know some great XC rides out from the town. They are a friendly bunch too.

Locals don't... Ride without pads, the speeds are higher on the open trails, so you will feel any crashes more than on slower courses.

Don't miss... The long summer nights mean you can fit in epic XC rides if you are fuelled up and prepared.

Remember to avoid... Forgetting adequate spares such as drop outs, disc pads and a spare rotor. There is little chance of picking up specialist items like these in town.

Practicalities

Oppdal is a small town of just 3500 inhabitants some 120 km southwest of Trondheim. The town sits just to the north of Dovrefjell, a lush national park with herds of muskoxen that were transported to the area from Greenland in the 1930s. The town now relies on tourism as one a major sources of employment and revenue and the area has become known as one of Norway's finest downhill skiing venues, a title that looks set to carry over into biking.

Sleeping Self-catering apartments are available in abundance in the summer months. Try the *Hovdin Apartments* (T+47 7240 0800) which sleep 4-8

people with a bike storage room. The *Oppdal Gjestetun* (T+47 7240 0800) is a hotel-cum-motel located in the centre of the town with rooms sleeping up to 6.

Eating There are a number of places to eat around the town together with some gourmet restaurants a short drive from the centre. *Mollen* restaurant in the centre has a broad menu of western foods, but for a meal to remember, try the *Kongvsold Fjeldstue*, a restaurant serving local delicacies in nearby Dovrefjell.

Bars and clubs Hardly a party town, even after it has dumped a load of

powder, Oppdal's bars are quieter still through the summer season.

Bike shop There are 3 shops in the town all stocking various bike brands and parts. Try *MX sport* (T+47 7242 0810) or *Intersport* (T+47 7242 1637) for spares and repairs.

Internet café *Oppdal Bowling* hall (T+47 7242 2750) has an internet café and serves food.

Bike map available? A map is not required for the bikepark due to the signed layout; maps are available from the tourist office for the longer XC rides.

Åre

ÅRE'

↘6 The trails

- **Cross country** Poor to fair/ beginner to intermediate
- **Downhill** Good to excellent/ beginner to advanced
- **Freeride** Good to excellent/ beginner to advanced
- **Uplift** There is a cablecar, 3 chairs and a gondola all servicing areas of the bikepark
- **Pros** One of the best funparks in Scandinavia and perhaps Europe; very good infrastructure for all types of people, and families
- **Cons** Can be very windy; always need ID to purchase any form of alcohol

Åre bikepark has been working hard to make an attractive resort, not only for riders from within their country, but also

Sweden's biggest and most varied resort and one of the locations striving for the title of best European bikepark.

increasingly for people from all over Europe. In this they have been successful, mainly thanks to the number of gravity trails on offer, the excellent terrain in the park, the number of lifts, the impressive freeride set up and a great festival every year. As a result of this, Åre is becoming recognised as one of the top resorts in Europe.

Cross country

The bikepark has been created to recreate the winter experience and is focused on lift-fed riding. As a result there are no XC loops in the park but the grading system and number of runs from green through blue, red and black mean that any XC rider aspiring to some bike park

fun would find this an ideal resort. There are some great back country trails outside the park which require guiding or a good map.

Downhill

The hill has some great natural features with huge slabs of exposed rock interlaced into the trails. Again the

Pronounced 'Ore-a', this Swedish gem is easy to mine for nuggets of fun.

ÅRE TOURISM

VICTOR LUCAS

VICTOR LUCAS

Top: The bikepark is a beaut.   **Bottom**: The DH course is a smasher.   **Right**: And the views are bobby-dazzling.

The Lowdown

Locals do... Use Snus, a type of chewing tobacco, instead of smoking.

Locals don't... Go out on Wednesdays.

Don't miss... The Åre Mountain Mayhem festival; good people, good trails and good parties.

Remember to avoid... Flying to a Swedish airport; you could have anything up to an eight-hour transfer to Åre. Better to fly to Trondheim in Norway, leaving you with a 90-minute drive.

grading system allows all riders to have fun and feel suitably challenged on the hill and there is even a world championship course here dating from 1999 when Nico Vouillioz collected one of his 10 world titles. Overall, Åre is a great place to ride downhill.

Easy Catch the recently built easy rider blue trail from the top lift.

Difficult Take the Östra Stjärnvägen black graded trail, this is a super flowy and rocky trail.

Freeride

Åre has all manner of freeride trails, complete with a slopestyle area that houses the yearly Mountain Mayhem festival and sets of dirt jumps. Whilst the trails down the hill are incredible and do feature some jumps and drops, the great natural terrain means they are best left that way, which is exactly what the bikepark crew have done, for the most part. New for '08 will be the machine-built A-line style Shimano Project trail to keep the flow from top to bottom of the hill. Many hours and days can be spent on the Fox slopestyle area dialling in drops, wallrides and tricks.

Practicalities

Although this is Sweden's most advanced resort in terms of infrastructure, it retains a mellow, friendly feel. The town is situated above the train station, making for easy access, and most accommodation is within close proximity to the lifts, and only a short walk from the station and centre. Unlike some other Swedish resorts, Åre has a good variety of bars, shops and restaurants, and is perched along the Aresjon lake.

Sleeping For self-catering and smaller budget options, contact *Ski Star* (skistar.com). They look after a wide variety of properties including the *Are Fjallby* and *Brunkulla* apartments which are convenient, modern and well-located and will suit all needs. A cheaper yet very nice hotel is the *Diplomat Ski Lodge* (diplomathotel.com). The *Tott Hotel* (totthotell.com) is a ski-in/ski-out luxury hotel that has extensive spa, gym and pool facilities, for those with bigger budgets.

Eating *Broken* serves Tex-Mex and *TT's* next door also serves food. For a quick cheap breakfast get a pastry and coffee at the kiosk next to the Olympia lift.

Bars and clubs Tuesday is the big local night at *Bygget* nightclub. On Thursdays visit the sophisticated booths of *Dippan*, part of the *Diplomat Ski Lodge*. Check out the *Broken Bar* for laid-back beers, while the *Wersens* is also worth a look in.

Bike shop You're spoilt for choice when it comes to bike shops and bike hire; we recommend the *Åre Mountainbike Centre* (T+46 6475 0888).

Internet café Wireless is available in practically all the apartments and hotels. Ask for details at the reception. Otherwise the *Telia* on Åre square or *Zebra Café* both have access.

Bike map available? A map is not required for the bikepark due to the signed layout.

Flottsbro

FLOTTSBRO

↘7 The trails

- **XC Cross country** Good/intermediate
- **DH Downhill** Good/Intermediate to advanced
- **FR Freeride** Poor/intermediate
- **↗ Uplift** Chairlifts transports riders to the top of the trails on weekends and holidays
- **✓ Pros** Very close to Stockholm; excellent vacation area with beaches, mountain, city and sunshine
- **✗ Cons** Limited number of trails

The hill overlooks the beach and the lake, and conditions through the summer are usually warm and sunny, making this a pleasant place to mountain bike. The cross country routes and downhill courses are both of a good standard though there is little to interest the freerider.

ⓘ OPENING TIMES

The bikepark opens from May to the end of Sep

Ⓢ RESORT PRICES

Day pass: 160 SEK

ⓘ DIRECTORY

Flottsbro Booking Office:
T+46 8535 32700
Website: flottsbro.com

Cross country

There are two XC trails marked out with reflective signs that allow for riding in the evening. There are also numerous unmarked trails that are used by the large and successful Swedish MTB club Sparvagen CF. The trails suit beginners and experienced riders.

Practicalities ⬛🔧♿

Flottsbro is a popular tourist area just 20 min south of Stockholm. The beach on the shores of Lake Alby is a haven for sun worshippers.

Sleeping There is a large campsite on the sight and 55 holiday cabins available for rent at *Flottsbro Cottages* (see Booking Office).

Eating *Flottsbrogarden* is a restaurant and café on the lakeside with a sun terrace making it the perfect spot for lunch and dinner.

Bike shop The nearest bike shops are in Stockholm.

Internet café No internet café in Flottsbro.

Bike map available? A trail map for the XC routes is available from the lift station.

Downhill

The downhill course in Flottsbro is a reasonably technical affair suited to intermediate riders and above. The ground is undulating and quite rocky and the trail hosts Swedish downhill races.

Freeride

There is only an old dual course which has been adapted to make a 4X trail, but it lacks the flow of design of modern 4X trails.

Locals do...

End a hot ride with a dip in Lake Alby.

Locals don't...

Wear normal loose fitting trail gear here; it's still full on Lycra for cross country amongst the locals.

Clockwise from top left:
1. Up and over. 2. Berm.
3. Bigger berm (this captioning lark is easy, eh?) 4. A shrubbery!

Sälen

↘8 The trails

- **XC Cross country** Fair/beginner to intermediate
- **DH Downhill** Poor to fair/beginner
- **FR Freeride** Fair/beginner to intermediate
- **Uplift** Chairlifts transport riders bikes to the top of the trails
- **Pros** Modern resort with good infrastructure; good family or beginner trails
- **Cons** Limited number of trails; not challenging for skilled riders

Sälen is a very simple set up when compared to its big brother Åre. The trails are limited and all relatively easy, new trails are being developed as the park has only been running for a couple of seasons. The park is well suited to beginners and families as the trails are designed to be fun for everybody but there is not enough to really challenge highly skilled riders.

Berm, baby, berm.

Cross country
There are no trails set out in the bikepark, but the descents are perfectly rideable on an XC bike. There are numerous gentle backcountry trails utilized by the local riders.

Downhill
The two descending trails are suited to less experienced downhill riders as they are not very steep and machine built which creates a smoother freeride style descent.

Freeride
The two gravity descents are a hybrid between a downhill and freeride trails and are great for less experienced riders, with sweeping berms, smoother surfaces and various size drops and jumps. There is also a small dirt jump area.

Locals do...
Come in all shapes and sizes – boys, girls young and old – all trying out the new activity at their ski resort.

Locals don't...
Ride through the week.

ⓘ OPENING TIMES
The bikepark opens from 21 Jun to the end of Sep

Ⓢ RESORT PRICES
Day pass: 160 SEK; Week pass: 655 SEK; Season pass: 13,000 SEK

Ⓓ DIRECTORY
Sälen Booking and information
Office: T+46 771-840000
Website: skistar.com/salen

Practicalities 🖿🍴🚲

The resort of Sälen is made up of four smaller lift areas; Lindvallen, Hogfjallet, Tandadalen and Hundfjallet. The bike trails are found in the Lindvallen resort, a modern and well laid-out town although perhaps not as interesting as some of the older traditional resorts in Europe. Having said that, it certainly has everything you may need during your stay.

Sleeping The modern resort has a wide range, from large apartments such as the *Snortorget* to the smaller rooms available in the *Skilodge aparthotel*.

Eating *Majken's* restaurant offers good food and Swedish waffles together with evening drinks and entertainment.

Bike shop *Bikepark Sälen* offer a range of bikes and kit to hire and also will service and repair customers bikes.

Internet café Wireless is available in practically all the apartments and hotels.

Bike map available? A map is not required for the bikepark due to the signed layout.

Gesundaberget

GESUNDABERGET

↘9 The trails

- **Cross country** Poor to fair/ intermediate
- **Downhill** Good to excellent/ intermediate to advanced
- **Freeride** Good to excellent/ intermediate
- **Uplift** A 2-man chairlift transports riders to the top of the trails
- **Pros** Excellent use of modest sized hill; trails that make you grin; out of the way backcountry location
- **Cons** Poor for XC; backcountry location won't suit everyone

Gesunda is working hard to become one of the top gravity resorts in Scandinavia, and at the rate they keep building quality trails they will soon be right there at the top.

The trails created here are a testament to what is possible on a modest hill. Expect it to be quiet: at 300 km away from Stockholm they're a bit off the beaten track; which is a shame, as they are lovely, flowing and technical trails in a beautiful setting. In short, Gesunda

The Lowdown

Locals do... Ride pretty fast; some of Sweden's top racers practise at this resort.

Locals don't... All ride big rigs as something a bit smaller means you can hit the downhills, the 4X and the slopestyle on one bike.

Don't miss... The Mayhem Festival weekend held at the resort. This is usually in July.

Remember to avoid... Travelling all that way without a spare drop out and pads.

makes a great alternative bike holiday for the gravity enthusiast.

Cross country

There are plenty of paths and trails on the hill for cross country riding and this is great terrain for mountain biking. That said, a lack of marked trails means it is a little tricky to turn up and ride, so there are better resorts elsewhere for cross country riding.

Downhill

The downhill trails in Gesunda are superb creations. With fresh loamy soils and steep sections they are primarily cut to make narrow, flowing and quite technical singletrack with some real steep sections. Most downhillers will have wide grins after riding these descents and they have just added a new downhill which adds to the appeal.

Freeride

The recently built magic carpet freeride descent is a true rip-off of Whistler's A-line,

SIMEN BERG/BERGPHOTO.NET

Top: Pinning it in the pine.
Bottom: Auburn lifts. Pretty, huh?

SIMEN BERG/BERGPHOTO.NET

ⓘ **OPENING TIMES**
The bikepark opens daily from 22 Jul to 20 Aug and from 1100 to 1800
Ⓢ **RESORT PRICES**
Day pass: 160 SEK
Ⓓ **DIRECTORY**
Gesundaberget Booking Office: T+46 2502 140008 **Website**: gesundaberget.se

but is that a bad thing? The flow, berms and tabletops will have riders taking the lift again and again. There is also a great 4X trail – the largest in Scandinavia – some long northshore runs from the top of the hill through the trees, a dirt and slopetyle area and a foampit.

Easy Take a cruise down the magic carpet freeride trail with smooth berms and mellow tabletops; it's a fun blast down the hill.

Difficult Give the great 4X track a crack, everything is rollable but there are some big doubles and triples when you get up to speed for the confident jumpers.

Scandinavia Gesundaberget

Practicalities 🔲🌀🌐

Gesunda is a small ski resort and hill that has taken to building some great bike trails. Once again it shows that you don't need a huge mountain to have some excellent riding: the peak at Gesunda is just over 500 m. The hill sits on the shores of Lake Siljan, one of the largest lakes in Sweden and formed by a meteor impact some 360 million years ago. The town itself is tiny but comfortable and has a nice peaceful backcountry feel. The nearest airport is Stockholm, 300 km away.

Sleeping The *Gesundaberget Ski Lodge* (T+46 2502 1400) is ideally situated just below the slopes. Or try the lovely *Gammerstugan Lodge*, a traditional alpine building that sleeps 8.

Eating The restaurants at the top and bottom of the ski runs are perfect for your stay and while riding in the park. *Toppstugan* is located up the hill and has great views out over Lake Siljan.

Bike shop Take any specialist parts with you. For basic spares and repairs head to *Bjorns Skidshop* (T+46 2502 1210).

Internet café There is no internet café in Gesundaberget.

Bike map available? There is no trail map, but the park is very compact and the routes are quite well marked.

Top: Northshore descent down to the lakes.
Bottom: Dirtjumping in the forest.

SIMEN BERG/BERGPHOTO.NET

Kanis Action Centre

KANIS ACTION CENTRE

⬊10 The trails

- ❌ **Cross country** Poor/intermediate
- 🔽 **Downhill** Fair/beginner to advanced
- **FR** **Freeride** Good/intermediate to advanced
- 🔼 **Uplift** A normal drag lift takes you all the way to the top
- ✅ **Pros** Good variety of gravity fed riding; great trails
- ❌ **Cons** The town is a little quiet; expensive to travel to from the UK

WWW.KANISACTIONCENTRE.SE

Kanis Action Centre has focused its attention in high quality gravity trails and the park mixes more traditional downhill routes with some interesting freeride areas and trails.

With Kanis being so far away from any other centres it gives a whole different experience where visitors mix really well with the local riders and there's a friendly, chilled yet progressive vibe on the hill.

Cross country
Kanis has not built any cross country trails.

Downhill
While Kanis is far from the largest mountain in Sweden and will never provide a long, arm-pumping descent, it does provide a good variety of trails that

WWW.KANISACTIONCENTRE.SE

allow you to ride at maximum pace top to bottom and mix up the runs.

Freeride
Kanis is a freeride park with a 4X track, a large area of dirt jumps and a slopestyle course that are all found on the lower slopes. The northshore gaps and trails are to be found higher up the hill. Some of the downhill routes contain man-made

features to allow the rocky terrain to flow better and carry speed.

Locals do...
Spend a lot of time in the beautiful surroundings.

Locals don't...
Have any strict laws stopping them from riding where they want.

ℹ️ OPENING TIMES
The park is open from mid-May to 11 Sep; from 1000 to 1600

💲 RESORT PRICES
Day pass: €7; Season pass: €700

🕐 DIRECTORY
Tourist Office: T+46 9291 0860
Medical Centre: T112
Website: kanisactioncenter.se

Left: Coming up for another go on the ladders.
Below: Northshore wooden shenanigans – quite good fun.

Practicalities 🖥️🚲♿

Älvsbyn is a small town in northern Sweden, set in beautiful surroundings and tailor-made for those who enjoy being out in unspoilt countryside as much as they enjoy the trails. A visit to the area gives an insight into Swedish rural life as this is a corner of the country that is pretty much untouched by tourism (though many locals do speak English). Be warned though, travel to Älvsbyn is expensive and time consuming from the UK, with the nearest airport in Umea, just under four hours away.

Sleeping There is no problem finding affordable accommodation. The town has a hotel (polarhotell.com) and 2 campsites. *Nyfors* camping ground (nyfors.nu) is found 1 km from the bikepark.

Eating The bikepark has a small restaurant on site that serves good, nutritious dishes for hungry bikers. In the town there is a large selection of pizzerias, burger grills and cafés.

Bars and clubs The town is small and has 2 places to go out in the evenings: the *Kanis Action Centre* has its own pub while there is also a discotheque in the town centre for some *Footloose* action.

Internet café No.

Bike shop There is a whole range of bikes available for hire from the bike park and it also has a well-equipped workshop for repairs.

Riders' tales
Dan Milner: the things I've learned

*Mountain Bike Photographer **Dan Milner** is well placed to take the long view on the development of the European scene; he's been riding since 1985 and having his pictures published since 1992. Here are some of his views on riding, travelling and bike photography.*

4000 m up in South America. Quite a descent.

The appeal of the mountains

DM For me mountains are about getting out there and losing yourself in the natural environment. I like the challenges, both mental and physical. On a bike you have to make decisions really quickly, because you have to adapt to the trail in front of you. It's quite liberating, especially if the rest of your life is a bit more controlled.

Favourite riding

DM No-one likes to pigeon hole themselves but if I had to I would say that I'm a back country mountainbiker. If you think about it, it's impossible to get off the beaten track as a mountain biker, but wherever I am on the mountains I like to be pushed, and not know what's coming up. It introduces adventure into your riding, and it really tests your confidence as a rider.

Favourite landscape

DM Corsica was surprising for the incredible variety of landscape formations you can use as backdrops for photos. And then you have the Alps – the rugged, spiky peaks of Chamonix can be way, way different to the moonscape of Les Deux Alpes or the monolithic outcrops of Livigno. Those three corners of the Alps are really different terrain for photos or riding. For me it's the subtleties that work. For a photograph to work it has to capture the essence of mountain biking. Like the obstacle challenges on the trails and the shape of the trials themselves.

How to shoot

DM If you're not shooting professionally, then carry something light and rugged like a 450D. That's probably the best amateur camera around; that or a decent splash-resistant point-and-shoot. Don't just shoot the action though, make sure you get a load of incidental shots. A grinning face covered in muds tells as much of a story.

My first published shot

DM It was a story on Majorca and it was a self portrait. It was 'set the camera up' and then ride on the track for a few seconds. I was freelancing stuff but there weren't that many people doing it. And then the next year I did a race called the Transalp, that you did in six days across the Alps. Back then it started in Italy. Four of us drove down from England to do it and that was for Mountain Biker International back in 1992.

Travel and riding

DM For me, mountain biking isn't just a job. I use it as an excuse to travel and explore places. Even if I didn't do this I'd be out there checking a bike in at an airport. Going riding is the ultimate excuse for getting out and discovering bits of the world. It's a great way to see the world, and it's a great excuse to do so. It can be a pain in the arse too: a great big heavy bike can be difficult to lug about, but the rewards far outweigh the difficulties. It's a great way of meeting people. It's like carrying a cricket bat in India; everyone wants to come and talk to you.

The secret for taking good shots

DM It's not about the best place it's about the time of day. An inner city wallride can look just as amazing as a crazy descent in Utah if you're shooting at the right time of day with the right light and the right people. Early morning and late in the evening is pretty much the best light. Getting good shots isn't just chance. You've got to get up early or stay out to get the shots.

Levi

LEVI

⬊11 The trails

- **⊗ Cross country** Fair to good/ beginner to intermediate
- **⊕ Downhill** Good/intermediate to advanced
- **⊕ Freeride** Good/beginner to advanced
- **⊘ Uplift** 1 gondola lift
- **⊘ Pros** Compact resort; the people in the resort will probably speak better English than you
- **⊗ Cons** No waymarked XC trails; lots of good trails but you need a good map; unforgiving surface on DH trails.

Levi bikepark is 170 km above the Arctic Circle, which means that during the summer months the sun literally never goes down. You can ride from sun up, to, well, sun up. The vertical drop in the park is 310 m and the summit is open as it sits 100 m or so above the treeline. The ground is made up of hard exposed rock near the top

Finland's flagship resort on a mellow hill within the Lappish Arctic Circle.

of the hill, and earthy loamy soils in the woods on the lower slopes.

Cross country

There are plenty of backcountry trails through exotic Lappish scenery, but unfortunately, as with many resorts, they have concentrated on the gravity trails mirroring their winter ski set-up, neglecting the XC routes. Buy a good map and you can find the trails and make some great loops, or alternatively try and hook up a ride with some locals. Visit the bike shop for details.

Downhill

Finland does not have big mountains and Levi is its best downhill and freeride resort. It hosts yearly downhill races on its most difficult trail which contains the steepest sections on the hill. All the trails are graded to suit a range of abilities,

ⓘ OPENING TIMES

The bikepark opens at the start of Jun and closes at the end of Sep; daily 1000 to 1900

Ⓢ RESORT PRICES

Day pass: €14.50

ⓘ DIRECTORY

Tourist Office: T+358 166-393300
Emergency medical number: T+358 400-356498
Website: levi.fi

Above: There's a moose, loose, about this trail centre.
Below: Uplift mechanics. But can you get tea on the gondola?

The Lowdown

Locals do... Enjoy their summer bike season making the most of the long evenings and chilled atmosphere.

Locals don't... Ride with single ply tyres, as they won't last one run on the rocky trails.

Don't miss... Riding under the midnight sun; the Levi 24 is one 24-hour event that you don't need lights for.

Remember to avoid... If you hate mosquitoes, come prepared as they can be out in force in the summer.

"Is this the way to the Levi store?"

"Actually it's pronounced Leh-vee."

from beginner's right through to the Kona DH race trail for experts.

Freeride

The gravity trails in Levi contain different features with some out-and-out downhill tracks and others with a more freeride feel, packed with hips, tabletops and drops. There's also a nice wallride and several ladder drops on the routes. The dirt park has been designed by the Kona clump team and features sets of trick jumps. The Kona team are also responsible for the 4X track.

Easy Try the newly constructed blue beginners trail, which is suitable for all abilities; Then try out the red run.

Difficult Check out the slopestyle park at the bottom of the run with the usual boxes, drops and wallrides. For more technical descending try the black downhill trail.

Practicalities ⬤🏃🚲

Levi is situated in western Lapland, in the municipality of Kittilä, about 180 km within the Arctic Circle. The forest Lapps first populated the region in the 17th century and nowadays Levi is widely known as the biggest skiing and recreation centre in Finland.

The resort has been built in typical Scandinavian style with special consideration towards its surroundings and, even when walking around Levi when it is busy, you still get a sense of open space. There are regular flights from Helsinki to Kittilä (KTT) airport, which is about 15 km from Levi. From there you can take a regular airport bus right into the centre of Levi.

Sleeping With Levi being Finland's main resort through the winter months there is plenty of accommodation for the summer bike season. The *Levitunturi Hotel* has a range of room types to suit most people; alternatively try the *Moonlight Apartments* which sleeps up to 6.

Eating Relax over lunch at the *Alpine Café Paulig* in the lower gondola area, or for an aerial view try the *Palovartija Restaurant* at the upper gondola station. When evening time comes around, look out for *Restaurant Myllyn Aija* or *Wanha Hullu Poro*, both in the centre of Levi.

Bars and clubs If you want to try out some traditional dances head for the *Taika Dancing Restaurant* at *Hotel Levitunturi*. Those with a less cultural bent should head for *Hullo Poro Areena*, a club with 6 bars and 2 main floors.

Bike shop Superior rentals are found at the gondola area. Levi also has good selection of Kona hire bikes.

Internet café There is an internet café in the *Hotel Levitunturi*.

Bike map available? A map is not required for the bikepark due to the signed layout.

Scandinavia Levi

KRISTIAN HENRIKSSON

KRISTIAN HENRIKSSON

Scotland

Opening it up on a clear section of forest.
Totally Scotland. [DAN MILNER]

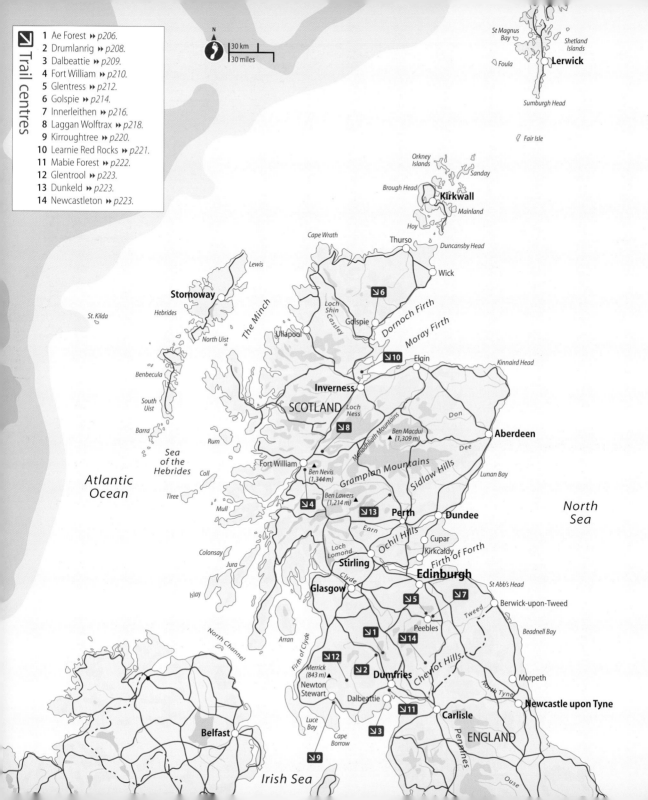

N

30 km
30 miles

St Magnus
Bay

Shetland
Islands

Foula

Lerwick

Sumburgh Head

Fair Isle

Orkney
Islands

Sanday

Brough Head

Kirkwall

Mainland

Cape Wrath

Hoy

Duncansby Head

Thurso

Wick

Lewis

↘ 6

Stornoway

Loch
Shin

Golspie

Dornoch Firth

St. Kilda

Hebrides

The Minch

Loch
Cassley

Moray Firth

North Uist

Ullapool

↘ 10

Elgin

Kinnaird Head

Benbecula

Inverness

South
Uist

SCOTLAND

Loch
Ness

Don

Aberdeen

Barra

↘ 8

Monadhliath Mountains

Ben Macdui
(1,309 m) ▲

Dee

Rum

Sea
of the
Hebrides

Coll

Fort William

▲

Grampian Mountains

Sidlaw Hills

Lunan Bay

**Atlantic
Ocean**

Tiree

Ben Nevis
(1,344 m) ▲

↘ 4

Ben Lawers
(1,214 m) ▲

↘ 13

Perth

Dundee

*North
Sea*

Mull

Earn

Ochil Hills

Cupar

Colonsay

Jura

Loch
Lomond

Stirling

Kirkcaldy

Firth of Forth

Edinburgh

Islay

Glasgow

Clyde

↘ 5

↘ 7

St Abb's Head

Berwick-upon-Tweed

Peebles

Tweed

Beadnell Bay

Arran

North Channel

Firth of Clyde

↘ 1

↘ 14

Cheviot Hills

↘ 12

Merrick
(843 m) ▲

↘ 2

Dumfries

Morpeth

Newton
Stewart

Dalbeattie

↘ 11

North Tyne

Newcastle upon Tyne

Luce
Bay

↘ 3

Carlisle

Pennines

ENGLAND

Belfast

Cape
Borrow

↘ 9

Ouse

Irish Sea

IAN LINTON

Ruaridh Cunningham at Innerleithen.

Scotland's wild rugged terrain could have been designed specifically with mountain biking in mind: it boasts the largest continuous area of high ground in the the UK, with a whopping 700 mountains over 2000 feet.

It come as no surprise then that this is big riding country with plenty to challenge the enthusiastic rider. One of the key factors here is also that the natural terrain is enhanced by its accessibility. Scotland's Outdoor Access Code, which gives everyone the right to have access to most land and inland water, providing they act responsibly, means the country has effectively opened up its countryside to adventurous riders.

The combination of these elements along, with world-class infrastructure and facilities, and a tourist board keen to promote the country's great outdoors, makes Scotland a world leader in mountain biking.

It is no coincidence that Scotland has twice been voted a 'Global Superstar' by the International Mountain Bike Association. One person well qualified to talk about Scotland is three-time world champion Steve Peat, who uses the country's downhill trails to hone his skills. "Scotland is the place I've used as a training ground for quite a few years and it's helped me go out and take on the rest of the world," says Peat. "A lot of leading mountain biking resorts around the world cater mainly for downhill riders – very few mountain biking locations build dedicated trails for downhill and cross country riding. That's what you have in Scotland and therefore it's Scotland that's really pushing the way forward in terms of catering for all levels of mountain bike riding."

Overview

Scotland's popularity as a mountain bike destination has been steadily increasing over the years, thanks no doubt to the increase in the number of trail centres and the raised awareness that the Fort William World Cup has brought to Scottish mountain biking. The country has a vast amount of open space in comparison to England and Wales, yet its centres are generally located quite conveniently close together, making it possible to tour the whole country in a packed two-week break. If you do have the motivation and nerve to trek across the open land now accessible to mountain bikers, then the possibilities are endless, but it is not for the inexperienced or unprepared as you can ride for days without seeing a soul in some of the more remote areas of the country.

Most riders will gain more instant thrills on the expertly designed trails featured in this chapter. If downhill or cross country is your thing, then Scotland has got it covered: when it comes to freeride the choice is rather more limited but spots like Glentress have some good play areas. If you had to take one bike then a 5 to 6" travel trail bike would allow you to not only enjoy the excellent XC trails but also tackle (albeit slightly slower) the World Cup DH course at Fort William and the infamous runs at Innerleithen.

Conditions

Scotland's position on the northern fringes of Europe with sea on three sides means that the weather is very varied. The driest months are May through August, with quite high rainfall levels through the winter. It is a common misconception, though, that it always rains in Scotland. In fact, Edinburgh's annual rainfall is only slightly greater than London's and many of the east coast towns have less precipitation than Rome.

Generally speaking, the east coast tends to be cool and dry, the west coast milder and wetter. July and August are normally the warmest months, with average temperatures of 15-19°C. The Scottish winter can be quite cold for bike riding, though this will depend on the conditions you're used to. Snowfall has steadily been declining over recent years and is quite unpredictable: bad news for the ski resorts but perhaps good news to mountain bikers as resorts look to increase their visitor numbers and turnover through other activities. Finally, a small consideration to be prepared for, are the armies of Scottish midges who love feasting on the blood of unexpected bikers. Midges are tiny blood-sucking insects with a voracious appetite, causing itching and swelling that can last several days. In summer they can make life unbearable in many parts of the Scottish Highlands. It is best to keep skin covered where possible and use midge repellent to help deter the little biters.

The scene

Scotland has a great scene on both social and competitive levels. The hub sites of Innerleithen and Fort William are developing internationally competitive riders; indeed Innerleithen is home to a Scottish Junior Downhill World Champion, Ruaridh Cunningham. At the trail centres, fed by the Central Lowlands where most of Scotland's population lives, there are regular meets between riders, often organized through the many web forums. The larger centres really encourage a chilled riding experience where you can hang out, with their onsite cafés and bike shops. There is both a Scottish downhill and a Scottish cross country race series which are very popular and use the best venues in the country. See sda-races.com and sxc.org.uk.

Top: Ruaridh Cunningham taking the Junior World Title at home in Fort William 2007.
Above left: Northshore surprise. Only the penitent man may cross. Wear your pads.
Above right: Gary Forrest at Innerleithen.

The industry

Scotland's mountain bike industry is somewhat limited, surprising when you consider the inspiration on the doorstep. Probably the most extensively used Scottish website is descent-

world.co.uk which is more focused on the downhill side of the sport, but the forums are full of trail meets. There are companies who are making the most of the landscape by offering guiding services off the beaten track; or try mountainbiketrax.co.uk and *Dirtschool* (dirtschool.co.uk) which offers coaching for all abilities.

ones with the most facilities on offer, and a variety of trails have been awarded double page spreads: these are Scotland's key destinations. Then there are single page centres which have some good trails but lack facilities. Then we have the best of the rest section where you will find downhill, cross country, dirt jump spots and four cross with brief explanations to point you in the right direction.

Scotland breakdown

While the UK can never compete in terms of uplift with the rest of Europe it still provides some fantastic destinations to ride your bike. We've aimed to pick out the best centre-based trails, the

Q&A with the experts

Chris Ball spent six years on the UCI Downhill circuit and is a former Scottish national champ. He now coaches the Scottish youth and junior MTB Teams (leading Ruaridh Cunningham to a gold at the Junior World Championships) as well as running a public coaching service named Dirt School. See the fantastic dirtschool.co.uk for more info.

You've got friends visiting for just one weekend and they can go anywhere in Scotland. Name the one place you'd definitely have to take them.

CB Scotland is small and compact enough to squeeze more than one trail into a weekend. Based from the Tweed valley, the trails at Glentress and Innerleithen are a must and could both be done in a long day or taken at an easier pace over a couple of days.

Which trail centre or resort has the best party scene or the best after-riding activities?

CB For pubs you want to choose the trails nearest to the bigger towns. You can have a good night in Peebles, not far from Glentress, or Fort William near Laggan and the Witches Trail. For a bigger night, get to Edinburgh, only 25 miles from Glentress and Innerleithen.

Where did you learn to ride, and where would you send beginners to ride?

CB The great thing about Scotland is its variety. I learnt on the massive roots and rocks of Dunkeld, the flat out fast straights of Fort William and the tight technical forestry of the Tweed Valley. There are more green and blue routes now than ever before so try the blue at Golspie for sandy trails and great sea views, or Glentress for a huge variety of all levels of trails.

In your opinion, which is the best downhill track in Scotland?

CB Fort William boasts the only World Cup track in the UK and gondola uplift too. The five-minute plus track sorts the men from the boys and you can ride knowing that the world's best have battled for the elusive rainbow stripes on the very same dirt you're riding on.

Where's best for total variety?

CB For the best variety try a road trip to as many venues as you can. The 7 Stanes trail network or Golspie, Learnie and Laggan are all grouped close enough that you'll find a huge variety all within an hour or so of each other.

Ae Forest

With both a quality downhill and an exciting XC trail, the riding here is at total odds with the tranquil setting.

◢1 The trails

- **⊗ Cross country** Fair to good/ beginner to intermediate
- **⊕ Downhill** Good/intermediate to advanced
- **⊕ Freeride** Fair/intermediate
- **⊘ Uplift** Service runs on some weekends and booking is essential; contact Uplift Scotland
- **⊘ Pros** Classic downhill track; trails never too busy
- **⊗ Cons** Not suited to novices; infrequent uplift service

① OPENING TIMES

The trails are open 365 days a year

ⓢ RESORT PRICES

All trails are free to ride

① DIRECTORY

Tourist Information Centre:
T+44 (0)1387-253862
Uplift Scotland: T+44 (0)7709-144299
Website: 7stanes.gov.uk

Scotland Ae Forest

Ae Forest is a venue traditionally associated with downhill events; the course has been hosting events for well over 10 years. The introduction of the excellent 7 Stanes project has seen Ae Forest developed into a more complete venue with the addition in 2005 of the red-graded XC loop. With a blue loop currently under construction it will soon have something to offer most types of rider. The trails here hold up well in all but the worst weather conditions.

Cross country

The red-graded Ae line XC trail lends much of its style and construction to the history of the downhill course in the forest. It leans heavily towards the freeride, fun style of riding with smaller versions of many of the obstacles that can be found on the downhill course. The 24-km trail will take between 1½ and three hours to complete, dependant on ability, and the series of jumps, drop-offs and tabletops towards the end are guaranteed to put a smile on any rider's face. There is also a short 4-km green-graded trail, but this is probably only suited to very young children as it does not contain much in the way of real off-road challenges.

Easy Currently the easiest trail is the red-graded Ae line trail. There is a blue route currently under construction so check the 7 Stanes website for latest updates on opening times.

Difficult If you're here for an XC ride then go for the Ae line trail; some sections are great fun to ride again and section, but make sure you are off the side of the trail when pushing back up.

Downhill

The downhill course at Ae is essentially one main line, but there are a few options that have been used to vary the line for different events over the years. It is not suited to beginners, but is a good course for riders with previous experience and

has a good mix of technical riding with the less technical berms and jumps.

Freeride

There are no specific stand-alone stunts or courses, but the jumps and drops on both the downhill and cross country trails will be fun to ride for any budding freerider, even if perhaps they won't challenge the expert rider.

ANDY MACANDLISH/FORESTRY COMMISSION

The Lowdown

Locals do... Grab a coffee and cake in the Ae café after a ride.

Locals don't... Hit the final descent of Ae line flat out as the jumps are too short; they cruise it.

Don't miss... The final drop in on the downhill course; a 25-ft almost vertical bank which is great to ride or watch.

Remember to avoid... Pushing directly up any of the trail sections as riders can approach at speed.

Opposite page left: Rocks, tape, speed. Perfect.
Opposite page right: Coming into land in the sweet spot at 30 mph. Go on!
Left: The XC isn't bad either.

Practicalities 🏕🍴🔧

Ae Forest is a 15-min drive from Dumfries, an ancient town with a long and turbulent history (English armies regularly sacked, plundered and occupied the town between the 1300s and 1700). Today, it is the largest town in southwest Scotland, the administrative centre for the region of Dumfries and Galloway and the focus of a large rural hinterland.

Sleeping There is plenty of accommodation in Dumfries. Try *Glencairn Villa* (T+44 (0)1387-262467), a B&B within walking distance of the town centre with wireless web connection, or for a self-catering cottage try the *Belmont Stables Cottage* (T+44 (0)1387- 268032) which has secure bike storage.

Eating There is no visitor centre at Ae Forest and nowhere to buy food so take some snacks with you. If you fancy eating out in Dumfries try the *Pancake*

Restaurant, (T+44 (0)1387-268523) or for a more formal meal *Casa Mia* (T+44 (0)1387-269619) offers à la carte cuisine.

Bars and clubs The *Globe Inn* (T+44 (0)1387-252335) was established in 1610 and was a regular haunt of the great bard, Robert Burns; check out the memorabilia. The *Venue* club (T+44 (0)1387-263623) has varied events from rock bands to house and techno nights.

Bike shop The *Cycle Centre* in Dumfries (T+44 (0)1387-259483) offers bike hire from Kona and has a workshop for repairs.

Internet café No, but try the libraries in Dumfries as they usually allow use of their workstations.

Bike map available? Yes, there are trail maps downloadable from the 7 Stanes website or you can pick one up from the bike shop.

Drumlanrig

⬎2 The trails

- ⓍⒸ **Cross country** Excellent/beginner to advanced
- ⒹⒽ **Downhill** Poor/n/a
- ⒻⓇ **Freeride** Poor/n/a
- Ⓩ **Uplift** None
- ✓ **Pros** Superb natural, technical singletrack
- ✕ **Cons** Not enough here to sustain a long visit but in close proximity to Ae Forest and Kirroughtree which makes a great round trip

In an area dominated by the Forestry Commission centres and their large budgets to create all-weather trails, what Rik Allsop has created on this private estate is both refreshing and remarkable. Due to the excellent mountain biking geology, the trails are all natural and challenging and have held up well despite their increased popularity. Add to this a stunning location with the impressive castle and lovely woodland and you have a great day's riding.

Cross country

There are lots of paths and fireroads suitable for young children and beginners, but what Drumlanrig is really famous for

The castle, spiritual home of the bike.

is the intensity of its red and black trails. At 15 and 23 km respectively, and with plenty of other options, there is plenty of ultra-rooty, tight and natural singletrack to keep you coming back for more.

Downhill

There is no downhill at Drumlanrig, but the highly technical nature of the trails makes them a great training ground and challenge for any aspiring downhiller.

Freeride

There are currently no freeride obstacles at Drumlanrig.

Locals do...

Ride in the wet, it makes the roots much more challenging and you can warm and clean up afterwards in the newly installed shower block.

Locals don't...

Disrespect the trails and the environment, they want the area to continue to grow.

The Lowdown

Locals do... Ride in the wet too, it makes the roots much more challenging and you can warm and clean up afterwards in the newly installed shower block.

Locals don't... Disrespect the trails and the environment. They want the area to continue to grow.

Don't miss... The final drop in on the downhill course; a 25-ft almost vertical bank which is great to ride or watch.

Remember to avoid... Pushing directly up any of the trail sections as riders can approach at speed.

Practicalities ⬛🍴♨

The nearest town to Drumlanrig is Dumfries.

Sleeping See page 207.

Eating There is a snack bar in the old stables on the estate which serves plenty of food for hungry riders. Dumfries also has a good choice of places to eat (see page 207).

Bars and clubs See page 207.

Bike shop Rik's Bike Shed is located in the grounds (T+44 (0)1848-330080) and offers bike hire as well as spares and repairs.

Internet café See page 207.

Bike map available? The routes are all well waymarked.

Dalbeattie

↘3 The trails

- ⊗ **Cross country** Good/beginner to advanced
- ⊕ **Downhill** Poor/intermediate to advanced
- ⊕ **Freeride** None/intermediate to advanced
- ⊘ **Uplift** None
- ✔ **Pros** Some interesting granite features
- ✘ **Cons** Quite a lot of forest road

Above: Up and over a bit of XC.
Below: With the Urr on your side, this is no time for caution.

The area has made an industry out of its granite reserves and no trail builder is going to pass on this as a major feature. Much of the trail is built up from, or runs on top of, the exposed granite which provides an incredibly grippy and bombproof trail. There isn't as much gradient change here so no prolonged climbs or descents, but plenty of features along the way.

Cross country

There are green, blue and red routes at Dalbeattie. The green loops are mainly on forest road and not suited to those looking to experience real mountain biking. The blue trail moves it on a level but it is the red Hardrock trail that is the flagship route here. It contains black-graded sections such as The Slab, a 15-m steeply angled bank of granite. There is a fair amount of forest road linking the sections of singletrack.

Downhill

There is no downhill at Dalbeattie.

Freeride

There are currently no freeride obstacles at Dalbeattie.

Locals do...

Meet up on Thursday evenings for group rides. Visitors are welcome.

Locals don't...

Ride too slow. Attack the trail, as speed is your friend over the rocks.

Practicalities ⊟🅿⚡♿

The trails are just a mile from Dalbeattie. Located on the beautiful Solway Coast, Dalbeattie is a modest town of about 6000 people sited in the sheltered valley of the River Urr, about 15 miles southwest of Dumfries. It is a comparatively recent settlement, having been founded in the 1790s as a planned town beside the water-power of the Dalbeattie Burn. Its industry has more recently been centred on tourism and, as is demonstrated on the trails, granite quarrying.

Sleeping Try the *Bellvue* (T+44 (0)1556-611833) a B&B in the town, or *Maidenholm Forge Mill* (T+44 (0)1556-611552) for a self-catering cottage.

Eating There is a choice of restaurants and pubs in Dalbeattie, try the *Sea Horse* (T+44 (0)1556-611173).

Bars and clubs There are no bars or clubs, just pubs with the more relaxed Scottish opening hours.

Bike shop *MPG Cycles* in Dalbeattie has bikes for hire, T+44 (0)1556-610659.

Internet café No.

Bike map available? Trail maps downloadable from the 7 stanes website.

ⓘ OPENING TIMES

The trails are open 365 days a year

Ⓢ RESORT PRICES

All trails are free to ride

ⓘ DIRECTORY

Tourist Information Centre: T+44 (0)1557-330494
Website: 7stanes.gov.uk

Scotland Dalbeattie

Fort William

☒4 The trails

- **Ⓧ Cross country** Good to excellent/ beginner to advanced
- **Ⓓ Downhill** Good to excellent/ intermediate to advanced
- **Ⓕ Freeride** Fair to good/ intermediate to advanced
- **Ⓤ Uplift** Yes; Britain's only gondola uplift
- **✔ Pros** Great facilities in town; ride some world-class courses; stunning setting when the weather is good
- **✘ Cons** Can be miserable in bad weather; not suited to beginners

Without doubt the most famous mountain biking destination in the UK. It hosted the 2007 world championships and is unique in having the only gondola-serviced downhill trail in the UK.

The DH course in all its snaking glory.

The trails are situated on and around Aonach Mor, Britain's eighth highest mountain (which stands adjacent to Ben Nevis, the highest). It's a typical rugged highland landscape and the downhill track starts from the top of the gondola with an impressive view. The ground up on the higher slopes is unforgiving, with soft waterlogged peat soils over the underlying bedrock. In order to overcome this the course has been built up out of stone and rock and the result is a rough and challenging track in keeping with the surroundings. There is also a huge following of riders who want to say they have ridden the World Cup courses (the venue has hosted 4X, cross country and downhill for several years).

Cross country

The main cross country trail at Fort William is the 15-km long Witches Trail. This fairly technical route stays on the lower wooded slopes of the hill in the Leanachan Forest. There are a further 40 km of trails in the forest ranging from easy, low level

Practicalities ⬤🍴🔧

The Nevis Range mountain bike and ski area is 7 miles north of Fort William. As the venue for the UCI Mountain Bike World Cup, the town is inundated with enthusiastic mountain bike fans and there can be up to 15,000 in the area at this time. Luckily 'Fort Bill' is very well equipped to accommodate so many people and there are loads of B&Bs, shops, restaraunts and pubs. This is all set in a location on the shores of Loch Linnhe, with Britain's highest mountain as a backdrop.

Sleeping Unless your stay coincides with the UCI Mountain Bike World Cup, you're not going to have any problems finding somewhere to stay in Fort William; there are plenty of hotels and B&Bs. The TIC in the centre of town will book something for you.

Eating There are plenty of takeaways, pubs and restaurants. The lochside *Crannog Seafood Restaurant* (T+44 (0)1397-705589) is well known for

its local fish and seafood. For pub grub try the *Grog and Gruel* (T+44 (0)1397-705078) on the main street.

Bars and cubs Fort William has plenty of bars to keep you busy through the evening. The *Grog and Gruel* serves a wide range of cask conditioned ales from Scotland, and the *Capercaillie* (T+44 (0)1397-706413) has a late licence and dancefloor.

Bike shop *Off Beat Bikes* (T+44 (0)1397-704008) is the specialist bike shop in the town. They have a fully equipped workshop and also hire bikes from both the shop on the High Street and also from the Nevis Range building itself.

Internet café *One World* internet café (T+44 (0)1397-702673) is on the High Street. There is also internet access at the town library.

Bike map available? Yes; trail maps are available from Nevis Range.

forest tracks and disused railway lines to technical purpose-built singletrack. In the car park there is a skills area to try out some of the obstacles that you might encounter out on the Witches Trail.

Easy The terrain and nature of the Fort William area means it doesn't really lend itself to easy rides for beginners. There are marked cross country trails in the woods that suit the less experienced rider but they are not purpose-built blue routes like you may find at other centres.

Difficult The Witches Trail is a great loop. At only 15 km you might think it's short, but remember that the world's best ride six laps of the trail, averaging 23 minutes a lap!

Downhill

The downhill at the Nevis Range is commonly known as simply the Fort William Downhill. It is one of the toughest on the downhill world circuit. Though it does not have many particularly steep

sections compared with some courses, the combination of the high speeds, big rocks and holes on the upper slopes and physicality on the bottom of the course make this a real tough test for riders and bikes. The top of the course is very exposed so can be difficult in very windy conditions. There is an easier route under construction down the hill.

Freeride

The 4X track at Fort William is a fun trail with all manner of jumps and obstacles of different sizes. Here you can learn to jump in a race environment where speed is needed to clear most of the jumps. There is also a dedicated dirt jump area near the quarry with three lines ranging from beginner to expert, with good progression throughout the sets.

Above left: The Witches Trail. Enchanting.
Above middle: More purpose-built XC. Cool, eh?
Above right: Fort Bill's play area.
Left: "Did I just see three men with green afros or is the length of the course playing tricks on my mind?"

Scotland Fort William

The Lowdown

Locals do... Section the downhill as it's a killer full run; float the rock sections.

Locals don't... Tend to travel up the the gondola in high winds as once at the top section of the downhill it can get pretty nasty; just ride the Nevis range, check the ride Fort William site for some of the other excellent trails in the area .

Don't miss... A trip to the top of Ben Nevis, if the weather is kind.

Remember to avoid... Riding on your own, always ride with a friend.

Glentress

Above: 7 Stanes perfection.
Below right: Like Goldilocks, you'll have to try all three drops to see which one is the right temperature.

GLENTRESS

N5 The trails

- **XC Cross country** Excellent/beginner to advanced
- **DH Downhill** Poor/n/a
- **FR Freeride** Good/beginner to intermediate
- **Uplift** None
- **Pros** Great for children and less experienced riders; good biking community atmosphere at the centre; well managed and maintained facility
- **Cons** Won't satisfy the diehard downhillers or freeriders due to lack of uplift and stunts; can be quite exposed when the weather closes in

Widely recognized amongst riders as the premier trail centre in the UK by virtue of its great location and varied trails.

Glentress is the flagship centre of the 7 Stanes and has a range of trails from green through to black. It is a great place for the inexperienced cyclist as the trails are well thought-out and riders can safely and slowly build their confidence here. The trails all run from the bottom car park and are predominantly through the forest, this does give way to some spectacular views on the more physical red and black trails. The ground is well drained and means these are all weather trails although the exposure in bad weather may prevent you riding. Most of the routes are surfaced with aggregates to really give a hard-wearing surface and the routes are well designed and fun to ride.

Cross country

The bulk of the riding here is cross country with green and blue routes designed to ease novices and younger children into off road riding before hitting the more physical and technical red and black trails. The red route is particularly popular as it has a good flow and some great sections: Spooky Wood is one such section containing tabletops, rock drops and 180° berms. The black route justifies its grading through its physical length and steep climbs rather than being any more technical than the red route. The black route will take you right out onto the hilltops and on a good day you will be rewarded with some stunning views.

Practicalities

The Glentress trail centre – flagship of the 7 Stanes development – is near the charming Borders town of Peebles, nestled in the picturesque Tweed Valley. Peebles makes the perfect base for riding the trails here.

Sleeping Peebles is a popular tourist hub so there is plenty of accommodation in the town. Try *Whities* (T+44 (0)1721-721605) for B&B, or the grand *Peebles Hotel Hydro* (T+44 (0)1721-720602).

Eating The *Hub in the Forest* is based at the trail centre in Glentress and they offer all manner of food for mountain bikers, most of it quite healthy. In Peebles try the *Sunflower* (T+44 (0)1721-722420) which produces award-winning food made from local produce.

Bars and clubs There are a number of pubs in Peebles. There is also a tiny late-night club/bar appropriately named the *Keg* for socializing into the early hours. Also hit *The Crown* pub (T+44 (0)1721-720239) which was frequented by the late Oliver Reed when filming 'The Bruce'.

Bike shop The *Hub in the Forest* (T+44 (0)1721-721736) has a wide range of bikes and stock of spares for repairs. They also have a fleet of hire bikes suitable for all the trails.

Internet café No.

Bike map available? Trail maps are available from the *Hub in the Forest* shop and café and also from the nearby tourist information offices.

Easy Start out on the skills loops found just beyond the Eagles Nest car park. It is a 1.5-km short loop to assess the skills of the less experienced riders. From here you can decide whether to head out on the green or blue cross country loops which are 4.5 km and 8 km respectively.

Difficult For an epic day in the saddle take on the 29-km black V trail which has some long and steep climbs in places. Stop at the northshore Ewok village and try out your balance skills there before heading back on the descents to the centre. If that hasn't tired you out completely then you should head up to Spooky Wood on the red trail or just play with your mates in the freeride area at the Buzzards Nest car park.

Downhill

There is no downhill in Glentress, but many downhill riders use the red and black cross country routes as training

ⓘ **OPENING TIMES**

Trails open all day, every day; may be closures for forest operations; check out the website

Ⓢ **RESORT PRICES**

All trails are free although the car park is pay and display

ⓘ **DIRECTORY**

The Hub in the Forest:
T+44 (0)1721-722104
Tourist Information Centre:
T+44 (0)8706-080404
Website: 7stanes.gov.uk

The Lowdown

Locals do... Head out on the trails early as it can be very busy; have some sneaky shortcuts and natural bits.

Locals don't... Ride long travel machines here, they're overkill for the trails; leave rubbish in the mountain shelter at the top of the black climb.

Don't miss... A fun blast racing your mates down Spooky Wood.

Remember to avoid... Holding riders up as the trails get busy; give way to faster riders.

rides and play in the freeride area. For downhill courses Innerleithen is only a short drive away.

Freeride

Glentress has a dedicated freeride area that is perfectly suited to beginners and skills progression. But that's not to say that the expert rider won't have a lot of fun on the tabletops, berms, drops and wallrides.

STEVE BEHR

Left: Northshore trickery with chicken wire help.

Golspie

SCOTTISHWOODLANDS.CO.UK

Scotland Golspie

⊠6 The trails

- **XC Cross country** Excellent/beginner to advanced
- **DH Downhill** Poor to fair/beginner
- **FR Freeride** Good/intermediate
- **Uplift** None
- **Pros** Varied trail that changes style through the gradings of the stacked loop; rugged, wild location; brilliant short stop vacation
- **Cons** If you ride the black trail on your first ride, you've covered everything already; maybe not enough to entertain a longer stay

The mountain of Ben Bhraggie stands imposingly overlooking the town and the infamous 1st Duke of Sutherland maintains a greedy eye over the trails from his monument near the start of the black descent. The trails here blur

The trails here are a long way away from anywhere, so something special is required to justify the journey to Golspie; luckily they do that and more.

the boundaries between cross country, downhill and freeride with features that will excite all riders. The material used to build the trails was all sourced on site and makes a great trail surface with huge slabs of sandstone to ride over and built up into technical features.

Cross country

The XC trails are built in a stacked loop format, which means that to reach the harder and longer black trail you have to first ride the red trail on the lower slopes. It works well and allows access to a blue, red and black trail in a reasonable sized area. There is also a family green trail, but it is the red and black trails that have gained Golspie its reputation as one of

SCOTTISHWOODLANDS.CO.UK

ⓘ OPENING TIMES

The trails are open 365 days a year

Ⓢ RESORT PRICES

There is a £4 charge to ride the trails

ⓘ DIRECTORY

Tourist Information centre:
T +44 (0)1549-402160
Website: highlandwildcat.com

Practicalities ⬛🚴⚙️

The town of Golspie sits on the shores of the Dornoch Firth in the county of Sutherland, a wild and beautiful place of high cliffs, islands, moorland and mountains, and some lovely sandy beaches. The town is overlooked by Ben Bhraggie, which is where you'll find the trails. Golspie has just enough to cater for your stay with hotels, pubs and places to eat out, and offers warm hospitality to visitors.

Sleeping There are 4 hotels and a few more B&Bs in the town. Try *Moray View* (T+44 (0)1408-634429) for B&B in the centre, or the *Ben Bhraggie Hotel* (T+44 (0)1408-633242).

Eating The *Ben Bhraggie Hotel* serves hot food. For good old fish and chips try the *Trawler* fish bar on the main street.

Bars and clubs There are no clubs in Golspie, but the pubs will stay open late during busy times.

Bike shop The nearest well-stocked bike shop is the *Highland Bicycle Co* (T+44 (0)1463-234789) which is 50 miles south in Inverness, so it is important to bring basic spares and tools with you.

Internet café No.

Bike map available? Yes, there are trail maps downloadable from the *Highland Wildcats* website.

The Lowdown

Locals do... Thank their lucky stars this is on their doorstep; section the best bits of the descent, it's a long way up from the car park.

Locals don't... Ride without spare tubes as the square edges on the rocks can easily shred a tube; smash their chainrings on the rocks in the climb – visitors, inevitably do.

Don't miss... A ride on what is clearly one of the very best man-made trails in the UK.

Remember to avoid... Getting caught out without any spares.

Far left to right:
1. There's something special in them thar hills.
2. Sharp bend coming up.
3. Goat track perfection. Although I doubt that the wooden bridge was built by goats.
4. But they definitely laid those stones.

SCOTTISHWOODLANDS.CO.UK

the very best in the UK. It is definitely worth combining a trip here with a trip to Learnie Red Rocks on the Black Isle, 52 miles away.

Easy Follow the easy blue route or, if you're feeling a little stronger, climb up onto the red trail which has some lovely flowing lines on the way down; easily rollable to all but complete novices.

Difficult Ride the full black loop. When you start coming back down, you'll want to do it again. Be warned though that this will require a high level of fitness.

Downhill

Golspie does not have a downhill trail, although on a shorter travel bike the descent from the top of Ben Bhraggie is worth every bit of effort put into the climb. Downhill riders will love this XC loop.

Freeride

Although there are no freeride courses or specific stunts, the trail from the top of the hill has various small drops, crests, tabletops and step-ups on its route that means a skilled rider will get the most out of it.

SCOTTISHWOODLANDS.CO.UK

Innerleithen

INNERLEITHEN

↘7 The trails

- **Cross country** Good/intermediate to advanced
- **Downhill** Excellent/intermediate to advanced
- **Freeride** Good/intermediate to advanced
- **Uplift** Uplift Scotland run transport to the top of the trails but only on certain weekends; pre-booking essential, see website for details
- **Pros** Great variety of downhill trails; technical riding; uplift available on some weekends
- **Cons** Not suited to novices or less confident riders; uplift only runs some weekends and is often oversubscribed

Innerleithen has a long history of mountain biking and it shows with a whole network of trails on the hill lovingly crafted by the local riders over the years and more recently by machine power. The area is definitely suited to the more advanced rider as the trails are all fairly technical whether it's XC, downhill or freeride. The geology here is also perfectly suited for mountain bike trails with an

ⓘ OPENING TIMES

The trails are open 365 days a year

Ⓢ RESORT PRICES

All trails free; uplift costs £30 per rider per day; car park is pay and display

ⓘ DIRECTORY

Tourist Information Centre:
T+44 (0)8706-080404
Uplift Scotland: T+44 (0)7709-144299; upliftscotland.com
Website: 7stanes.gov.uk

Innerleithen shale turn.

STEVE BEHR

This venue, steeped in downhill history, has been hosting national races since the beginning of time.

excellent hard stony soil that drains well making this a great all weather venue, though it can be very exposed at the top of the XC trail in bad weather.

Cross country

The XC trail is graded black and is both physically and technically challenging, so is only suited to more experienced riders. The climb is long, with multiple false summits, but the views are outstanding. Currently under construction are new red sections to make the option of a shorter

red graded loop which will open up this hill to more riders. Those who love natural riding will be spoilt with a plethora of paths on this and the surrounding hills, all unmarked, so they require some exploration.

Downhill

The downhill trails on Plora Rig are infamous. While there are only four main marked runs it's like a rabbit warren really with so many lines linking different sections. You could easily spend a day on

Practicalities 🛏🍴🔧

The village of Innerleithen, or Traquir as it is sometimes called, lies in the Tweed Valley, close to the Glentress trail centre. Their close proximity means they are sometimes referred to together as the Tweed Valley centres. However, the 2 centres cater for quite different groups of riders. Innerleithen was once a busy textile marketing town but nowadays trade is more focused on its beautiful surroundings and outdoor activities and it has for some time been one of the major mountain bike venues in the UK.

Sleeping There are a few hotels and guest houses in Innerleithen such as the *Traquir Arms Hotel* (T+44 (0)1896-830229) or for self-catering accommodation try *The Bothy* (T+44 (0)1896-831227) which is ideal for groups of riders.

Eating In Innerleithen there are loads of bakeries and don't forget to try the award-winning ice cream in the paper shop. Also worth a visit is the *Traquair House Tea Rooms* or the *Riverbank Restaurant* (T+44 (0)1896-831221) for hot food.

Bars and clubs There are no clubs in Innerleithen and there is a wider choice of pubs in Peebles. In Innerleithen you could try the *Tweedside Hotel*.

Bike shop *Alpine bikes* (T+44 (0)1896-830880) can be found in an old church in Innerleithen and are well equipped for all the riders using the testing trails in the area.

Internet café No.

Bike map available? Yes, there are trail maps downloadable from the 7 Stanes website or you can pick one up from the bike shop.

the hill and not hit the same line twice; not that you'd want to as many of the runs are steep and technical and require some learning. On many of the more natural style downhill runs expect plenty of roots and tight turns through the conifer trees (an Innerleithen trademark). The trails all run down to the bombhole jump, which has seen many of the world's finest racers launching into the finish arena over the years.

Easy None of the routes are too easy at Innerleithen, perhaps the easiest route down the hill being Make or Brake. Although the trail is made up of multiple jumps, they are all rollable for the novice who can cruise down what is probably the least technical trail on the hill if you keep your wheels on the ground.

Difficult If you're looking to downhill all day, why don't you book in advance onto one of the uplift weekends and spend a day mastering the downhill tracks, tackling the roots and pinning the turns.

Freeride

From the top of the downhill routes there is a trail called 'Make or Brake' which is a freeride trail made up of loads of tabletops, rollers and berms. It runs down to the middle forest road and is easy to section and push back up. A mid travel bike will get the most out of this trail. From the forest road you have the option of heading on down the final descent of the XC known as Caddon Bank which has a great flow on anything other than a long travel DH bike, or riding across to the left and picking up one of the downhill routes.

The Lowdown

Locals do... Rip! Innerleithen has raised some of the world's fastest riders; section the downhills, it's a long push from the bottom back to the top.

Locals don't... Hit the jumps when it's windy, Caddon Bank has a wind sock at the top just to warn you; ride without appropriate gear as the top of the black route is way up there.

Don't miss... A run down Make or Break linked into Caddon Bank.

Remember to avoid... Pushing directly up any of the downhill courses as riders can approach at speed.

Laggan Wolftrax

Short, fun and challenging trails in the Scottish Highlands with something for all abilities.

⅀ 8 The trails

- ⓍⒸ **Cross country** Excellent/beginner to advanced
- ⒹⒽ **Downhill** Poor/n/a
- ⒻⓇ **Freeride** Good/beginner
- 🚡 **Uplift** Uplift runs from the Base Camp MTB on weekends and busy periods; call to check on availablilty
- ✔ **Pros** Great compact venue; peaceful area
- ✖ **Cons** The trails are only short so you may exhaust the riding in a few days

Pick your line. Then pin it.

NICK BAYLISS

ⓘ OPENING TIMES
The trails are open 365 days a year

$ RESORT PRICES
All trails are free

ⓘ DIRECTORY
Base Camp MTB: T+44 (0)1528-544786
Website: laggan.com

Practicalities 🏨⚡🚠

The Laggan Wolftrax centre is just outside the village of Laggan, which adopted the fictitious name of 'Glenbogle' during the filming of the BBC drama 'Monarch of the Glen'. Found in the Central Highlands of Scotland and surrounded by the Monadhliath and Grampian ranges, it provides the opportunity to explore the peaceful countryside and spot a range of wildlife, from golden eagle or osprey to red deer, stags and pine martin.

Sleeping For bed and breakfast try the *Rumblie* (T+44 (0)1528-544766) in the village or if you are looking for a self-catered cottage try *Rowan Cottage* (T+44 (0)1226-383258) also in Laggan.

Eating There's not much choice when it comes to eating out in the village. The *Base Camp MTB* centre at the Laggan Wolftrax trail has a café selling wholesome foods. Laggan has two hotels/pubs serving food: try the *Monadhliath Hotel* (T+44 (0)1528-544276) on the Dalwhinnie road, which offers bar meals and a restaurant.

Bars and clubs There are no bars and clubs in Laggan but the two pubs will quench your thirst in the evenings.

Bike shop *Base Camp MTB* (T+44 (0)1528-544786) are based at the Laggan Wolftrax trails; they have a good workshop and hire bikes from Giant and Kona.

Internet café No.

Bike map available? Yes, trail maps are available from the *Base Camp* shop.

Wolftrax offers three main trails which are all cross country, but by their own admission they are trails with bite. They offer real variety ranging from flowing, easy and fun to highly technical double black runs. The highland terrain is ideal, with plenty of exposed bedrock and wild heather up on the hills. The trails have been designed to maximise the natural features on the hill and reflect the rugged terrain. *Base Camp* offer an uplift service at busy periods so you can make the most of the trails again and again.

Cross country

The three main trails are cross country orientated: the blue trail is in the funpark theme with great flow and berms; the red trail takes you up onto the hill and incorporates much more of the natural features of the hill with some great sections to attack; the black route expands on this, heading out further onto the hilltop and descending down over section after section of rock rolls and stone-pitched technical trail and requires good handling skills and reading of the trail to clean the full loop.

Easy Head out on the blue trail trying, the small jumps on the funpark descent. If you tackled this loop easily then after some lunch head out on the red trail which features more climbing and steeper and more technical descents; most mountain bikers with some off road experience should be able to tackle this..

Difficult Only one choice really; head out on the testing black trail, anything you don't clear first time round you can conquer on your second run after lunch.

If you still want some more look for the uplift bus and go around again.

Downhill

There are no downhill trails at Laggan, but swing your leg over a cross country bike and the black route will challenge even the best downhill riders, as it contains lots of technical rock features.

Freeride

The blue cross country descent has been built in the style of a funpark with big berms, tabletop jumps and sweeping lines, it will suit the learner freerider. Apart from this Laggan does not offer much in the way of catching air but the technicality of the black trail should interest most.

Smooth wood.

Open XC.

The Lowdown

Locals do... Incorporate all three trails into one loop; ask in the shop and they'll show you how to do it.

Locals don't... Ride long travel machines here, they're overkill for the trails.

Don't miss... A run down Air's Rock, a steep black optional rock-roll on the red route.

Remember to avoid... Riding the black route if you're not technically proficient.

Smooth wood.

Rock section.

Kirroughtree

📍9 The trails

- 🚵 **Cross country** Good to excellent/ beginner to advanced
- 🚴 **Downhill** Poor/n/a
- 🚵 **Freeride** Poor/n/a
- 🚡 **Uplift** None
- ✔ **Pros** Good rock features and sinuous singletrack
- ✖ **Cons** Not many descents so will not appeal to everyone

The cross country trails at Kirroughtree have gained a good reputation for their excellent contouring lines and the large granite rock features incorporated into the harder red and black routes. The surfacing used to build the trails makes for a very artificial road-type surface, but the curves and lines make up for this, mixed in with the exposed areas of rock. There is also a skills loop featuring multiple options of different gradings which is a great place to progress and try out harder lines.

Cross country

There are four XC trails at Kirroughtree: one green, one blue, one red and one black. The green and blue are ideal for younger riders and novices while the red and black trails pose more of a challenge for experienced riders with features such as the well known McMoab, a huge granite slab reminiscent of the Slick Rock trails in Moab, Utah.

Downhill

There is no downhill in Kirroughtree.

Freeride

No freeride at Kirroughtree.

Locals do…

Loop back up the forest road to ride the final descent of the climax again.

Locals don't…

Ride off the marked trails as the ground is soft and easily damaged by bikes.

ⓘ OPENING TIMES

The trails are open 365 days a year

💲 RESORT PRICES

All trails are free; car park is pay and display

① DIRECTORY

Visit Dumfries & Galloway:
T+44 (0)1387-253862
Website: 7stanes.gov.uk

Easy on the front brake, boss.

Practicalities 🛏🔧🍴

The nearest town to Kirroughtree is Newton Stewart, which lies about 3 miles to the west of the forest in Galloway. Newton Stewart is a small, friendly market town that accommodates all manner of outdoor enthusiasts looking to explore the Galloway hills.

Sleeping Try *Eskdale B&B* (T+44 (0)1671- 404195), one of many in the town.

Eating There is a tea room on the site which closes quite early so check times before you head out on your ride. In town try the *Galloway Arms Hotel* (T+44 (0)1671-402653).

Bars and clubs There are no bars or clubs in Newton Stewart, but there is a handful of pubs.

Bike shop *The Break Pad* (T+44 (0)1671-401303) is found at Kirroughtree Visitor Centre where all the trails start. They have hire bikes and carry out repair work.

Internet café No.

Bike map available? There are trail maps available from the visitor centre or from: himba.org.uk

Rock 'n' roll.

Learnie Red Rocks

LEARNIE RED ROCKS

⬃10 The trails

- ⓧⓒ **Cross country** Good to excellent/ beginner to advanced
- ⓓⓗ **Downhill** Good to excellent/ intermediate to advanced
- ⓕⓡ **Freeride** Good/intermediate to advanced
- ⓩ **Uplift** None
- ✔ **Pros** Good mix of flowing singletrack and tough challenging trail
- ✖ **Cons** You'll probably be able to ride it all in a day

The trails in Learnie Forest have been built by both machine and crafted by hand and you soon get the feeling as to which is which: from swoopy flowing singletrack to super-technical rock staircases, steep descents and power climbs, the riding at Learnie is really varied. There is a range of short but intense XC trails and a small jump spot.

Rock stair drop. Turn shocks to full absorption.

ANDY MCANDLISH/FORESTRY COMMISSION

Cross country

The XC trails range from sweeping blue grades and bermed reds to super physical black routes. The black does not have much height gain or loss, but when it does climb or descend you can be guaranteed it will be steep. There are some great views out over the Moray Firth from the top of the hill.

Easy Start out on the skills area at the car park before climbing up onto the blue route which has some great singletrack with constant left and right turns; you'll learn a lot about how to handle your bike here while having a blast doing it.

Difficult Head out on the black Learnie Hill Trail which contains steep climbs and technical sections. If you manage to clean all of this then go onto the Firhill trail, it's much tighter and requires good physical strength and skill.

Downhill

There is no downhill in Learnie, but the challenging hand-built Firhill will test any rider's ability.

Freeride

There is a small jump spot at the main car park and some skills obstacles there. Some of the northshore pieces in the black Firhill section of trail are challenging freeride pieces.

Locals do...

Know how to build a testing trail; they built the Firhill trail by hand.

Locals don't...

Ride single chainrings; you'll need your gears for the steep climbs.

ⓘ **OPENING TIMES**

The trails are open 365 days a year

💲 **RESORT PRICES**

All trails are free

ⓘ **DIRECTORY**

Tourist Information Centre: T+44 (0)0870-608 0404
Website: forestry.gov.uk

Practicalities 🛏💰🔧

The red rock trails are found in Learnie Forest on the Black Isle, which is not an island, but a peninsula jutting out between the Firths of Moray and Dornoch. The nearest town is Cromarty, an amazingly well preserved town at the tip of the Black Isle which serves as a quiet retreat while riding the trails away from the main tourist routes.

Sleeping Denoon Villa (T+44 (0)1381- 600297) and the Cromarty Arms (T+44 (0)1381-600230); both offer B&B.

Eating The Cromarty Arms serves home-made meals.

Bars and clubs There are no bars and clubs, only pubs in Cromarty.

Bike shop Mountain Bike Highlands and Islands (T+44 (0)1381-600386) is found in Cromarty only 4 miles from the trails and offer bike hire, guiding and servicing.

Internet café No.

Bike map available? Yes, trail maps are downloadable at himba.org.uk

Mabie Forest

Left to right: "I said Mabieeeee. You're gonna be the northshore that saaaves me."

MABIE

🚲11 The trails

- ⊗ **Cross country** Fair/beginner to intermediate
- ⊗ **Downhill** Poor/n/a
- ⊗ **Freeride** Fair/intermediate to advanced
- ⊗ **Uplift** None
- ⊗ **Pros** Traditional singletrack feel
- ⊗ **Cons** Not as exciting as some trails

Mabie Forest has boasted a small mountain bike centre from way back in the '80s, yet it was only when the 7 Stanes project kicked off that they gained some longer and more challenging singletrack routes to bring it up to date with the current riding scene. The trails are a mixture of natural and surfaced sections and are undulating while never involving too much climbing.

Cross country
The main route at Mabie is the 17-km red-graded Phoenix trail. There are also green and blue trails, although they are slightly disappointing, sticking largely to forest roads and established paths.

The real singletrack is to be found on the Phoenix trail and this is what most people will come to ride.

Downhill
There is no downhill at Mabie.

Freeride
The double black diamond graded (the toughest grading) Kona darkside is a 2-km northshore trail that climbs and contours along the hill over rocks and stumps. It is for experts only and requires excellent balance and trails-like skills to ride the wood, which is as narrow as 10 cm in places, and make the tight turns. There is also a small freeride area with doubles, tabletops and berms.

Locals do…
Meet up for regular Thursday evening rides at the centre.

Locals don't…
Clean the darkside section very often, despite the local knowledge: it's that tough.

Practicalities 🔧🚴🌲

Mabie Forest, the original mountain biking venue in the southwest of Scotland, lies just a few miles south of Dumfries. It is part of the 7 Stanes bike project and is easily accessible from Dumfries, the region's biggest town.

Sleeping See page 207.

Eating Mabie has a small cafe on site which sells some hot food and plenty of cakes and snacks. Dumfries has a good choice of places to eat (see page 207).

Bars and clubs See page 207.

Bike shop *The Shed* (T+44 (0)1387-270275) is on site at Mabie and offers bike hire as well as spares and repairs.

Internet café See page 207.

Bike map available? Yes, there are trail maps downloadable from the 7 Stanes website or you can pick one up from the bike shop.

ⓘ OPENING TIMES
The trails are open 365 days a year.

Ⓢ RESORT PRICES
All trails are free to ride.

ⓘ DIRECTORY
Tourist Information Centre:
T+44 (0)1387-253862
Website: 7stanes.gov.uk

Best of the rest

⊗12 Glentrool

- ⊖ **Difficulty** Very low
- ⊕ **Ability range** Low to high
- ⊕ **Length** 9-km blue or a long-distance 58-km trail
- ⓘ **More Info** 7stanes.gov.uk
- ★ **USP** Easy riding with great views of lochs and rolling hills

Glentrool is the family and novice orientated centre of the 7 Stanes. With a 58-km ride, all on forest road and minor public roads, there is no technical challenge, it's just a nice way to get out into some great countryside with friends or family. The 9-km blue route is 65% on singletrack but again this is of no great technical difficulty as it is fully surfaced with no rocks or roots and as such is suitable for novices.

⊗13 Dunkeld

- ⊖ **Difficulty** High
- ⊗ **No of Runs** 1
- ⊘ **Uplift** Only at organized events (upliftscotland.com)
- ⓘ **More info** sda-races.com
- ★ **USP** A good test of bike skills and a great training ground for downhill racers.

Dunkeld firmly holds the mantle as the UK's most technical downhill trails. It is made up of numerous rock gardens, with the upper ones on steep gradients and the lower ones mellower in gradient. That doesn't make them easy; there are roots and rocks aplenty to keep you on your guard. You can ride this venue anytime but can only uplift on organized days.

⊗14 Newcastleton

- ⊖ **Difficulty** Low
- ⊕ **Ability range** Low to medium
- ⊕ **Length** The longest loop trail is 10 km
- ⓘ **More info** 7stanes.gov.uk
- ★ **USP** A good beginner's introduction to trail centre singletrack

The trails at Newcastleton have been built with novices in mind. They feature more singletrack than those at Glentrool but are simple so are perfect beginner XC trails. They even feature some simple boardwalk and northshore section. For stronger riders, there's also the opportunity to ride across the Scottish/English border and into Kielder Forest in Northumbria (see page 66).

CHRIS MORAN

Scotland Best of the rest

Spain, Andorra and Portugal

Sam Dale and Josh Bryceland take on some Iberian rock. [VICTOR LUCAS]

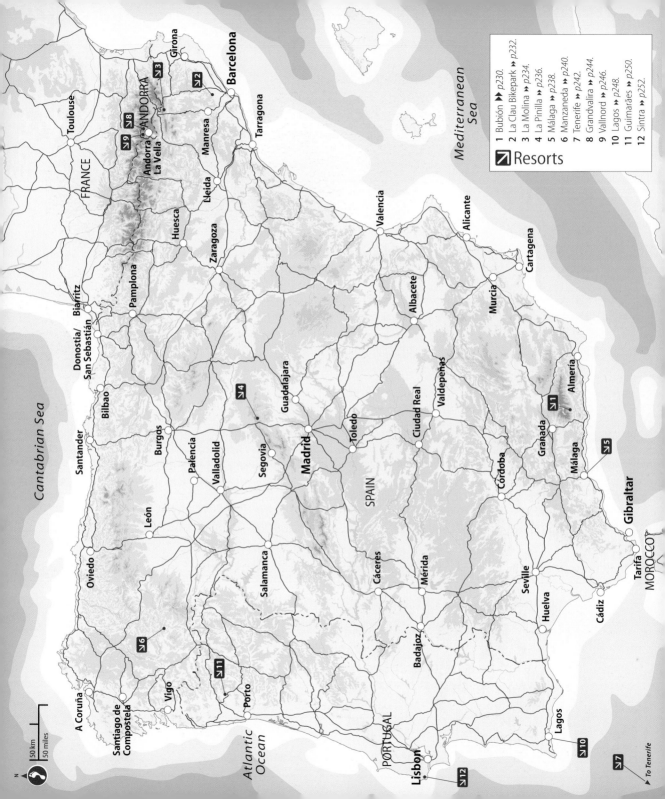

Cantabrian Sea

Atlantic Ocean

Mediterranean Sea

FRANCE

Toulouse
Biarritz
Donostia/ San Sebastián

ANDORRA
Andorra La Vella

Girona
Barcelona
Manresa
Tarragona
Lleida
Huesca
Zaragoza
Pamplona

Santander
Bilbao
Burgos
Palencia
Valladolid
Segovia
León
Oviedo
A Coruña
Santiago de Compostela
Vigo
Salamanca

Guadalajara
Madrid
Toledo
SPAIN
Cáceres
Mérida
Badajoz

Valencia
Alicante
Cartagena
Murcia
Albacete
Ciudad Real
Valdepeñas
Córdoba
Almería
Granada
Málaga
Gibraltar
Tarifa
MOROCCO
Seville
Huelva
Cádiz

PORTUGAL
Porto
Lisbon
Lagos

To Tenerife

50 km
50 miles

N

CHRIS MORAN

"I remember when all this was fields. About 3 million years ago."

Andorra, in the east of the Pyrenees range, is mostly famous as a winter destination, although is now coming into its own as a biking destination. These mountains are actually older than the Alps, and equally as rugged. The result is a bounty of biking opportunities married to some high-standard holidaying infrastructure. Certainly, the duty free possibilities in Andorra are legendary.

It's a similar story in Spain, which might rival France as one of the continent's most versatile riding destinations. It is a diverse country, with cultures to match, ranging from the whitewashed coast of Andalucia to the high-rise holiday apartments of the Costa del Sol. The options for riders are similarly wide-ranging and you'll be able to pick your trip depending on which side of the country you want to experience.

Portugal is also forging quite a reputation as a forward-thinking bike destination. With its long history as a premium surf spot it is perhaps not surprising that mountain bikers have taken to the country with such enthusiasm. Again, diversity is the key, with the laid-back surf town of Lagos and the metropolitan delights of Sintra and Lisbon both amazing options. Sun blessed, with a fascinating hybrid culture and incredible partying and cuisine, it is no wonder that the Iberian peninsula is fast becoming the centre of European cycling through the winter months. Here you'll find mountain biking of every type, fast developing riding scenes and three distinct cultures in which to experience them.

Overview

Sam Dale, Portugal, and what looks like a radioactive fart.

JOSH KNOX

JOSH KNOX

ROWAN SORRELL

Above: The thrill of two wheels is too hard to resist for most.
Bottom left: Dust – the staple diet in Iberia.
Bottom right: One day they'll finish that northshore line in Bubión.

Spain is a huge country full of varying landscapes. The riding here is similarly mixed, predominantly based on the differing climate and geography of the north and south. In northern Spain, the ski resorts can provide luscious pastures and lift access reminiscent of Alpine riding, though limited compared to French resorts.

In contrast, the temperate climate of the south provides a perfect environment for cyclists of all kinds and has long been a popular area for road cyclists in training. Until recently, the mountain bike scene has been reasonably low-key in the south, but a major influx of downhillers looking for winter training, and cross country riders wishing to rip up some of the world's best singletracks, has led to a real boom in the riding scene. Such has been the explosion in interest, numbers and trails, this is now the epicentre of Spanish, and perhaps European, bike riding.

Conditions

The country is full of high mountains and backcountry riding, and dangerous conditions come as standard. Although sunshine and dust spring to mind when Spain is mentioned, much of the country experiences cold winters and even snow, so make sure to visit the right region or you'd be better off packing your skis! The drier areas generally have deep, dusty and loose rocky trails where wider, more aggressive tyres will cope better in the conditions.

The south of the country may provide consistent warmth and sunshine, but, as with any mountains, this can change rapidly so pack well and be careful to check for severe weather warnings before heading off on that epic ride. Flash floods are common in Spain and being caught out in one will tend to affect your enjoyment of the ride.

The scene

Spaniards are mostly laid-back and welcoming people and the riding scene here is perhaps one of the friendliest anywhere. Turn up at any track, trail or jump park and make sure to say hi to the locals, shake their hands and you will be treated like royalty! The riders in Spain live for their bikes and love to build their own trails, which they will be more than happy to show any weary traveller.

Having said that, as laid-back as they are, the Spaniards also like to compete and there is now a flourishing race scene that encompasses downhill, cross country and particularly endurance events. There are several major series that are based in, or visit Spain, through the year so check the race calendars and plan your trip around an event to get a full feel of the fantastic riding scene here.

The industry

Though the majority of cycling industry is based in the richer European countries, Spain has its own manufacturers keen to get their products out there, and is home to MSC bikes, the European importer and distributor of Maxxis tyres. The warmth and variety of riding in the south is becoming a major attraction to bike companies the world over as a testing centre and the mighty SRAM hold an annual testing camp around Málaga to put their new products (and riders!) through their paces.

Spain breakdown

Scan through the Spain chapter and you will surely come across something to whet your appetite. However, it would be wise to think carefully on how to maximise your trip, as different areas will appeal to differing styles. Remember to avoid summer months in the south as the sun will be truly scorching, and don't assume that Spain equals sunshine – spring in the north can be wet and in winter time check for forecast snow.

Q&A with the experts

Tomi Misser is Spain's most accomplished downhill rider, and co-owner of GUAK with his brother Pau.

You've got friends visiting for just one weekend and they can go anywhere in Spain. Name the one place you'd definitely have to take them.

TM At home in Llinars del Valles where we have some good short downill (around two to three minutes long) and all kinds of XC and freeride trails. There's two natural resorts around the village, El Montseny, with longer downhills which are more rocky and fireroad trails. There's also El Corredor which is where I ride the most with good singletrack and terrain. But nothing is marked; you just need some locals to guide you.

Which trail centre or resort has the best party scene or the best after-riding activities?

TM If you really like to party you can go to Ibiza where you have one good downhill. We did one of the GPGUAK in 2007, which starts on the highest mountain on Sant Josep de sa Talaia and you can also find some XC routes. It's a beautiful place too.

Where did you learn to ride, and where would you send beginners to ride?

TM I learned in Linars del Valles where I live. All resorts right now are pretty difficult. I think the best to start is around your zone and doing a bit of all kind of mountain biking, but if you're looking for an easy pedalling ride you can go to the route of Carrilet which starts in Olot and finishes in Sant Feliu. All the vias verdes are interesting as they use to be the railroad network, so they don't have many steep uphills or downhills and they go through nice places.

In your opinion, which is the best downhill track in Spain?

TM La Pinilla which every year holds one of the Grand Prix GUAK and should be one of the best courses through the trees. It's got some open corners, and very little pedalling. The Catalunya DH in La Molina – on which we organized some GUAK competitions too – is a really good downhill for highly skilled riders.

Where's the best place to avoid pedalling uphill? Where has the best uplifts? Would you avoid anywhere?

TM We only have three real resorts with uplifts: La Molina, which opens all summer, La Pinilla in the centre and Manzaneda. Otherwise, it's pedalling for sure.

Where's best for total variety?

TM La Molina – it's got some really good downhills, good roads and XC rides. To get the most out of it though your riding level should be high.

Bubión

Donkeys, beautiful traditional buildings and epic rides.

BUBIÓN

↘1 The trails

- **XC Cross country** Excellent/beginner to advanced
- **DH Downhill** Excellent/ intermediate to advanced
- **FR Freeride** Poor/beginner
- **↗ Uplift** switch-backs.com offers an uplift and guiding service all year round and will show you the best spots to ride
- **✓ Pros** Escaping from the outside world – this area really is as secluded as it gets
- **✗ Cons** Lack of bike shops

Bubión, the Alpujarra and the Sierra Nevada region are stacked full of incredible singletracks, trails and downhill tracks. You could spend a lifetime exploring the mountains here and barely scratch the surface of what's possible. The trail network has been developing and that is still continuing now; expect rocks, dust and luscious forested trails. A guide is necessary in this region even for downhillers, otherwise you could spend all week getting lost, looking for the trails.

ⓘ OPENING TIMES

Open all year but note that weather in Dec can be treacherous and Aug can be dangerously hot

Ⓢ RESORT PRICES

n/a

Ⓓ DIRECTORY

Website: switch-backs.com

Spain, Andorra & Portugal Bubión

Josh Knox saw enormous spots for about 6 weeks after this photo was taken. Pretty trees though.

JOSH KNOX

WIG WORLAND

Poor shrubs. They properly get it eh?

Pinning the cobbles. Spanish style.

Practicalities ⬤🔧🔩

Bubión is a small timewarp village in La Alpujarra, a mountain region of southern Spain, home to tapas bars, hippies and the last hiding place of the Moors. The typically whitewashed and beautiful little villages of this region are a far cry from the highrises of the coastal resorts and act as great retreats for those wishing to escape modern life. As an indication of the pace of life here, local transport is commonly by donkey as opposed to the car.

Sleeping Look for 'Hostal' signs for cheap, yet usually quite high standard accommodation, or for a package try *Switchbacks* (switch-backs.com) who offer accommodation with their guided ride weeks.

Eating All around the Alpujarra you can find great tapas bars. The *Pizzeria* in Capileira serves great food at reasonable prices and the service is top quality.

Bars and clubs This isn't the place for a banging night out, though drinks are very cheap and bartenders in this region are usually more intent on seeing you have a good time than taking your money. There is a club in Capileira which comes to life at weekends but don't go expecting Ibiza sound quality!

Bike shop Bike shops don't exist in this area, for spares you have to travel to Granada, so carry the usual spares and any specialist parts for your bike.

Internet café The *Estanco* in Bubión has some stone-age computers, all of which adds to the great feeling of remoteness and distance from the outside world, though won't make sending a large file any less painful.

Bike map available? Bike riding isn't strictly allowed in this national park, so bike maps certainly don't exist! However, guiding outfit switch-backs.com is a registered company and has permitted access to the sublime trails – the only company that runs legally in this region.

Below: Rowan Sorrell
Bottom: Going for the overtake on some loose ground.

Spain, Andorra & Portugal Bubión

Cross country

To fully enjoy the mountains of this region you need a good bike set up with strong tyres and plenty of suspension. The trails can be pretty brutal to say the least which is part of what makes the riding so special; you ride up high into the mountains to gain some absolutely epic descents which have been described as the best around.

Easy There are plenty of fireroads and smooth rolling trails to keep even complete beginners smiling.

Difficult Try Lemmings, a trail named by the local riders that plunges into a gorge with rocks, water and cliffs aplenty; certainly not for the faint-hearted.

Downhill

In Bubión itself there are no specific downhill tracks, but the trails in this region are largely uplift suitable and nearby there are purpose-built tracks in Motril, La Zubia (a popular training track with pro riders from all over the world) and Pradallano (summer only-chairlift and home to the 1999 World Championship downhill).

Freeride

There are no freeride trails in and around Bubión, only miles of endless singletrack.

The Lowdown

Locals do... Ride prepared – this is the backcountry and you can easily get caught out in very severe weather. Always take spares and check for weather warnings before setting out on that epic ride!

Locals don't... Finish a ride anywhere but a tapas bar to take in some free snacks, soothing local beer and the natural beauty of this incredible area.

Don't miss... Local fiestas throughout summer; the towns essentially close down for a week and everybody parties!

Remember to avoid... Riding without a pack for fluids and to carry some basic spares as the trails can be miles from base and it can get very hot.

La Clau Bikepark

LA CLAU BIKEPARK

↘2 The trails

- **XC Cross country** Fair/beginner to intermediate
- **DH Downhill** Fair/beginner to intermediate
- **FR Freeride** Good/beginner to intermediate
- **Uplift** There is no uplift here as the trails don't require one
- **Pros** Quiet Spanish mountain village; variety of circuits and obstacles to choose from
- **Cons** There are no hotels and if you don´t have transport you won´t be able to catch a bus or a train here

La Clau is all about the fun elements and playing on your bike. There are no serious downhill routes or waymarked XC but plenty of drops, jumps and obstacles crammed into a modest area. It is best suited to less experienced and intermediate riders who will learn a lot on the progressive range of trails.

Cross country

There are a number of XC loops in the area around the park but they are not

Gap transfer over 'The Claw'.

waymarked so it is best to contact the park in advance to arrange for directions or to hook up with some of the friendly local riders.

Downhill

There are small downhill sections of trail in the park, but no downhill tracks per se. Most riders will enjoy playing on the different jumps and freeride areas,

though a downhill bike is not the best suited for this.

Freeride

There is a national standard BMX track, various natural step-down and play areas with drops etc, a dual course, a set of dirt jumps with various easier and harder lines, trials sections, a jump box and a foam pit. For riders looking to chill out in the sun while having a blast on the trails and dialling tricks on the box and pit this is paradise.

① OPENING TIMES

The park is open 365 days a year

⑤ RESORT PRICES

Day pass: €10; Season pass: €50

① DIRECTORY

Taxi: T+93 735-7777
Website: bikelaclau.com

The Lowdown

Locals do... Always wear a helmet in the park and when riding the dirt jumps.

Locals don't... Ride when it has been raining as the trails cut up badly.

Don't miss... The festival held at the venue once a year in November.

Remember to avoid... You should make sure you leave the park before six in the evening or you may find your car has been locked in.

Practicalities 🏠🚲🏃

The nearest town to the park is the tiny Sant Llorenc Savall, a small town halfway up the mountainside. With a population of just 2000, everybody knows everybody and there is little to no accommodation. However, this is the true Spain and spending some time here getting to know the locals is a must. The river Ripoll and adjacent national park is full of wildlife and is worth checking out at the foot of the valley. La Clau is a great stopover if you fly into Barcelona airport en route to any of the resorts in the Pyrenees.

Sleeping With no choice in the village try *Fonda Huix* in Sabadell (T+93 716-0275) 20 km away.

Eating If you are visiting La Clau on the weekends, there is a bar on site serving food and drinks and also with a small workshop area. The village is built around bar culture so you will be

spoilt for choice. Try *Cal Ramon* in the centre of the village and ask for their menu of the day. Three plates with a dessert and coffee for under €10 is a delicious steal.

Bars and clubs Head for the interestingly named club, *El Crack*, which opens from dusk till dawn.

Bike shop There is no bike shop in the town so make sure you bring any supplies and spares with you. The nearest shops are in Sabadell town 20 km away.

Internet café Bring your pen and paper as there are no internet cafés here.

Bike map available? Bike maps are not required in the park; to get directions for longer XC loops you will need to email via the web page bikelaclau.com.

Riders' tales
Road bikes v mountain bikes by Stuart Millar (*The Guardian*)

About halfway up the hour-long first climb, it occurred to me that this might not turn out to be the roaring triumph I had hoped for. The plan had been simple: take two friends who are hardcore road riders – one of them a former London cycle courier – and transplant them on to bikes with suspension and knobbly tyres and convert them to the one true path that is mountain biking.

Then came reality. Almost from the start, one of them was struggling on the sharp, slippery uphills that kick off the 15-km Twrch Trail at Cwmcarn. After one tricky section, he threw down his gleaming new Trek full-suspension rig – the same one he'd been lovingly stroking in the car park – and growled: "First thing Monday morning, that bastard is going on eBay!"

The Twrch Trail climb is a test for experienced riders, so it's fair to say I was chucking them in at the deep end. Yet I had assumed that all those hours in the saddle would be more than enough to carry him through the initial shock of not being on smooth asphalt. That's when it dawned on me that the differences between mountain biking and road riding may be more fundamental than I had anticipated.

The biggest, of course, is the terrain. Riding off road requires three-dimensional thinking: it's not enough just to be able to propel the bike forward; you also have to propel it over a surface that can change with every pedal stroke. On narrow sections of singletrack, with steep drops to the side, there is always the nagging thought that any mistake on the rocks and roots will have consequences. Exposure, the trail-builders call it.

There is also the technique issue. Having 27 gears is only useful if you know when to drop down through them to make it up a short, sharp climb, or how to use the drive-train to punch the bike over obstacles such as logs and rock steps. Suspension is great for soaking up the bumps, but it also helps to know how to use it to pump the trail for speed. Hydraulic discs provide reliable, instant stopping power but grab them at the wrong time and you could end up teeth down in the dirt.

And then there's the different physical challenge: maintaining speed and line on constantly shifting terrain involves constantly shifting your body weight and moving the bike beneath your body. So balance and core strength are just as important as leg power and stamina.

Laid out on paper these all sound more than a touch daunting. But these ingredients are exactly what make it such a brilliant sport; unpredictability, speed, nature and a constant element of danger. There is no better feeling than flowing fast down a twisty natural trail, just on the right side of control, feeling the bike float over obstacles and rail around corners.

Just ask my mate. Suddenly it all clicked into place and for the next couple of hours he threw himself and his bike at the trail, attacking climbs and charging at the descents – even the loose, off-camber, super-exposed sections that complete the loop. Back in the car park, the huge grin on his mud-caked face said it all: his bike won't be on eBay any time soon.

La Molina

LA MOLINA

↘3 The trails

XC Cross country Fair to good/ beginner to intermediate

DH Downhill Excellent/intermediate to advanced

FR Freeride Good/beginner to advanced

Uplift There is a telecabin to take you to the top of the Tosas for all downhill trails

✓ Pros Excellent maintained trails; fantastic panorama of valley and neighbouring areas; created with all abilities in mind; learning areas to develop skills before heading down the trails

✗ Cons Be sure to stick to the marked trails; big cliffs and drop offs if you go astray!

The La Molina resort has a variety of trails for all levels. Extensive development over the last summers on the Tosas, the resort's highest mountain peak, has opened up a variety of exciting downhill riding. All trails can be accessed by the Telecabin Alp 2500, a 10-minute ride to

The Lowdown

Locals do... Go out hard and are your best guides, if you can catch them!

Locals don't... Ride without suitable helmets and armour as safety is number one.

Don't miss... Catalunya National BTT Championship.

Remember to avoid... Late-night sangria parties...it makes riding tough the next day!

Spain's premier freeride resort.

More leaning in Molina. Sorry.

the top with fantastic views to Alp and the Cerdanya Valley. In the lower part of the resort there is a variety of XC trails ranging in difficulty from experts to children, and includes challenging routes involving man-made obstacles, ramps and jumps. All the trails begin and finish at the base of the Telecabin Alp 2500.

Cross country

There is a variety of trails crossing the base of the resort. They loop through forested areas and across *prados* and are so well signposted it's impossible to get lost!

Downhill

The bikepark has several downhill courses through the forested hillside, made up of rock gardens, drops, and plenty of drifty turns, as well as ramps and jumps. All the routes are gravity fed and clearly signposted to determine difficulty level although there are some very challenging tails only for the fearless! New downhill trails have been created linking La Molina resort with the town of Alp, a 1200 m vertical drop of fast downhilling through forest and single tracks. Return transport to La Molina can be made by prior arrangement.

"I told you I was going to wear the red t-shirt."

WWW.LAMOLINA.CAT

Practicalities ⬤⬤⬤

The resort of La Molina was established as a mountain sports destination over 100 years ago as the Ferrocarils, the national railway, offered easy and rapid access to the Pyrenees from Barcelona. As you'd expect, winter sports dominated the area until the development in the last few decades of summer facilities which made La Molina a year-round sporting destination. La Molina is located in the Cerdanya valley, a fertile valley running east to west which allows for long sunlight hours in summer. Tourism is fundamental to the area, with sports enthusiasts attracted to its tall peaks, favourable climate and the development of a variety of summer sporting opportunities such as the La Molina Kona Bikepark. The valley has a number of villages offering authentic Spanish cuisine, all linked by an extensive network of country roads and excellent biking routes for all ages and abilities. The nearest city airports are Girona, Barcelona and Toulouse (France).

Sleeping A huge range of hotels, hostels and apartments is located within a short driving or walking distance of the resort. *Guitart Hotel* and *HG Hotel* were recently built with 4-star facilities located within minutes of the bikepark. They offer extensive views of the valley and surrounds, first-class service with wellness suites, indoor pool, gymnasium and fine cuisine. Several other hotels are located at La Molina.

Eating Relax at *El Bosc*, the mountain resort restaurant only metres from the base of the Telecabin Alp 2500. Unwind at the end of the day with a swim, relax on the terrace or replenish the energy reserves with some local specialities and hearty mountain food.

Bars and clubs Spain is renowned for its bars and nightlife, with the bars offering tapas to the hungry and thirsty at about 2000, with late-night dining and a continuation of good food and music well into the early hours. The resort has a variety of small local bars, while the town of Puigcerda, some 10 minutes down the valley, has an extensive variety of *discotecas* for all your nightlife needs.

Bike shop Bikes can be hired from the bike shop at the Telecabin Alp 2500 in La Molina, also providing accessory and repair facilities.

Internet café There is internet access at the many hotels in La Molina, and also at the Telecabin Alp 2500.

Bike map available? A map is available from the ticket offices and on the website pagelamolina.cat , but usually this is not required as the bikepark is well signposted.

Freeride

Freeriders will find all their needs met with an extensive development of a slope-style freeride course at the base of the Telecabin Alp 2500. The freecross course offers ramps, jumps, berms, fast bends and wall rides. One park (Txiquipark) is especially designed for family needs and is very attractive for children and learners who want to develop and enhance their riding skills.

Easy Start out on the Txiquipark or Woodpark areas which contain all types of jumps, drops and ramps.

Difficult The toughest trails will really test your skills; the more confident will be nailing the road ramps that cross the fire trails and playing in the slopestyle course.

ⓘ **OPENING TIMES**

The bikepark opens 14 Jun 2008 until 14 Sep; also last 2 weekends of Sep, daily 1000-1800

Ⓢ **RESORT PRICES**

Day pass: €20.50; Week pass: €84.50; Season pass: €155

ⓘ **DIRECTORY**

Tourist Office: reserves@lamolina.cat
Central de reservas: T+93 972-892031
RENFE: T+93 902-240202; renfe.es
Website: lamolina.cat

La Pinilla

A good all-round riding spot with fun flowing trails, all within an hour of Madrid airport.

LA PINILLA

↘4 The trails

- **XC** **Cross country** Good/beginner to advanced
- **DH** **Downhill** Good to excellent/ intermediate
- **FR** **Freeride** Good/intermediate
- **↗** **Uplift** There is a 4-man chairlift to the top of the trails
- **✓** **Pros** Nice gradient to the hill; well marked out and designed descents
- **✗** **Cons** Quite weak for freeride at the moment, though they are adding new features through the seasons; not open during the week

SIMEB BERG/BERGPHOTO.NET

La Pinilla bikepark is Europe's most southerly. It is in its fourth season and plays host to predominantly Spanish riders from the central and southern areas. There are now seven trails in total running in and out of the woods between the pistes and the park is continuing to develop the trails each year.

Cross country

Every Sunday there is a guided ride leaving from La Pinilla (at 1500 m), which costs €10 but is well worth enrolling on as they can show you some of the many trails from La Pinilla down and around the Riaza valley.

Downhill

La Pinilla is all set up for downhill with permanent descents taped out for

ⓘ OPENING TIMES

The park is open every weekend of Jul and Aug; lifts run in that typical relaxed Spanish fashion from 1100 to 1900

Ⓢ RESORT PRICES

Day pass: €19

ⓘ DIRECTORY

Lift Station: T+34 921-551113
Website: lapinilla.es/multiaventura

Practicalities 🎿🚴⚡

La Pinilla is located in the Sierra de Ayllon, just 50 mins' drive from the capital Madrid. The bikepark currently only opens its lifts at weekends and holidays, so this is perhaps a better choice for a weekend break on a budget flight to Madrid. The Panilla station is 8 km from the town of Riaza and linked by road, but if you are just here for the weekend to ride then staying at the station will allow you to get the most out of your visit.

Sleeping Stay at the *Hostal La Pinilla* up at the lower station at 1500 m which is set up to cater for bikers through the summer riding season.

Eating The bar *Mont Blanc* at the bottom of the ski lift serves a variety of quality hot and cold dishes and is a great place to grab a bit of lunch and eat after a long day on the hill. For typical local food and dishes try out *Bar Pico del Lobo*, also at 1500 m.

Bars and cubs The resort is pretty quiet through the summer, however you could grab a few drinks after riding in *Pica del Lobo* or bar *La Olla*, but for a more exciting night you really should plan a stopover in Madrid.

Bike shop The resort has specialized big hit bikes for hire but there is no well-equipped shop at the resort. As such it would be wise to carry any specialist parts, as otherwise the only option would be a trip back to Madrid.

Internet café There are no Wi-Fi hotspots listed for La Pinilla.

Bike map available? There is not a map for the downhill trails as they are all marked out and the best way to explore the XC riding around the valley is to hook up on one of the guided rides.

different abilities. The downhills have had design input by Spanish legends the Misser brothers, and have great flow while remaining challenging enough to not become boring. If you time your visit right you can coincide with one of the downhill endurance runs which start higher up the mountain and are between 10 and 15 km long. Check the website for more details.

Easy The red graded trail from the top is perfect to get into the flow of the hill but is pretty easy to ride for most abilities.

Difficult Try the GUAK race trail, a longer and more technical run down the mountain.

Freeride

The northshore section of the bikepark has been redesigned to better suit the different abilities, from complete beginners through to advanced riders, and the brand new 4X trail, which is also serviced by the ski lift, means there is more playing at the park.

Right: Here's a soil shot for all those doing Geography GCSEs.
Opposite page: If you're going to pin some DH, do it in Pinilla.

The Lowdown

Locals do... All head up from the city on the weekends.

Locals don't... Get up early; the hill seems deserted until the afternoon.

Don't miss... The Maxi avalanche when it comes to town. This is a mass start downhill endurance race that is always popular.

Remember to avoid... Travelling out here without a spare dropout or brake pads as you could be stuck.

SIMEN BERG/BERGPHOTO.NET

Spain, Andorra & Portugal La Pinilla

Málaga

JAMES MCKNIGHT

Sitting amidst the tacky Brits' love of egg and chips, football shirts and gold jewellery, Málaga is, in terms of both temperature and popularity, one of the hottest places to ride a bike .

Above: Take a puncture repair kit.
Below: Downhill madness all the way to the classic Spanish tapas restaurant 'The Union Bulldog's Bollocks'.

JAMES MCKNIGHT

MALÁGA

⇘5 The trails

- **Cross country** Fair/intermediate
- **Downhill** Excellent/beginner to advanced
- **Freeride** Excellent/intermediate
- **Uplift** The teleférico in Benalmadena; switch-backsdh.com for guiding and shuttle service
- **Pros** Endless amounts of fantastic riding; year-round sunshine; full English breakfasts
- **Cons** Security can be an issue on the Costa – keep it locked; full English breakfasts

Being such a dry climate, the trails around the Costa del Sol are mostly dusty, sandy and rock-infested, and even with a bit of rain nothing much changes. This predictable terrain is part of the attraction to teams and individual downhill racers coming here to train and test equipment.

The Lowdown

Locals do... Live for it. These guys are seriously passionate about bikes of all sorts and the strong BMX scene in Málaga makes for many top trails, skateparks and street spots, allowing locals to ride 24/7.

Locals don't... Sleep. If the floodlit BMX jumps don't keep them awake, the 24-hour party life does.

Don't miss... Easter Celebrations – the week-long party is crazy, typically Spanish, and has to be seen to be believed.

Remember to avoid... Leaving any of your possessions on display to thieves; you have to be aware of crime here.

Cross country

Benalmadena and the Costa don't have
any specific XC trails as such, but head
inland to the reserves of El Chorro or
Sierra de las Nieves and you'll find some
superb scenery, traditional villages and
lush singletracks aplenty.

Downhill

A thriving scene of locals and travellers
has developed a huge amount of
downhill tracks, spreading from the
mountains east of Málaga all the way
down the Costa as far as the racetracks
in Estepona. The teleférico itself has three
superb runs that are easily accessible, but
to ride the best of the Costa a guide and
shuttle service is needed.

Easy Easy tracks are hard to come by with
all these rocks floating around, but behind
the city of Málaga are several easier tracks
with hardpack soil and lots of fun jumps
and berms to play on.

Difficult The Montes de Málaga hide
some secret test tracks that are deadly to
all but the most experienced of riders.

Freeride

The teleférico hill has its own take on
a freeride park – a long succession
of doubles, tables and hips, and in
Benalmadena Pueblo there is a huge
area devoted to local mountain bikers
with trails-style jumps, drops and a huge
wooden wallride. Again its a little hard to
find, so ask the locals and they might be
nice to you.

"Scorchio!"

JAMES MCKNIGHT

Practicalities ⬤⚫⚫

Málaga is not the most aesthetically
pleasing model of modern
architecture. In no more than half
a century the Costa del Sol has
exploded from small towns into the
purpose-built collection of high rises
and golf clubs that it is today. Rest
assured though, that amongst this
sea of sunburnt Brits and pints of
San Miguel you can come across rare
pockets of sanity and some lovely
little towns. Probably the best thing
to come out of the development of
the Costa is the gondola (teleférico)
in Benalmadena; now open to keen
bike riders wanting to get the most
out of the year-round sunshine.

Sleeping This is the Costa del Sol,
so accommodation is never going
to be difficult to come across. We
recommend staying in the smaller
towns of Benalmadena Pueblo or
Mijas to avoid the beer-swilling
holiday makers of the coastal towns;
unless that's your thing!

Eating Have a snoop around in
Benalmadena Pueblo and you'll
come by some great little restaurants
with plenty of character and friendly
prices. *Restaurante Sal y Limon* in
Pueblo is a favourite with its mix
of traditional exterior and warm and
welcoming staff, great food

and supply of Spanish and
international beers.

Bars and clubs Where to start?
Málaga itself is worth the train trip
or short taxi ride if you fancy some
nice bars and a great atmosphere
at weekends, or for a slightly tackier
night out visit *Plaza Solimar* in
Benalmadena for cheap drinks, an
array of very samey bars and Spain's
biggest night club, *Disco Kiu*, which is
spread over 3 sq km!

Bike shop There are plenty of shops
scattered around the towns on the
Costa, but for quality service and a
good supply of spares it's necessary
to travel inland a little to *Fon Bike* in
Alhaurin (fonbike.com).

Internet café There are plenty of
internet 'booths' scattered around
with usually at least one on every
street and provide cheap internet
and phone calls.

Bike map available? A very basic
map can be obtained from the
ticket office at the gondola in
Benalmadena, yet it won't really
help with finding any of the riding.
The best bet is to hook up with one
of the local guiding services as the
riding is spread across many different
mountains.

Manzaneda

☑6 The trails

- ⓧⓒ **Cross country** Poor/intermediate
- ⓓⓗ **Downhill** Excellent/beginner
- ⓕⓡ **Freeride** Good/beginner
- 🚡 **Uplift** There is a 4-man detachable chairlift to the top of the trails
- ✅ **Pros** Laid-back, gentle and fun bikepark riding; great beginner resort
- ❌ **Cons** Resort lacks much life; not open during the week

Fun and mellow trails over mixed ground perfect for free ride and downhill beginners.

The Lowdown

Locals do... Travel to this resort from all around Galicia and northern Portugal.

Locals don't... Ride without basic pads as the park doesn't allow you on the lift without them.

Don't miss... Look out on the website for the avalanche race dates where they mark out a 10-15 minute descent with short climbs.

Remember to avoid... If you are a racer-head, this is probably too mellow for you.

The park trails run between 1400 and 1800 m and have been laid out to try and cater as best as possible for all abilities. So while there are plenty of wooden ladder drops and jumps, there are always runs around them offering small and big options. There are six separate runs plus a number of different ways of linking different section of each route giving a whole load of choices. The uplift is quick and with just

ⓘ OPENING TIMES

The park is open on weekends from May through till Sep; lifts operate between 1000 and 1730

Ⓢ RESORT PRICES

Day pass: €23; 2-day pass: €39

ⓘ DIRECTORY

Lift Station: T+34 988-309080
Reservations: T+34 988-309090
Website: manzanedabikepark.com

400 m vertical height some riders have managed up to 30 runs in a day here!

Cross Country

The park's emphasis is very much on the gravity side of the sport, so cross country doesn't really get a look in here. That said, this is not a steep hill and most XC riders will have fun on the downs and playing in the park or riding the Los Miradores enduro trail.

Downhill

There are five downhill/freeride runs all built in a fun bikepark style with obstacles thrown in for good measure. The hill is pretty mellow, so this is good terrain for beginners and intermediate riders. The quick uplift and ability to mix up the runs allows for a whole load or runs to be sessioned.

Easy Take the Cannondale Cut trail, which runs through the scrub land on the upper slopes with plenty of nice turns.

Difficult The Burn trail is the most direct route down the hill and the trail that they hold local races on.

Freeride

The park's descents run mostly over natural terrain with loose dry soil, rocks and roots and have spiced this up to appeal to the bikepark crowd by adding in drops, jumps and little road gaps. The combination makes some mellow and fun freeride descents, perfect for those just getting into the sport and learning the ropes.

Above right: 'Give way to mountain bikes'. Yaaay!!
Opposite page from top:
1. If that sign was in Mississippi it'd be riddled with bullet holes.
2. That road sign has definitely been nicked.
3. The 'Evil Eye' is watching. Make it a good run.

Practicalities

Manzaneda is a tiny community in the eastern Ourense province in the Galicia region of northwest Spain, about a 2½-hr drive from Vigo airport. It is a predominantly rural, unspoilt region and only in recent years has it been linked by motorway to the more populated coastal region around Vigo. It is this isolation from the rest of the country, a result of the mountains surrounding it on all sides, that has caused the region to be economically challenged, but which now fuels a growing tourist sector with travellers coming to see the spectacular scenery of the river valleys. Manzaneda is now one of Spain's better winter ski resorts and an emerging popular bikepark.

Sleeping The 2 recommended places to stay in Manzaneda are the *Apartment Galacia* and *Albergue Turístico Queixa*. Both are similarly priced and can be booked half board with access to the heated indoor swimming pool. Queixa places are small separate chalets with lots of character, sleeping 2-6. Both can be booked through the resort's reservation line on T+34 988-309090.

Eating *The Ploughing* restaurant by the lift station is a good choice; it serves traditional local food such as veal, locally picked mushrooms and fresh honey. Alternatively the bike-friendly meals and staff at *As Maceiras* (T+34 988-330034) will look after you with a discount for riders.

Bars and clubs You certainly won't be hitting the dancefloor in Manzaneda; this is a subdued, peaceful resort. You can share a few drinks with the locals at the bar by the lift station but there is no nightlife beyond that.

Bike shop The ski station hire out basic bikes and have just set up a sponsorship deal with Cannondale so expect to see Cannondale suspension bikes available to hire soon. There is no decent shop in the area though so it would be wise to travel with some basic spares.

Internet café There is no internet cafe in the resort.

Bike map available? There is a simple trail leaflet available from the lift station and all the descents are marked.

Tenerife

Year-round sunshine and unique riding surfaces.

TENERIFE

↘7 The trails

- **XC Cross country** Good/beginner and advanced
- **DH Downhill** Good/advanced
- **FR Freeride** Fair to good/intermediate
- **Uplift** The uplift in the bikepark is super quick and efficient, but for the natural trails you will either need to hire a van or use the bus service which runs once a day
- ✔ **Pros** Great winter riding venue with year-round sunshine and varied terrain
- ✖ **Cons** The island has been slow on the uptake with mountain biking so many of the best trails are not marked out and require someone to point you in the right direction

ROWAN SORRELL

ℹ OPENING TIMES

The park is open Fri-Sun year round from 1000 to sunset; the rest of the trails you can ride anytime

$ RESORT PRICES

Day pass: €20

ℹ DIRECTORY

Tourist Office: T+ 34 902-003121
Medical Centre: T+112
Website: bikeparktenerife.com

(sidebar, vertical) Spain, Andorra & Portugal Tenerife

Practicalities ▭✎☺

There are plenty of options of where to stay in Tenerife, but most of the trails and the bikepark is located on the north side of the island. The capital, Puerto de la Cruz is handy for Mount Teide, an area popular with older holidaymakers. If you're here to ride that won't worry you, but if you are allergic to geriatrics, it may be worth considering the livelier and generally quite naff resorts on the south of the island.

Sleeping You are spoilt for choice when it comes to accommodation in Puerto de la Cruz, the *Casablanca Apartments* being one of the better choices. Bikepark Tenerife is currently restoring a lodge for guests so you will be able to stay on site in a more authentic corner of the island at the quiet village of Tegueste.

Eating There is everything from local, Italian, Chinese and tapas through to British food. Head to the main square in the resort where there is a good choice of restaurants.

Bars and clubs Puerto de la Cruz is not a lively place for bars and clubs, as the town is mostly frequented by a much older clientele. If you're looking for lively all-night bars and clubs you should head for Playas de las Americas on the south side of the Island. Alternatively, coincide your trip with Santa Cruz Carnival (the world's second largest after Rio De Janeiro) in the first two weeks of Feb, where everyone parties beyond the limits of what is humanly possible.

Bike shop *Inter Sport* in Santa Cruz is well stocked with most major spares available, plus there are shops in Puerto de la Cruz, though with less choice. *Mountain Bike Active* hire out Ghost trail bikes and also take guided rides (T+34 922-376081).

Internet café Most of the hotels and apartments have terminals or wireless connection.

Bike map available? There are currently no bike-specific maps. Buy a hiking trails map which will have the cross country tours marked on and downhill routes can be identified following descending hiking routes.

The set up in Tenerife is a little different to many resorts in Europe and to ride the dry, dusty, rocky and loose trails all year round requires a little bit more work, as there are no specific bike trail maps. As it stands now, riders have to put in the work to find and get to the top of the trails. You will have to buy a map, speak to locals, pay a guide (try Mountain Bike Activ in Puerto de la Cruz) and go to the bikepark where they will point you in the right direction. If you do that, you will ride some of the most varied, technical trails in some of the most amazing volcanic landscapes. The trails are only suited to advanced riders due to the amount of loose volcanic rock.

Cross country

There are miles and miles of cross country tour marked out on some of the maps available to buy. Much of the route is on double track and dirt roads, but it also takes in some sublime contouring singletrack through the Coronal Forestal and some amazing volcanic landscapes. Marked trails are relatively easy; the numerous unmarked routes that can be linked in are far more technical.

Downhill

Take the bus from Puerto de la Cruz up to Mount Teide (summit is 12,000 ft+) and take the trail from Portillo back down

The Lowdown

Locals do... Get to the bus very early and they know where the best trails are so get chatting to them.

Locals don't... Rush. Apart from nailing the bus, the pace of life and riding is very relaxed.

Don't miss... The carnival at the start of February where the whole island parties. Don the fancy dress (as everyone else does) and you'll also earn yourself half price entry at the bikepark.

Remember to avoid... The buses up to Mount Teide can be very busy any day but especially on weekends so make sure you are there early.

which is an hour plus descent. Other runs ending in Guimar and Arafo are of similar lengths but require shuttling. Hiring a van between groups of four or more and shuttling is the best way to ride the trails. Fridays, Saturdays and Sundays should be spent in the fun bikepark.

Easy The descents on the whole aren't easy on Tenerife as the surface is so rocky and loose but on the weekends

when the bikepark is open there are some easier runs.

Difficult The trail from high up in the national park down to Arafo is a highly technical route over very varied terrain.

Freeride

Bikepark Tenerife has a whole range of jumps, drops and northshore obstacles, together with three downhill runs and a kilometre-long biker cross track. There are some dirt jump trails under construction and some in the nearby town along with a skatepark and BMX track. The bikepark owner will point you in the direction if you have a hardtail and want to ride the tracks.

Above: The local wood merchant drives a Ferrari.
Left: "Skiiiiiiiiiiiid!!!!"
Opposite page: Rushin' in the bushes.

Grandvalira

New bikepark in Andorra's largest ski area.

GRANDVALIRA

↘8 The trails

- **Cross country** Good/advanced
- **Downhill** Good/beginner to advanced
- **Freeride** Fair to good/intermediate
- **Uplift** The Soldeu gondola and the Solana chairlift are the main lifts for the bikepark
- **Pros** Fun trails for a range of abilities; skills schools available to improve technique; very affordable
- **Cons** Grandvalira is still developing and will take some years to be a big player in its own right

Practicalities

Soldeu is just part of the much larger Andorran resort of Grandvalira, which is in fact made up of 6 individual resorts linked by the mountain roads below: these are Pas de la Casa, Grau Roig, Soldeu, El Tarter, Canillo and Encamp. The general feel of the entire Grandvalira resort is one of fun and friendliness and they have carried this element into their new bikepark at Soldeu.

Sleeping There are some good accommodation choices in Soldeu, ranging from the top of the line *Sport Hotel Village* (T+376 870500) to the *Hotel Piolets* (T+376 872787).

Eating The best of the restaurants are probably in Andorra la Vella, but locally there's *Fat Albert's* serving local cuisine,

or British-run *Slim Jims*. A little further up the price scale is *Borda del Rector* (T+376 852606) serving fantastic local cuisine.

Bars and clubs Soldeu is famed for its nightlife through the snow season and although summer is much quieter, there are still the usual seasonaire's haunts to try out such as *Fat Albert's*, *The Pussycat* or *Aspen*.

Bike shop *Grandvalira Mountain Bikepark* offers bikes to hire for freeride, downhill and cross country. They are found at Pla d'Espiolets.

Internet café *Slim Jim's* has good internet access.

Bike map available? There are bike maps available from the lift station and bike shop.

Andorra is a current hotspot for mountain biking and there's a whole lot of riding in this tiny country that has, remarkably, remained a well-kept secret too. With Vallnord only a short drive away, these two resorts offer trails to suit most riders no matter what your preference. The bikepark is managed by Oscar Saiz who has for many years been one of Spain's top downhillers and who has graced the Top 10 sheet at World Cups many times. It is awesome to see people like this involved with the parks, and with Gracia working as a consultant at Vallnord, Andorra has a great set up that oozes credibility.

Cross country

Whether you choose to ease the climbs by utilizing the lifts or take the full aerobic workout, Grandvalira has enough choice to keep you busy with 75 km of trails running between the Canillo, Soldeu and El Tarter sectors.

The terrain here is very steep so the riding is only suited to those with a high level of fitness.

The Lowdown

Locals do... Buy the Andorra 5-day bike pass which allows them to ride Grandvalira and Vallnord on the same pass.

Locals don't... Often ride XC here as the hills are so steep to climb. Everyone bar the very fittest uses the lift.

Don't miss... The Nou Obac blue all-mountain trail, a good 10-15 minute natural trail that is a great varied trail starting up on the open piste and working its way down into the woods.

Remember to avoid... It's all pretty positive at Grandvalira bikepark.

Downhill

The downhill routes managed by Oscar vary between wide, open, fast and dusty pisted runs that are graded easy but become trickier the faster you go, to steeper, technical wooded trails graded red and black for advanced and expert riders. There are 11 gravity-assisted runs in total.

Easy Take the Parabolica trails down the hill, fast and open is the order of the day here with some great berms to rail.

Difficult The black Avet trail is enough to challenge the most experienced riders with a super steep top section and some pretty tasty drop options along it's length.

Freeride

The downhill trails are all labelled as freeride trails but the only true freeride route is the Roller Coaster trail. It is a short trail made up of rollers, doubles, tabletops and wallrides. The park is expanding each year with more features being added.

ⓘ **OPENING TIMES**

The park is open from 6 Jul to 9 Sep; from 1000 to 1700

$ **RESORT PRICES**

Day pass: €20; Season pass: €150

ⓒ **DIRECTORY**

Tourist Office: T+376 801060
Medical Centre: T+112
Website: grandvalira.com

Below: Tax-free northshore.
Bottom: "Shooooopppping!"
Opposite page: Grandvalira DH on course.

Vallnord

VALLNORD

↘9 The trails

- **XC Cross country** Good to excellent/ beginner to advanced
- **DH Downhill** Good to excellent/ intermediate to advanced
- **FR Freeride** Good/intermediate to advanced
- **Uplift** There is a gondola to midway and various chairlifts on the upper slopes
- ✔ **Pros** Excellent variety of riding; great trails and location
- ✖ **Cons** Difficult to find a bad point at Vallnord; perhaps not enough trails yet for stays of more than 10 days

Vallnord is the pride of the Pyrenees.

Above: "Did I puncture on that corner?"
Bottom left: Bikepark hop.
Bottom right: Sweet, sweet gondola.
Opposite page: Vallnord wall-lord. Sorry again.

The Vallnord bikepark is fast becoming one of the premier spots in Europe, with great terrain, stunning views and local rider Cédric Gracia behind many of the developments. The park is new, exciting and growing. Hosting the World Cup has given the resort a further boost pushing the envelope with their trail design for both downhill and 4X. The ground here is usually loose and dusty as the summers are hot and dry, and it can be a strange feeling surfing through the dust, making you think you have punctured. The park is not suited to beginners, as the lower face of the hill is very steep.

Cross country

Vallnord is a great place to ride XC; the trails are interesting, the vistas inspiring and the ground loose and lively. The weather in the summer is usually very warm which means that hydro packs are essential when putting in some miles. There are seven marked routes of varying difficulty and if you want to ride out to the surrounding hills you can make up many more. The venue has hosted a UCI World Cup XC round and the trails on offer can be as testing as you like as there are some huge mountains to test your lung capacity.

Downhill

The downhill routes have hosted several international races, from Maxxis to World Cups, a testament to their quality. The trails are long, loose and testing,

ⓘ OPENING TIMES

The park is open from 2 Jun to 11 Sep; 1000-1830

ⓢ RESORT PRICES

Day pass: €18.50; Season pass: €180

ⓓ DIRECTORY

Tourist Office: T+376 737017
Medical Centre: T+112
Website: vallnordbikepark.com

with steep chutes. Strong brakes are essential at Vallnord due to the steep slopes under the gondola. There is also a Maxi Avalanche trail from the top of the mountain; the winners finish in some 25 minutes of leg-burning and arm-pumped gruelling descending.

Easy The Skippy Track DH and La Carbonera are two easy downhill runs.

Difficult Take the Cédric Gracia World Cup trail. It is not steep but has plenty of roots and rocks to sharpen your reactions.

Freeride

The four cross trail designed by Phil Saxena and Cédric Gracia is top quality and will be fun for all riders while still managing to test the best. There is a trials section, which contains sections of varying difficulties and it is great to see young kids learning their bike handling skills here. The woodpark up on the hill is well made and combines loamy turns on the dirt with all manner of wood ramps, wallrides, step-downs and gaps. It's a lot of fun, but not for beginners.

The Lowdown

Locals do... Kick back and make the most of their sunny climate; midday is too hot to ride, but just perfect for chillin' in the café.

Locals don't... Have any strict laws stopping them from riding where they want.

Don't miss... Make sure you have a go at the maxi avalanche trail, a fun ride when you're cruising but a totally different beast when racing hundreds of others.

Remember to avoid... The bars in the evening if you don't like smoking; no such thing as a smoking ban here just yet.

Practicalities

The principality of Andorra is a small yet perfectly formed country with the rugged Pyrenees mountains offering a stunning landscape overlooking the towns and villages in and around the valley bases. It is prosperous partly due to the increase in tourism over the years and perhaps more so due to its status as a tax haven. The town of La Massana houses the gondola that serves the bikepark. It is a small yet bustling little area that gives you a taste of Catalan and Andorran living.

Sleeping The hotels that are usually full to bursting through the winter season are much quieter and subsequently cheaper in the summer. *Hotel Palanques* offers overnight from just €19 and *Hotel Font* from €20, both are found in La Massana town.

Eating Cafés bars and restaurant are a mainstay of Andorran culture.

Try *La Bona Taula* or *Border D L'avi*, both near the town centre.

Bars and clubs The resort on the whole is pretty quiet in the summer so any nights out are going to be shared with the locals and give you a taste of local life. Try a few drinks in *El Món Bohemi*, a relaxed bar, before moving onto the livelier disco pub *El Còctel de l'Avi*.

Bike shop There is a whole range of bikes available for hire from the *Pic Negre* bike shop, which is found next to the La Massana gondola, and has a well-equipped workshop.

Internet café The cyber café in La Massana is the place to log onto the web and enjoy some tapas.

Bike map available? There are bike maps available from the lift station and bikeshop.

Lagos

A mountain biking gem hidden in the corner of Europe. Originally made famous as a surfer town, Lagos now has a burgeoning underground mountain biking scene, with amazing singletrack by the coast and some incredible downhill on a nearby volcano.

CHRIS MORAN

CHRIS MORAN

LAGOS

↘10 The trails

- ⓧ **Cross Country** Good/beginner to intermediate
- ⓓ **Downhill** Excellent/beginner to intermediate
- ⓕ **Freeride** Good/beginner to intermediate
- ⓪ **Uplift** The Mountain Bike Adventure Nissan, a hire car, or your own legs
- ✔ **Pros** Fantastic holiday feel, with a vibrant, fun town; sun tan guaranteed year round; amazing volcano riding with surprisingly good downhill and singletrack; no queues, very few riders, and incredible scenery
- ✘ **Cons** You'll need a bike bag or have to rent a bike from *The Mountain Bike Adventure* – it's really too far to drive from anywhere in Europe; gets incredibly hot in the summer months.

About 45 minutes drive north of Lagos town lies the volcano of Monchique (the peak itself is known as 'Foia'). A 1000-m high, 15-km descent awaits those who drive to the top. There are numerous trails in every direction, continuously upgraded by the burgeoning local mountain bike scene. The downhill ranges from

Above: "The GPS says turn left at the wind turbine. Where's that?"
Above right: Prepare to get covered in red dust.
Below right: Room for one more bike.

fairly challenging all the way down to intermediate. It's not highly recommended for beginners as the top section is basically exposed rock with several tricky sections, although there are gentle trails under the mighty wind turbines that would suit those looking for a mellow ride.

Cross country

There are coastal routes spreading out both east and west from Lagos town. Perhaps the most scenic is the 30 km stretch west towards Zavial. There is a network of easy rides on the outskirts of town, right next to the Portuguese coast, where huge sea cliffs are dotted with lighthouses, picturesque cafés and the odd dirt jump.

Downhill

Monchique commands the most respect, but there is downhill to be had all around, with short bursts of steep, shaley cliffs stretching all the way to Sagres – some 60 km to the west. There's also a new area opening up in the pine forests around 10 km north of Lagos town. Jim and Toby of *The Mountain Bike Adventure* are behind it and it's a secret unless you go with them.

The Lowdown

Locals do... Enjoy the cheapest food, wine, beer and general living in western Europe.

Locals don't... Ride these trails without paying them the respect they deserve; bikes need to be well set up and maintained and protection is advised.

Don't miss... A day surfing in the Atlantic; the sea-cliffs next to the O Camillo Lighthouse.

Remember to avoid... If dust and heat aren't your thing.

Practicalities ⊖🚲🚵

The town of Lagos is around an hour's drive from the low-cost carrier airport of Faro, bang in the middle of Portugal's Algarve region. Most people on your flight will no doubt be carrying golf bags, which is a boon for those wishing to take advantage of the area's less managed countryside. Empty trails here can be virtually guaranteed. The nightlife is a different story: Lagos has always been popular as a local hangout, and has nightlife to reflect that. A beautiful fishing port, lovingly built in white soapstone, with terracotta roofs jostling for the best view of the sea, it is the embodiment of an old-world town. From the late 1980s onwards, the town was invaded by surfers looking to take advantage of the fantastic waves. Today, virtually every bar has a surf theme, and Lagos has become a must-do stop on the Euro backpacker tour. Expect to meet a lot of liberal-minded folk! Mountain biking is new to the area, but the athletic locals and impressively large expat community have taken to it as the best thing to do when the surf is flat. Get there before the crowds do.

Sleeping As one of the most popular backpacking towns in Europe, there is plenty on offer. For any visitors to Lagos the first number to call should be that of *The Mountain Bike Adventure* (T+351 918-502663, themountainbikeadventure.com) a company set up by Toby Gornell, a long-time Lagos resident, and Jim

Carroll, who helped to build Hopton Castle's trails before decamping to the sunnier climes of Portugal. They have a network of B&Bs on their books and are guaranteed to get you a better price than anything over the internet.

Eating As a tourist hotspot, all tastes are covered, whether it's Thai at *The Lemongrass*, or the variety of *Mullen's* (where Prince William and George Galloway are considered locals). Traditionalists should head to *A Forja* where amazing locally caught fish is served, and a trip to Lagos without visiting *O Franguinha* is a wasted trip indeed; they serve the best roast chicken in the whole of Portugal.

Bars and clubs The *Three Monkeys*, *Nah Nah Bar* and *DC's* are all popular hang-outs, but you'll undoubtedly spend your time at *Eddies* drinking 'bocks and playing darts.

Bike shop There are a couple of decently equipped bike shops in town, but if you want the best servicing and parts, you'll need the garaging services of *The Mountain Bike Adventure*.

Internet café Pretty much every café, restaurant and bar in town is hooked up with Wi-Fi.

Bike map available? Nope. This is truly remote riding, and you'll need the guiding services of *The Mountain Bike Adventure* if it's your first trip.

CHRIS MORAN

ⓘ OPENING TIMES

24/7; if you're planning on simply riding the singletrack around Lagos you'll have no need for an uplift; to ride on the Moncheque Volcano, home of some incredible downhill trails, you'll need either a hire car or the guiding services (and Nissan 4x4) of *The Mountain Bike Adventure*

Ⓢ RESORT PRICES

The Mountain Bike Adventure charge €45 per person per day for full guiding services, including all uplifts, lunch, and the use of a fleet of Specialized Hard Rock Sports and protective equipment; weekly prices start at €300 per person including accommodation.

ⓘ DIRECTORY

Tourist Office: portugalvirtual.pt/
Jim Carroll: T+351 918-502663
Website:
themountainbikeadventure.com

Easy The repair track for the wind turbines on Monchique provides some perfect easy pinning.

Difficult This is true old-school downhill. The runs don't even have names.

Freeride

Lagos has a skatepark and a dirt jumping course, but serves as a nice addition to the XC and downhill on Monchique and along the coast. No one would travel this far for what is very much a collection of small local jumps.

Guimarães

A taste of the real old Portugal, with churchgoers and tea shops aplenty.

GUIMARÃES

↘11 The trails

- **Cross country** Fair/beginner to intermediate
- **Downhill** Excellent/intermediate to advanced
- **Freeride** Excellent/intermediate
- **Uplift** Gondola in the town; van uplift is advised to get the most of the trails
- **Pros** Year-round gondola access; amazing cake shops; friendly locals
- **Cons** Can get very busy

Used for many a national downhill round, the tracks in Guimarães are big and fierce with road gaps, drops and massive boulder fields aplenty. Summertime is hot and dry here and the tracks turn to pure dust in no time. Racers run spiked tyres for the events to combat the axle-deep loose soil.

Cross Country

Although there are no specific marked XC trails in the area, there is plenty of XC riding to be found for those who don't need to follow the arrows. Just ask at Bike Zone and the friendly locals will point you in the right direction. Used for years for motocross endurance events, the mountains surrounding Guimarães are riddled with trails. Just make sure you have an idea where you're heading as it is very easy to get lost!

Downhill

The gondola access is a little limiting, but two superb downhill tracks can be reached, one of which runs directly underneath the cabins and which is used

Practicalities

Guimarães is a lovely old town near Porto, the self-proclaimed founding city of Portugal. It has a great friendly feel to it and attracts bikers and tourists. The town is vibrant all year round, particularly in the summer months when the wealth of teahouses and patisseries are full to the brim with tourists from all round the world. Surrounding the city are several mountains with the main hill behind the town capped not by snow, but by a huge church and gardens. No snow, but there is a gondola there to get you up to church, or perhaps to the start of some of the country's best mountain biking.

Sleeping A popular tourist area, so make sure to visit outside the summer months if you wish to find a place to stay without booking. The *hostal* in town is a great budget place to stay, costing as as little as €12 a night and equipped with internet service and a bar. A little more expensive, though still reasonable, is the *Santa Marinha Pousada*, an elegant building with 51 rooms only minutes from the centre of town.

Eating If there's something Guimarães is great for, it's food. Scout around and you'll find some fantastic places to eat a range of different styles. Daytime is best spent in one of the many teahouses which are renowned for their supreme cakes.

Bars and clubs Right in the centre of town you can find a great courtyard area which is packed full of great bars and in the summer months turns into an all-night outdoor party, every night!

Bike Shop *Bike Zone* is Portugal's chain of shops dedicated to quality mountain bikes and components. Check out *Bike Zone Guimarães* for all your spares and to drool over the latest Troy Lee kit. This is also the hang-out for local riders who'll be more than happy to help you out and show you all the trails.

Internet café Guimarães is a Wi-Fi free town so no problems there.

Bike map available? Although there isn't a great map, just ask in *Bike Zone* and you'll get more info than any map could provide!

Kicking up some dust on the DH.

Below: Rocking in the rocks.
Bottom left: Boing!
Bottom right: The New Age centre is gutted their bamboo fence is next to the DH course.

JAMES MCKNIGHT

JAMES MCKNIGHT

ⓘ **OPENING TIMES**

The gondola runs all year round, but try to avoid holiday periods and times of religious importance as the gondola will be packed with people ascending to the church

Ⓢ **RESORT PRICES**

Gondola tickets are sold by the trip (€6) which can work out to be quite expensive so try to get chatting with the locals and organize some shuttle uplifts

Ⓓ **DIRECTORY**

Tourist Office: T+351 253-518394

The Lowdown

Locals do... Like to build. Riders here have bikes running through their veins and put a lot of effort in to the town's array of tracks and jump spots.

Locals don't... Turn their noses up. Everyone is welcome here and you can be guaranteed a good time as a passing mountain biker.

Don't miss... Portuguese National round in September of every year – huge crowds, television broadcasts and cheap entry fees make this one of Europe's best race series.

Remember to avoid... The freeride section if you're a beginner. You might be out of your depth.

for a round of the national series every September. Again Guimarães is all about asking the locals, as they'll be more than happy to help with uplifting some of the less obvious tracks and will point you in the direction of some absolute gems.

Freeride

The local scene here is all about the freeride. Riders love to watch all the latest films and then recreate their own versions of what they see. Dotted around the hillsides are many huge wooden structures, hucks and gap jumps. The town has a freeride trail – which is kept tucked away and is one of Europe's best secrets – a succession of berms, natural wallrides and super steep sections to keep you smiling!

Easy The downhill tracks aren't difficult to ride and will keep every level of rider happy.

Difficult The freeride trail has some daunting drops and technical wallrides and isn't for the inexperienced.

Sintra

SINTRA

↘12 The trails

- **Cross country** Fair/beginner to intermediate
- **Downhill** Excellent/beginner to advanced
- **Freeride** Excellent/beginner to advanced
- **Uplift** No specific uplift – a van and a share of the driving is required to access the downhill tracks
- **Pros** Wealth of trails enough to keep you happy for a lifetime
- **Cons** Can be treacherous in the rain

Not a resort in the sense of many of the areas in this guide, Sintra is more of a DIY riding area: a combination of passionate locals and pro racers have helped to craft Sintra into what is has become; a heaven for riders of all levels. Expect rocks, tree roots and terrain not too dissimilar to that of South Wales. Trails are nearly entirely under cover of trees giving the riding here a great relaxing quality as you swoop from berm to jump through sun-dappled forest.

The Lowdown

Locals do... Build jumps; lots of them.

Locals don't... Overdo things in the rain, as the trails can get dodgy.

Don't miss... The Freeride structures; there are some brilliantly elaborate contraptions.

Remember to avoid... Getting stuck for spares. Take what you need as it can be a drive to sort them out.

South Wales riding transferred to the sunny terrain of Portugal? Sintra is full of surprises.

Check out that line.

The Sintra New Age Centre got an email from their sister Guimaraes branch about fencing just as they put the last post in the ground. Gutted.

Cross country

There are plenty of local cross country riders also frequent Sintra, and although it is not perhaps the greatest destination for a trail-riding holiday, if you have a bike capable of pedalling and riding the downhill trails.

Downhill

The forest is literally riddled with downhill tracks; at least 10 or perhaps a few more if you know where to look. From the top of the hill, the general rule is that tracks more to the right are much more severe, including extreme rock sections and big jumps, while tracks to the left of the hill are more flowing with a nice blend of berms, jumps and root sections.

Freeride

Portuguese are mad for building jumps and wooden features, and the locals of Sintra are no exception to this rule. There is an incredible array of structures scattered around the forest ranging from lines of doubles, to the proclaimed longest northshore (suspended) trail in Europe.

Easy Tracks to the left as you look down the hill are generally the easier ones.

Difficult Ask locals to show you the hidden northshore trail for a test of your balance and balls.

Bush ranger.

Top and above: Evil Knievel's attempt to jump 18 bikes AND a Portuguese café drew a pathetic crowd.

Practicalities

The Sierra de Sintra is a forested countryside location only a stone's throw from the city of Lisbon, and a popular weekend destination with bike riders and city escapers. This little slice of bike-riding heaven hides a huge variety of bike rideable terrain; from craggy rocks to kilometres of suspended northshore trails there is something for everyone and riders travel the length of the country to ride these legendary trails week in, week out.

Sleeping Although there is a small town at the foot of the trails, accommodation is limited so why not stay in the heart of one of the most interesting and historic cities in Europe? Here you have a huge choice of accommodation, from super cheap hostels through to 5-star chic hotels.

Eating Breakfast and lunch can be bought at the fantastic bakery perfectly positioned at the foot of the hill. For

dinner, why not drive to one of Lisbon's beautiful beachside restaurants in the Expo area for a view and some fantastic international cuisine.

Bars and clubs Lisbon has a wealth of bars and clubs and is the most affluent city in Portugal, so a party isn't hard to come by. Party riverside at one of the boat clubs for a classy night out with a mix of tourists, businessmen and riders. Be warned though most of the clubs don't even open till 0100, so don't expect an early night.

Bike Shop There isn't a bike shop any nearer then Lisbon so for spares a short drive is necessary.

Internet café Internet access is easy to come by in the city.

Bike map available? No map available, but head to Sintra and drive up the tarmac road used by numerous riders every day of the week and you can't fail to find a range of varied trails.

switzerland

Another Wile E Coyote route, this time above the picturesque town of Zermatt. [ENDRE LOVASS]

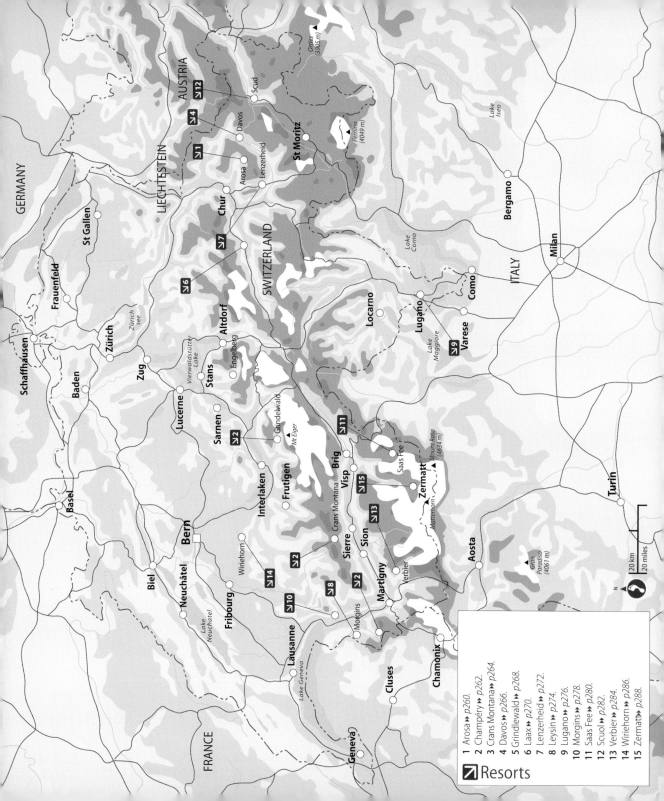

GERMANY

AUSTRIA

LIECHTENSTEIN

SWITZERLAND

ITALY

FRANCE

Schaffhausen

St Gallen

Frauenfeld

Baden

Zürich

Zürich see

Basel

Biel

Neuchâtel

Lake Neuchâtel

Fribourg

Bern

Lausanne

Geneva

Lake Geneva

Cluses

Chamonix

Morgins

Martigny

Verbier

Sion

Sierre

Crans Montana

Frutigen

Interlaken

Lucerne

Zug

Sarnen

Stans

Vierwaldstätter Lake

Altdorf

Engelberg

Grindelwald

Mt Eiger

Brig

Visp

Saas Fee

Mount Rosa
(4634 m)

Zermatt

Matterhorn

Aosta

Gran Paradiso
(4061 m)

Turin

Wiriehorn

Chur

Arosa

Lenzerheid

Davos

Scud

St Moritz

Bernina
(4049 m)

Ordlus
(3905 m)

Locarno

Lugano

Lake Maggiore

Lake Como

Como

Varese

Milan

Bergamo

Lake Iseo

N

20 km
20 miles

1 ↗12

4 ↗4

↗1

↗7

6 ↗

↗2

↗11

↗15

↗13

9 ↗

8 ↗

↗2

10 ↗

14 ↗

↗2

ENDRE LOVAAS

The high Alps. Seriously captivating.

The Swiss today are quintessential modern Europeans: they're multilingual (speaking four national languages), yet determined to hold onto their own culture; they've moved with the times to enjoy one of the highest standards of living in the developed world, and have done so without sacrificing any of the tradition and beauty that characterizes the place for the rest of the world.

For many, Switzerland's iconic mountains and valleys define the European Alps. The terms 'Heidi country' and 'chocolate box' are overused, and the stereotypes – ornate chalets, a clockwork train system and cloyingly pretty valleys overlooked by fearsome peaks – are well known. For sure, there's something in each of those stereotypes (as any visit to, say, Grindelwald will testify) and it is these uplifting landscapes that have allowed Switzerland to become one of the trail riding greats on the planet.

On the downside, the elephant in the room when it comes to Switzerland, is the cost. Even by usual mountain standards, it's an expensive place to go riding, and some resorts suffer from a complete lack of mountain bike culture. Those who rank their resorts in terms of hedonistic potential must also choose carefully, as most of the Swiss resorts are a whole lot quieter through the summer months. But for a quintessentially European experience and a winning combination of history, culture and facilities, Switzerland must be a serious option.

Overview

The riding in Switzerland is perhaps as you might expect from a highly conservative and traditional Alpine nation; it is mainly centred around the more natural paths and trails that dissect these mountains. That said, it hasn't escaped the building boom that has characterized some of the French resorts. This has helped to create loads of runs and a variety of trails for beginners through to experts.

The heart of Swiss mountain biking, though, lies with XC trail riding, and while they have been a little slow on the uptake some resorts are now starting to open up and see the benefits of providing for the other areas of mountain biking. There are new bikeparks at Verbier and Leysin and purpose-built downhill tracks in Saas Fee and Crans Montana. These have added choice and contrast to the amazing singletracks that offer trail paradise, not only to the discerning XC rider but also to any downhiller who is prepared to step away from the constant shuttle runs and get stuck into some more technical epic trails.

On the freeride scene, and taking the country as a whole, it is left wanting a little as no resorts truly cater for the slopestyle and stunt culture. If freeride alone is your thing, perhaps Switzerland is not the best choice for you.

However, bringing your bike here opens up a whole wealth of trail riding in some of the most inspiring Alpine settings. Just be prepared to work a little for your pleasures; there is no carrot on a stick in Switzerland, but if you appreciate great trails in magnificent settings then this country is one hell of a place to mountain bike.

Conditions

The southernmost parts of Switzerland enjoy the warmest weather through the summer months and most of the resorts featured in the guide are fortunately located in the southern cantons of Vallais (such as Zermatt) and Graubünden (such as Davos). They enjoy a Mediterranean climate with warm temperatures and lower periodic rainfall. The rest of the country to the north has a temperate climate which is still very pleasant through the summer months. Precipitation is hard to predict in Switzerland and varies from year to year, but on the whole the wettest areas are those of the high Alps and in the Canton of Tocino (where Lugano is found). These areas typically enjoy many days of sun and heavy bursts of rain from time to time.

The scene

The Swiss mountain bike scene is not as thriving and passionate as some of its European counterparts, but it does have a core group of enthusiasts and over recent years many foreigners have set up camp having discovered the unspoilt trails and superb singletrack. Many of the Swiss resorts have companies offering bike packages; they will show you around the trails in their resort and organize point-to-point tours. The most popular European race series, the IXS Cup, visits many resorts in Switzerland through the season and brings the travelling race circus into the resorts. Events are becoming more and more popular with each resort coming up with their own slant on the mass mountain bike race. Probably the standout event in the country is the unique Saas Fee Glacier race with riders racing down a 14-km piste descent at speeds of over 60 mph.

The industry

The suspension manufacturer giants of Fox racing shocks have their European HQ in Switzerland and the suspension centre is a well respected Swiss tuning and service centre for the company. The largest Swiss mountain bike company, DT Swiss, are best known for their manufacture of quality spokes, hubs and rims for lightweight XC use through to the heavier and stronger downhill ones. They have recently ventured out into the suspension market as well as buying out British company Pace to produce a new line of suspension forks together with a new ultra lightweight carbon rear shock.

Switzerland breakdown

There was only really one thing to focus on it Switzerland and that was the big mountain resorts that offer spectacular trails riding with amazing backdrops. So, with Zermatt overlooked by the Matterhorn, and Davos in the shadow of the Eiger, they were easy choices. The rest of the picks were due to the trails they offer and to provide a few choices of venues slightly more downhill- or freeride-orientated to compliment the great XC resorts.

Trains, castles, mountain tops and religion. What a heady mix.

Q&A with the experts

Christophe Ritzler *is a Swiss Mountain Bike pioneer and now heads up FOX European Management.*

You've got friends visiting for just one weekend and they can go anywhere in Switzerland. Name the one place you'd definitely have to take them.

CR Number one place? Phew that's tough. It would probably be somewhere in the Engadin region. That's the best place for biking, at least with your own pedalling. The region of Graubünden, like St Moritz and around there, has absolutely fantastic trails.

Which trail centre or resort has the best party scene or the best after-riding activities?

CR That's a good question. I'm too old to answer that. I like to go to bed after riding these days! I guess though in the end if you're looking for partying then you're best going to Valais in the French part: resorts like Verbier which have great trails and are very touristy. Or any of the Portes du Soleil resorts work for sure.

Where did you learn to ride, and where would you send beginners to ride?

CR I learned around Basle, but that's just foothills. I'd say that if you were learning to ride then Verbier or anything in the Portes du Soleil would work because they've got different levels of trails and definitely have lots of great learner routes.

In your opinion, which is the best downhill track in Switzerland?

CR It really depends one what your looking for. The technical one that I personally like is Wiriehorn, with northshore stuff and some cool sections. It's kind of old-school technical downhill: rooty, rocky, lots of natural riding. And the lift is new and it's cheap and super friendly. One other I really like – but it's a more prepared track with perfect radius in the corners – is Crans Montana. You ride from really high up and all the way down it's a well-made purpose-built downhill track.

Where's the best place to avoid pedalling uphill? Where has the best uplifts? Would you avoid anywhere?

CR Anywhere in the Portes du Soleil is definitely the best for lifts. If you don't like pedalling then avoid Davos; it's a place with fantastic trails but they clearly don't want gravity riders, so they don't want trail conflicts with the hikers. You can't even take your bike on the lifts. If you go there you're definitely going to have to learn how to pedal!

Switzerland Overview

Arosa

A picturesque high-altitude resort with some great cross country trails.

AROSA

⇘1 The trails

- **XC Cross country** Good/beginner to intermediate
- **DH Downhill** Fair/beginner
- **FR Freeride** Poor/ n/a
- **⑦ Uplift** There are 2 cablecars and a mountain railway to transport you to the top of the mountains around Arosa and all are free
- **✔ Pros** Scenic setting; open terrain; very quiet on the hills
- **✘ Cons** Lack of wooded riding; still early days for MTB in Arosa

The terrain in Arosa is open with little to no trees resulting in plenty of open, fast runs and singletrack routes running through the valleys linking to the other nearby Swiss resorts. Arosa is an ideal place for a mid travel trail bike or light freeride bike. Perhaps one of the main incentives to visit Arosa is that at present all cablecars and the mountain railway are free to use during the summer when staying in the resort.

ⓘ OPENING TIMES

The main lifts run from 14 Jun to 19 Oct and from 0900-1645

Ⓢ RESORT PRICES

The lifts are free when you stay in Arosa

ⓒ DIRECTORY

Tourist Office: T+41 81-378 7020
Medical Centre: T+41 81-377 2728
Website: arosa.ch

Switzerland Arosa

ENDRE LÖVAAS

It's hard to keep your eye on the singletrack with those kind of views.

Cross country

The Grischa trail is a great adventure route that links Davos, Arosa and Lenzerheide in a loop and can be extended out as far as Chur. There are a few companies offering guided rides but the route is relatively easy to follow if you pick up the guides available. You will need to think about booking accommodation in the neighbouring resorts on this ride.

Easy Take the Schwellisee, one of the shortest mapped tours available at under 10 km.

Difficult Take the Grischa trail through some great landscapes.

Downhill

The downhill track in Arosa is very natural and fast and doesn't contain many technical features; it is more of a wide open piste affair. Most riders will love the ease of going fast on this descent but advanced riders may find the lack of tighter technical sections limits their challenge on this trail; they'd be advised to track down some of the steeper hiking and biking routes.

Freeride

Arosa is far from a freeride haven; only the downhill track offers some very small jumps. Freeride fanatics would be better off heading elsewhere.

Shingle city.

The Lowdown

Locals do... Take in the longer tours through the valley and over into the other resorts.

Locals don't... Spook the cows often lining the course on the downhill.

Don't miss... The free uplifts through the summer. Even the most hardened climber will want to make the most of this offer.

Remember to avoid... If you're a budding freerider or downhiller who doesn't want to pedal and explore.

Practicalities ⊜🚴🚵

The beautiful Alpine village of Arosa is situated on the river Plessur in a high glacial valley in the canton of Graubünden. The village, at a height of 1734 m, is surrounded by mountains ranging up to 2653 m. A popular winter resort, Arosa is now working hard to expand its summer offerings, listing an increasing number of tours or cross country rides for bikers and free lift access through the summer.

Sleeping For budget accommodation try the *Backpackers Mountain Lodge* (T+41 81-378 8423) with rooms sleeping 2, 4 and 6 people. Next up the scale is the 2-star *Carmenna* (T+41 81-377 1766) offers adequate accommodation if you're going to be spending more time on your bike than in the bar or spa. For a bit of style upgrade to *The Sporthotel Valsana* (T+41 81-378 6363) which has everything in place to make your stay slightly more luxurious.

Eating The *Heimeli Restaurant* offers both traditional dishes and international plates, or try the *Hornlihut* mountain restaurant.

Bars and clubs Arosa is still a very quiet summer resort at present with few riders in the resort. Try the *Los* bar or *NUTS* discoteque, but don't expect pumping après-ski to continue through the summer.

Bike shop *Arosa Bike* (T+41 81-377 2377) has basic bikes available to hire and some spares, but be advised to carry spare parts specific to your bike.

Internet café Wi-Fi is available in most hotels in Arosa.

Bike map available? There are a number of cross country loops and tours marked and available from the tourist office. The Grischatrail has its own guide available.

Check out the switchbacks! Better give that brake finger some exercise.

Switzerland Arosa

Champéry

Home to the craziest World Cup competition ever and the sickest downhill course used for an event.

CHAMPERY

↘2 The trails

- **⊗ Cross country** Excellent/ intermediate to advanced
- **⊕ Downhill** Good/advanced
- **⊕ Freeride** Poor to fair/beginner to intermediate
- **⊘ Uplift** There is a cablecar and 3 chairs in the immediate area around Champéry, these are part of the 24 lifts open to bikes in the region
- **⊘ Pros** Stunning setting; lovely town; challenging riding
- **⊗ Cons** Not suitable for beginners; not a good freeride destination

Champéry is set in impressive surroundings; the scale of everything at this end of the Portes du Soleil seems massive in comparison to the green rolling hills of Les Gets. It means that the trail riding is generally tougher and the downhills also require a certain amount of basic bike skills. Be wary of some of the singletracks as they are closed to bikes. The benefit from a guide here is in getting you out to the best trails without too much messing around.

Cross country

There is some truly picture-book singletrack around Champéry. From flowing curves in mountain pastures to testing ridge runs, there is something to test the most advanced riders in this valley. Riders prepared to hike as well as bike can open up even longer trails in the hidden corners of the valley which have remained all but untouched.

Practicalities 🔌🍴🥾

Champéry is at the opposite end of the Portes du Soleil to Morzine and Les Gets and is a good place to base yourself for XC riding and the more extreme end of the spectrum for downhill riding. The resort sits in the valley bottom with the impressive and somewhat imposing Dents du Midi mountain range overlooking the town. The riding area is on the mountain opposite where you take the cablecar from the centre of town up to 'le Mur Suisse', or the Swiss wall, where you can access the trails and the Swiss bikepark lift areas of Les Crosets and Champoussin.

Sleeping The resort has plenty of bed space during the summer and the buildings have retained much of their Alpine charm. We would recommend you stay with a company that offer guiding to get the most out of the area. *Alpine Tracks* (T+41 800-028 2546) have a large chalet in the centre of town with a secure garage, bikewash facilities, jacuzzi and a bar.

Eating *Café Du Centre* is located in the old town hall building and has a good mix of dishes from around the globe. For a popular and more traditional restaurant head to the *Café Du Nordon* in the high street which specializes in local cuisine.

Bars and clubs The bars are still quiet in the summer months and there won't be any late-night disco antics in Champéry. The bars to head for are *Bar des Guides*, for a more formal environment, or *La Cravasse Bar* and *Café du Levant* for a fun, relaxed evening.

Bike shop The *Bikepark Shop* is by the main cablecar station in the centre of town and hires out XC and downhill bikes as well as offering spares and repairs.

Internet café *The Chalet Rose des Alpes* at *Alpine Tracks* has Wi-Fi connection.

Bike map available? A map of the Portes du Soleil is available from the lift station and the tourist office free of charge.

Downhill

Home to the most technical, steep and downright scary World Cup track (this was where Sam Hill defied belief by riding the life out of his Iron Horse Sunday in torrential rain), this should only be even considered by absolute experts. The main riding is in the Les Crosets valley the long Grand Conche descent and the Les Crosets 2 gentler descent. Like the rest of the Portes du Soleil, you can then explore out to the trails at Morgins and Châtel.

Easy Les Crosets 2 is the easiest descent in the immediate area, it has long sweeping corners and can be ridden

Ritchie Schley and Hans Rey taking on the DH course.

The XC has some staggering backdrops.

The Lowdown

Locals do... Take excursions to Rochers de Naye to ride awesome descents overlooking Lake Geneva. You can get there by train and details are available in the tourist office.

Locals don't... Ride the hiking trails.

Don't miss... The ridge singletrack from Col de Cou down to Balme then back to Champéry. Classic singletrack.

Remember to avoid... Even thinking of riding the World Cup downhill course here unless you are a World Cup rider!

steady and then allows you to build up to full pace runs.

Difficult Bash out the runs on the Grand Conche, a big track with high speeds and big holes; great fun for the racers.

Freeride

There is a basic 4X track in Les Crosets and there are often some basic jumps and balance beams set up in the car park outside the front of the cablecar in town but really Champéry is not the best base for freeride in the region. Châtel would be a better choice.

ⓘ OPENING TIMES

The Champéry cable car is open from 14 Jun to 19 Oct and the Mossettes and Les Crosets lifts are open from 27 Jun to 3 Sep

Ⓢ RESORT PRICES

Day pass 26 CHF; 6 days 140 CHF; Season pass 208 CHF

ⓞ DIRECTORY

Tourist Office: T+41 24-479 2020
Website: bikepark.ch; portesdusoleil.com

Switzerland Champéry

Crans Montana

CRANS MONTANA

↘3 The trails

- **Cross country** Good/beginner to intermediate
- **Downhill** Good/intermediate to advanced
- **Freeride** Fair/intermediate
- **Uplift** There are 2 main gondolas feeding the mountains above Crans and Montana
- **Pros** Great downhill course; trails haven't been hammered
- **Cons** Not enough for the freeride enthusiast; town not as attractive as some

Crans has a bit of everything; some classic singletrack and marked

DANMILNER.COM

The Lowdown

Locals do... Wonder how they've managed to keep this to themselves for so long.

Locals don't... Follow too close through the northshore trail or the see-saw will take you clean out.

Don't miss... The main downhill run, a great trail with a bit of everything along its route.

Remember to avoid... Watch out for the out of control kids on their monster scooter monstrosities!

A small resort that lacks in quantity but makes up for it in the quality of its trails.

ENDRE LOVAAS

Above left: A rolling bike gathers no moss.
Above: That's Henry Kelly at the back. Playing 'Catch Up'.

out cross country tours, some real quality downhill trails and a great little bikepark with northshore. Whether it has enough to sustain more than a week's riding is debatable, but as a shorter destination or part of a tour, it's a must.

Cross country

There are a number of marked XC routes and they are graded from easy through to very difficult. There is even the chance to ride the first ever mountain bike world championship course, held in Crans Montana in 1988, and this is a more physical route.

Practicalities ⊞📷🏠

Crans Montana (also known as Crans sur Sierre) is a ski resort in the heart of the Swiss Alps made famous from its role in the Bond movie 'For Your Eyes Only'. Roger Moore was so struck by the area he bought a property after filming in the resort. The resort is an amalgamation of the 2 separate villages of Crans and Montana. Along with Verbier and St Moritz, it is one of Switzerland's glitziest resorts, and perhaps best known for hosting the European Masters golf on an incredibly scenic and tough course. The town itself lacks the Alpine charm or atmosphere of many of its counterparts as it contains too many dreary apartment blocks, but on the bike front, the resort is now working hard to map out routes and develop facilities to create a summer season worthy of the town's strong winter reputation.

Sleeping Crans Montana is in a beautiful location and is a great place to camp and enjoy the full nature experience – *Camping La Moubra* is your best bet (campingmoubra.ch).

Alternatively there are stacks of high quality chalets and apartments to rent such as the pretty *Chalet Paprika* (T+41 33-336 5180).

Eating Heading off the trails, stop in *Chez Cucu*, a quality little crêperie with plenty of lighter dishes to enjoy before you put in some more kays. In the evenings *Le Raphaele*, near the town centre, is quite popular with the locals, serving local and Italian cuisine.

Bars and clubs If you're missing that feel of your local back home then a quick stop in the *George and Dragon* is in order. *Monk's Bar* and *Leo's* are both

a good call for a few drinks and the late-night action is at the *VIP* and *Club Xellent*.

Bike shop For bike hire and a good service workshop head down to *Crans Montana Mountain Freeride Shop* (T+41 27-480 3030). The staff here are also well clued up on their trails if you want any insider tips.

Internet café The *New Pub* (T+41 27-480 2598) or *A Net Point* (T+41 27-480 4500) are both open till late evening.

Bike map available? There is a trail map available for the XC routes from the tourist office and the lift stations.

Downhill

With two purpose-built downhills and a further 35 km of downhill trails that are shared with other users, there is some good riding for the gravity set in Crans Montana. The main downhill runs are pretty sweet and great for intermediate to advanced riders as they are laced with steep wooded switchback sections, plenty of roots, fun fade and fly off jumps and a great rocky gullied section.

① OPENING TIMES

The lifts open on 7 Jul and close on 22 Sep; from 0830-1645

⑤ RESORT PRICES

Day pass: 30 CHF;
Season pass: 160 CHF

① DIRECTORY

Tourist Office: T+41 27-485 0404
Website: crans-montana.ch

Easy Take the red downhill; with no steep sections it leaves you the choice of letting off the brakes and going with the gradient. Fast and flowing.

Difficult The black route is a flat-out hardpack affair, not too steep but fast with some decent kickers and rock slabs.

Freeride

Though Crans Montana say they have a 'bikepark' in reality it is like so many European resorts in that it is really just a small area set aside from the trails for the more freeride aspects of the sport. In Crans Montana they have focused on the northshore area of freeride with a trail built up in the trees with multiple lines and including skinnies, drops, berms and a see-saw. Great fun for northshore aficionados and all well built

but there isn't much to do once you have nailed all the lines there.

Another rock shot for the geologists out there.

DANMILNER.COM

Davos

The highest city in Europe offers some quality trail riding.

DAVOS

⩒4 The trails

- **⊗ Cross country** Excellent/beginner to advanced
- **⊗ Downhill** Fair/intermediate
- **⊗ Freeride** Poor/beginner to advanced
- **⊘ Uplift** With mountain railways and numerous gondolas all allowing bike transportation Davos has an efficient, modern set up
- **✔ Pros** Lots of bars and restaurants; miles and miles of singletrack
- **✖ Cons** The resort is still finding its feet and developing its biking offer; constant use of the gondolas can be expensive

Davos has been working its publicity engine to try and build on the number of mountain bikers coming to town over the summer. In the last few years they have done this by holding a 4X race on snow at

The Lowdown

Locals do... Tend to ride lighter trail bikes allowing the best riding to be accessed.

Locals don't... Know how to jump; the resort just hasn't had any until recently.

Don't miss... The IXS cup when it rolls into town in August, bringing hundreds of riders and spectators.

Remember to avoid... If you're looking for a bikepark, Davos is all about big mountain riding.

night under floodlights which has proved popular and broadened the awareness of what can be an exciting resort. The mountain terrain around Davos is inspiring and perfect for the adventurous rider; with a little effort you can access some sublime trails. Definitely not an out and out downhill resort, Davos offers excellent riding for the trail rider while any downhiller prepared to work for their thrills will have a good experience here.

Cross country

The Grischa trail runs through the high national park area and over to the resorts

of Lenzerheide and Arosa. It is a three-day ride and the resort offers packages with accommodation provided and luggage transfer. Staying closer to the resort, there are a number of good singletrack trails and loops marked out on the bike explorer map available in the town for a small fee, and the resort have provided their own routes to follow. Trail riding around Davos is a superb experience with the good terrain and great landscapes.

Easy Take the Clavedar Alp loop, a short 16-km route, all on wide, easy trails or mountain roads that will take you up to

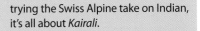

Practicalities

Like a lot of Swiss resorts, Davos has roots. Compared to many North American resorts, its history makes it practically Precambrian, and it continues to dine out on this heritage today. Initially famed as a sanatorium, then as a resort, it's been written about by Conan Doyle and Thomas Mann and been popular for well over 100 years. Even today, the associations are many, from the World Economic Forum (Davos hosts the symposium each year) to its claim to be the highest city in Europe.

Sleeping Stay at the heart of the action at the riders hotel, the *Bahnhof-Terminus* (T+41 81-414 9797). Similarly set up to cater for mountain bikers is the *Sunstar Park Hotel* (T+41 81-413 1414).

Eating *Padrinos* do cheap pizzas, while *Parma* is a slightly posher, authentic Italian. And if you fancy trying the Swiss Alpine take on Indian, it's all about *Kairali*.

Bars and clubs The *Bolgenschanze* is definitely the social hub of the resort. *Villa Palatina* has some full-on House nights, and *La Onda* is also popular with the locals.

Bike shop In Davos look for *Beat Metz* (T+41 81-413 3909) or in Klosters go to *Bardill Sport* (T+41 81-422 1040); both have spares and a workshop while *Beat Metz* hire XC bikes.

Internet café *Villa Palatini* has good internet access as well as being a Wi-Fi hotspot. Almost every hotel has free internet access, as does the Davos tourist office.

Bike map available? The excellent bike explorer series of maps has produced a guide for Davos which is available for 12 CHF.

contouring, fast and flowing descents possible back down. Of course there are steep hiking trails that are used as well, but these are not official bike trails and the new downhill course has been added to try and draw bikers away from the hiking routes.

Freeride

There are no freeride areas in Davos.

a panoramic viewpoint before looping back down to Davos town.

Difficult Book yourself in for the Grischa trail, a three-day ride through awesome scenery.

Downhill

While Davos has only just built its first downhill specific course in order to host the IXS Cup in 2008, it has for some years been popular among the Swiss on long travel trail bikes and for downhillers who don't mind to pedalling. This is due to the good transport system and the long,

DANMILNER.COM

Above left: Nicolas Sarkozy takes a break from the World Economic Forum with a bit of XC R&R. **Left**: Rustic.

ⓘ OPENING TIMES

1 May-31 Oct

Ⓢ RESORT PRICES

Day pass: 30 CHF;
Season pass: 80 CHF

ⓘ DIRECTORY

Tourist Office: T+41 81-415 2121
Medical Centre: T+41 81-414 8888
Taxi: T+41 81-416 7373
Website: davos.ch

Switzerland Davos

Grindelwald

↘5 The trails

- **XC Cross country** Good/beginner to advanced
- **DH Downhill** Good/intermediate
- **FR Freeride** Poor/beginner
- **Uplift** Grindelwald has a modern and efficient lift system with mountain railways and gondolas
- **Pros** Rich history to dip into; some good technical singletracks; the views of the surrounding peaks are awe inspiring
- **Cons** Expensive; no good for freeriders

The riding in Grindelwald involves some picture-book Alpine terrain, and there is a good mix of routes, from mapped trails suitable for beginners and novices through to long, tough tours that are both physically and technically demanding. The area is still fairly quiet through the summer but the Swiss have been wising up to some of the incredible descents possible from way up above the treeline. The great thing here is the fact that all the hiking trails are open to bikes as well, so long as you have the skill and are respectful of hikers and the trail. This opens up a lot of technical routes, but if

ⓘ OPENING TIMES

The lifts are open from the end of Jun to the end of Aug

Ⓢ RESORT PRICES

Day pass: 100 CHF

Ⓒ DIRECTORY

Tourist Office: T+41 33-854 1212
Medical Centre: T+41 33-854 1010
Taxi: T+41 33-853 1177
Website: grindelwald.com

Pretty much defining the term 'chocolate box', the pastures around pretty Grindelwald provide a mellow counterpoint to the fearsome Eiger looking over the village.

Top: Effort going up...
Above: ...equals fun going down!

you want guidance it can be arranged through privat-bike.ch.

Cross country

There are 27 routes available for GPS download and they range from easy routes using wide Alpine tracks and dirt roads to highly technical, eroded rocky runs. There is something to suit most abilities here and GPS units can be hired from the tourist office (if you'd rather have the ease of following the machine as opposed to stopping and getting out the map every 10 minutes).

Downhill

There are two new downhill courses being constructed through the summer season 2008, running from the Schrekfield lift station. These new man-made additions should complement the more natural and highly technical descents that can be found in the resort

You could take the cable car.

with a little exploration. If you like the singletrack in Verbier or Les Arcs you'll enjoy Grindelwald.

Easy Try out the new downhill run at the Schrekfield lift. A warm up for the more technical challenges of the hiking singletracks.

Or stay in town and get leathered.

Difficult Take the awesome Schynige Platte descent. It begins way up in the moonscape high up above the treeline, and is a long enduro style descent containing some really technical rock sections that wind down into wooded switchbacks. It's an epic ride.

Freeride

There are no freeride trails in Grindelwald.

Practicalities ⬤🚲🔧

Overlooked by the Jungfrau and the Eiger, two Swiss peaks steeped in modern and ancient folklore, Grindelwald should be in the same rarefied rank as Zermatt or Chamonix. And yet, in common with the rest of the Berner Oberland, Grindelwald pretty much defines the term 'Heidi Country'. The area that lies beneath these fearsome peaks has some versatile and fun riding.

Sleeping If you're on a budget there are plenty of low-end hostels and dorms in town, but the *Mountain Hostel* (mountainhostel.ch) is well situated, across the road from the Mannlichen gondola. The *Downtown Lodge* (downtown-lodge.ch) has rooms for 8 people and is centrally located. If you're flush then stay at *The Eiger* (eiger-grindelwald.ch) or the *Spinne* (spinee.grindelwald.com) hotels.

Eating As well as the best views of the Eiger, the *Central Hotel Wolter* serves vegetarian options (T+81 33-854 3333). The *Spinne* is also a renowned culinary experience, with an international menu of kangaroo, moose and other strange meats. Try *C and M* for snacks.

Bars and clubs Head to the 'Bermuda Triangle' area of town, where clubs and bars centred around the *Spinne* and *Eiger* hotels are the liveliest.

Bike shop The hostels in Grindelwald rent out basic bikes, but these are not suited to the more technical trails.

Internet café Grindelwald is a wireless village so no worries there.

Bike map available? Yes, maps are available from the tourist office.

The Lowdown

Locals do... Eat at the Mongolian barbecue at the *Eiger* – all you can eat for 30 CHF.

Locals don't... Ride! On the whole the town has been a little slow on the uptake, but there is a small emerging local scene now.

Don't miss... The Jungfraujoch station, Europe's highest indoor train station, with its incredible views of the Eiger and Jungfrau.

Remember to avoid... The menu in the *Spinne*, if you're veggie.

Switzerland Grindelwald

Laax

Where else has a marketing slogan 'Flims is crap'?

LAAX

↘6 The trails

- **XC Cross country** Excellent/beginner to intermediate
- **DH Downhill** Good/intermediate
- **FR Freeride** Good/intermediate
- **↗ Uplift** There are 2 main lifts serving the freeride and enduro trails; but there are other lifts that can be used to link the resort to Lenzerheide
- **✓ Pros** 90 mins from Zürich Airport; no queues and unspoilt trails; all bases covered
- **✗ Cons** Very quiet resort; quite a spread-out town

Laax really should make more fuss over their trails. There's a huge variety here, with some really well-made freeriding lines packed with jumps and drops, steep and technical downhills and over 300 km of cross country, from novice to expert routes. This place could easily gain renown as one of the best in Switzerland, with most trails finishing up at the swimming lake – a perfect place to cool off before hitting another run. Another plus point is that biking is allowed on all trails here.

ⓘ OPENING TIMES

The Foppa chairlift runs from 31 May to 19 Oct and from 0830 to 1715

Ⓢ RESORT PRICES

1 day: 44 CHF;
Season pass: 260 CHF

ⓘ DIRECTORY

Tourist Office: T+41 81-920 9200
Website: flims.com

Practicalities

Laax is in the Swiss canton of Graubünden, and is part of the Alpenarena resort which combines the formerly separate resort of Flims, Laax and Falera. The resort has a well set up summer mountain bike trail network though it has remained a secret to most. It can be very quiet during the week, and it is virtually unknown outside the Swiss and German markets. It deserves to have more riders, although they are perhaps put off by the unfortunate local name for peak – 'crap'. As a result pretty much everything in town has 'crap' as a prefix. The main bar is called the 'Crap Bar', the peaks are 'Crap' and the tourist board uses the slogan 'Flims is Crap' in its marketing. Genius.

Sleeping The *Arena lodge* (T+41 81-911 2400) is in the centre of Flims opposite the gondola station and is a bike hotel set up to cater for mountain bikers. Likewise, the *Backpacker Hotel Capricorn* (T+41 81-921 2120) caters for mountain bikers.

Eating For a touch of the west head to *Barstows Steak House* where they serve tasty steaks and generous burgers. In Laax, *Pizzeria Cristallina* is the best of the bunch and serves thin crust pizzas from a wood-burning oven.

Bars and clubs The *Crap Bar* is the definite focal point, although like the rest of the resort it tends to be extremely quiet at the weekend. The *Capri Lounge* at the *Backpacker's Deluxe* are also lively.

Bike shop Head to *Boarder World* in Flims (T+41 81-927 7077), they hire bikes as well as carrying the usual spares and can also organize a guide.

Internet café Most of the larger hotels have Wi-Fi, as does the *Capri Lounge* and the *Living Room* in Flims.

Bike map available? There are small trail maps available for free from the tourist office but they only outline some of the basic beginner routes. A detailed trail map is available from the same place for 12 CHF.

RED BULL TRAILFOX

A crap wallride.

FLIMS LAAX FALERA TOURISM

Cross country

Over 300 km of signposted XC and enduro trails around Laax make it a serious contender. They range from mellow family routes to technical routes for experts only. The whole area uses its own Flims signage system which identifies the discipline and its physical and technical difficulty.

Downhill

Laax actually label all their downhill trails as 'freeride' trails, and while they do contain some freeride features they are really downhill runs. Downhillers with trail bikes will enjoy the enduro trails as well – you take a lift up and take a longer run back down to the bottom. Riders with rounded skills will be able to take on the major freeride line with all its gaps. There is also a more traditional race downhill with some big rock and root technical sections which is pretty steep in places too.

Easy Take the Flims 247 run, a long 12.1-km descent that, while not necessarily 'easy', is a good challenging ride without being too over-facing.

Difficult Take the Red Bull Trail Fox route; you'll need to be a flying fox to hit all the lines as this trail mixes up the speed of a traditional downhill with the jumps and gaps of a freeride line.

Freeride

The freeride trail has various stunts and northshore features along its length, from step-downs and drops to wallrides and gaps. It's a really good trail for intermediate to advanced riders but as with most of the Swiss resorts there are not enough standalone freeride features to sustain a longer visit. Mix it up with the enduro trails and you'll find some great riding to enjoy here with a small slopestyle area at the bottom and a set of trick jumps for sessioning.

Above: Rugged landscape. Don't forget the puncture kit.
Below: The Red Bull Trail Fox.

RED BULL TRAILFOX

The Lowdown

Locals do... Rip through the steep rock sections on the technical downhill. Stop and watch to pick up some lines.

Locals don't... Rush, you will often see them feet up on the sun terrace or stopped at the lakes.

Don't miss... The Red Bull Trail Fox Competition each Jun is an awesome event with three downhill runs over two days (one of them at night); the fastest cumulative time takes the prize purse.

Remember to avoid... The Flying Fox trail in the wet; it can be lethal.

Lenzerheide

LENZERHEIDE

↘7 The trails

- **XC Cross country** Excellent/beginner to advanced
- **DH Downhill** Fair/intermediate
- **FR Freeride** Poor/beginner
- **⚡ Uplift** With funiculars, cablecars and chairlifts Lenzerheide is well adapted to carry mountain bikes
- **✓ Pros** Close to Zürich airport; linked to other bikeresorts of Aros and Davos; resort runs a special TREK women's bike festival (womensbikefestival.ch)
- **✗ Cons** Won't keep the shuttle-happy downhillers busy

More cross country trails than you can shake a cuckoo clock at.

Lenzerheide is an XC rider's dream, but it still offers some good trails for those of you who are a little ascent-shy. Every year they host the Bike Attack descent which rivals any of the spots in the Alps and which can be accessed from the mountain lifts. At its highest point the terrain is bare, rocky and barren and as you descend it becomes more and more lush with mountain pastures, deeper soils, forests and eventually you reach the shores of the lake which is the perfect way to cool after a hard ride. Lenzerheide

The lifts open at the end of Jun and run through till the end of Oct: most run 0900-1630

$ RESORT PRICES
Day pass: 44 CHF;
Season pass: 190 CHF

ⓘ DIRECTORY
Tourist information:
T+41 81-385 1120
Mountain Bike Information:
T+41 81-385 1151
Website: lenzerheide.com

is spot on for those who enjoy their environment as much as the riding itself.

Cross country

With 250 km of signposted bike tours and a further 900 km of GPS tours, the resort has plenty to fill a week or two of riding.

Left: Checking out the view halfway down.
Below: "Moo? I was going to say that."

WWW.KURHAUS-LENZERHEIDE.CH

Switzerland Lenzerheide

Practicalities

Near to Zürich in eastern Switzerland's canton of Grisons is Lenzerheide, a modest resort located at the end of the pretty Lake Heidsee. Now as much a summer resort as a winter destination, the town is long-established and traditional. Hotels are built in the traditional Swiss style and their setting is stunning with lake, woodland and mountain views. Set in a high altitude valley at 1500 m the area is a real playground offering a wide range of mountain bike trails. In Lenzerheide, you stay overnight in 1 of 4 bike hotels, eat in 1 of the biker friendly restaurants on the bike tour, improve your technique in the bike obstacle course, take the mountain train to the summit in order to enjoy the travelling wind and never lose your way, thanks to GPS and first-class maps.

Sleeping In Lenzerheide there are 4 special bike hotels that offer a great package and if you stay at any of them your tickets for the lifts are free for the duration of your visit. You can't go wrong with that offer, so check out *Hotel Collina* (hotelcollina.ch), *Hotel Alpina* (hotelalpinaparpan.ch), *Hotel Waldhaus am* (waldhausvalbella.ch), or *Sporthotel Dieschen* (hotel-dieschen.ch).

Eating There are a number of bike friendly restaurants along the many tours around the resort which are a great place to take a break, fill up on food and fill your water bottles or camelbacks. In the town head to *La Scala* (schweizerhof-lenzerheide.ch) or *La Riva* (la-riva.ch).

Bars and clubs With a slightly busier summer season than most ski resorts, the bars have a little more going on. The *Larchen Lounge* found in the *Hotel Kurhaus* is a good place to kick off with a few tales over some drinks. Later in the night head on to *Nino's Bar* where the locals like to hang out.

Bike shops There are 4 main bike shops in the resort which all hire bikes and equipment; they will also help you out with GPS routes and are quite knowledgeable on the area. They are *Activ Sport Baselgia* (activ-sport.ch), *Louis Sport* (louissport.ch), *Pesko Sport Peak* (pesko.ch), and *Seeli Sportshop* in Churwalden (seelisportshop.ch).

Internet café The hotel *Schweizerhof* has a coffee bar where you can grab a drink and log onto the web.

Bike map available? The resort has produced some great maps of the XC routes and has also set up a GPS download service from their website, lenzerheide.com, or you can download them in the resort.

Downhill

Head over to the Rothorn where you can race down the Bike Attack race track, which is like a mini mega avalanche. Starting up on the rocks and scree and winding down through into the forests, it drops some 1600 m over 18 km of descent. Many of the tours can be followed cutting out the climbs and riding only the descents by using the lifts, it also allows you to tour around the area. Don't come expecting race tracks and shuttle runs, but come prepared to enjoy the trails and put a bit of effort in and Lenzerheide is perfect for beginners and intermediate riders.

Freeride

Despite a couple of small pieces built at the bottom of the run, Lenzerheide does not really offer anything for the freerider.

The view from the top. Not bad, eh?

The Lowdown

Locals do... Every so often take on the 3-day trip of the Grischa trail that loops through the bike resorts of Lenzerheide, Arosa, Davos and then back round to Lenzerheide, an epic ride (www.grischatrail.ch).

Locals don't... Ride solo, if you want to join up for a ride they meet on Wednesday evenings at 1900 at *Activ Sport* for free.

Don't miss... The views from the Rothorn summit and then of course the Bike Attack trail back down.

Remember to avoid... Riding trails that are not signed. There are so many marked trails there really is no excuse.

Many of the tours are marked out on easier gentle routes that take in roads and doubletrack. But with each one graded for both physicality and technique you can choose one to suit you. The tougher routes taking in some quality pieces of singletrack and great views. Those looking for guiding or to hire a GPS unit should head to Activ Sport (T+41 81-384 2534) or Bike Explorer (T+41 81-356 2244).

Easy The west side of the Rothorn (Scalottas) is a lot flatter than the east and is the ideal terrain for XC tracks and easier rides. This side is very popular with families and beginners.

Difficult The east side of the Rothorn is steep and has much more technical trails.

Leysin

◺8 The trails

◉ Cross country Good/beginner to intermediate

◉ Downhill Fair to good/beginner to intermediate

◉ Freeride Fair/beginner to intermediate

◉ Uplift There is a gondola to carry riders and bikes to the top of the trails

◉ Pros Very quick transfer time; great views; good short break destination

◉ Cons Small resort where you will exhaust all possibilities in less than a week; bikepark still developing

For what is seemingly a pretty tiny resort, Leysin has a hidden fund of XC terrain. Although the Kona bikepark is still under construction, this will give the riding area a much more rounded package. It's not the biggest area in the world, but the scope is definitely there for some fun, creative lines. For its proximity to Geneva, and simple up-mountain access, we think this resort is perfect for a mid-season quick getaway.

Cross country

With 110 km of marked trails – from mellow, easy routes through to the leg burning most difficult ones – there is plenty to keep most abilities challenged

Great views and a fund of riding from this tiny Swiss riding centre.

ENDRE LÖVAAS

Above: Chocolate box scenery in the woods.
Opposite page: The farmer's wall was stolen stone by stone by thieves on bikes.

Practicalities ◼◢◔

Compared to some of its more illustrious Swiss resort cousins such as Verbier and Zermatt, Leysin suffers from a lack of profile in the wider world. This is a shame as it punches well above its weight. Somewhere between a pretty Alpine village like Vars and a developed resort town along the lines of Morzine, Leysin is friendly, compact and has some nice trail riding within its scant boundaries. Another trump card is its closeness to Geneva and the new Kona bikepark, which makes it a real option for a short break getaway.

Sleeping Best for riders on a budget and looking for a hostel or equivalent is the wonderfully named *Hiking Sheep* (T+41 24-494 3535). Families or groups of friends should try the *Central-Résidence* (T+41 24-494 1339), a classic Alpine hotel. A more upmarket shout is the 4-star *Le Classic* (T+41 24-493 0606).

Eating Eat at *Le Leysin* (leleysin.com) at least once to experience the local cuisine. Elsewhere, the *Lynx* and the *Yeti* are recommended for cheap eats and a good atmosphere.

Bars and clubs The *Yeti Bar* is popular with the younger crowd, as is the *Lynx* and *La Calèche*. Later, everyone heads to *Club 94* in *Central-Résidence* which opens on weekends through the summer.

Bike shop *Endless Ride* (T+41 24-494 1131) is the best shop to head to, with bikes for hire; a good workshop and knowledge of the trails. Make sure you pop in for a chat.

Internet café There are 2 cyber cafés in town: the *Tea Room* (T+41 24-494 2706) and the *Lynx* (T+41 24-494 1532)

Bike map available? There is a trail map showing some of the 110 km of XC tours around Leysin.

ⓘ OPENING TIMES

The lifts are open from 7 Jun to 19 Oct and from 0900-1700

ⓢ RESORT PRICES

Day pass: 27 CHF

ⓞ DIRECTORY

Tourist Office: T+41 24-494 2244
Medical Centre: T+41 24-493 2929
Taxi: T+41 0800-802333
Website: leysin.ch

in Leysin. Riders who enjoy the more technical singletrack trails can then turn their hand to the 200 km of hiking routes that are mapped out in the area and which contain some significantly more technical sections than the VTT routes. *Endless ride* in the village are a great source of trail knowledge.

Downhill

Leysin was brought to the attention of the downhill scene way back in 2000 and 2001 when it hosted a round of the UCI World Cup (the race of 2000 being one of the great World Cup winning margins when Cédric Gracia posted a nine-second victory over the greatest rider of all time, Nicolas Voillioz). The courses then were true old-school affairs, flat out across pistes and long off cambers with run times of over six minutes. And it's great to see downhill returning to Leysin with the new Kona bikepark opening for 2008 (konabikeparks.com).

Easy The wooden northshore/slopestyle park has plenty of easy lines through it so beginners can learn to hit drops and gaps in a safe environment.

Difficult There are some harder lines through the bottom northshore area with step-on/step-off features – some quite high off the ground – so it's suitable for more experienced riders.

Freeride

The Kona bikepark contains the usual sets of drops, northshore and jumps but at this stage the park is only small and needs to expand further to become an attraction in its own right. Riders who have a mid travel bike capable of hitting the trails, the downhills and the freeride drops and jumps will have a great time but there is not enough at present in Leysin to attract core freeriders.

The Lowdown

Locals do... Take five minutes to look at the breathtaking view, one of the best in the Alps.

Locals don't... Tend to ride on their own; you will see groups of locals shooting off together at the top of the trails; if you're lucky they may let you follow.

Don't miss... Stop in the *Kuklos* restaurant for lunch at least once. It's that Alpine special, a revolving restaurant, and, unsurprisngly, has great views of the area.

Remember to avoid... Some of the hiking routes have exposed drops and steep technical sections which should only be tackled by advanced riders.

Lugano

The deluxe lakeside city in the excellent cross country region of Tocino.

LUGANO

↘9 The trails

- **Cross country** Good to excellent/ beginner to intermediate
- **Downhill** Fair to good/beginner
- **Freeride** Poor/beginner
- **Uplift** There are 4 lifts: the Monte Bre, Monte Tamaro, Monte Lema and Monte Generosa
- **Pros** Beautiful city and area; great XC area
- **Cons** It's not all laid out for you here like at some ski resorts; quite dispersed riding area; expensive lifts for multiple runs

Lugano is a beautiful part of Switzerland and is a different experience to many of the more traditional ski resorts in the country. In Lugano you stay in a wonderful city and the trails all head out across the hills and mountains in the region with a perfect topography for mountain biking. It is not as steep as in many places in the Alps; the hills are more rolling and lush here allowing you to cover longer distances and gain vantage points overlooking the city and lake. The tourist board are working hard to improve

The Lowdown

Locals do... Enjoy the technical challenge of the World Cup course.

Locals don't... Ride the marked trails so much on Monte Tamaro, there are much better routes off the hill.

Don't miss... A trip up into the valley of Valcolla above Lugano; a great place to ride XC and has had a lot of its routes recently signed to improve access to the trails.

Remember to avoid... Bringing a heavy out and out downhill bike and gear; there's some great descending to be done, but better done on a trail bike that can be pedalled as well (the lifts are pretty pricey).

Above: The classic 'branch duck' stance.
Below: Three dwarf riders approached the giant zebra with caution.

the amount of waymarked bike trails in the area and it's starting to pay off.

Cross country

A beautiful wide area to enjoy XC riding with trails heading out from all parts of the city and around the surrounding hills and valleys. Lugano is an unspoilt XC mecca. While on the whole the trails are not as technical or exposed as say Verbier or Chamonix, they are flowing and run through some beautiful landscapes. Until recently the trails were poorly marked out and some still require map skills or local knowledge. If you want a guide to show you around contact Sport&Turismo (T+41 91-924 9653), which organized different excursions for the beginner through to the expert biker. They can also arrange to take you to the valley of Valcolla, above Lugano in the Tocino region, which has some great trails.

Easy Pick up the trail map from the tourist office and hit the number 5 and 6 trails, a short hour loop around the Monte Croce peak to the south of the City.

Difficult Head northwest out of the city up to the 2003 World Championship course at Monte Tamaro; the loop there will test your strength and technique.

Downhill

Lugano will not satisfy the racer heads as the long and steep World Championship course is not open to ride anymore, but it does have bags of quality singletrack and, with four lifts all on different mountains around the city that carry bikes, there are loads of trails to take down the hills. Just be aware that the main marked descents are pretty tame; the better trails that the locals ride are little-used old footpaths. You will need a car to get to the different lifts and the lifts do not offer day and week passes as they would at the ski resorts, so most are single trip tickets.

Lugano is best suited to the rider who is prepared to put in some pedal power as well as use the lifts over their stay.

Freeride

There are no freeride facilities in Lugano.

"Six cheese McNuggets and a Filet-O-Emmental please."

Practicalities

Lugano is a stunning city set on the shores of Lake Lugano and surrounded by mountains in the Italian-speaking region of Tocino, in south Switzerland. The city has earned the nickname the 'Monte Carlo of Switzerland' due to the large number of celebrities and sportsmen drawn to the place. It enjoys a temperate climate with a high number of sunny days; perfect trail riding weather to hit the many trails surrounding the city and lake.

Sleeping Lugano is a city with a thriving tourist industry, so you can choose from cheap and cheerful to full bling here. *Hotel Pestalozzi* (T+41 91-921 4646) is a clean, family-run hotel with some ensuite rooms in the budget range. *Villa Sassa Hotel & SPA* (T+41 91-911 4111) is found on the hills overlooking Lugano, yet just a few minutes' walk from the centre of town, a slightly more luxurious option and more expensive.

Eating The cafeteria in the *Manor* department store offers a wide variety of tempting international dishes, ranging from sushi to pasta. Wine and beer are available along with

a wide range of other beverages. While *Argentino* (T+41 91-922 9049) is perhaps the best example of the many quality pizzerias in the city with great service; prices range from 15-20 CHF.

Bars and clubs In the summer your best bet is to wander along the lakeside promenade and check out open-air bars and cafés. Check local listings for clubs and shows as venues come and go with the seasons. There are 3 clubs in the city: *Privilege*, *Club One* and *Desperado's* are all located downtown near the *Manor* department store. *Oops* is a great place to have a few beers in the evening near the University .

Bike shop For bike hire and basic repairs head to *Balmelli Sport* (T+41 91-923 5867).

Internet café *Café Studio B2 Network* (T+41 91-976 1220) offer 30 mins free internet use when you buy a drink there.

Bike map available? A map of the trails around Lugano is available from the tourist office.

Morgins

A charming small Swiss town with good links to Châtel and the rest of the Portes du Soleil.

MORGINS

↘10 The trails

- **Cross country** Good/beginner to advanced
- **Downhill** Good to excellent/ beginner to advanced
- **Freeride** Good/intermediate to advanced
- **Uplift** Just 1 chairlift serving the town of Morgins as part of the 24 lifts of the Portes du Soleil
- **Pros** Lovely quiet village; no crime
- **Cons** Difficult to ride back to Les Crosets and Champéry on a DH bike; may be too quiet for some

While Morgins may be the smallest and quietest town in the area, it has some cracking trails and is a peaceful base from which to ride out onto the wider Portes du Soleil trails. The one chairlift in the town gives access to Morgins trails and also to head out to Champoussin and Les Crosets. Or it is a short spin across the border to Châtel in France.

Cross country

There are some great cross country trails on this side of the Portes du Soleil region. Taking the lift up out of Morgins allows

① OPENING TIMES

The lifts run daily from 27 Jun to 31 Aug

⑤ RESORT PRICES

Day pass: €16; week pass: €64; Season pass: €128

① DIRECTORY

Tourist Office: T+41 24-477 2361
Medical Centre: T+ 41 24-473 1731
Taxi: T+ 41 796-382250
Website: portesdusoleil.com; morgins.ch

Practicalities 🍴🚲🔧

Morgins is a chocolate-box mountain village on the Swiss/French border nestled in the valley between mountains with expanse of forest and green Alpine meadows. It really is a pretty village and one to unwind and relax in as it is perhaps one of the quietest of the whole Portes du Soleil region while still allowing access to all the great trails. The hills of Morgins itself do not feature as many purpose-built trails, but Morgins is close to Châtel, Champoussin and Champéry.

Sleeping *Camping La mare au Diable* (T+41 79-301 3333) is a nice campsite with all the necessary facilities including Wi-Fi, it is a nice place to sleep in the open air. *L'Echappe Belle* offer bed and breakfast accommodation, or book into the *Hôtel Beau Site* (T+41 24-477 1138) which is close to the lift and with space to store your bikes.

Eating *Chez Tonio* and *C'la Pizzeria* are both popular amongst the locals with a European menu, and make for good evening haunts. Most riders will be found at lunchtime congregated around the large musical clock, making rolls with meat and cheese from the convenience store.

Bars and clubs Morgins is perhaps the quietest resort in the Portes du Soleil, so riders seeking nightlife should stay in Morzine. Occasionally at weekends the *Yucatan* or *Le Saf* will open for some late-night drinks.

Bike shop *Snowline* sports shop (T+41 24-477 2906) have the usual rental bikes, together with a well-equipped workshop and most of the spares that you may need.

Internet café The central *Sportif* and the *T bar* both have computer terminals and Wi-Fi access.

Bike map available? A trail map of the Portes du Soleil is available from the tourist office and lift station.

The Lowdown

Locals do... Know some good trails not on the trail map, off the back of the hill.

Locals don't... Ride when there has been heavy rain as the rain ruts and steepness of the hill make it tough going.

Don't miss... The freeride trail is challenging and good fun with various obstacles to try out on the way down.

Remember to avoid... Missing the bus back from Pré-La-Joux.

you to spin around to Champoussin, Les Crosets and Champéry and ultimately you can ride the whole of the loop over to France in either direction, depending on whether you head first to France and Châtel or over to Champoussin.

Downhill

The two routes down of the hill in Morgins are super fun: one a classic downhill race style course with mix of fast sections and tighter wooded roots sections and bus stops; the other trail, labelled the northshore or freeride trail, is a lot steeper and will have your brakes glowing by the time you reach the bottom.

Easy The main downhill run is suitable for most riders with some previous experience and doesn't get as hammered as some of the other trails in the Portes du Soleil.

Difficult The freeride track doubles up as a steep and challenging downhill when ridden with a bit of pace. The discs on your bike will be glowing by the time you hit the bottom.

Freeride

The freeride trails in Morgins are essentially steep downhill routes with some wooden jumps and drops built along their length. There are different options of varying difficulty as you head down the hill but the sheer steepness of the route means this is only really for riders with a reasonable level of skill. For more freeride fun spin over the hill to Châtel bikepark in Pré-La-Joux.

Switzerland Morgins

DANMILNER.COM

Saas Fee

SAAS FEE

↘11 The trails

- **Cross country** Good/beginner to intermediate
- **Downhill** Fair to good/beginner to intermediate
- **Freeride** Poor/beginner
- **Uplift** There are 3 lifts through the Saas Fee valley open to bikers: the Morenia, the Hannig and the Furggstalden
- **Pros** No cars make for a peaceful valley; a cheaper alternative to next door Zermatt; everyone speaks English
- **Cons** The resort is not really geared up to all types of mountain biking, though there are plenty of killer natural trails

Saas Fee is a prime location with an unusually high treeline that allows many of the trails to run through the pine forests despite the high altitude. Above the treeline there are moraine fields and above that the glaciers which provide year-round skiing. This is also where the crazy Saas Fee Glacier race is held, on the first week of April, down a 9-km piste run

ⓘ OPENING TIMES

The lifts start running in mid Jun and close at the end of Sep; each has its own schedule so see the Saas Fee website for more information

ⓢ RESORT PRICES

Day pass: 32 CHF

ⓘ DIRECTORY

Tourist Office: T+41 27-958 1858
Medical Centre: T+41 27-957 5859
Taxi: T+41 27-957 3344
Website: saasfee.ch

Home of the crazy Glacier race, Saas Fee offers some classic trail riding in unspoilt surroundings.

with the fastest guys hitting speeds of over 60 mph. The resort is quite close to Zermatt and the two make a perfect trail riding break.

Cross country

There are 70 km of marked routes through the Saas Fee valley and many have the option of skipping out the climbs by using the lifts, while others head out into corners of the valley where you will have to climb under your own steam. The routes are all mapped but you can arrange for an MTB guide from the tourist office and companies such as

The Lowdown

Locals do... Enjoy a good night out in the *Popcorn* bar.

Locals don't... Drive. Cars are banned in the resort. Take your ticket to the hotel and get a reduction on parking rates.

Don't miss... The Saas Fee Allanin Glacier Race, with a Le Mans-style mass start and speeds of over 60 mph. This unique race down 9-km of piste each April has been gaining a lot of interest.

Remember to avoid... A car-free village, drivers must park at the end of the village and then make their own way to their hotel or apartment. Find out where you are beforehand and, if necessary, book a taxi. Some hotels can be 15 minutes' walk away from the car park – a nightmare with lots of bags.

ENDRE LOVAAS

Practicalities ⊟🚲🏔

Saas Fee is an insanely picturesque resort. Sitting in the next valley along from Zermatt, it's a traditional Swiss village with beautifully winding, car-free streets surrounded by towering 4000-m peaks such as the Allalinhorn and the Dom and a glacier that appears to hang right over the town. The singletrack is world class, and the resort manages to balance the demands of the modern summer and winter sports scene with the needs of the fondue-supping tourists who also make up a large part of the Saas Fee's clientèle.

Sleeping Saas Fee has a loads of self-catering apartments that are typically family owned and rented out through the tourist board. Contact them on saas-fee.ch/en/reservations.cfm to secure a booking.

Eating The pizzeria in the *Ferienart-Walliserhof* (T+41 27-958 1902) is reputedly one of the best in the Alps and has an amazing salad bar. A slightly cheaper Italian option can be found at the *Spaghetteria* (T+41 27-957 1526), underneath the *Hôtel Brittania*. Elsewhere, the *Hôtel Dom* (T+41 27-957 5101) is good for traditional Swiss food.

Bars and clubs *Popcorn* is a boardsports shop that turns into a bar each evening and is popular with locals, bands and DJs. The *Happy Bar* is also popular, and is a little cheaper and quieter, as is *The Lounge/Living Room*, above *Popcorn*.

Bike shop Head to *Anselm Bumann* (T+41 27-957 2680) for a store that will carry out repairs as well as hire out bikes.

Internet café There's an internet café close to the *Migros* supermarket, and wireless in many hotels. If all else fails you can also get online in the *Hôtel Dom* (uniquedom.com).

Bike map available? There is a trail map which shows the marked bike routes in the valley, available from the ticket office.

Below: It's hard to keep focused on the track when there's a valley shot like that in distance.
Below right: Evening dust. Perfect.

OTP in Zermatt can show you some great trails that you probably won't find without assistance.

Easy The easiest tour around Saas Fee is labelled No 1 which is just 6.6 km and suitable for families as it is on gentle and easy terrain.

Difficult The number 11 Trail is one of the more technical and strenuous of the short loops as it climbs and descends from 1500 m to 2100 m.

Downhill

The main downhill route in Saas Fee is the Morenia run which starts at the intermediate station at 2500 m and drops 800 m vertically over 7.8 km. The other trails that can be accessed from the lifts are best suited to a freeride or longer travel trail bike as most contain some climbing along their route.

Freeride

Saas Fee has no facilities for freeride.

ENDRE LOVAAS

Scuol

A popular venue of the IXS Swiss race series that is oh-so quiet the rest of the season.

SCUOL

⌄12 The trails

- ⓧⓒ **Cross country** Fair to good/ beginner to intermediate
- ⓓⓗ **Downhill** Good/intermediate to advanced
- ⓕⓡ **Freeride** Poor/beginner
- ⓩ **Uplift** There is a gondola to the top of the downhill trails
- ✔ **Pros** Picturesque valley; quiet, no queues and unspoilt trails
- ✖ **Cons** Not enough trails for a longer stay

While Scuol does not have bags of trail, it does feature some great traditional touring style XC and some technical singletracks, as well as some quality downhill runs that have gained a solid underground following amongst some of the European seasonaires who make trips over to Scuol to session the trail.

Cross country

There are a number of routes available, either on a map or downloadable for GPS units for the easier option, as well as several marked trails. The highlight of the area is the organized four-day tour from Scuol across the national park to Livigno in Italy and back.

ⓘ OPENING TIMES

The lifts open on 30 May and close 19 Oct and run from 0900-1645

ⓢ RESORT PRICES

Day pass: 38 CHF; Week pass: 175 CHF; Season pass: 375 CHF

ⓘ DIRECTORY

Tourist Office: T+ 41 81-861 2222
Website: Scuol.ch

Downhill

The downhill track in Scuol was featured on the 'Illusionary Lines' DVD being shredded to pieces by Chris Kovarik. If you've seen that you'll have a good idea

"You need Scuolling! Baby I'm not foooling."

ENDRE LOVAAS

Switzerland's famous 'sideways tree' draws another crowd.

of what we're talking about here. It's a fast singletrack with countless switchbacks, some tech wooded sections and plenty of drops and jumps along its route. They are long runs too in the region of

10 minutes top to bottom. This is Swiss rider Claudio Calouri's local ride spot and he has helped design the routes.

Easy Take the blue route, a shorter and mellower downhill run suitable for novices.

Difficult Take the black route as featured in *Illusionary Lines* and which regularly hosts a round of the IXS downhill race series.

Freeride
While Scuol does not have any freeride trails or a bikepark area, the black downhill route does feature some drops and jumps. However, unless you are a keen downhiller as well, best to look elsewhere.

The Lowdown

Locals do... Use the spa to unwind after a weekend of hard riding.

Locals don't... Party hard, it's not that sort of place.

Don't miss... The national park guided 4-day tour through some stunning landscapes.

Remember to avoid... For longer stays unless you have booked into the tour.

Practicalities

Scuol is a small town in the Engadin Valley, a peaceful unspoilt corner of Switzerland. It is a quiet resort, but one that has had mountain bike trails longer than any of the other Swiss resorts, with the first trails added way back in 1997. Many of the visitors to the town come to sample the deluxe spa site of Engadin Bad Scuol, where you can unwind and recharge your batteries surrounded by stunning scenery.

Sleeping Perhaps one of the best offers for accommodation for XC riders is the National Bike Park Tour, a 4-day guided tour over some stunning terrain starting out from Scuol. This can be booked through the Scuol website (Scuol.ch).

Eating When out on the bike, *Café Erni* in the town is a good place to take 30 mins, and grab a tasty snack before getting back to the trails. In the evening many of the restaurants serve Endadin local specialities with the *Alegre Restaurant* at the *Belvédère Hotel* being one of the best.

Bars and clubs *Bar Dialect* and the *Alerta* bar are the places to head for a few drinks as they both have a relaxed vibe. On the weekend try out the *Galleria* which is the disco in town.

Bike shop Head to the *Engadin* adventure shop (T+41 81-861 1419) where you can hire bikes and arrange for a guided day's riding.

Internet café There is no internet café in Scuol.

Bike map available? A trail map is available from the tourist office with 20 routes for 12 CHF.

Switzerland Scuol

Verbier

Previously one of Europe's best-kept secrets, it is now regarded as one of Europe's best mountain biking locations.

VERBIER

↘13 The trails

- **Cross country** Excellent/beginner to intermediate
- **Downhill** Excellent/beginner to advanced
- **Freeride** Good/beginner to advanced
- **Uplift** There are 2 gondolas serving the main riding area; there is talk of the other side of the valley opening its lift and further cablecars opening at selected dates
- **Pros** Beautiful setting; resort is a sun trap; superb technical riding
- **Cons** Quite expensive; not for beginners

The bowl of Verbier is the perfect shape for mountain bikes as it allows you to easily gain height using the gondola and then spin out to either end of its reach along a variety of mellow doubletrack

ⓘ OPENING TIMES

The lifts run daily from 5 Jul to 22 Sep but the companies mentioned here also offer shuttles at other times of the year

Ⓢ RESORT PRICES

Day pass: 39 CHF

ⓘ DIRECTORY

Tourist Office: T+41 27-775 3888
Medical Centre: T+41 27-771 7020
Pisteurs: T+41 27-775 2511
Taxi: T+41 79-332 4545
Website: verbier.ch

Practicalities ⬛🚲🚵

Situated in a sun-drenched south-western facing bowl in the canton of the Valais, Verbier is perched high up on the mountainside at an altitude of 1500 m, bordered by France to the west and Italy to the south. Verbier by summer is a different beast to the winter time. While winter sees the well-to-do out in their Dior shades and Prada clothes, summers are a lot more grounded with just the seasonaires who truly love the resort and its environment left in the town. To these is added a steady influx of real enthusiast riders looking to shred some of the best trails in the Alps.

Sleeping Verbier draws its Alpine charm from its traditional chalet-style buildings which blend in with the hillside and their natural setting. The southwesterly orientation means you benefit from maximum sun exposure so most chalets have sun terraces for you to kick back and relax on. There are several mountain bike holiday companies based in Verbier, who all have essential knowledge of the trails. Try *Bike Verbier* (bikeverbier.com) or *Powder and Dust* (powderanddust.com) who both have chalets all geared up for biking.

Eating *En Bas at the Pub Mont Fort* (T+41 27-771 1834) is cheap and caters well for vegetarians. *Al Capone's* (T+41 27-771 6774) is open for great pizza for lunch and dinner. *Le Hameau* (+41 27-771 4580) does an unbeatable 25 CHF midday menu with a salad.

Bars and clubs The *Pub Mont Fort* has a tasty snack menu, while *Le Farinet* has a sun deck and a lounge bar. *Wonderbar* is relaxed, while *Le Fer a Cheval* is reliably busy. Later, *Le Casbah* is always busy.

Bike shop In nearby Le Châble there is the *Happy Sport* shop with a range of brands including La Pierre and Scott. In Verbier *No Bounds* is probably the best stocked shop with a good workshop and includes Iron Horse, Kona and Mondraker among its roster of brands.

Internet café Check your emails in *Harold's*, *Pub Mont Fort*, *Verbier Beach* and the *Wonderbar*.

Bike map available? There is a simple trail map available from the lift office, but it does not show many of the better trails. It is necessary for a guide to show you these routes.

and technical singletracks and pick off routes along the way. With little effort you can ride a different trail each time, although you will need a shuttle to complete the longest DH runs which take you beyond Verbier right down to the valley floor. The trails in Verbier are mostly narrow technical singletracks that are not hammered by bikes. Most contain steep sections and often have significant sections with exposure or sheer drops near the trail edge.

Cross country

The resort has produced a trail map with 16 marked routes around Verbier and while some of these take in spectacular views they are not a patch on some of the singletrack around the mountains which are not marked on the cycle trail. The Kona bikepark also has marked out a cross country itinerary which features some nice trail. To get the most out of Verbier we recommend you take a guide and hit some of the longer epic climb and descent trails such as The Ultimate Descent.

STEVE JONES

on a smaller trail bike, but make sure you have good brakes for the hour-long descents. Riders looking for the more traditional downhill course will enjoy the tracks in the Kona bikepark which have fast bermed turns, rough braking bumps and technical wooded sections.

Easy One of the easier descents, but maybe the most fun you will have, is on the Tobboggan run. You will need a shuttle to the top of this trail so hook up with one of the guiding companies.

Difficult Vertigo or Jackass will test the very best riders with countless steep switchbacks, roots and big exposures along their route.

Freeride
Verbier does not feature a whole lot of freeride. The bikepark does have drops, see-saws, doubles and northshore running down through the trails, but the main spirit of riding in Verbier is in the challenge of riding the steep and highly technical trails in the wider Verbier basin away from the bikepark. Riders looking for slopestyle and session spots would be left a little disappointed.

Downhill
There is so much downhill available to ride in Verbier and the great thing is as many of the routes are old hiking and trading paths they have worn down to a firm base of rock or roots and do

not become packed with huge braking bumps like some of the downhill trails. A downhill bike is not a necessity here as many of the tight switchbacks are easier

The Lowdown

Locals do... Make the really steep hard switchbacks look annoyingly simple.

Locals don't... Get stranded on the back side of the Verbier resort after the lifts have closed.

Don't miss... The Ultimate Descent, an epic ride through a varied terrain.

Remember to avoid... The jumps at the top of the bikepark run have very steep lips that catch out a lot of riders. Play safe on these unless a confident jumper.

Switzerland Verbier

STEVE JONES

Top: Colour co-ordination is important but matching yourself to the surrounding vista is going too far.
Above: Knock and run. Bike style.

Wiriehorn

A sleepy Swiss town that comes to life for the race events held here each year. Don't forget though, the trails are open most of the year with zero queueing.

WIRIEHORN

↘14 The trails

- **XC Cross country** Poor to fair/beginner to intermediate
- **DH Downhill** Good/beginner to advanced
- **FR Freeride** Fair/intermediate
- **Uplift** A new and fast 6-man chairlift transports riders to the top of the Wiriehorn mountain
- **✓ Pros** Good quality downhill trails; long bike season
- **✗ Cons** A lack of marked cross country trails; low-key resort; very few trails

The Lowdown

Locals do... Nail the wooden 270° berm into step-down road gap. It's easy when you see someone do it.

Locals don't... Take the chainless races too seriously, it's a chance to meet up and party.

Don't miss... The chainless races which the resort holds on the main downhill course. These are always light-hearted and good fun.

Remember to avoid... Putting in a reactive pedal stroke in the above race or it'll be a trip over the bars for sure.

The wallride is a popular shot in this book you'll notice. Gotta love 'em though eh?

Wiriehorn has a very small but good quality bike offer, it is aimed more at the downhill/freeride market, but that shouldn't put XC riders off, it's just the riding here requires a little more head work than some of the other resorts. All in all, Wiriehorn has a relaxed and fun feel to it and is great as part of a multi trip tour.

Cross country

The resort has focused its attention on gravity trails and not put so much effort as some of the other Swiss areas into marked XC routes. The new XC route is a welcome addition, but there is not enough here to justify anything more than a weekend stop without heading out under your own steam with a map.

Downhill

The main downhill line in Wiriehorn is a regular fixture of the IXS downhill series and tests some of the best riders. With high speeds and tighter, more technical root sections it has a good mix of terrain. Local Swiss downhiller Thomas Rysser has had a lot of input in the trails over the past few years building lines to challenge beginners through to pros. All of the hardest parts of the course can be avoided making the line work for less experienced riders as well as the racers out there. They are good trails, but there's

Practicalities ⬛🔧♻

Wiriehorn is a small Alpine town and a tiny ski resort through the winter months. Its one chairlift has been used to good effect through the summer months by the resort, which has built some downhill and freeride trails to provide a summer season. Though this is by no means a Les Gets or Morzine, it has a mellow relaxed vibe that makes it an enjoyable place to spend a few days.

Sleeping Wiriehorn has a few chalets and apartments on offer but the best offer in the town is undoubtedly at the *Berghaus Nuegg* (T+33 684 1242) where they have a special biker package of bed and breakfast plus a day's lift Pass for 49 CHF. Unbeatable really.

Eating *Restaurant Wirieblick* (T+33 684 0100) is the place to sit back and relax on the sunloungers watching the riders coming down the final section of the course. They have a light menu for lunches and also serve up a range of local dishes late into the evening.

Bars and clubs Wiriehorn is not the place to come if you're looking for a party; the town is small and quiet, though if you come when the resort is hosting one of their chainless races the atmosphere picks up around the *Berghauss Nuegg*.

Bike shop The *Hot Trail* shop hire bikes, has a downhill workshop and you can also book days of instruction on the trails.

Internet café No internet café in Wiriehorn.

Bike map available? There is a bike leaflet available from the lift station.

a limited choice; great for a weekend but any longer and you would feel burnt out on the same trail.

Easy Take the red line from the lift station which is of medium difficulty

and there is plenty of choice to hit the jumps and gaps or work your way around them.

Difficult Take the black downhill route when the trail splits; this is a steeper and more direct run as used for the races held here.

Freeride

Wiriehorn has a new freeride descent with more northshore and jumps than the main race downhill, though even that trail is littered with drops and small gaps and there is a 400-m northshore section. It's a fun place to session the downhill trails and hit the various stunts and gaps that have been put in on the hill, but if you don't enjoy shredding the downhills as well then there isn't enough to keep you busy here. If you do enjoy the downhills, then you'll enjoy Wiriehorn.

Three of those planks are loose and there's a pit of crocodiles rubbing their stomachs in anticipation.

Zermatt

↘15 The trails

- **XC Cross country** Excellent/intermediate to advanced
- **DH Downhill** Fair to good/intermediate
- **FR Freeride** Poor/beginner
- **⤴ Uplift** There are several lifts open to bikes in the Zermatt and Matter valley; up to 9 lifts can be used to access the longer rides and return journeys
- **✔ Pros** Some of the most awe-inspiring views in the Alps; when you're shown the way there are some fantastic XC and descending trails
- **✘ Cons** Expensive lifts; poor set up for bikes so guide required

Why Fox Racing haven't brought out a Glacier race and called it 'The Mint' I don't know.

DANMILNER.COM

Switzerland Zermatt

With incredible views, a large riding area, a cosmopolitan town and a mixture of modern and Victorian lift facilities, Zermatt is the purest of Swiss resorts.

Zermatt remains a long way behind the rest of Europe in terms of providing facilities for mountain bikers; there are few marked out routes and the ones that are are far from the best. It's a shame, as the resort has some superb riding, but until it is more proactive in its approach you will need to stay with a guide and use their knowledge to access some of the fantastic trails.

Practicalities 🏨🍴🚲

Sitting right beneath one of the world's most iconic mountains, the Matterhorn, Zermatt is one of the wintersports world's major players. Alpine history seeps from every part here, and the town buzzes with mountaineers, tourists and more recently an increasing number of mountain bikers. The town is impressive, but it's the Matterhorn looming over the village that really raises Zermatt above and beyond its 'resort' status. It is truly an awe-inspiring sight.

Sleeping *Zermatt's Youth Hostel* (youthhostel.ch/zermatt) is clean, architecturally impressive – and predictably busy and expensive. At around 70 CHF a night, the 1-star *Hotel Weisshorn* (holidaynet.ch/weisshorn) is about as cheap and cheerful as Zermatt gets. This is another resort where finding the best trails is down to knowing where to look, so it's best to stay with a company that can offer guiding; *OTP* are probably the best in the town (otp.co.uk).

Eating If *McDonald's* (reputedly the most expensive in Europe!) won't suffice, the *Pizzeria Broken* at the *Hotel*

Post (hotelpost.ch) is a better option. *The Pipe*, known locally as the 'Surfer's Cantina' is also good for a sit-down meal, while locals swear by the *North Wall Bar*.

Bars and clubs *Grampi's Pub* on the high street is expensive, but worth checking out for the piano man who plays twice a night, as well as the food and drinks. Other ports of call to check out are the *Papperia Pub* and the *Brown Cow Snack Bar*.

Bike shop *Slalom Sports* and *Julen Sports* both hire bikes and have very basic workshops. The town is not as geared up for bikes as some of the other Alpine resorts, so be prepared with some spares.

Internet café The wonderfully named *Stoked* (stoked.ch) is as good as they get. Terminals and laptop points are in the basement.

Bike map available? The bike map available from the tourist office does not really map out the best routes, unless you enjoy riding up and down gravel roads. Scenic yes, but engaging? Well, not particularly.

Switzerland Zermatt

ⓘ OPENING TIMES

The Gornergrat or Matterhorn railway runs on weekends from the 12 Jun to 16 Sep

ⓢ RESORT PRICES

Day pass: 78 CHF

ⓓ DIRECTORY

Tourist Office: T+41 27-966 8100
Medical Centre: T+41 27-967 1188
Taxi Number: T+41 0848-111212
Website: zermatt.ch;
mountainbiking.uk.com

Cross country

Zermatt is a fantastic place to ride but it is not well laid out for visitors yet so we highly recommend the use of a guiding service in this resort to get onto the best trail. Two of the best are *OTP* (mountainbiking.uk.com) and Big Mountain Adventures (ridebig.com).

Downhill

While typically not a downhill venue, Zermatt does offer some great natural downhill runs around the town and *OTP* are offering downhill specific holidays now guiding you to the best descents and including days to the nearby resorts of Crans Montana and Saastal.

Freeride

Zermatt does not offer any freeride trails or bikeparks.

The Lowdown

Locals do... Go to the *North Wall Bar* for a low-priced pizza and a few beers.

Locals don't... Drive. Cars are banned in Zermatt. Park at Tasch, further down the valley, and catch the train up.

Don't miss... The view from the Gornergrat station on a clear day, with Monte Rosa, the Matterhorn and Breithorn in sharp relief. Breathtaking.

Remember to avoid... The trails around Zermatt town at midday are packed with hikers, so get out early and head out on longer all day rides away from the crowds.

Wales

Author Rowan Sorrell takes on a secret Welsh rock garden. [ANDY LLOYD]

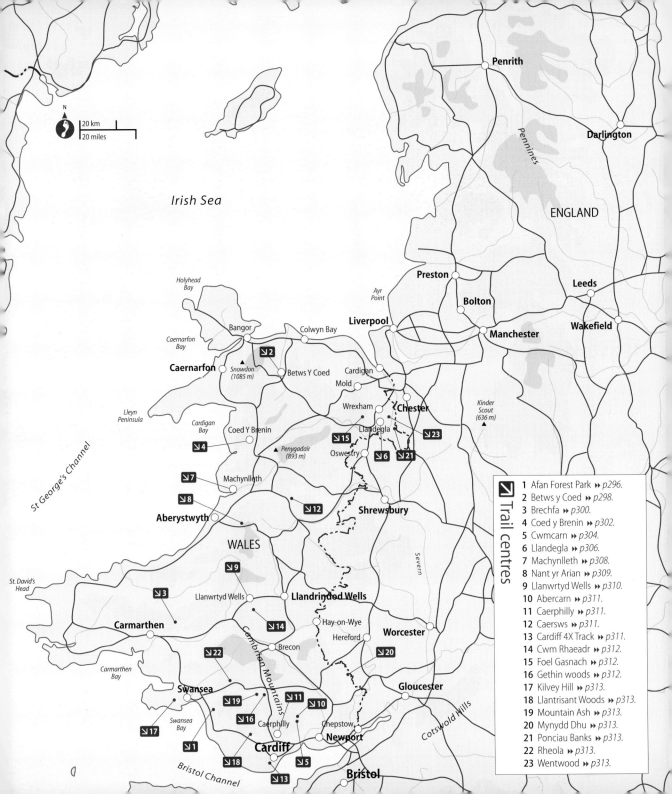

N
20 km
20 miles

Irish Sea

Holyhead Bay

Bangor

Caernarfon Bay

Caernarfon

Snowdon (1085 m)

Betws Y Coed

Lleyn Peninsula

Cardigan Bay

Coed Y Brenin

⊿ 4

⊿ 7

Machynlleth

⊿ 8

Aberystwyth

Colwyn Bay

Ayr Point

Cardigan

Mold

Wrexham

Llandegla

⊿ 15

Oswestry

⊿ 6

⊿ 21

⊿ 23

Penygadair (893 m)

⊿ 12

Shrewsbury

St. David's Head

WALES

⊿ 9

⊿ 3

Llanwrtyd Wells

Carmarthen

⊿ 22

Carmarthen Bay

⊿ 17

⊿ 19

⊿ 16

Swansea Bay

⊿ 1

⊿ 18

Swansea

⊿ 14

Brecon

Cambrian Mountains

Hay-on-Wye

Hereford

Llandrindod Wells

⊿ 11

⊿ 10

Caerphilly

Cardiff

⊿ 13

⊿ 5

Chepstow

Newport

Worcester

⊿ 20

Gloucester

Cotswold Hills

Bristol

Bristol Channel

Preston

Bolton

Liverpool

Manchester

Chester

Kinder Scout (636 m)

Pennines

ENGLAND

Penrith

Darlington

Leeds

Wakefield

St George's Channel

Severn

Alan Muldoon taking on a Welsh hairpin.

Wales is largely responsible as the place that kick-started the trail centre experience in the UK. The original centres of north Wales have shaped how and where we ride today. Not that it was ever a case of age before beauty; the original centres sparkle in the shadows of the Snowdonia National Parks Mountains and still cut it today. In addition to this are the many new centres that have opened over the years throughout Wales, resulting in a strong scene as diverse in its riding styles as it is in its landscapes.

The craggy, rocky and rugged beauty of the north combine with the strong industrial past of the south to make an interesting tour of what, in real terms, is a relatively small country. Luckily for us it is has a big heart and lots to offer the mountain biker.

Culturally, visitors can learn about the heavy industrial past that typifies many regions, and even go down a former working mine at the Big Pit, in Blaenafon Torfaen. It is also a pleasure to hear the most widely used Celtic language, Welsh, spoken by so many natives as much as it is to visit the many beautiful beaches along the Pembrokeshire coast.

As a mountain bike destination Wales seems to serve two distinct markets; the day trippers from the many nearby English towns and cities and those on long weekend or week breaks who tend to base themselves around one or two centres. Look slightly beyond this and you will find a country that offers a great variety of terrain across the different disciplines of biking, from the family holiday to the thrill-seeking downhillers. Wales has got it all covered.

Overview

Andrew Denham, Cwmcarn XC.

Llandeglla energy snack.

"Giz a lift, mate"

When you think of the bigger mountain ranges in the UK, it is the countries of Scotland and Wales that will often come to mind. With very little flat ground this is a land that almost seems designed for the invention of the modern-day trail bike; the gears will get you up the hills and your suspension and disks will be working overtime coming back down them.

Coed Y Brenin is considered the true innovator, and it was here that the first big scale sustainable mountain bike trails were established some 15 years ago. A lot has changed in such a small time with mountain biking booming and the Welsh Assembly right behind its continued development. You could spend two weeks travelling throughout the country and ride a different man-made trail every day and we're not even scratching the surface of all the possibilities. Just open out the map and explore.

Perhaps the most important quality of Wales is its size; being a small country you can soon skip from trail to trail with very short journeys in between. With coastal paths, national parks, rock strewn bridleways and secret trails, it is almost a crime that most of the country's riders themselves seldom pull themselves away from the trail centres, but that says a lot about their quality and convenience. You will always enjoy yourself and it's a safe bet you will be back for more.

Conditions

The UK's prevailing winds and weather systems work their way uninterrupted over the Atlantic for over a 1000 miles, and though this is great news for surfers, for bikers and residents in general it is a mixed blessing. The prevailing wind combined with the surrounding warming effect of the sea leads to a mild climate that rarely becomes anything like as cold as equivalent latitudes in mainland Europe. What comes with this mild weather, though, is rainfall, and lots of it. Wales is first in line for much of this and the hills exacerbate the precipitation with relief rainfall. It must be said, though, that through late spring to early autumn clear days can be gorgeous and temperatures are usually comfortable enough for short-sleeves. Having said that, it is always advisable to be prepared when heading onto the hills as weather can change rapidly and leave you exposed.

The geology of the country varies as you travel through it, but the soils generally have a high mineral content and allow for great riding come rain or shine.

The scene

Nowadays everyone knows someone who mountain bikes in Wales. It has grown from a minority sport to a major pastime. Cross country is primarily centred around the many superb forestry centres such as Glyncorrwg, Coed y Brenin and Cwmcarn, but those in the know have regular meets and head out across the hills. Go to mtb-wales.com for meets and rides off the beaten track. The race scene is also good with a Welsh downhill series and Wales playing host to many of the UK national series rounds. This translates into great places for people to train and ride and there's a bunch of talented young riders ripping around the Welsh hills. If you're looking for something a little different and a real challenge then consider the biennial Trans Wales 7-day event across the country which provides a great introduction to the mixture of riding that's out there.

The industry

With internationally renowned downhill magazine *Dirt* setting up their offices in the Welsh countryside for reasons more imperative to the magazine's production than cheap rent, Wales has played host to a few big players in the UK bike industry, and they are all drawn to the ease of access to the countryside. Howies (howies.co.uk) have this philosophy at the forefront in their ethos: located in the beautiful Cardigan area of west Wales their positive outlook on life and their business is perfectly mirrored by their location. Mojo Suspension is located just off the M4 corridor and being the UK importer and distributor for Fox racing shox must service half of the UK's front or rear suspension units. They also play a big part in supporting local talent and have sponsored many local events. For a forum to discuss all things Welsh mountain bike related, try mtb-wales.com.

Wales breakdown

The information for Wales has been split into three groups relating to what the trails and/or centre can offer. While the UK can never compete in terms of uplift with the rest of Europe, it still provides some fantastic destinations to ride your bike. We've aimed to pick out the best centre-based trails, with the most facilities on offer, each deserving one or two pages. All those places with just a good trail have been collated into the 'Best of the rest' section. In here you will find downhill, cross country, dirt jump spots and four cross with brief explanations to point you in the right direction.

Q&A with the experts

*At 20 years old **Rachel Atherton** is already one of the most established riders in the worldwide scene. The youngest of the Atherton clan (brothers Dan and Gee make up the trio), she regularly wins UCI Downhill World Cups, won the Junior Downhill World Champs and was voted* The Times *'Young Sportsperson of the Year' in 2005. Originally from Somerset, she has called Bala home since she was 15. Rachel is currently sponsored by Animal Clothing and Commencal.*

You've got friends visiting for just one weekend and they can go anywhere in Wales. Name the one place you'd definitely have to take them.

RA   Probably Betws Y Coed. Normally I'd say Coed Y Brenin, but that's big time already. Betws Y sums up Wales. To get to the riding centre you go over a really cool river and the place is surrounded by really steep hills. It's beautiful.

Which trail centre or resort has the best party scene or the best after riding activities?

RA   Probably Llandegla as it's handy for Manchester. It's not super local and there's lots of diversity, from mums all the way up to girlfriends and pro riders. It's a mixed, friendly bag

Where did you learn to ride, and where would you send beginners to ride?

RA   I learned to ride on the local track that my brother built on some common land. I think I'd probably send learners to one of the the cross country centres with the family loops and the beginners loops. The more fun you have the faster you learn. Llandegla is a bit too easy, so I'd say Coed Y Brenin again.

In your opinion, which is the best downhill track in Wales?

RA   Again, I'd say Betws Y Coed. There are some downhill tracks there that we ride and they're pretty gnarly. All the black runs basically. If you want something more out of the way there's a place called Penmachno on the other side of the hill from Betws Y Coed that's amazing. There's no trail centre there it's just a loop with some wicked downhill sections.

Where's the best place to avoid pedalling uphill? Where has the best uplifts? Would you avoid anywhere?

RA   Best uplifts? I think Molfrie is best for downhill, and Farmer Jack runs uplifts there. You just phone him and he'll do uplifts for five or ten pounds. If you don't want to pedal then avoid Snowdon, the walk up is a killer.

Afan Forest Park

ROWAN SORRELL

Ex-South Wales mining area revitalized by new biking centres offering stacks of singletrack for the enthusiast biker.

↘1 The trails

- **XC Cross country** Excellent/ intermediate to advanced
- **DH Downhill** Poor to fair/beginner
- **FR Freeride** Poor to fair/beginner
- **Uplift** Uplift service at has ceased to operate though it is hopeful that with the inclusion of a new downhill route it will restart; possible to uplift The Wall final descent using your own vehicle on the public road
- ✓ **Pros** The trails will give most riders a wide grin; all-weather riding surface; very friendly atmosphere at the centres and on the trails
- ✕ **Cons** Won't satisfy the diehard downhillers or freeriders due to lack of uplift and stunts; can be quite exposed when the weather closes in

With four trails and more all-weather singletrack than any of the other Welsh mountain bike centres, this is a must-do for any keen trail rider. The forest block is also one of Wales' largest and the trails really do get you into the thick of it. The four trails are all of a similar style – flowing singletrack trail riding – but it is a great riding venue for all bikers as there are as many thrills on the way down as there are views on the climb up. The terrain here is mainly stable mineral soils that hold up well in all weathers with plenty of small rocks and exposed roots to keep you on your toes.

Cross country

The trails are predominantly aimed at the trail riding XC rider, with long climbs and contouring flowing descents. Inexperienced riders should start with the short blue trail and longer Penhydd route out of the Afan Argoed centre. Technically proficient riders will love the speed they can achieve on The Wall and The Whytes level trails. For those looking

Practicalities ⬛⚡♺

Afan Forest Park is affectionately known as 'little Switzerland' and it offers two visitor centres and start/ finish points at Afan Argoed and Glyncorrwg. The former is better suited to the daytripper with Glyncorrwg taking on the flagship role. Glyncorrwg was previously a one-horse town left out on a limb after the closure of the mines a few decades ago. With no through road, the town had to look for alternative ways to increase visitors and revenue. It's achieved this through a stunning visitor centre and a bike-friendly attitude, resulting in Glyncorrwg now being somewhere you can easily escape for the weekend, whether it be with friends, or riding solo deep in the South Wales valleys.

Sleeping There are a number of bike-friendly B&Bs in the area perfect for individuals and small groups, as well as camping and caravan spots with electric hook up available at the *Glyncorrwg Mountain Bike Centre*. If you're travelling in a group of four or more try out the superb log cabins at *Bryn Bettws* (T+44 (0)1639-642040) situated on the side of The Wall trail.

Eating Both visitor centres offer hot and cold food, although the bike-friendly sized meals and healthy menu in the *Drop Off* café are not to be missed. Nearest supermarket is in Port Talbot so best to stock up before you drive up the valley.

Bars and clubs Clubs are thin on the ground in the Afan Forest Park area, although you will feel welcome in the *Glyncorrwg Rugby Club*, where beer is nice and cheap. After that kick back and watch mountain bike DVDs on the big screen at the *Drop Off* café while draining the fridge of its many continental beers.

Bike shop *Skyline Cycles* (T+44 (0)1639-850011) are based at both centres; they are very well stocked with excellent mechanics. Both shops also hire bikes and have test bikes from top brands.

Internet café The *Glyncorrwg Mountain Bike Centre* is a wireless hot spot.

Bike map available? Yes, there are waterproof trail maps available from both centre for a small fee.

OPENING TIMES

The trails are open 365 days a year, day and night; the only closures are due to forest operations; details on the website below

RESORT PRICES

All trails are free although there is a car park charge of £2.60

DIRECTORY

Afan Argoed Centre:
T+44 (0)1639-850864
Glyncorrwg Centre:
T+44 (0)1639-851900
Website: mtbwales.com

for a more tranquil, scenic experience the Skyline trail, at 46 km, is the longest and has long forest road stretches linking singletrack sections.

Easy Starting from Afon Argoed take on the brand new blue beginner trails with their modular sections where you can build up your skill and confidence. After lunch take a steady ride around the 22-km Penhydd trail.

Difficult Starting at either centre the W2 trail is a challenge; linking both The Wall and The Whytes level trail you will ride 43 km taking in all the best sections of singletrack in the valley. Whichever

way you ride it you will have a café at the halfway point and somewhere to have a cup of tea and tell your tales after.

Downhill

Glyncorrwg does not at present offer any downhill specific trails, although many of the descents built into the four trails offer plenty of challenges for the average rider (many riders quote the final descent of the Wall as their favourite). There are future plans to construct a permanent downhill course in Glyncorrwg so contact the centre for the latest information.

Freeride

Glyncorrwg does not have any specific freeride trails although the black run and energy section on the Whytes level trail both contain various jumps, berms and small drops to session. Looking around the hills there are huge glacial boulders stranded on the hillsides which the skilful and imaginative can put to good use.

Below: Rowan Sorrell being watched by the windmills.
Bottom: Opening the throttle in the clearing.
Opposite page: Everyone's a fan of Afan.

The Lowdown

Locals do... Ride the fun bits on The Whytes level before cutting across to the Skyline descent; have regular evening rides and night rides through the winter; relax in the *Drop Off* café afterwards and into the evening.

Locals don't... Always ride the trails the way they are waymarked, they find their own routes around the forest; ride when it's chucking it down.

Don't miss... The Wall final descent should be done by all who visit the forest park.

Remember to avoid... The long forest road ride along the old railway at the start of the wall – tag onto someone who knows the shortcut!

Betws Y Coed

A truly epic location, Gwydwr Forest sits on the doorstep of Betws Y Coed, the outdoor adventure capital of Wales.

BETWS Y COED

⬇2 The trails

- 🚵 **Cross country** Excellent/ intermediate to advanced
- 🚵 **Downhill** Good/advanced
- 🚵 **Freeride** Poor/beginner
- 🚵 **Uplift** There is no uplift at Gwydwr, though it is possible to use your own vehicle on the public road to reach the top and shuttle some of the descents
- ✔ **Pros** Penmachno trail is built to help the local community grow its economy; stunning setting
- ✘ **Cons** Not as many waymarked trails as some other centres; some people will consider there to be too much fireroad on the Marin trail

Top: "I thought I had the only orange kagoul in the village?"
Bottom: "Oi! Come back her with that orange kagoul you."

The Lowdown

Locals do... Find lines you didn't even see on the Penmachno descent; ride as much natural as man-made terrain.

Locals don't... Ride without a spares kit; park in the wrong place in Penmachno causing obstructions.

Don't miss... An ascent of Snowdon.

Remember to avoid... Trying the above in less than perfect conditions.

The attractions for the mountain biker visiting Betws Y Coed can be split into three main areas: Gwydwr Forest, Penmachno and the national park itself. Gwydwr offers the 24-km Marin trail and plenty more if you get out and explore beyond the confines of the coloured arrows.

Penmachno has two of the newest additions to the Welsh XC trails and they are both regarded as belters. The outreaching possibilities of Snowdonia National Park are only limited by your imagination and fitness. The geology in this region is truly ancient with some of the oldest rocks in the world found which translates into trails with many rocky sections and makes for great singletrack.

Cross country

Penmachno's XC trails have been well received and there are now two trails starting there; the village is four miles south of Betws so can be cycled to or driven. The main Penmachno trail is 22 km long and suited to experienced riders; it is worth noting that the trail was built as part of a community funded scheme to help regenerate poor areas, so riders should make an effort to spend some money in the village of Penmachno itself. The Marin trail in Gwydwr Forest contains a lot of forest road that won't be to everyone's taste, but the singletrack is good. A novice cyclist should be able to complete the loop, perhaps walking the odd section, in around two to four hours.

Easy Follow the Gwydwr Forest's Marin trail. This will take you at least half a day at a slow pace, enjoying the scenery, then rolling back to Betws and find a watering hole to rehydrate.

Practicalities 🛏️⚡🚲

Betws Y Coed is the main centre of the 800-sq mile Snowdonia National Park, situated where the River Conwy meets its three tributaries flowing from the west, the Llugwy, the Lledr and the Machno. Surrounded by mountains with cascading waterfalls, hilltop lakes, river pools and ancient bridges, it is clear why Betws is such a popular destination. With all this rugged beauty and terrain, it wasn't long before bikers caught on and started riding in the area and the Forestry Commission developed a purpose-built trail first at Gwydwr Forest and later added to it with the Penmachno trails.

Sleeping There is plenty of accommodation in Betws Y Coed and the town is more than used to looking after people who love the outdoors, so mountain bikers are more than welcome in most places. For bed and breakfast try the *Meas Y Garth* (T+44 (0)1690-710441) or for large groups you can try dorm style accommodation at the *Woodlands* outdoor centre (T+44 (0)8707-873326). More choices available at visitwales.co.uk.

Eating There is no visitor centre at the forestry car park where the trail starts from, but you will find plenty of choices for good food in the town of Betws. Try the *Dragon Hotel* (T+44 (0)1690-710334) for hearty pub grub. Or if you feel flash as well as flush, then go for the *Waterloo Hotel* (T+44 (0)1690-710411) for a relaxing evening meal.

Bars and clubs Betws has many hotels and bars. There are no clubs, but the bars will keep you topped up. *The Stables* (T+44 (0)1690-710011) puts on some live entertainment, and is the favourite hang-out for most tourists.

Bike shop *Beics Betws* (T+44 (0)1690-710766) will hire bikes and have a fully equipped workshop for any running repairs on your own.

Internet café *Café Active* (T+44 (0)1690-710999) is in Betws Y Coed and the price is currently £0.50 per 15 mins.

Bike map available? There are bike maps available online at mtbwales.com. All routes are waymarked from the car park.

Difficult Ride to Penmachno and try out the number 1 loop, stop there for lunch. Cycle back up to Gwydwr Forest and seek out some of the natural riding. Day two, try loop 2 at Penmachno and search for more trails in Gwydwr.

Downhill

There are no official downhill courses at these venues; however Gwydwr Forest is littered with downhill trails, from flowing to super steep and technical. It has long been a stomping ground and training place for much of north Wales' downhill contingent, who have developed some pretty crazy runs. It is important to realise that these are not officially recognized, so you will require some local knowledge to find them.

Freeride

Apart from the challenge of some of the hidden downhills, which are very technical, Betws Y Coed does not offer the freerider any features.

Brechfa

↘3 **The mountain**

- **XC Cross country** Excellent/beginner to advanced
- **DH Downhill** Fair/beginner to intermediate
- **FR Freeride** Good/beginner to intermediate
- ⊘ **Uplift** No uplift
- ✔ **Pros** Pretty, quiet part or rural Wales with some of the best riding out there; best beginner green and blue trails for novices and kids that contain real mountain biking singletrack
- ✖ **Cons** Limited facilities on site; the shale can be slippery when it's very wet

The Lowdown

Locals do... Link the red and blue loops by riding across the top of the hill; ride most of the more challenging optional sections on the trail; always take in the blue descent as part of their rides.

Locals don't... Hang about, the style of trail and the multiple climbs soon develop fitness, skill and speed.

Don't miss... For more experienced riders, it has to be a loop around the black Raven trail, a challenging loop with a great variety of sections that will call on all your riding skills.

Remember to avoid... Leaving the area without some food and a drink from the excellent *Black Lion* in Abergorlech, a quiet country pub that serves the best lunch!

The smoothest trail centre in Wales, with tracks that stay rideable in all but the worst weather conditions.

The trails at Brechfa have caused quite a stir in both their design and their construction. Traversing through stunning mixed woodland of oak, beech and conifer and the routes are fast and flowing and sure to bring a grin to any rider, from novices up to experts. The varied style of the Raven Black trial combines steeper natural sections and the huge berms and tabletops of the more new-school trails. The Gorlech red route will challenge the experienced cyclist while the green and blue Derwen trails starting at Brwrgwm car park are gentler but still flow amazingly well and are great for novice riders. Brechfa is a shale area and the trails have been built using this shale mixed with the soils to

Top: Singletrack as far as the eye can see.
Above: The Bank of Wales, Brechfa branch.

give a really smooth, hard and fast trail surface that never gets muddy.

NICK BAYLISS/ROYAL RACING

ROWAN SORRELL

OPENING TIMES

The trails are open 365 days a year, day and night; the only closures are due to forest operations; details on the website below

RESORT PRICES

All trails are free

DIRECTORY

Aberystwyth Tourist Information:
T+44 (0)1970-612125
Website: mtbwales.com;
bikebrechfa.co.uk

Cross country

Brechfa is a fantastic area for cross country riding. The 60 km of waymarked trails take you through this stunning forest and there are plenty more trails away from the waymarkers to find and explore. Brechfa is a different style of trail to its Welsh counterparts, with a much smoother surface and more obvious descents with features to maintain flow. The green trail is 7 km, the blue 11 km, the red 19 km and

Practicalities

Brechfa forest is set in a rural location with Llandeilo to the east and Carmarthen to the west. The area is made up of rolling hills and some steeper-sided river valleys that the trails work their way around. It is a very green area of farmland and mixed forestry and subsequently a visit to Brechfa gives the opportunity to really get away from it all for a weekend and stay in some lovely, quiet country villages that are close to the trails.

Sleeping There are a few bed and breakfasts but try local bike enthusiasts Carl and Ivy at *Bike Brechfa* (T+44 (0)1558-685811) who can accommodate you and guide you around Brechfa's hidden corners.

the black a gruelling 20 km with steep climbs and fantastic descents.

Downhill

There are no official downhill trails in Brechfa forest but the descents on the black, blue and red trails, especially the natural descents on the black and the final descent of the red, have earned a popular following among the downhill crowd when riding short travel bikes due to their speed, features and flow.

Eating You'll do well to beat the food in the *Black Lion* (T+44 (0)1558-685271) in Abergorlech where the red Gorlech trail starts.

Bars and clubs For beer head to the *Black Lion*, Abergorlech. Nearest nightclubs are in Carmarthen.

Bike shop There is no bike shop in the Brechfa forest area so make sure you bring spare tubes etc. The nearest shop with a good range of stock for repairing high end bikes is *Summit Cycles* in Aberstwyth (T+44 (0)1970-626061).

Internet café No.

Bike map available? Yes, leaflets available from the car parks.

Freeride

No freeride specific course, though obstacles have been designed into the cross country trails such as tabletops and step-up jumps, natural wallrides and northshore obstacles. The additions make these trails fun for all to ride.

Easy Start out on the green Derwen trail and head for the blue extension loop. This is still within the easy skills level, so continue out on this, following the blue waymarkers. The blue descent back down to the green trail is one of the best in the forest.

Difficult Starting in Bwrgwm it is possible to follow the black trail out from the car park and link it into the red route before returning back following the black waymarkers. This will, however, be one big ride; around 45 km with five climbs. Anyone completing this will be feeling it for days to come, but it takes in all the best sections and has some amazing views.

Above: You could be here.
Below: The 'Bodecia Chariot Course Downhill' cut quite a clearing.

Coed Y Brenin

For many years this was the UK's flagship trail centre. It is the trails at Coed Y Brenin that have led to the evolution of many new venues across the country. Just because it was the first, doesn't mean it is any way outdated though.

The path or righteousness is beset on both sides by the tyranny of trees.

NICK BAYLISS

FORESTRY COMMISSION

FORESTRY COMMISSION

Top: The rack of righteousness is beset on both sides by bike mechanics and visitor centres.
Bottom: The forks of righteousness are.... oh, I can't go on with this.

COED Y BRENIN

↘4 The trails

- **XC Cross country** Excellent/ beginner to advanced
- **DH Downhill** Poor/beginner
- **FR Freeride** Poor/beginner
- **Uplift** There is no uplift at Coed Y Brenin
- **Pros** Unique stone pitching throughout the trails, interesting to ride and weatherproof; stunning new visitor centre to start and finish your rides; area is very bike friendly
- **Cons** Won't satisfy the diehard downhillers or freeriders due to lack of uplift and features

Coed Y Brenin, translated as 'Forest of the Kings', covers a vast area of over 21,000 acres. It's an ancient volcanic region with many mineral deposits that have been mined for years. Those interested in the rockier side of life can follow a geology trail from the visitor centre. For

ⓘ OPENING TIMES

The trails are open 365 days a year, day and night; the only closures are due to forest operations; details on the website below

$ RESORT PRICES

All trails are free; there is a small car park fee

ⓘ DIRECTORY

Coed Y Brenin Visitor Centre:
T+44 (0)1341-440742
Dolgellau Tourist info:
T+44 (0)1341-422888
Website: mtbwales.com

the biker, these same rocks means there is an incredibly hard wearing surface to rip through the forest on. The trails hug beautiful, river-carved valleys with technical rock features and climb out over untamed mountain tops.

Mountain biking is huge in Coed Y Brenin and the whole region has really taken to the development of the bike centre and its trails. When you add the drama of southern Snowdonia's mountain views and the very real possibility of seeing the magnificent red kites circling overhead, it makes for a great day's riding. Although many of the trails have been recently renamed, it's their older labels that most are familiar with and

the ones you will hear in most rider's conversations. So you don't get too confused on the hill, the Red Bull trail is now known as the Tarw (Welsh for bull), the MBR route remains and the old Karrimor trail is now affectionately known as The Beast!

Cross country

Coed Y Brenin is the original British cross country trail centre and is an XC rider's mecca, with the new Yr Afon trail suiting family and novice riders and the red graded Temptiwr trail giving a great short loop to test out whether the longer trails are within your grasp. With one green graded trail, three red trails and two graded black, there's a bit of everything for the XC rider. Remember the trails are rocky and contain small drop offs, but any regular mountain biker will relish the challenge.

Easy If you consider yourself a novice either hit the family trail (Yr Afon) or the red-graded Temptiwr. Experienced riders looking for an easier day should ride the MBR trail; at 18 km long it won't leave you too tired.

Difficult Only one real option here and that is to take on the physically challenging black trail, The Beast; at 38 km long and with a ride time of between three and six hours depending on fitness, it will leave you ready for some coffee and cake back at the café.

Downhill

Coed Y Brenin does not have any downhill courses or trails that are suited to downhill bikes as there is no uplift and the trails all are built with gentle gradients. Downhillers often ride here on trail or cross country bikes as the terrain offers some technical challenge and the loops offer a good day's riding away from the downhill bike.

The Lowdown

Locals do... Ride the rocks very well; layer up in winter as it can be cold on the hilltops.

Locals don't... Ride much else other than cross country; use super lightweight tyres – they will tear and puncture.

Don't miss... Just take a look at how much work has gone into creating these trails built up from stone!

Remember to avoid... Heading out on the longer rides without a spare tube and pump – it's a long walk back.

Freeride

Although Coed Y Brenin does list a dual slalom course among its assets, it really isn't up to modern-day expectations. Built a long time ago and without input from expert riders, a trip purely for this would leave you very disappointed. It is now used by XC riders on their way out or back from longer rides. Unless you're a budding freerider who simply wants a good day's aerobic exercise then Coed Y Brenin is not for you.

FORESTRY COMMISSION

Woods. They're just cool, aren't they?

Practicalities ⚏🍴🚲

Dolgellau is the nearest town to Coed Y Brenin, just 6 miles away, a small market town situated at the foot of the Cader Idris mountain range of south Snowdonia. The town dates back to the 12th century with many of the narrow streets linking the various town squares still reflecting this history. It also played a central part in the Welsh gold rush of the 19th century with some 500 miners employed in the gold mines towards the end of the century. Nowadays the town is an ideal tourist destination with many places to stay, eat and shop. It is also a great base for exploring the rest of Snowdonia.

Sleeping There are a number of places to stay in Dolgellau such as the *Ty Seren Bed & Breakfast* (T+44 (0)1341-423407) or for a self-catering cottage try the *Isfryn House* (T+44 (0)1229-583761). If you want to stay closer to the trails try *Ferndale* (T+44 (0)1341-440247) which can accommodate up to 24 people and is bike friendly and reasonably priced.

Eating On site there is the *Bwyd y Brenin* café which serves good food to hungry bikers. In the town try *Y Sospan* (T+44 (0)1341-423174), once the town courthouse and jail, where you can get all-day food. The *Callanish Restaurant* (T+44 (0)1341-422008) is a popular choice, or try *Frankies* fish and chip bar.

Bars and clubs There are a few pubs to drink away the evening in but don't be expecting nightclubs in this small town. Try the *Cross Keys Inn* or the *Halfway House*.

Bike shop *Beics Brenin* will be your best call for spares, repairs and bike hire (T+44 (0)1341-440728).

Internet café There is an internet café in Dolgellau called *The Web*.

Bike map available? Yes, trail maps available from the visitor centre.

Wales Coed Y Brenin

Cwmcarn

⬊5 The trails

Ⓧ Cross country Good/intermediate to advanced

Ⓓ Downhill Good/beginner to advanced

Ⓕ Freeride Fair/beginner to intermediate

Ⓤ Uplift Probably the best uplift service in the UK; Cwmdown can transport up to 40 riders on a weekend; book at cwmdown.co.uk; see below for prices

✔ Pros Offers all kinds of riding; a great local riding scene with lots of trails

✖ Cons You'll wish you had 3 bikes; not all the village locals are bike friendly; theft of bikes and bike gear from the car park can be a problem car park

What the village lacks in on-site après ride entertainment, the hill more than makes up for with its trails. In addition, Cwmcarn is one of the UK's few permanent uplift facilities.

Cwmcarn Forest Drive runs through a pretty little valley tucked away above the terraced housing. Up here you'll find excellent trails that cling to the contours of the valley or dive down steeply to the valley floor, and with the most efficient uplift service currently operating in the

DANNY MILNER

UK, you will be able to make the most out of your time on this hill. The terrain is made up of steep-sided valleys while the soil is excellent; loamy and buff on the lesser known local trials and super hardpacked on the main routes, ensuring it drains well and making Cwmcarn a great place to get out on the bike when the weather isn't so kind.

Cross country

With just one waymarked XC trail, you'd think the offer is limited here. The Twrch trail is very good, but explore a little further afield and the riding is epic in every direction. The Twrch trail is suited to those with some previous off-road experience and high level of fitness as the climb is quite tough.

Easy For complete novices and young children make use of the Brecon-Monmouth canal, which is perfect for gentle rides. Riders with off-road experience should take in the Twrch trail.

ⓘ OPENING TIMES

The trails are open 365 days a year, day and night; the only closures are due to forest operations; check website below

Ⓢ RESORT PRICES

All trails are free; uplift pass £22-25 per day

ⓘ DIRECTORY

Cwmcarn Forest Drive: T+44 (0)1633-850864
Taxi: T+44 (0)1633-614615
Website: mtbwales.com

ANDY LLOYD

Top: Nice rack!!!
Above: High speed bush avoidance.
Opposite page: Sunset riding. You can't beat it for shots.

Wales Cwmcarn

The Lowdown

Locals do... Have lots of secret trails; use the Cwmdown uplift service to get the most out of their days and get some extra descents in; ride to a high standard.

Locals don't... Always park at the centre, many incorporate the centre's trails into longer rides, parking elsewhere.

Don't miss... Watching someone hit the infamous quarry jump on the downhill course.

Remember to avoid... Riding the freeride section in the wind, it's a waste of time and dangerous if there is a cross wind.

Difficult Head out on the Twrch trail, climbing up to the highest point, then cut up onto the open hill and moorland. Here you can extend your ride as far as your body and mind will allow before finishing your loop back down to the forest drive.

Downhill

The downhill track at Cwmcarn is one of extremes; super fast and with some big lines as well as the availability of smaller, easier jumps. One fact is constant though; everything is rollable. It's probably not suited to the total beginner, but anyone with previous downhill experience will get plenty of thrills out of this course.

Freeride

Cwmcarn has a small freeride area with some drops, tabletops and a superb curved wallride. Many freeriders will be found sessioning the bottom section of the downhill course perfecting their jumping skills.

Practicalities ⬚🍴🌙

The village of Cwmcarn itself does not offer much to the overnight visitor; its facilities are a little disjointed, but the lure is still strong due to the excellent facilities on the hill. Many punters stay in nearby Newport, which is only a 15-min drive away, or base themselves slightly further afield in Cardiff where they can enjoy the best of both worlds. Back in Cwmcarn, there is the usual range of small local shops. And while the town may not be pretty, the surrounding hills certainly are and have created a real hub for mountain bikers.

Sleeping For bed and breakfast try the bike-friendly *Coed Mamgu Guest House* (T+44 (0)1495-270657) situated in the village at the foot of the forest drive. The forest drive has a campsite with electrical hook up. For those looking for a more cosmopolitan stay, nearby Cardiff and Newport offer plenty of accommodation for all budgets.

Eating Snacks and meals are available at the visitor centre during opening hours. Evening meals are available in local pubs and restaurants; try the *Cross Keys* for simple bar meals, or *Vittorio's* (T+44 (0)1633-840261) in Newport for a good restaurant meal. *Morrisons* is the nearest supermarket, on the A469 between Newport and Cwmcarn.

Bars and clubs There is no bar at the visitor centre itself, but there are plenty of pubs in Cwmcarn and more in neighbouring Cross Keys and Risca. For a local après-ride pint try the *Cross Keys*, but for real nightlife it is a trip by taxi to Newport or Cardiff. Be warned though that return fares will be expensive.

Bike shop There is a small shop in the visitor centre carrying basic spares to keep you on the hill. For more urgent repairs and hire see *Martin Ashfield Cycles* in Risca, and for specialist parts see *Sunset MTB* or *Don Skene Cycles* in Cardiff.

Internet café Abercarn Library (T+44 (0)1495-244393) has free internet use but limited workstations. *Zoo* internet café in Newport has more (T+44 (0)1633-212453).

Bike map available? Yes, there are waterproof trail maps available from the forest drive visitor centre for a small charge.

ANDY LLOYD

Wales Cwmcarn

Llandegla

A great location accessible to many of the larger towns and cities in the midlands and north of England. The area's trails cater for family groups and novices right through to the black-run enthusiasts.

LLANDEGLA

↘6 The trails

- ⓧ **Cross country** Excellent/ beginner to advanced
- ⓓ **Downhill** Poor to fair/beginner to intermediate
- ⓕ **Freeride** Poor to fair/beginner to intermediate
- ⓩ **Uplift** There is no uplift at Llandegla, but on the right bike this is no problem as most of the fun bits are easily climbed around to hit again and again
- ✔ **Pros** The trails are enjoyable to all; very relaxed vibe
- ✖ **Cons** You will have to stay elsewhere and commute; some doubletrack stretches can be quite boring

The Lowdown

Locals do... Heavily session the black bits; learn to manual over the wooden northshore bridge; socialize at the centre.

Locals don't... Always ride the trails the way they are waymarked, they find their own shortcuts to their favourite bits; try and out-jump local builder Jason Rennie (he set the world long jump record here at 134 ft!).

Don't miss... Those pumpy, swoopy black sections.

Remember to avoid... Annoying the locals – pay you're parking fee.

All tracks are completely self-contained in the 650-ha forest. What you can expect to find out on these trails is a mix of double and singletrack purpose-built mountain bike trails; all built using sound construction techniques that give a solid all-weather and fast rolling surface that flows well throughout the woods. What Llandegla does not offer is the expanse of natural trails that can be discovered at many other venues, but the trails that have been built have plenty to keep your mind and body working overtime. The stable all-weather surface means that the trails don't get too muddy in winter.

ⓘ **OPENING TIMES**

The trails are open 365 days a year and technically you can ride them any time; the café and bike shop have varied opening times from Tue to Sun

Ⓢ **RESORT PRICES**

All trails are free although there is an all-day car park fee of £2.50

ⓘ **DIRECTORY**

One Planet Centre: T+44 (0)1978-751656
Chester Tourist Information: T+44 (0)1244-402111
Wrexham Tourist Information: T+44 (0)1978-292015
Website: coedllandegla.com

Cross country

All the trails at Llandegla are suitable for the XC rider and XC bikes as even the more technical black sections can be rolled through safely at a moderate speed. The trails range from short family loops of 5 km to the black loop at

Sweet drop in the woods.

Left: Left.
Right: Right.

21 km with a blue novice trail and red intermediate slotting in between.

Easy Follow the novice (blue) trail around the loop and back to the centre. Too easy? Take the intermediate (red) loop as well after lunch.

Difficult Take the black route. Each black section is a loop branching off the intermediate trail, so if you enjoy it, loop back around and hit the section again. You'll soon find you're running low on energy but the fun will keep you going back to the centre.

Downhill

In keeping with most of the Welsh trail centres Llandegla does not offer any specific downhill runs, but it does have plenty to keep downhill rider entertained. Used by many pro riders to have a fun blast while keeping the fitness levels up, Llandegla throws berms, tabletops and plenty of whoops that will keep you manualling and jumping through the fun black sections. Not suited to long travel DH bikes though.

Freeride

For the aspiring freerider looking to develop their jumping skills the black runs at Llandegla are perfect as they have various jumps of different sizes to learn and progress on. There are no big obstacles though so more skilled riders will not be challenged, but for the majority there is plenty of fun to be had.

Practicalities ●🍴🚲

Llandegla Forest is 7 miles from Wrexham and 14 miles from Chester. There are a lot of small villages closer to the centre that offer bed and breakfast accommodation and pubs for food and drink. Chester mixes the old and the new perfectly with stunning medieval architecture on display in the shopping area of the Rows and bang up to date shops and amenities. It is also a student city with a young, vibrant feel. Wrexham offers a slightly closer alternative, nestled in the Dee valley between the lush Cheshire plains of England and the hills of Wales.

Sleeping There is no accommodation on the Llandegla site itself, but nearby Wrexham and Chester offer a wide range, from bed and breakfast to hotels. In Wrexham try the Scandinavian self-catering cottages of *Three Tops County Leisure*

(T+44 (0)1352-770648) and also the *Windings* (T+44 (0)1978-720503) for bed and breakfast. In Chester there is lots of good accommodation; try the *Comfort Inn* (T+44 (0)1244-327542) for reasonable prices check out visitchester.com.

Eating *The One Planet* café in the log-cabin style visitor centre is the place to eat when you're hitting the trails, run by enthusiastic bikers, they know exactly what you need. For the evenings you should hit the country pubs or restaurants in the nearby towns.

Bars and clubs If you're looking for something lively, then you really should base yourself in Chester as there are bars and clubs there to suit most tastes. If you like live music try *Telfords Warehouse*. For clubbing you should check out the flyers in

the city as there are many different nights catering for the large student population.

Bike shop *The One Planet* bike shop (T+44 (0)1978-751656) at the Llandegla visitor centre stocks many parts and accessories and you can hire one of the Kona bikes there. Elsewhere, there is a good shop in Chester, *The Edge Cycleworks* (T+44 (0)1244-399888) which stocks a wide range of brands.

Internet café There are a few internet cafés in Chester. Try *Cafenet* (T+44 (0)1244-401116).

Bike map available? Yes, there are trail maps available from the *One Planet* visitor centre and downloadable from their website: coedllandegla.com.

Machynlleth

↘7 The trails

- ⊗ **Cross Country** Good/intermediate
- ⊕ **Downhill** Poor/beginner
- ⊕ **Freeride** Poor/beginner
- ⊘ **Uplift** No uplift
- ✓ **Pros** Healthy living, alternative, bike friendly town
- ✗ **Cons** Limited without exploration or guide

Riding from Machynlleth itself there are three waymarked trails; the Mach 1, 2 and 3. These are suitable for the bikers who enjoy a steadier form of biking: Mach 1 being the shortest at 16 km and Mach 3 being the longest at 30 km. The thrill seekers amongst you will do better to head up the Dyfi valley to the Climax trail in Dyfi forest. This 16-km loop is packed with fast sweeping singletrack and the final descent just keeps on going.

Cross country

The three Mach trails will get you out into the hills but to truly make the most of the Dyfi valley, go and speak to the guys in the bike shop for some great natural XC riding.

Bush running.

Practicalities 🛏🍴🚲

The town of Machynlleth is the ancient capital of Wales and is now well known for its Centre for Alternative Technology and the town's eco-friendly slant on modern living. Don't look for major chain stores here, nearly every one of the shops and stores on the high streets of Machynlleth, Aberdyfi and Tywyn are owner-occupied traders and businesses. As British towns become more and more like clones of each other, it is a refreshing change walking around Machynlleth.

Sleeping There's a range of accommodation available in this popular tourist town. Try the bike-friendly, well situated *Dyfi Guesthouse* (T+44 (0)1654-702562)

Downhill

There are no downhill specific trails in the area although on a short travel suspension bike you can have a lot of fun on the Climax trails descents.

Freeride

No freeride trails although the 'eye of the needle' drop on the climax trail would challenge some of the best riders.

Eating There are no big commercial chains, so expect quality local produce and while you'll pay a little more, it's so much better. Try the *Maengwyn Café* (T+44 (0)1654-702126).

Bars and clubs There are plenty of pubs in Machynlleth; nearest clubs are to be found in Aberystwyth.

Bike shop The *Holy Trail Bike Shop* (T+44 (0)1654-700411) will look after you.

Internet café No café's, so hit the Machynlleth Library.

Bike map available? Yes, in the *Holy Trail Bike Shop*.

Locals do...

Loop back up the forest road to ride the final descent of the climax again. Have a wealth of natural riding in the Dyfi valley.

Locals don't...

Ride when there has been heavy frost – the trail gets very sticky.

ⓘ OPENING TIMES

The trails are open 365 days a year, day and night; the only closures are due to forest operations; details on mtbwales.com

Ⓢ RESORT PRICES

All trails are free; there is a pay and display car park in Machynlleth centre and an honesty box at the Climax trail

⊙ DIRECTORY

Machynlleth Tourist Information: T+44 (0)1654-702401
Website: dyfimountainbiking.org.uk

Nant Yr Arian

NANT YR ARIAN

↘8 The trails

- ⓧⓒ **Cross country** Good/ intermediate to advanced
- ⓓⓗ **Downhill** Poor to fair/beginner
- ⓕⓡ **Freeride** Poor to fair/beginner
- ⓐ **Uplift** No uplift
- ✔ **Pros** Varied trail riding and vibrant seaside town
- ✖ **Cons** Limited facilities for non-XC riders

Above: Gentle climb.
Above right: Gentle descent.

ⓘ OPENING TIMES

The trails are open 365 days a year, day and night; the only closures are due to forest operations; details posted on the website below

ⓢ RESORT PRICES

All trails are free; parking is £1

ⓘ DIRECTORY

Aberystwyth Tourist Information: T+44 (0)1970-612125
Website: mtbwales.com; aberystwyth-online.co.uk

Nant Yr Arian forest sits high on the mountains just inland from Aberystwyth, and offers stunning high-level wilderness riding. With trails heading out into the epic scenery of the Cambrian Mountains, this is a fantastic area for those who like their riding rugged. Just be prepared for everything from true mountain climbs to river crossings and technical rocky descents.

Cross country

The trails in Nant Yr Arian offer up some true mountain riding and run across exposed moorland and through tight technical singletrack. There is a short (9 km) blue graded taster trail the Pendam, the longer singletrack (16 km) Summit trail and then the epic Syfydrin trail at 35 km long, both are graded red.

Downhill

There are no official downhill trails in Nant Yr Arian, but call into Summit Cycles in Aberstwyth and they can take you to where the locals have their downhill courses.

Freeride

No freeride trails, though there is a dirt jump spot in Aberystwyth. If you befriend the locals they may show you.

Locals do...

Rip down the Mask of Zorro descent; ride in groups.

Locals don't...

Ride the Syfydrin trail without appropriate gear.

Practicalities ⓐⓑⓒ

There is no town at Nant Yr Arian forest itself. The nearest is Aberystwyth, a busy student town on the coast, about a 15-min drive away from the trails, with some 50 pubs and a friendly community feel.

Sleeping There are plenty of places to stay in Aberystwyth. You should be able to book into the *Marine Hotel* at any time (T+44 (0)1970-612444).

Eating The *Honoured Guest* (T+44 (0)1970-617617) Chinese restaurant comes recommended, but you will find Indian, Italian and Mediterranean cuisine in the town alongside traditional dishes.

Bars and clubs With so many pubs in a relatively small town it shows that they like to have a good time. *Inn On The Pier* is a more relaxed venue, or you could go to one of the many student nights.

Bike shop The excellent *Summit Cycles* (T+44 (0)1970-626061) are based in Aberystwyth and sponsor the Summit trail at Nant Yr Arian.

Internet café *Caffi'r Web Café* on 13 Terrace Road, Aberystwyth.

Bike map available? Yes, from the Nant Yr Arian visitor centre.

Wales Nant Yr Arian

Llanwyrtd Wells

LLANWYRTD WELLS

N9 The trails

- **XC Cross country** Good/intermediate to advanced
- **DH Downhill** Poor/n/a
- **FR Freeride** Poor/n/a
- **Uplift** No uplift
- **Pros** Quiet trails, perfect for families; a different ride experience to the other centres
- **Cons** The trails won't be exciting or challenging enough for some riders used to the thrills of man-made singletrack

Llanwyrtd differs from the other featured Welsh sites in that its riding is not focused on a Forestry Commision centre, rather on the surrounding open hills around the town. Some trails are waymarked and maps can be collected from the town, others routes are not and require a bit of headwork. There is also a small trail centre set up called Coed Trallwm with three short forest trails and a lovely cafe. Other trails around the town tend to be out in the open country and can be quite soft going if it has been very wet. Many people base themselves in Llanwrtyd to head over to the excellent Elan Valley

OPENING TIMES

The trails are open 365 days a year, day and night; the only closures are due to forest operations; details on the website below

RESORT PRICES

All trails are free

DIRECTORY

Llanwrytd Wells Visitor Centre:
T+44 (0)1591-610666
Website: mtbwales.com;
coedtrawllm.co.uk

Carrying the tag of 'Britain's smallest town' you may well think that this has little to offer, but the town is big on beer festivals and big on mountain biking; a winning combination if there ever was one.

Practicalities ▪◉🍴🔧

Sitting astride the river Irfon, Llanwyrtd Wells is tucked down in the valley between the Cambrian Mountains and the Mynydd Epynt, a wild plateau covered largely by blanket bog and grass, but intersected by several stream valleys. Its fame, once built on the mineral springs, is now firmly in the bog snorkelling world championships, a peculiar but brilliantly entertaining event that has now sprung an off shoot – the bike bog snorkelling event. Bog snorkelling aside, it is just one of many attractions that make this unique town stand out; rolling hills and rugged mountains, spectacular passes and gentle valleys, open pastures and thick forest, trickling streams and, of course, the mid Wales beer festival.

Sleeping It may be the smallest town in Britain, but there are plenty of places to stay and eat and the hospitality is always warm to bikers. For bed and breakfast try the *Plas Newydd* (T+44 (0)1591-610293) or if you are interested in hiring a cottage on wooded grounds try the *Cwm Irfon Lodge* (T+44 (0)1591-610849).

Eating There are a number of suitable places to get a hearty meal, try the *Drovers Rest Restaurant* (T+44

(0)1591-610264) or for something different The *Carlton House Hotel* French restaurant (T+44 (0)1591-610248). If you're riding at the Coed Trallwm trails there's a great café there for bikers with a wood burning stove to keep it cosy in the winter.

Bars and clubs There are no clubs in Llawrtyd but you won't be worried about that with all the warm and cosy traditional pubs. There are many beer and ale festivals in the town and it prides itself on good ale. The *Neuadd Arms* (T+44 (0)1591-610236) is a popular biker haunt.

Bike shop You can hire basic mountain bikes from *Irfon Cycles* (T+44 (0)1591-610668) in the town and they also carry out repairs. *Biped Cycles* (T+44 (0)1874-622296) in nearby Brecon have a slightly more specialist stock if specific parts are needed.

Internet café There is web access available at the tourist information centre (T+44 (0)1591-610666). You can't miss it, its bright pink!

Bike map available? Yes, trail maps available from the tourist information centre.

singletracks. Perhaps the best way to learn the multitude of tracks here is to combine your visit with an event such as the Red Kite Mountain Bike Bash or the Real Ale Wobble.

Cross country

A great place for the purist cross country rider as so many of the trails follow old bridleways and paths and it really does have a different feel to the other Welsh trail centres. The forestry at Coed Trallwm provides a few shorter loops

The Lowdown

in the woods with a visitor centre there but it is up on the surrounding hills that the real riding can be found. There's no better way to explore than to book into the Real Ale Wobble. This is held once a year and is a non-competitive event based on having a good time. Half pints of ale are provided at check points and the route is marked out so that hopefully even the most inebriated will find their way home...

Easy For family and novice groups the blue trail at Coed Trallwm provides an enjoyable yet relatively easy mountain bike ride. After home-made soup and bread in the café head out for a second loop or if ability allows try the red loop.

Difficult Head out on the Mynydd Trawsnant route, its 27.6 km will take you over undulating terrain with some stunning views. Expect a ride time of 3-4 hours and to feel slightly drained afterwards.

Downhill

Although there are numerous big hills and mountains around Llanwyrtd Wells, there are no downhill trails and no downhill scene in the surrounding towns.

Freeride

There are no trails or facilities suited to freeriders.

Best of the rest

DOWNHILL
⬂10 Abercarn

- **❓ Number of runs** One main track that is used regularly for downhill races
- **⬇ Uplift** No day-to-day uplift but see dragondownhill.co.uk for organized uplift days
- **ⓘ More info** dragondownhill.co.uk

Fast and flowing downhill course with numerous switchbacks cutting down the hill. Rides well in all weathers, though can be quite loose and rocky at times. Can be ridden comfortably on trail bikes but is quite steep. Situated very close to Cwmcarn; riders staying in the area should try out Abercarn as well. Also some great XC riding to be found in the surrounding hills; can be linked across the hilltop to the Cwmcarn Twrch trail which is a local riders favourite loop combining DH and XC. For a beer head to the *Black Lion*, Abergorlech. Nearest nightclubs are in Carmarthen.

DIRT JUMPS
⬂11 Caerphilly

- **📍 Location** Coed Park Van Woodland on Vann Rd, Caerphilly; park in the Forestry Commission car park; the jumps are 250 m up the forest road on the right
- **❖ Ability Range** Novice to expert

This public dirt jump spot has a range of jumps, from small tabletop and roller tables to big lines with step-up jumps and gaps. Steep transitions and tight bowls on some of the larger jumps make them quite technical jumps.

DOWNHILL
⬂12 Caersws

- **❖ Ability range** Range from intermediate to national standard trails; previous downhill experience advised
- **❓ Number of runs** 3 completely separate courses with lots of options to make up many more different runs
- **⬇ Uplift** Regular monthly uplifts run by the landowner, call T+44 (0)7977-987755

A great place to ride and with three downhill runs and tons of different sections on each you could make up a different trail every run. The ground always tends to be drier here than surrounding areas and somehow Cearsws seems to have its own microclimate. A super efficient uplift and a good mix of roots, fast trail, jumps and technical sections means it's a great place to spend the day. Uplifts can be organized with the landowner, you will need a group of 15 or more to book the day.

↘13 **Cardiff 4X Track**

- ⊕ **Ability range** Track suited to beginners and novices and also to more experienced riders; some of the more technical lines designed for experts
- ⬥ **Length** 400 m, 25-m vertical drop
- ⊿ **Uplift** Monthly uplift planned

The trail is built to encourage learners and novices whilst still having enough technical jumps and turns to test expert riders. Can be easily pushed back to the top and has organized uplifts from time to time. Small fee to ride, currently a couple of quid for the whole day. Also worth heading for Maindee in Cardiff to ride the pump track there which is great on a jump bike.

↘14 **Cwm Rhaeadr**

- ⊕ **Ability range** 7-km trail is graded red and is medium technicality; a steady climb that steepens at the end

The trail starts and finishes in a small forestry car park, from there it's a long gentle climb up the forest road until you reach the singletrack which steepens and switches back up the steep hillside. This takes you to the highest point and the views out over the valley and waterfall are stunning. From here there is an option to leave the waymarked trail and follow the bridleway out onto the Mynydd Mallaen for a much longer ride. Sticking with the main trail it's a fun blast all the way back to the car park with berms, jumps, bombholes and

loose shale. Whilst in the area it is worth riding some of the natural trails up at Llyn Brianne.

↘15 **Foel Gasnach**

- ⊕ **Ability range** Medium to high
- ⊗ **Number of runs** 3
- ⊿ **Uplift** It is possible to shuttle run the Foel venue with your own transport
- ⓘ **More info** foelgasnach.co.uk

Foel Gasnach was formed after the loss of the infamous Scouse track in Nannarch. The group have now developed three downhill trails of varying technicality but in general the trails are rooty and can be pretty slick in the wet. It is possible to do a lot of runs in a day here and there is a good local scene.

↘16 Gethin Woods

- ⊕ **Ability range** Intermediate
- ⊗ **Number of Runs** 1
- ⊘ **Uplift** Only on organized uplift days
- ⓘ **More info** dragondownhill.co.uk

The trail has evolved over the years but remains one that can be enjoyed by trail bikers as well as downhill riders. Gethin is well known for its rock garden on the lower section of the track and its switchback section higher up the hill. The woods offer various trails for cross country riding but the downhill trail is the best way back down.

↘17 Kilvey Hill

- ⊕ **Ability range** Intermediate
- ⊗ **Number of Runs** 2
- ⊘ **Uplift** No uplift

Kilvey Hill has long been the local stomping ground for Swansea residents and its student biking fraternity. The trail, though technically a downhill route, will appeal to freeriders with its numerous jumps. The trail does not require much technical skill to roll down but some of the optional jumps are for more advanced riders. The hill drains amazingly well and is great in all weathers. Freeriders will also enjoy the nearby Cline woods with its drops and jumps.

↘18 Llantrisant Woods

- ⊕ **Ability range** Intermediate
- ⊗ **Number of Runs** 2
- ⊘ **Uplift** No

Llantrisant, just north of Cardiff, offers a good place to ride cross country on the many paths and trails in the wood and two built downhill tracks which are both of intermediate difficulty. Lots of roots make it slick in the wet. Best ridden in the dry when the trails are running fast, as the hill is not too steep. Many riders trail ride here and come down the downhill routes as part of a longer XC ride.

↘19 Mountain Ash

- ⊕ **Ability range** Intermediate
- ⊗ **Number of Runs** 1
- ⊘ **Uplift** Only on organized uplift days with dragon downhill
- ⓘ **More info** dragondownhill.co.uk

A fast downhill course without too many obstacles, fun to ride on any bike but fastest on a downhill set up. Park on the road at the bottom and then either ride up the forest road to the top or push up the trail to section it bit by bit.

↘20 Mynydd Ddu

- ⊕ **Ability range** Hard
- ⊗ **Number of Runs** 1
- ⊘ **Uplift** On organized days
- ⓘ **More info** dragondownhill.co.uk

One of the bigger British courses, this trail takes a route one approach down the dark wooded hillside with fast chutes and plenty of rocks and roots. Contains several steep banks that require competent downhill skills to ride but for all keen downhillers it's a must ride.

↘21 Ponciau Banks

- ⊕ **Ability range** easy to roll – expert to jump
- ⊕ **Length** Approx 200 m
- ⓘ **More info** dragondownhill.co.uk/ 2004site/ponciaubanks.htm

A beautifully sculpted pump track that's great on a mountain bike or a BMX, and will polish up those jumping, manualing and pumping skills in no time. Some of the jumps are quite advanced but most will have a great time riding this track. Situated about 10 minutes from Llandegla trail centre so can be incorporated into a trip there.

↘22 Rheola

- ⊕ **Ability range** Hard
- ⊗ **Number of Runs** 1
- ⊘ **Uplift** Only on organized uplift days
- ⓘ **More info** dragondownhill.co.uk

Rheola has hosted many rounds of the British national series and also the National Championships. It is a technical downhill course that is overall quite fast but has a few slower tricky sections. The trail contains lots of bus stops and is quite rough with lots of rock exposed in the ground. Nearest town is Resolven or Glynneath.

↘23 Wentwood

- ⊕ **Ability range** Intermediate to hard
- ⊗ **Number of Runs** 1 downhill
- ⊘ **Uplift** No
- ⓘ **More info** dragondownhill.co.uk

Wentwood has a lot to offer the rider who is prepared to get out and explore. With so many natural trails it is a good place for cross country and the downhill trail just complements this being great to ride on a trail bike or a downhill set up. The red clay in this area is very slick when wet so it's best to stick to dry days in Wentwood.

Tread your own path

Saddle up, check the view, ride the world

Footprint story

1921
Ireland had just been partitioned, the British miners were striking for more pay and the federation of British industry had an idea. Exports were booming in South America – how about a handbook for businessmen trading in that faraway continent? The Anglo-South American Handbook was born that year, written by W Koebel, the most prolific writer on Latin America of his day.

1924
Two editions later the book was 'privatized' and, in 1924, in the hands of Royal Mail, the steamship company for South America, it became The South American Handbook, subtitled 'South America in a nutshell'. This annual publication became the 'bible' for generations of travellers to South America and remains so to this day. In the early days travel was by sea and the Handbook gave all the details needed for the long voyage from Europe. What to wear for dinner; how to arrange a cricket match with the Cable & Wireless staff on the Cape Verde Islands and a full account of the journey from Liverpool up the Amazon to Manaus: 5898 miles without changing cabin!

1939
As the continent opened up, The South American Handbook reported the new Pan Am flying boat services, and the fortnightly airship service from Rio to Europe on the Graf Zeppelin. For reasons still unclear but with extraordinary determination, the annual editions continued through the Second World War.

1970s
Many more people discovered South America and the backpacking trail started to develop. All the while the Handbook was gathering fans, including literary vagabonds such as Paul Theroux and Graham Greene (who once sent some updates addressed to "The publishers of the best travel guide in the world, Bath, England").

1990s
During the 1990s the company set about developing a new travel guide series using this legendary title as the flagship. By 1997 there were over a dozen guides in the series and the Footprint imprint was launched.

2000s
The series grew quickly and there were soon Footprint travel guides covering more than 150 countries. In 2004, Footprint launched its first thematic guide: Surfing Europe, packed with colour photographs, maps and charts. This was followed by further thematic guides such as Diving the World, Snowboarding the World, Body and Soul escapes, Travel with Kids and European City Breaks.

2008
Today we continue the traditions of the last 87 years that has served legions of travellers so well. We believe that these help to make Footprint guides different. Our policy is to use authors who are genuine experts who write for independent travellers; people possessing a spirt of adventure, looking to get off the beaten track.

Index

Index

Credits

Footprint credits

Text editor: Alan Murphy
Layout and production: Angus Dawson

Managing Director: Andy Riddle
Publisher: Patrick Dawson
Editorial: Sara Chare, Ria Gane, Jenny Haddington, Felicity Laughton, Nicola Jones
Cartography: Robert Lunn, Kevin Feeney, Kassia Gawronski
Design: Mytton Williams
Sales and marketing: Hannah Bonnell
Advertising: Renu Sibal
Business Development: Zoë Jackson
Finance and Administration: Elizabeth Taylor

Maps: Netmaps, SA. 2008
http://www.digitalmaps.co.uk

Photography credits

Title page: Chris Moran (Josh Bryceland)
Front cover: Seb Rogers (Chamonix)
Back cover: Chris Moran (Josh Bryceland)

Print

Manufactured in Italy by EuroGrafica
Pulp from sustainable forests

Footprint Feedback

We try as hard as we can to make each Footprint guide as up to date as possible but, of course, things always change. If you want to let us know about your experiences – good, bad or ugly – then don't delay, go to www.footprintbooks.com and send in your comments.

Every effort has been made to ensure that the facts in this guidebook are accurate. However, travellers should still obtain advice from consulates, airlines etc about travel and visa requirements before travelling. The authors and publishers cannot accept responsibility for any loss, injury or inconvenience however caused.

Publishing information

Footprint Mountain Biking Europe
1st edition
© Footprint Handbooks Ltd
August 2008

ISBN 978-1-906098-31-5
CIP DATA: A catalogue record for this book is available from the British Library

® Footprint Handbooks and the Footprint mark are a registered trademark of Footprint Handbooks Ltd

Published by Footprint

6 Riverside Court
Lower Bristol Road
Bath BA2 3DZ, UK
T +44 (0)1225 469141
F +44 (0)1225 469461
discover@footprintbooks.com
www.footprintbooks.com

Distributed in North America by

Globe Pequot Press